Bards, Bohemians, and Bookmen

Bards, Bohemians, and Bookmen

Essays in Australian Literature

Edited by
LEON CANTRELL

University of Queensland Press

© University of Queensland Press
St. Lucia, Queensland, 1976

Printed and bound by Silex Enterprise & Printing Co.,
Hong Kong

Distributed in the United Kingdom, Europe,
the Middle East, Africa, and the Caribbean
by Prentice-Hall International, International Book
Distributors Ltd., 66 Wood Lane End,
Hemel Hempstead, Herts., England

*National Library of Australia
Cataloguing-in-publication data*

Bards, bohemians and bookmen.

   ISBN 0 7022 1321 7.

   1. Australian writers – History and criticism –
   Addresses, essays, lectures. I. Cantrell, Leon
   Nicolas, 1943–, ed.

820.9

for Cecil Hadgraft

Contents

CONTENTS

CECIL HADGRAFT

Preface

The essays in this book are a cross-section of work currently being done in Australian literary history and criticism. They are published to honour Cecil Hadgraft on his retirement and represent an attempt to cover, not the whole field of Australian literature, but those areas in which Cecil has been especially interested during his writing and teaching career over the last forty years.

The collection does not suggest a canon of Australian writing though many of the essays offer a reinterpretation of material or a redirection of critical interests. Particularly, several open up areas in nineteenth-century Australian literature, a neglected field until recently, but one to which Cecil Hadgraft has made a distinguished contribution.

All the contributors trust their piece is at least a token of their affection and esteem.

Leon Cantrell
Brisbane
January 1976

Contributors

John Barnes, Reader in English, La Trobe University, Melbourne, is the author of *Joseph Furphy* (1963), *The Writer in Australia: A Collection of Literary Documents 1856 to 1964* (1969), *Henry Kingsley and Colonial Fiction* (1971), and *An Australian Selection* (1974).

Leon Cantrell is Lecturer in English, University of Queensland. His edition of A.G. Stephens's work will be published soon.

Dennis Douglas is Senior Lecturer in English, Monash University, Melbourne.

P.D. Edwards is Professor of English, University of Queensland. His books include Trollope's *Australia* (edited with Roger Joyce, 1967), *Anthony Trollope* (1968), *Some Mid-Victorian Thrillers* (1971), and an edition of Trollope's *He Knew He Was Right* (1974).

Brian Elliott is Reader in English, University of Adelaide. His books include *Leviathan's Inch* (1946), *Singing to the Cattle* (1947), *Marcus Clarke* (1958), *The Landscape of Australian Poetry*

(1967), and *Bards in the Wilderness: Australian Colonial Poetry to 1920* (with Adrian Mitchell, 1970). In 1976 he was made a Member of the Order of Australia for academic service in the field of Australian literature.

Reba Gostand is Lecturer in English, Department of External Studies, University of Queensland.

L.T. Hergenhan, Reader in English, University of Queensland, is the founding editor of *Australian Literary Studies*. His edition of Marcus Clarke's journalism, *A Colonial City: High and Low Life* was published in 1972.

H.P. Heseltine is Associate Professor of English, University of New South Wales. His books include *John le Gay Brereton* (1965), *Vance Palmer* (1970), *The Penguin Book of Australian Verse* (1972), and *Xavier Herbert* (1973).

Brian Kiernan, Lecturer in English, University of Sydney, is the author of *Images of Society and Nature: Seven Essays on Australian Novels* (1971) and *Criticism* (1974).

Jack Lindsay is the author of well over one hundred books, among the most recent being *Helen of Troy* (1973), *The Normans and Their World* (1973), and *William Morris* (1975).

Brian Matthews, Lecturer in English, University of Adelaide, is the author of *The Receding Wave: Henry Lawson's Prose* (1972).

Elizabeth Perkins is Lecturer in English, James Cook University of North Queensland.

Colin Roderick is Professor of English, James Cook University of North Queensland. Among his many books are recent editions of Henry Lawson's *Short Stories and Sketches 1888—1922*, *Autobiographical and Other Writings 1887—1922*, and *Henry Lawson Criticism 1894—1971* (1972).

Spencer Routh is Reference Librarian, University of Queensland Library.

Vivian Smith, Senior Lecturer in English, University of Sydney, is the author of *The Other Meaning* (1956), *James McAuley* (1965), *An Island South* (1967), *Vance Palmer* (1971), and *The Poetry of Robert Lowell* (1974).

Terry Sturm, Senior Lecturer in English, University of Sydney, has been an editor of *New Poetry*.

Alrene Sykes, Senior Lecturer in English, University of Queensland, is the author of *Harold Pinter* (1970), and the editor of *Five Plays for Radio* (1975).

Elizabeth Webby is Lecturer in English, University of Sydney.

Michael Wilding is Reader in English, University of Sydney. His books include *Marvell: Modern Judgements* (1969), *Milton's Paradise Lost* (1969), two novels, *Living Together* (1974) and *The Short Story Embassy* (1975), and two collections of his stories, *Aspects of the Dying Process* (1972) and *The West Midland Underground* (1975).

R.B.J. Wilson is Senior Lecturer in English, University of Queensland. With Cecil Hadgraft he edited *A Century of Australian Short Stories* (1963).

Acknowledgments

Acknowledgment is made to the National Library of Australia (Canberra), the Mitchell Library (Sydney), and the Fryer Memorial Library of Australian Literature within the University of Queensland for permission to reproduce material in their collections.

Acknowledgment is also made to Mr. Walter Stone for use of photographs from his collection.

1

Literature, History, and Literary History: Perspectives on the Nineteenth Century in Australia

BRIAN KIERNAN

To trace the growth of letters in the community, from the earliest period of our history to the present time, and to show in what manner that growth had been influenced by the productions of the Mother Country ... would amount to a literary history of the country, and it was hoped that such a history would serve more than one useful service. It would enable the reader to form an exact idea of the progress, extent and prospects of literary enterprise among us, more readily than could be done by means of any general statement; it would constitute a bibliographical account that might be practically useful, not only to those who are interested in our literature, but also to those who may hereafter be engaged in historical enquiries; it would serve to throw some light, from a new point of view, on our social history; and lastly, it would preserve the memory, and give some notion of the achievement, of men whose name could scarcely be expected to survive their generation.

So wrote G.B. Barton, Reader in English at the University of Sydney, in the introduction to his *Literature in New South Wales* (1866). This and his critical anthology *The Poets and Prose Writers of New South Wales* (also 1866) were the first books on Australian literature. Although Barton recorded much valuable bibliographical information, he did not provide any systematic review along the lines he suggests in the above passage; however, his ideal of what literary history ought to provide comprehends the intentions of many who were to follow him with their accounts of the "growth of letters" in this country.

Barton's intention of enabling the reader to form an opinion of the "progress" of literature in this country reminds us that he was writing in the mid-Victorian period—and three years after the first appearance of Taine's *History of English Literature*. "Progress" in accordance with the universal laws of evolution was assumed by most nineteenth century (and perhaps later) commentators on Australian literature. As a new society, a new race, evolved in response to the new environment, so would a new literature, which (ambiguously) would be an agent in and a product of this evolution. And "prospects" had a particular poignancy for the scholar turning his attention to the literature of his own colony; what he surveyed could be only the first fruits plucked from a vine that had scarce taken root in this thin soil; it would be a later age that reaped the harvest. Later literary historians have traced the extent of the Mother Country's influence on local writing, and of Europe's and America's. Bibliographies have been compiled, and the memories of men whose names could scarcely be expected to survive their generation have been preserved. Here, I want to consider the success with which Barton's other, and elusive, aim—that of throwing some light "from a new point of view" on our social history—has been fulfilled.

Broadly, one can imagine a literary "history" that has no awareness of social history at all. The various "Histories of English Literature" written for schools and civil service examinations in England last century approach this extreme, being chronological listings of authors and descriptions of their works, located in time by reference to ruling monarchs or wars. Then there is the "social history" of literature itself: literary movements, literary influences, even the lives of writers do not always correspond with the periods postulated on economic or other grounds. But at the point that even the most ahistorical of literary historians moves beyond texts and chronology to considerations of conditions of authorship, the writer's expression of social values, or other relationships between the writer, his work, and his society, he is encountering history and, consciously or otherwise, offering an interpretation of the past and of the nature of these cultural relationships. At the opposite extreme from the literary chronicle would be a work—such as Taine's—highly aware of literature as a social institution. In Australia, although there were no attempts to provide inclusive literary histories between Barton's books and H.M. Green's *Outline of Australian Literature* in 1930, many of the problems, assumptions, and issues of Australian literary history had emerged by then.

The first of these problems was that of defining the field—what is *Australian* literature? ("What is Australian *literature?*" and the issue of whether the historian should confine himself to an Arnoldian notion of literature or adopt an anthropological approach to literary culture did not, for obvious reasons, preoccupy early historians like Barton or Walker.) Although we most usually think of the concept of a national literature emerging in the eighties and nineties of last century, it is a concept that was present almost from the beginning of the century in literary expectations—expectations because these all but preceded the literature. Romantic literary theory in England and on the Continent had seen literature as the history of the national mind and as the expression of the genius of the individual race. The peculiar problems of a country sharing the language and cultural inheritance of the English but encountering and mastering a different environment, and developing a new culture, had been experienced in America. There the issue of a national literature—the issue, simply of whether a writer's obligations were to be American or a writer first of all—remained contentious at least until the Civil War; and the contention was not diminished by English observers such as Sidney Smith enquiring in the *Edinburgh* in 1820: "Who in the four quarters of the globe reads an American book?" William Ellery Channing, who felt that it were "better to have no literature than form ourselves unresistingly on a foreign one" addressed the issue in 1823 in his lecture "The Importance and Means of a National Literature". In this he defined literature as "the expression of a nation's mind" and claimed that "literature is plainly among the powerful methods of exalting the character of a nation, of forming a better race of men".

Such exalted views of literature's function were quite orthodox on both sides of the Atlantic—and soon after on the other side of the Pacific. For as George Nadel documents in *Australia's Colonial Culture*, these were also the principles of those who took upon themselves the education and moral improvement of the Australian colonies. Literature and culture were virtually co-extensive terms, and the propagation of literature was expected to alleviate the depressingly materialistic tone of the Australian colonies, restore a lost sense of community, and morally elevate the masses. Nadel shows how, from the 1830s onwards, literary culture was related to nationalism: "In whatever fashion the argument was disseminated the basic point seemed to be that sheep and acres did not give a country nationality, but that literature did: indeed there could be no patriotism without literature"[1] and he quotes the essay "Literature—Its Advancement and Results" from the first issue of the *Australian Era* (1850). The author of the essay saw Australia "as standing on the brink of nationality ... Literature created nationality, because nationality presupposed national thought and a national intelligence, themselves the product of literature".

The connection between literature and nationality came early—we might say it was imported before much imaginative writing had appeared in Australia. One of the first (of many, as it turned out) to proclaim the emergence of a national literature was William Walker in his lecture "Australian Literature" delivered at the Windsor School of Arts in 1864. His historical survey, he felt, showed that Australia had a "a literature of her own of a progressive and promising character", and one, his title implied, that transcended colonial borders and jealousies. So impressed was Walker with the progress already made that he felt another lecture would be necessary to do full justice to the poetry, and that there was every probability that Australia would produce writers worthy to be placed alongside Bacon, Shakespeare, Byron, and Scott. Such optimism reminds one of Melville in America earlier—"Believe me, my friends, men not very inferior to Shakespeare are being born this day on the banks of the Ohio"—and the American parallel was one that occurred naturally to critics as Australia enjoyed its own debate over a national literature in the last quarter of the nineteenth century. While "universalists" agonized over whether one could meaningfully speak of American literature (if a work were good enough it surely belonged to English literature?), the "nationalists" were inspired with confidence, as were the republicans in politics, by the American precedent. The confident national literature they saw as emerging with Hawthorne, Longfellow, Bret Harte, and others seemed an important indication of the most likely course of Australia's own literary maturation. The invariable analogies between literary and biological or organic growth (mothers and daughters, trees and branches, with America always at a later stage of development) fitted the general belief in the inevitability of evolutionary progress and must have seemed, subconsciously, to guarantee eventual social and literary maturation. The American parallel provided the historical model which was to be employed by later historians of Australian literature. After a colonial period in which immigrant writers discovered a strange new land, native-born writers would emerge to express their acceptance of this land and society as their own; eventually, after a period of nationalistic selfconsciousness, a mature, assured, unselfconsciously national literature would be established. Consistently, from about 1870 onwards (and well into this century) Australian critics were proclaiming the beginning of this second stage, the emergence of distinctively Australian writers; just as in this century they have proclaimed the achievement of the final stage, the coming of age.

Although, for obvious reasons, there were no full-scale literary histories written in the nineteenth century, critical discussions in books and periodicals presupposed views of the development of Australia and literature's relationship to this. Australia had done well for a pioneering country with a small population which, of necessity, had to get on with more immediate matters than pursuing culture; on the other hand, Australia was too materialistic (a view that Barton questioned) and its prosperous class that could afford time and money for culture was too philistine, too nouveau-riche to offer the traditional patronage of the European aristocracy and haute-bourgeoisie. Whichever way the argument ran, this sense of literature as an index of cultural attainment and social history was common to a number of books that appeared around the turn of the century. These were not literary histories in the sense that they pretended to any systematic inclusiveness, but their assumptions concerning the relationships between literature and the society in which it was produced, like those in many other studies of particular writers or partial views of Australian writing in the periodicals, contributed to an awareness of literature as part of our general or cultural history. Indeed, the most frequent assumptions, issues, and phrases, of later literary history can be found in these books which appeared within a brief space of time at the end of last century: Patchett Martin's *The Beginnings of Australian Literature* (1898), a pamphlet originally delivered in London as a lecture by a former editor of the *Melbourne Review*; Desmond Byrne's *Australian Writers* (1896), a collection of biographical and critical discussions of Clarke, Kingsley, Cambridge, Gordon, Boldrewood, Praed and "Tasma" introduced by a general discussion; and Turner and Sutherland's *The Development of Australian Literature* (1898), the only one to be published in Australia with primarily an Australian audience in mind.

Turner's introductory "General Sketch of Australian Literature", (which is then followed by Sutherland's biographies of Clarke, Gordon, and Kendall) expresses the conventional literary historical assumptions about the relationship between the size of the population, the country's stage of development, and its literature. Turner, writing at a time when the population was four million, says that the growth of a large population sharing local experience "must inevitably bring strength and maturity to a national literature". The present stage in cultural development Turner sees as restricted by the necessity for culture to take a second place in a pioneering community and the lack of national feeling. Until leisure is possible and a national spirit is developed ("as it will be unless the tradition of our race suffers decay") we must be content "with the productions of local literature, essentially English in its characteristics, but moulded by climatic and scenic surroundings into a form that gives it sufficient distinctiveness to justify the term 'Australian'."

Scepticism towards this attitude that linked the "development" of Australian literature with the expansion of society, and its corollary that what literature had been produced was admirable for a society at such an early stage of its development, was also expressed. Professor T.G. Tucker, an editor of the *Australasian Critic*, constantly attacked this attitude, as also did Byrne in his introduction to *Australian Writers*. Taking up the parallel with America which had been used so often to prophesy the inevitable emergence of an Australian literature, Byrne inverts it to question its assumptions (Benjamin Franklin, he points out, appeared considerably before America achieved nationhood) and to shatter any complacency about Australian cultural life. Australians, he says, take no pride in creative intellectual work; despite Government provision of education and cultural establishments public taste has not improved; clubs and societies devoted to literature are elitist; the lack of support for local periodicals and books, because of public preference for what is approved by the English public, has meant that it is impossible to live by writing in Australia. These facts, Byrne suggests: "may not be found to explain why there is yet no sign of the coming of an Antipodean Franklin or Irving, or Hawthorne or Emerson; but they will help to show why the literature of the country grows so unevenly, why it is chiefly of the objective order and leaves large tracks of the lives of the people untouched."[2]

In later literary historical accounts, the years in which these views of the relationships between society and culture in Australia were being advanced were also the years when a national feeling (and a politically unified nation) was emerging, and finding expression, particularly in the *Bulletin*. Byrne, writing in England, seemed unaware of the *Bulletin* writers; the others however were not, though their contemporary view was not that of later generations. Turner's conservatism made him critical of Lawson's radicalism and wary of exaggerating the place of the *Bulletin* writers; Patchett Martin was more warmly disposed towards them as indicating the commencement of an Australian school of writing; Francis Adams employed by the *Bulletin* in the late eighties was contemptuous of local poetry and prose. It would be interesting to establish when the view of the *Bulletin*'s central role in the development of a national literature—a view shared by many of its writers and, presumably, readers also—became a historical view. Nettie Palmer's *Modern Australian Literature* (1924) would seem to have been very influential here. As its title suggests, it is concerned with the first quarter of the twentieth century, and its necessarily summary treatment of the previous century became orthodox in many later accounts. Nettie Palmer was among the first to take a historical view of the decades before and after Federation and to draw a sharp division between the "colonial" literature which presented Australia through the eyes of expatriate Englishmen (or "bias-bleared spectacles" as A.G. Stephens had expressed it characteristically in 1901) and the "Australian" literature that had emerged with the new nation. Of course writers involved in the conscious movement to establish a national literature—Stephens, Lawson, Vance Palmer—felt that the *Bulletin* schools had achieved those long anticipated characteristics by which the national literature would be recognized: a lack of selfconsciousness in the use of Australian experience and the assumption of a local rather than an English audience. As Jose wrote in his *History of Australasia* in

1909: "during the last twenty years there has sprung up a school of young Australians who tell of their own life in their own natural way, and describe their own country as men who love it; so that through them a stranger can get at the heart of the people, not merely at the ideas about the people formed by interested outsiders."[3] *Modern Australian Literature* endorsed such contemporary views as historically accurate. The long-awaited nationhood and national literature had been achieved. For the literary historian the task was to reveal what was essentially Australian in the literature, and the elusive relationships between the land, the people, and the literature that for a long time it had been presupposed would emerge.

Although literary historical issues had been discussed for the best part of a century, it was not until 1930 that the first attempt to provide a comprehensive account of imaginative writing appeared with H.M. Green's *Outline of Australian Literature*. It was presented, in its introduction, as preliminary to "a short history of Australian literature" in which an attempt would be made "to relate the literature of each period to its social, political and other conditions". As we now know, it was to be another thirty years before that work, which attempted the higher literary historical aim of exploring the relationships between literature and society, appeared. The earlier *Outline*, however, is conceptually unadventurous. It is a "pure" literary history, and a history of "pure" literature, which makes only passing references to historical events and developments and is concerned only with "high" literary culture. The interpretative framework remains vague and general, and its opening sentence retains the favourite metaphor and the guarded stance of the "colonial" critic: "Australian literature is a branch of English literature, and however great it may become and whatever characteristics it may develop, it will remain a branch." For Green, as for so many of the nineteenth century critics, "the literature of a country is obviously an expression of the characteristic qualities of its life", and he lists the characteristics he discerns:

> Most apparent are the qualities, positive and negative, which one would expect to find in the literary work of any young and comparatively undeveloped country, such as vigour and freshness, crudity and lack of architecture and craftsmanship generally; these last, however, no longer mark the best Australian work. But there is also apparent at times a richness, an almost tropical warmth and colouring which may be noticed particularly in the verse of Hugh McCrae

and Dorothea Mackellar. More widely spread are certain other qualities which are only in part literary, since their presence in any work which involves representation of character will be derived from the characters represented as well as from the temperament and experience of the writer and their result upon his literary method and point of view. These qualities are an independence of spirit, a kind of humorous disillusion, a careless willingness to take a risk, a slightly sardonic good nature and a certain underlying hardness of texture.[4]

The first two sets of characteristics are conventionally evolutionist and synthesize much nineteenth century discussion which emphasized the difficulties encountered by a pioneering society, and speculated that climatic and other environmental factors would mould the people and their culture. The third set relates to national character and its expression through literature, and although he does not develop these here it is these characteristics and their relationship to historical experience and social institutions, including literature, that were to become so important in later accounts, including Green's own.

In the same year as the *Outline* another book appeared which was to affect views of Australian social history, culture, and literary history for generations to come—W.K. Hancock's *Australia*. Like Tocqueville, who "tried to explain to cultivated Europeans the characteristics of democracy in a 'new' country", Hancock tried to explain to cultivated Europeans the paradoxes of Australian life. His success can be gauged from the fact that *Australia* has assumed something of the same classic status for historians and commentators on society here as *Democracy in America* has in that country. Although not a history, being as much concerned with what could be considered separately as politics, economics, culture, or sociology (for each of which areas it contributed concepts), it was the first study to seek "dominant themes" in Australian life that would relate the past to the present. It provided an interpretative framework that related the social, economic, and cultural in bold hypotheses which many later scholars have examined. For example, the statement that "Australian nationalism took definite form in the class struggle between the landless majority and the land monopolizing squatters", although it synthesizes attitudes that had been expressed many times at various stages in the past, confers a historical validation upon them, and anticipates the major theme of Australian historians in later decades. Hancock's influence on historians and social commentators has been discussed and criticized by R.W. Connell (in *Quadrant*, vol. 12, no. 2, 1968): here I want only to draw attention to its similar influence on the concept of history found in the work of literary critics. Again as an example of the bold generalization that anticipates or stimulated later writers we could take his statement that "Recurrent in Australian poetry is a note of renunciation, sometimes regretful, sometimes defiant ... and a note of expectation, of waiting upon the future for an Australia which has not been known to the past ... "[5] which accords with Judith Wright's later study of the preoccupations with exile and utopia in Australian poetry.

Hancock sees literature as part of the total cultural development he traces and analyzes, and sees it as expressing "the prevailing ideology of Australian democracy": "in Lawson and Collins, and almost every other writer of the *Bulletin* school, Australian nationalism expressed itself as a repudiation of English conventions and standards, as a vindication of equality and democracy and an assertion of the supreme worth of the average man."[6] Hancock is synthesizing the nationalism and egalitarian democracy that were expressed (however more complexly) by these writers. But he is also defining in social and political terms what was "characteristic" of Australian literature and providing the literary historian with the link between literature and society in terms of the values expressed in the literature of the nationalist period. These were not the links perceived, or so explicitly formulated, by literary historians (for example, Nettie Palmer or H.M. Green) up to this time. However, the tradition Hancock postulated was to be elaborated by historians and critics from then on. It provided the opportunity to interpret the development of literature in terms of social history and to use literature to illustrate the formation of an egalitarian national culture and character. By the time H.M. Green's full history appeared this had become an orthodoxy—though already an orthodoxy under attack—which provided in numerous summaries a stereotyped view of literature developing in accordance with national consciousness. It is also an orthodoxy that clearly affects Green's consideration of the relationship of "the literature of each period to its social, political and other conditions".

The *History of Australian Literature* (1961) opens with much more confidence in its subject as an entity than does the *Outline* with its branch-of-the-tree image: "It is scarcely necessary to argue nowadays that the literature of Australia is worth discussing on its own account, and not merely as part of the great literature in English, of which it is an outgrowth. This great literature is like a banyan-tree, whose branches bend down, and, striking the ground, take root and grow up as independent individuals."[7] And the *History* reflects the growth of interest in, and re-interpretation of, the nineteenth century that had developed since 1930. Green in his concluding section mentions key contributors to this greater awareness of the past, as much historical and broadly cultural as specifically literary: Russel Ward, A.A. Phillips, Cecil Hadgraft, whose own history of Australian literature had appeared in 1960, Vincent Buckley, and others. A.A. Phillips in *Meanjin* (in essays later collected in *The Australian Tradition*) and other contributors to that journal including Manning Clark had elaborated the connections between literature and society Hancock had discerned. Vance Palmer, whose first essay on an Australian national literature had appeared in 1905, and Russel Ward had both explored the social historical bases of the "legend" that linked the past to the present in a national consciousness. And in the criticism of Buckley and others a reaction against the democratic nationalist interpretation of literature and social history had emerged, so that Green in introducing his discussion of the period "Self-Conscious Nationalism" could observe "a tendency nowadays to underrate the achievement of the third Period of Australian literature".

In the *History* Green's sympathies are on the side of those who had expounded an Australian social and literary tradition. He confesses, in a footnote, of having made the mistake in his *Outline* of "concentrating too much upon literature in its more aesthetic aspect". This "aesthetic" writing in earlier periods was thin and nostalgic in comparison with the "rough spun" indigenous material: "beyond the world of books ... material was accumulating that was to form the basis of important elements in the literature to be ... yarns and anecdotes ... old bush songs ... sketches ... recollections, diaries, memoirs ... "[8] Following Russel Ward and other historians, Green perceives in the popular culture of the earlier nineteenth century the bases of an Australian tradition. In dealing with the nineties, his analysis seems to owe more to Hancock and his influence than to what had already been written in the *Outline*: "In

Australia, the spirit of the nineties and early nineteen-hundreds was a spirit ... which took the form in literary as well as in the social and political worlds, of a fervent democratic nationalism: it was based upon a broad social consciousness, a feeling of mutual relationship, that found its most characteristic expression in Lawson's doctrine of mateship".[9] Here, the characteristics of a distinctive Australian literature are defined in social and political terms, although the vaguer perceptions of the pre-Hancock *Outline* are retained also— "a kind of warmth and glow which seems to be a reflection of heat and light and the colour-effects of the landscape". After his period of "Self-Conscious Nationalism", Green abandons the attempt to relate social and literary developments closely. His promise to discuss national types and characteristics at the end is not fulfilled; perhaps because, as the introduction to the "Modern Period" suggests, the democratic idealism of those earlier decades had become dissipated in cosmopolitanism and superficiality.

The *History of Australian Literature* most fully achieves the aims Barton had suggested nearly a century before. The mass of information it assembles on the press, the social groupings of writers, and the economics of authorship make it an important contribution to social and cultural history as well as a more narrowly literary study. So comprehensive, in fact, is Green that the broad interpretation he offers on social and literary relationships in the nineties is qualified by his recognition that there were many periodicals other than the *Bulletin*, writers like Brennan, Baylebridge, and Richardson as well as Lawson, Furphy, and Paterson, and the influences of the Celtic twilight as well as democratic nationalism on a host of minor writers. In these ways, the *History* avoids the stereotyped account of the development of a national literature that had been advanced by wedding Hancock's social analysis to literary history. Now that the major role for the literary historian was no longer to provide the basic biographical and bibliographical information (as had been necessary in 1930), critical interpretations of the stereotypes appeared. Cecil Hadgraft's *Australian Literature* was published the year before Green's *History*. It concentrates on "pure" literature and the methodological problems of establishing "periods" that will reconcile the temper of a particular time with the literary works of distinction produced within it. Thus on his first period, Hadgraft writes: "The name Colonial Period has been suggested for these

seventy years. If poetry alone is considered then the name is perti-
nent. But to apply it to a period that includes Clarke's masterpiece
seems almost defamatory. It is worth noting, however, that the
literature of the period does not much express Australian ideals."[10]
For his second period 1880—1930 Hadgraft postulates two "sub-
periods", 1880—1914 and 1900—1930, to account for the diversity
of writing, some consciously nationalistic, some unconcerned with
issues of nationality, and for the stubborn refusal of facts to fit the
stereotypes neatly: "the nineties, often thought of as prolific in
valuable and representative works are really rather thin. Only two
volumes of Lawson's tales and one of his verse and only one volume
of Paterson's verse, for instance, appeared before 1900."[11]

A similar awareness that the courses of literary and social
history did not always run parallel had already been expressed by
G.A. Wilkes, in an essay on the decade that is the focus of literary
historical interpretation—the 1890s:

> Was there a literary period "the nineties" in Australia? The stages of
> Australian literary history have still to be determined. The present
> tendency is to fix them in accordance with existing political or
> economic divisions, so that a new age is dated from the gold-rushes of
> 1851, for instance, another from the nineties or the attainment of
> Federation in 1901, and another from the Great War of 1914—18.
> This is to determine periods of literary development by reference to
> non-literary critera, and the boundaries that result are often fal-
> lacious.[12]

Wilkes sees the literature of the period having been distorted by the
emphasis placed on democratic and nationalistic writing, which was
not the only kind of writing, was not necessarily the best—and was
certainly not the best because it was democratic. He combines a
historian's responsibility to take account of all relevant evidence
with a critic's attention to the interpretation of texts (for example,
what Furphy was concerned with) and their artistic quality (the best
of Lawson's work would not include his political verse). "The Eighteen Nineties" is the only critically conscious discussion of the
hybrid nature of literary history by an Australian critic, and the
same awareness of conceptual and methodological problems is
found in Wilkes's later *Australian Literature: A Conspectus*, (1969).
Like Hadgraft's *Australian Literature* this admirably fulfils the
literary historian's traditional role of providing a guide for the non-
specialist, while establishing an interpretative framework that is

critical of received and stereotyped formulations. By implication, the opening sentence which sees the continual interaction of two cultural strands—European and indigenous—as operating throughout the course of Australian literature, dismisses as irrelevant the riddle "What is *Australian* literature" with which most previous historians had felt compelled to begin. There is no attempt at an explanation of literary developments in social terms, and wariness of such explanations is suggested by the observation on Neilson and McCrae that they remind us how "literature at any period may escape parochialism through the artist with the vitality and perception to create his own imaginative world".

As well as these comprehensive literary histories there have been other studies which suggest that the earlier nineteenth century was not as discontinuous with the nineties and the twentieth century as earlier accounts had assumed. Historical studies such as George Nadel's *Australia's Colonial Culture* (1957), Michael Roe's *The Quest for Authority in Eastern Australia* (1965), Henry Mayer's *Marx and Engels in Australia* (1964), and Manning Clark's *History of Australia* (1962) made it clear that Australia had a more complex and vital culture than the stereotype of generations awaiting the coming of the *Bulletin* allowed. It was, of course, a "literary" culture in the fullest sense of that word, and most of its literature assumes most interest for us today in relation to that culture and its issues. Judith Wright in her *Preoccupations in Australian Poetry* (1965), which searches for correspondences between literary attitudes towards Australia and the historical social reality, also questions assumptions of cultural discontinuity. The dual vision she traces as a recurrent theme of poets throughout the nineteenth century and later sees Australia as a land of exile and a utopia simultaneously in each period, rather than each aspect representing a different stage of development.

Other reinterpretations of a deliberately provocative kind have appeared more recently. Humphrey McQueen's *A New Britannia* (1970) although not a literary study (despite its title) impinges on literary history because of his attack on Russel Ward's *The Australian Legend* (1958), the democratic egalitarianism of the social and literary tradition postulated by critics and historians in the forties and fifties, and his iconoclastic assault on its most "representative" literary figure, Henry Lawson. Since the appearance of the third volume of Manning Clark's *History* (1973) it would seem any point in McQueen's diatribe against Australian society as capitalist, racist and militaristic that is relevant to Australian culture in the first half of the nineteenth century has found more substantial and responsible expression in Clark's analysis of the conflicts in this period and the ensuing dominance of bourgeois values of Australian society. Coral Lansbury's *Arcady in Australia* (1970) argues that recurrent images of Australia in literature before the "nationalist" period were formed in fact in England and represented expectations there that the colonial writer observed. The facts Coral Lansbury adduces have been questioned; her argument is partial, but it has the virtue of suggesting the complexity of social forces that enter into the forming of literary images and conventions. The image of idyllic possibilities of life in the Australian landscape is a persistent one that her study stimulatingly draws attention to—even though the stimulus might be to disagreement and qualification. Barry Argyle's *The Australian Novel : 1830—1930* (1972) is also partial, reckless in its procedures, and desperate to assert a continuity in Australian literature and society of the violence and cruelty established in the convict era; but like the others it is most interesting in manifesting a concern to revalue the past, to discover continuities with the nineteenth century, and to depart from received stereotypes (though each of these writers seems equally anxious to establish his own).

The attitudes of historians, literary or otherwise, towards culture in nineteenth century Australia have acquired a history of their own by now. The closing decades of the century especially provide a focal point for any general account of Australian culture, so that, today, we cannot look back directly to the nineteenth century itself without being conscious of the interpretations and evaluations of it that have been offered in the seventy years that intervene between its close and our own vantage point in time. The "colonial" period probably seems more interesting now than it has in earlier decades this century. Its literature may not be granted any intrinsically higher value than it has been accorded previously, but when the different later perspectives are taken into account, the period raises interesting issues for cultural history. These issues concern the social ramifications of literature and culture generally, and here most later commentators have much in common with nineteenth century critics, who were similarly concerned with relating social and cultural development and with suggesting formative and causal connections. The basic assumptions here, and the forms of the arguments advanced, have not changed essentially over more than a century, and these are valuably rehearsed in Geoffrey Serle's *From Deserts the Prophets Come* (1973), the first book to provide a comprehensive cultural history of Australia.

One of the many virtues of Serle's outline is that, like Desmond Byrne's earlier analysis, it brings into the open assumptions which prefer to shelter shyly behind a hedge of organicist analogies. "Culture is a highly perishable growth which, transplanted, cannot bloom as before", Serle himself writes, and quotes from James's *Hawthorne*, the now classic statement about the thinness of the soil in which the American novelist found himself planted. The analogy, implicit in our uses of the word "culture", between man's cultivation of the natural world and his "cultivation" of what he has created himself begs many questions. Talk of "transplanting", of tending slips or seedlings in the new soil in the expectation of a later harvest, follow naturally—such tropes come as second nature to literary men. But what sort of growth is being presupposed—qualitative or quantitative—and is there any essential relationship between the two? What ensures this growth—are "natural" processes involved, is time essential? Or is this a pseudo-explanation that disguises only a confidence that what has happened elsewhere will happen here, eventually? What is the "soil"—the people, all the people, or culturally conscious groups and individuals? James's emphasis on the need for "an accumulation of history and custom ... a complexity of manners and types, to form a fund of suggestion for a novelist" has been very influential in later discussions of the relationship of the individual talent to a social tradition. It tells us a lot about the position James felt himself to be in, but he was clearly wrong about the writer in mid-nineteenth century America: not only was there Hawthorne, there were Emerson, Melville, Whitman, Poe, and others producing one of the most vital periods in any national literature in that century. These writers did not go unobserved in Australia, by Harpur, by Kendall, by many critics. As Frederick Sinnett intimated in 1856, the Australian writer, deprived of such properties of romance as ivied ruins or even a house with seven gables, could better concentrate on the serious concerns of fiction.

16

The need for Australia to grow in scale and diversity and to move towards nationhood Serle also lists as important factors in the "theory of cultural growth" he advances. Again, nineteenth century critics (for example, the historian Turner in 1898) had nominated these as essential for the eventual development of a national literature; but are these "essential factors", do they contribute to an explanation of how culture "grows", or do they provide a description of the social conditions against which it grew in America or Australia? If, as did the majority of Australian critics in the nineteenth century, we assume a natural evolution or growth at work, how do we explain the relative lack of "progress" in the 1920s in Australia? Was the federationist and nationalist idealism which has been seen as the stimulus behind the literature of the preceding decades in advance of actual social conditions, and did this become apparent in the twenties? Are the arts really active agents in social change, or are they, like seeds waiting for the right season, soil, and water, passively dependent on fertile social conditions? Serle himself sees not only "growth" but "maturity" as important, and argues that the delayed development in literature and painting in the twenties is related to the delayed development of national independence and to the continuation of cultural isolation. This is a succinct, accurate expression of one's "sense" of the period but how is "maturity" (as distinguished from "growth", which is thereby assigned a more quantitative or descriptive role) determined: is *For the Term of His Natural Life*, by all accounts the finest novel of the "colonial" period, necessarily a lesser achievement than the novels (all of them, or the best of them) that were produced at a more "mature" stage of our cultural development?

A general pattern of links connecting literature and society in a causal way remains as elusive as ever. At one level there are the abstractions of "society", "culture", and "literature", at another level the particular works of individual writers (in dealing with these the critic and biographer can also contribute to our historical understanding, by bringing these abstractions to life in the case of his chosen subject). Too much insistence on social and economic conditions, publishing outlets and markets, political ideology and established conventions can lead to a deterministic sense that the "age" has produced the literature; at the other extreme too great an insistence on the autonomy of imaginative literature can ignore the involvement, direct or indirect, of writers with their society. In confronting this dilemma and attempting to find a point of balance, Australian literary historians have thrown, in Barton's words, "some light, from a new point of view, on our social history". They have contributed to our awareness of the culture of the past and raised issues of its interpretation from a later vantage point in time and its relevance to the present. These are not issues that can be disposed of finally, because they reconstitute themselves for each generation. Beyond recording biographical and bibliographical facts, what the literary historian can do most successfully is register his understanding—and to some extent this will be the understanding of his time—of the past. What the nineteenth century or earlier twentieth century critics had to say about individual writers and works is most interesting today as a record of their understanding of and attitudes towards the past. In this way literary historians themselves have some claim on posterity: for later generations the best of them will become part of what they have described, part of literary history.

2

"Parents rather than Critics": Some Early Reviews of Australian Literature

ELIZABETH WEBBY

The first decade of the nineteenth century saw the beginning of two famous English *Reviews*, the *Edinburgh* (1802) and the *Quarterly* (1809). Between these dates, the *Sydney Gazette* (1803) printed the first pieces of Australian literature. Being thus born in an age of reviews, even its infant burblings could not escape criticism. Early reviewers were, however, highly conscious of the tender age of their subject, of the need, as one of them wrote, "to estimate rather as parents than as critics". Although their reviews varied widely in quality, the prevailing tone was moralistic and paternal. Works were usually praised for their sentiments rather than style, authors for their efforts rather than achievements. When publications were condemned, it was generally for personal or political, rather than literary, reasons. Here, too, a parental voice could often be heard: that of the angry father bemoaning disgrace to the family name. The smallness and interdependence of colonial literary circles naturally fostered this familial relationship of reviewer and writer, making objective criticism almost impossible.

Excellent examples of these various prejudices at work may be seen in the critical reception of Charles Tompson's *Wild Notes from the Lyre of a Native Minstrel* (1826). It had been published by Robert Howe and so, hardly surprisingly, his *Sydney Gazette* for 1

November 1826 gave Tompson high praise:

> ... when a young man modestly offers the offspring of his muse to the world, he has something like a claim upon the public notice, and the more so when that production evidently bears the stamp of genius. What perhaps may seem to be somewhat singular is, that although the author of the present poem is a young man, we find in the whole of his writings a great chasteness of expression ... From the chaste style of the present writer, we expect that at an after period he will furnish us with something of the classical elegance of a Pope. We are always fond of seeing what is natural either in young or old, because nature is the language which constitutes real poetry.

The specific praise of Tompson's "Retrospect; or, A Review of My Scholastic Days"—"we think no one will rise from the perusal of the piece without respecting the ingenuous feelings of the writer"—shows the emphasis on "right sentiments" then so pervasive in contemporary Australian, and English, literary criticism. There was, however, more originality in the conclusion:

> ... we will merely suggest to Mr. Tompson the propriety of letting his similes and metaphors be purely Australian. He will soon find his account in doing so, as they will infallibly possess all the freshness of originality. In this respect he has a decided advantage over all European poets, because here nature has an entirely different aspect. Let him select from the treasures by which he is surrounded—let nature be his exclusive study—and Australia will have it in her power to boast of the productions of her bard.

As often when reading the newspapers of this time, one is surprised by the early introduction of an idea that was later to prove so important for Australian literature.

Just as the *Sydney Gazette* was bound to give Tompson a favourable review, so, granted the continuous rivalry between colonial editors, the other newspapers and magazines were equally bound to find as many faults as possible. A reviewer in the *Sydney Monitor* for 24 November 1826 took a much more critical view of "Retrospect", commenting on Tompson's imitation of Goldsmith and finding the poem "void of originality, either in design or expression". Mr. Tompson was further advised:

> ... miscellaneous productions afford but an uncertain criticism by which to try poetic merit. Such are not calculated to call forth the latent sparks of real genius. An historically descriptive poem, not in the beaten track of odes, or the worn-out numbers of an elegy—but

warmed and enlivened by descriptions true to nature, and ornamented by metaphors and similes, easy and unrestrained; and avoiding those nicely measured rhymes which only jingle in the ear like pack-horse bells, would go farther to advance Mr. Thompson's fame than a closely printed quarto of birthday sonnets, although inscribed to Venus herself.

This call for Australian poets to try their hands at longer pieces was often repeated; even the *Gazette* reviewer had looked forward to Tompson's production of a "heroic poem ... which will enable him to display his real abilities".

Wild Notes was also given a poor reception in the first number of Australia's second magazine, the *South-Asian Register*, in October 1827. The *Sydney Gazette*, challenged by the *Monitor* to justify its harsh remarks on the *Register*, lost no time in proving, in a review of 24 October, that the *Register*'s critic knew nothing of poetry or criticism:

> After quoting sixteen lines from one of the poems, entitled "Retrospect", as "a favourable specimen of the whole", the opinion of the quotation, because it cannot be called a criticism, is contained in the three words "this is pretty", which anybody might have said without evincing any extraordinary degree of acumen. Fourteen lines more are immediately quoted, and in order to counterbalance the "this is pretty" with a spice of critical censure, the Reviewer says, "There are many instances in which the nominative is very dubious and the sense consequently obscure". Now in order to illustrate this other mere assertion without proof, eighteen lines are quoted from the "Pleasures of Memory", in which, as well as in the former quotation, the reader is left to form his own conjectures of truth or fallacy of what the pretended critic has asserted, without even the scanty assistance which an italic word might have afforded.

The type of labour-saving criticism censured here was, however, extremely common in Australian and English newspapers in the early nineteenth century. Such reviewers made a few, often a very few, general and meaningless remarks and then devoted the rest of their space to quotation of "beauties" or, with prose, touching or exciting incidents.

Following the general pattern of attack and counterattack then current, the *Monitor* was provoked to reply to the *Gazette* in the form of a letter to the editor from "Chathamville", printed on 29 October 1827. Here the *South-Asian Register* reviewer was defended and Tompson once more charged with unoriginality:

Had Dr. Oldfield in reviewing Tompson's poems cut where he *could*, mercy might have arraigned him as a severe critic;—but he "felt for another's woes", and therefore spared the young man's Zephyrs and Bowers, Nymphs and Flowers, with all the other pretty little *poetical* etceteras which might well be termed "wild" and uncultivated;—jingling weeds that are excluded from the parterres of true poetry, and which only serve to mark the barrenness of the soil in which they flourish. I have read these "poems", and cannot call to mind a single idea which the boy of 12 years might not with the greatest facility have conceived. "Black Town" is quoted by the "South Asian" as the highest flight of the Poet's pegasus. And what have we here? A canting rhapsody of *speculative* patriotism and philanthrophy; an idea or two, that have been ten thousand times metamorphosed, to preserve a show of originality, and presented to the public, and now again *transposed* and laid before us as the *unsuggested* thoughts of the writer. When Mr. Tompson ventured to publish his "*poems*", he listened with too attentive an ear to the flattery of his friends who praised the fluttering attempts (to use an Australian simile) of the yet callow emu, which alas! was NEVER created to fly. I am not singular in my opinion; the public voice goes with me, of which presumptive evidence may be seen on the shelves of the Australian Stationery Warehouse. The Public will no doubt acquit the editor of the Sydney Gazette of disinterestedness in becoming the panegyrist of Tompson's Poems, when they are informed, that he printed them, and that the payment of a pretty round sum for so doing, may be said to be contingent upon their sale.

Thus even in 1827 Sydney was not devoid of literary talent—consciously or not, the writer heeded the advice of the *Gazette* critic and made his remarks more telling by the use of local colour! He also gives one of the few pieces of evidence as to the popularity of early Australian poetry. Little wonder more publishers did not take a chance on a slim volume or two.

Nothing is known of the sale of John Dunmore Lang's *Aurora Australis, or Specimens of Sacred Poetry, for the Colonists of Australia* (1826). It appeared soon after Tompson's volume, to be greeted by a similar amount of newspaper criticism. Since Lang's verses deserve the title of "poetry" even less than Tompson's, one's sympathies are strongly on the side of "Spectator", whose "Lines Written on Reading Those Luminous Poems Designated Aurora Australis", in the *Australian* for 13 January 1827, opened:

> Go, little book! my mind is much imbued,
> To doom thee to eternal solitude;
> Or in the flood of Phlegethon's fierce flames;

Or Lethe's rolling, dark, oblivious streams;
With other reams of foolscap much befool'd,
Lost to all light, the day they once have rul'd,
Perversion strange! to dare assume the name
Of bright Aurora, in this land of fame;
Where dawn of talent spreads the eager wing,
To which aspiring minds with ardour cling.

The editor of the *Australian* had been careful to dissociate himself from this possible "harsh treatment" of poems he "had not perused" personally. And on 24 January 1827 he published a counter to "Spectator's" arguments from "An Onlooker". Although consisting mainly of a selection of "beauties", the sound point was made that " ... it was, perhaps, unfortunate for the Scotch Parson's muse, though it showed his desire to turn her to good account, that he confined his attention to sacred and devotional subjects, for Dr. Johnson tells us somewhere that such subjects are not fit for poetry; and besides, they are of all subjects the least adapted to Colonial taste." Three days later, however, a critic in the *Monitor* complained that Lang had chosen to write on trivial subjects unsuited to the dignity of sacred poetry.

The *South-Asian Register* for October 1827 gave a much better review of *Aurora Australia* than of Tompson's *Wild Notes*, showing a rare early recognition of the need for objective criticism of Australian literature: "We are disposed to make much of our Colonial productions, and not to be over fastidious when their number is so small: but we, notwithstanding, take it to be our province, to preserve a record of their merits and defects, for the guidance of public opinion." Lang's characteristic metres were beautifully summed up in the sentence, "Most of these poems were written, it appears, on ship board; we therefore do not wonder at their having a certain qualminess, every now and then, which is so commonly felt in the motion of a cross sea."

Little of poetic interest appeared in volume form in Australia during the 1830s. The young William Woolls, seemingly agreeing that long poems were the test of a poet's art, published two, *The Voyage; A Moral Poem Written During, and Descriptive of, A Voyage from England to New South Wales* (1832) and *Australia: A Moral and Descriptive Poem* (1833), but their reception was not encouraging. On 1 May 1833, for example, the *Monitor* wrote " ... we think 'Australia' inferior to the 'Voyage'; and we would advise the author, if he love composition, to turn his attention to prose ... The poetry appears to us mere jingling rhymes, such as a rhyme-making friend might set down to amuse his correspondent with extemporaneously. The TONE of 'Australia' is lofty—while the language and subject are quite common-place."

Even the *New South Wales Magazine* for August 1833, while objecting to the *Monitor*'s "sweeping and ill-natured sarcasms", had to allow Woolls "an occasional poverty of poetical phraseology, and slovenliness of versification". This review, probably by the magazine's editor, Ralph Mansfield, opened with the usual explanation for the lack of a sturdy literary culture in the colony:

> ... however true the charge may be (and it is advanced by many), of the little encouragement that is given to the intellectual efforts of literary men in New South Wales; we cannot but think that it is somewhat out of place and exaggerated. The fact is, that in *all* young countries, men's minds are too exclusively occupied in overcoming unlooked-for obstacles, and in forming the foundation of future personal comfort and competency, to take much interest in the quiet and peaceable pursuits of literature.
>
> ... with whatever crudeness or defects Mr. Wools' [sic] poem may be charged, we cannot but think it displays a very great portion of poetical spirit and promising talent (the author, we understand, is yet a minor) ...

Woolls appears to have heeded the *Monitor*'s strictures for his third publication, *Miscellanies in Prose and Verse* (1838), was made up of essays on moral and colonial topics, along with a few short poems, most of them reprinted from local newspapers. A lengthy review was printed in the *Colonist* on 11 August 1838. As Woolls had been a frequent contributor to this paper it was naturally predisposed to find in his favour but even so had to allow that his essays lacked "variety of sentiment", while his verse did "not exhibit the brilliance of a BYRON or a CAMPBELL". Though so needing to qualify his praise of the results, the reviewer could not speak highly enough of the attempt:

> ... when we consider the usual employments of young men in New South Wales, and the sad want of taste which they manifest in literary and scientific pursuits, we should be wanting in justice to the author if we were not to congratulate him on the profitable manner in which he has spent his vacant hours. Too many, we are well aware, in this colony, surrender their whole time and attention to occupations of a mercenary character—they pay no regard to the engagements which

should excite the energies of a moral and intellectual being—they bury themselves in sloth and indolence, intent only on gratifying their animal nature—and, strange to say, through the love of money, or the allurements of dissipation, they entirely overlook the grand end and object of their existence. Such a state of things is certainly deplorable, inasmuch as it shows the tendency which prevails to depreciate the efforts of the mind, and those employments which have for their object the amelioration and exaltation of mankind. To our author, therefore, some attention is due on account of his perseverance in the paths of literature, for, while others have consumed their evenings in scenes of riot and dissipation, it is manifest that he has spent his hours by the "midnight oil", and, with no common care and anxiety, turned over the "the ponderous tomes" of the ancients.

Just over a month later, and also in the *Colonist*, Woolls himself was expressing similar paternal sentiments about James Martin's *The Australian Sketch Book* (1838)[1]:

... when we consider that the book, now before us, is the composition of one whose "down is yet upon his cheek," and all whose opportunities of improvement or observation have been confined within the narrow limits of colonial society, we are quite disarmed of the fearful shafts of criticism ... Mr. Martin's example, too, affords a salutary lesson to many of our colonial striplings. Let them imitate him in his meritorious search after knowledge, and, instead of endeavouring to attain celebrity by their superior skill in horse racing and boating, let them labour, with all their might to secure their moral and intellectual improvement.

The other local reviewers, however, were not so sparing of Martin's efforts, most of them justly pointing to the extremely derivative nature of *The Australian Sketch Book*. His lack of originality in subject matter—topics included "The Sublime in Nature", "A Visit to the Scenes of Youth", and "A Church Yard Reverie"—was the chief complaint of the *Sydney Gazette* for 29 September 1838: "The great fault we have to find with this and similar productions, is that great portions of the space are occupied with dissertations on subjects which have already occupied the attention of minds of a superior calibre to any we can expect to find in the Colonies, while the great mines of Colonial materials are in great measure left unexplored."

Although equally derivative in conception, Martin's attack on colonial writers, "The Pseudo-Poets", did at least have local content and is the most interesting of his collection. Many of his general descriptions of early Australian verse are all too apt: "ridiculous and unmeaning trash"; "Literary fragments—sober tragedies— didactic poems—and fugitive pieces of every description"; "love is the principal—almost the only topic, on which their productions are composed". In his treatment of individual poets, however, Martin became unbearably superior. Charles Tompson had not read widely enough, while Henry Halloran had not selected his subjects wisely or "carefully revised and corrected" his verses. He was told to study more and to "beware of vanity". Charles Harpur was also directed to "the illustrious sages of antiquity": "You may have innate genius, I dispute it not—you may have talent for poetic composition, but that talent, let me inform you, is useless without proper cultivation."

Martin's heavy emphasis on the need to read before one writes, so obviously his own practice, was turned against him by the reviewer of *The Australian Sketch Book* in the *Australian* for 27 October 1838:

> In the "Sublime in Nature", the "Thunder Storm", and "Genius", "Sun-rise", and "Sun-set", the author shews no mean powers of description, but his reflections seem rather the result of reading than of thought. The "Pseudo-Poets", we like least of all; it is commendable neither on matter nor form. The position of literary censor is one which Mr. Martin's modesty should just now prevent him from assuming, even if his abilities qualified him for the task. There is, no doubt, much trash put forth, in this Colony, under the name of poetry. But it is not *all* trash—and we could wish Mr. Martin's acumen had led him rather to discover gold, than to expose the dross. "Your reading", says Mr. Martin to one of the luckless wights condemned by Apollo, "appears not to have been sufficiently extensive." Does Mr. Martin, then, imagine that extensive reading will make a poet? Did Burns get his poetry from books? From our author's admiration of Gray and Goldsmith, we infer both his reading and his taste, but we suspect that his judgment in these matters is yet far from being mature. We have spoken candidly on this subject, because Mr. Martin seems to treat with something like contempt, all whose productions do not bear internal evidence of the "reading" of their authors. His own writings are not chargeable with this fault—and, to deal plainly with him, we wish there *had been* some deficiency in this respect. He has ability enough to be original; and we would rather have his own thoughts properly matured, than the reflected ones of Paley or Washington Irving.

James Martin's criticisms of Harpur were based on poems contributed to Sydney newspapers during the 1830s. Harpur's first

volume, *Thoughts, A Series of Sonnets*, published in 1845, received
only two local reviews but both were highly favourable. A notice in
the *Morning Chronicle* for 5 November 1845 opened with the usual
hope that Australia would soon arise from the slough of
materialism:

> We are glad to perceive that a love of literary pursuits is gradual-
> ly springing up amongst us; and though the incipient efforts which
> have hitherto been made by our press have not been attended with any
> very great degree of success, we hail them with satisfaction, as being
> the prelude to a happier and more abundant consummation.
> We have been hitherto too much engaged in building up fortunes,
> in "adding field to field, and house to house," to pay much attention
> to the cultivation of literary tastes and pursuits. Those few individuals
> who have stepped out from the common mass, and have occasionally
> diverted our attention, though even for a short time, from the pursuit
> of Mammon, deserve to be esteemed and honoured. Amongst those,
> we know of no one who has been more ardent in his devotions to the
> Muses, or with whose effusions we have at various times been more
> delighted, than Charles Harpur. We have often regretted that he has
> not earnestly set himself to work to frame something worthy of
> himself, and of the bright and sunny land from whose soil he sprung.
> His great flow of words, his rich stores of imagination, and the
> strain of unaffected piety and pure patriotism which run through all
> his effusions, point him out as one well fitted to crown his country
> with a diadem of poetry worthy of herself, and of her children.
> The unpretending little work now before us, we have perused
> with much pleasure; it contains twenty-three sonnets; on various sub-
> jects, all of them very pretty, and several really beautiful, abounding
> in rich imagery and poetic feeling.

On 22 November, Harpur's friend Henry Parkes wrote in even
more glowing terms in the *Weekly Register*:

> The "Thoughts" of Mr. Harpur occupy only sixteen pages, con-
> sisting of twenty-three Sonnets, all of which we think are beautiful,
> and some of them such as will bear comparison with the productions,
> in the same kind, of illustrious names. The English language is rich in
> its number of fine sonnets: our great bards, Milton, Shakspeare,
> Wordsworth, and others, have minted some of their grandest thoughts
> into this unpretending fashion of mental coinage—have planted, in
> moments of pure inspiration, the rarest as well as the most delicate of
> poetry's immortal flowers in this "scanty plot of ground." Mr. Har-
> pur is a poet not unworthy to be named with these august sons of
> genius, though he may never attain to their universal fame. As a
> native bard, Australia ought to be proud of him. When the day arrives
> that some wanderer of Europe shall gather up the first fruits of

Australian literature, the lines "To an Echo on the Banks of the Hunter", "The Message", "The Dream by the Fountain", and other poems bearing the name of Charles Harpur, in the Sydney journals, will be held in admiration in our fatherland, to the shame of the country and the age that could neglect them. As a sonnet-writer, in particular, we think Mr. Harpur excels so far, that we are inclined to question whether from Wordsworth's "Sonnets dedicated to Liberty", there could be taken any twenty-three, consecutively arranged, superior, "all in all", to the twenty-three before us. We cannot enter into the merits of his poetry here to the extent we wish; but whoever has a capability to appreciate the passion and energy divine of song, needs only to obtain a copy of Mr. Harpur's publication, to be convinced that Australia has now produced a poet all her own, to atone for the indiscretions of poetasters among her adopted sons.

Parkes's high praise, however, resulted in further public humilation for Harpur in the following year when a certain R.K. Ewing delivered three lectures on "Modern Poetry" at the Sydney Mechanics' School of Arts. His final lecture included some remarks on colonial poetry, in particular, an attack on the *Weekly Register* review of *Thoughts*. As the *Spectator* for 27 June 1846 reported, mistakenly printing "Parkes" for "Harpur" and wrongly attributing the review to W.A. Duncan.

> Whilst the claims of Messrs. H. Halloran, R. Lynd, Lowe, and other colonial writers of deserved celebrity, were hastily disposed of, the lecturer rather cruelly lingered over a most severe, though nobly minded, castigation of Mr. H. Parkes, the pet *protege* of the late editor of the *Weekly Register*. Mr. Duncan's comparison of Parkes with Milton was a glaring piece of absurdity which did not require the exposure Mr. Ewing thought proper to give it; and although we joined heartily in the laugh which he raised at the expense of the *Register Sonnetteer* and his friendly critic, we could have wished that the writings of the authors we have just named had received the attention which they assuredly demand from any one who professes to analyse the pretensions, and expiate on the merits, of colonial poetry.

In daring to mention Harpur in the same breath as English poets, Parkes was, of course, only following a practice fairly common among local reviewers. Of his own *Stolen Moments: a short series of poems* (1842), the *Sydney Gazette* had opined on 14 July 1842:

> Although we do not meet with, in the "Stolen Moments" of our author, the soul searching energy of a Byron, the melodious lays of Moore, or the impassioned breathings of the gorgeous Wordsworth,

we not infrequently find some fine passages which would not disgrace any of these great men, and strongly indicate, that by proper cultivation, the author will one day reach no humble position in the "temple of fame".

Given the relative merits of Harpur's and Parkes's poem, one imagined what Mr. Ewing would have made of these comparisons if he had been lecturing in 1842! A more accurate estimation of *Stolen Moments* appeared in the *New South Wales Examiner* for 18 July 1842[2]:

> ... we have read Mr. PARKES' book from beginning to end, with every disposition to do justice to its merits: but, out of the whole of his forty-nine pieces, we can find but one, which, in our judgement, bears the impress of a poetical mind. If it were our intention to deal with the book in the style of minute criticism, there are few passages which could be pointed out, and exhibited as entirely free from fault. At one time, the meaning seems threadbare—at another time, the sense is obscure; and throughout, there is a general absence of pure poetic diction—which, cojoined with feeble redundancies of expression, and a style the most prosaic that can well be imagined, leave Mr. PARKES without a single one of the several attributes requisite to form the poetical character.

All the works and reviews mentioned so far were printed in Sydney. Some of the best Australian criticism of the 1840s is, however, to be found in the *Launceston Examiner*. On 27 January 1847, the reviewer of A.C. Stonor's *Poetical Fragments* (1846) put forward the most cogent of all early arguments for the patronage of Australian literature.

> THOSE who nurse the fortunes of an infant community should deal tenderly with aspirants to literary fame. They are bound to estimate rather as parents than as critics—to treat attempts at excellence with a liberality of praise, which in a land of mental opulence may be proper only to those who have excelled. The tendency of colonial life to chain the thoughts and interests of men to material pursuits and sensual pleasures, or to confine the sympathies to professional or sectarian objects, requires a powerful counteraction. The intellect of a young community is sharp but stunted: it moves rapidly but seldom soars; its vision, though clear, is limited. The competition and bustle of all classes throw an air of absurdity and romance on everything abstract and sentimental, and those who offer the embellishments of mind may be rated with those who anciently "cast pearls" before a body not remarkable for nice discrimination.
> The utmost partiality will not enable us to hope that colonial

authors can early rank among the *literati* of Britain. Had they the intellectual resources and talent of older societies, the expense of publication would be an impassable obstacle in their path. The number of readers is too small to ensure a sale for the most useful and entertaining volumes—to secure their author from pecuniary loss—without condescending to solicitations they are apt to disdain. It may be asked why encourage inferior and high priced works, when the British press teems with an infinite variety on every topic? Certainly, if the province of mind is to be delivered over to the maxims of economists, the answer may be difficult. But there are pleasures not included in bills of lading. It is useless to tell a parent that the embroidery and wool work of his daughters, or the painting of his sons, could be substituted at a fraction of their school account. If given to vindicate what he prefers he will imagine a future utility to compensate the present cost. But the fact undoubtedly is that he finds a charm in these specimens of industry which the productions of the most skilful artist could not afford. Thus local talent may have its attractions. A colony is assuredly acquiring the consistency of an established state when a writer can find patrons in his neighbours—when they cheer his efforts to naturalise the Muses, and to transplant the flowers of poesy to regions adopted as their home.

Despite this predisposition to kindness, the reviewer was not uncritical of Stonor, making a fair assessment of the defects of his volume:

> ... we are disposed to estimate its worth as an indication of talents, which, if employed on a better theme might command more unqualified praise. The principal part of the publication is a translation of LUCAN'S PHARSALIA. There is a deficiency of interest in the subject for which great powers could hardly compensate ...
>
> The versification is extremely unequal in merit. Some passages might be compared with our best translations; but too often the fatigue of the poet is shared by the reader. The unlicensed collocation of words confuses the understanding, and the sense is realised with difficulty. These defects are the more to be censured because the author has shown they were not inevitable. A sprawling verse, through which the meaning lingers is bad enough, but better than hopeless obscurity.

Later in 1847, the publication of Bassett Dickson's *Honi Heki, in Two Cantos; Warbeck, in Two Cantos; and Miscellaneous Pieces* gave the *Examiner*'s reviewer an opportunity for some amusing remarks on English and Australian poetry. Again the review, printed on 4 December, was of much higher literary quality than its subject:

> THE British reviews have long ceased to look for poetry. The reading public have been estranged from the Muses by the seduction of gain.

The way to make money and to spend it is the sole business of the modern Carthage. Those who remember the raptures which hailed the works of Scott, and the still deeper, because mingled interest, which attended the successive publications of Byron, will feel that the glory of Apollo is departed—at least, in the poetical line. Not but occasionally a votary of the god appears, and presents a song worthy of fame: but it is useless. We have now no hero who would be a popular subject for song. To make an ode to Mr. Hudson, or a pastoral for Baron Rothschild, would require that the education of the Muses should be entirely reformed. They must remodel their plan, and recast their figures. Instead of swords they must have spades and wheelbarrows—for castles, bridges and embankments; the dashing of cavalry must be abandoned for the rushing and rumbling of engines. Such is the fate of British poets: they die off as mechanism advances—just as the aboriginal tribes vanish before a white face.

But not so in Van Diemen's Land. If we may fancy that Tasmania really understands the apostrophes addressed to her, with what gladness must she observe the increase of poets cherished in her own bosom. We have, during the last year or two, seen several burst on the astonished public—Kentish, Kemp, Stonor, and now last, not least, Dickson. If we compare the number with the population, we shall learn how large is our proportion of poets: the United Kingdom would require six thousand volumes of poetry to overtake the fertility of the Tasmanian muse. We by no means disapprove the aspirations of our local bards. Nothing can be more innocent. The very attempt indicates a generosity of mind. No one need be ashamed of making verses, or of being in love—if both are pure: they are kindred passions. Our author seems to be imbued with both, and we should almost fancy that in making verses he was making love.

Mr. Dickson desires criticism; of this we are glad: it will entitle us to enlarge with more freedom on the merits of his productions. If a writer pleads his youth, pays his printer, gives away his works, and observes the laws of good breeding in his verse, we are bound to be exceedingly indulgent. He has sought a rational amusement, he has improved his mind, he has pleased himself, and perhaps gratified his friends. This is worth doing. As to future or distant fame, that is not always to be thought of by a wise man. We live by the day—enough if it is innocent and happy. If we compare the work of Mr. Dickson with colonial poetry, he may be entitled to a distinguished place. We certainly should dread another standard. We can fancy the awful havoc which the *Quarterly* or some such dissector of genius would make were the tale of "Warbeck" or "Honi Heki" before him. We do not doubt the magnanimity of Mr. Dickson; he would not, like poor Keats, die of a review: but we congratulate him on his happier position, where nothing more terrible than the publisher's account will await the aspirant to literary honour.

Our author has been a reader of Byron. We have not only an imitation of his rapid transitions, his gossiping parentheses, but something more. Perhaps no poet can be exempt from the charge of plagiarism—the same ideas will recur—the same words will present themselves; and the malice of criticism will often attribute to literary fraud the undesigned coincidences of thought—the inevitable similarity of a recollection. The story of WARBECK is of a settler who arrived in the early days; he gets a grant—builds a hut—plants a garden—and falls in love, with perfect regularity—first with "Emelina", who is a coquette, but whose person combined several of the attactions which are not novel, but extremely pleasing. Her eyes shoot love's darts—they are black—shine like stars; her hair is profuse; her teeth whiter than ivory: but she is given to tight lacing. Such was Warbeck's first love. Her name was Andrews. Her father was

"A plain, straightforward, plodding sort of man."
Warbeck buys his sheep, and woos his daughter, who jilts him, and marries a sot: notwithstanding he depicts her ungratefulness in a song, of which the author says;

"———so now his thoughts I'll show them,
As he described them in a pastoral poem."
This poem was lost upon the hard-hearted Emelina, but it serves to bring out an agreeable fact in our natural history—namely, that woods and zephyrs, which have always shown the utmost attention to poetry and love in other countries, are not less sensitive here ... However, all things have an end, and thus the grief of Warbeck. It was partly attenuated by time, but more by "sweet Maria" ...

But no doubt the author intended the poem to depict the neighbourhood around the favoured couple, and to trace the progress of colonial life. We might easily point out bad lines and bad rhyme, but the great defect of the production is its want of character. It belongs to any state or country: it describes lawns, woods, gardens and society as they have been described since the days of Spencer [sic]: it saunters on in hacknied phrases. Now a poem of real interest might be written on unoccupied colonial ground: our natural history and scenery—the details of those difficulties which the first settlers encountered—the extraordinary incidents of bush life, might be wrought up into a pleasing if not deeply impressive song. But this requires some invention, and especially a very vigorous supervision.

Here the critic correctly points to the absence of individuality and the over-reliance on generalities which vitiate most early colonial poetry.

A work having some of the needed originality and particularity, Edward Kemp's *A Voice from Tasmania* (1846), was, because of its satirical nature, almost universally attacked by the local press. The *Launceston Advertiser* for 29 October 1846 thought it "conceived in the worst possible spirit" while on 14 November the *Cornwall Chronicle* thundered at Kemp: "his madness cannot be questioned, for publishing the blasphemous ribaldry and obscenity now before us: Happily, the chance is small of such trash being read ... we denounce 'The Poem' as an insult to the colony". After derisively quoting many lines, sometimes with quite unjust criticisms, this reviewer concluded:

> We can follow this Tasmanian poet—this misguided aspirant after disgrace no farther; his production merits burning by the hands of the common hangman and himself branded with infamy. The inhabitants of this colony cannot be other than heartily disgusted with the person who voluntarily attempts to lower them in the estimation of all right minded people; earnestly do we hope that the "Voice from Tasmania" will never find its way from this colony.

Although not advocating such a public book-burning, the *Colonial Times* for 30 October had been equally insulting towards Kemp:

> But nothing can exceed the presumption and self-sufficiency of this conceited rhymster: over and over again, he presumes upon the ignorance of his readers, and "flares up"—we must address him in his own flash language—in the style and character of a would-be second Byron: the lowness of the man, however, exposes the cloven foot; his gross vulgarity is emblazoned in every page of what he calls his "Poem" ...

The only note of sympathy came from John Morgan's *Britannia and Trades' Advocate*, which on 29 October called *A Voice from Tasmania* "a very clever production". A longer notice in the next issue, though also objecting to the imitation of Byron, concluded "In the Poem there are many clever evidences of ability. The running fire of attack is in general well kept up, and the meter well sustained. There are of course exceptions, which might have been avoided by care, and experience."

Some equally vituperative criticism had greeted one of the most readable prose works of this decade, John Lang's *Legends of Australia* (1842). Again, the objections were chiefly on non-literary grounds, particularly the damage the work would do to Australia's reputation in England. Lang's work was published anonymously in serial form, but it is evident that his authorship was widely known. Thus "*Judex damnatur*", writing of No. 1 in the *Australian* for 8

ELIZABETH WEBBY

February 1842, complained:

> ANXIOUS as we are and ever have been to see the growth and ex-
> pansion of literature amongst our colonial youth, we confess we
> opened the pages of this work with every disposition to be gratified by
> their perusal. Having heard that the author was one of the native born
> of Australia, whose abilities had been highly spoken of, and who had
> received a university education, we hailed the appearance of this
> number as an affair of national importance. Looking back upon the
> dreary waste which our history presents in the field of letters, we
> hoped every thing from the pen of one who, unlike the rest of his
> countrymen, was fortunate enough to be thrown in the way of receiv-
> ing all the advantages which the best of education could afford.
> Knowing how few of the youth of Australia have received other than
> the mere rudiments of instruction, and at the same time aware of their
> cleverness, which under these disadvantages they still generally ex-
> hibit, we did expect something worthy of perusal from an Australian
> whose opportunities have been as great.
>
> We regret to say that we have been disappointed. A more trashy
> production than these self-same legends we certainly have never met
> with. Hurried, unconnected, abrupt, without sentiment, wit, pathos,
> or humour, and withal, a kind of self-sufficient futile aiming at
> dramatic effect running through, and pervading the whole work, they
> are in our opinion, the most childish *legends* that ever issued from a
> printing office.
>
> ... the author does not possess that delicate talent for dressing up low
> and disgusting scenes in the humourous and pleasing manner, which
> alone can render them worthy of being tolerated by persons of educa-
> tion and refinement.

The *New South Wales Examiner* more judiciously kept back its
comments until all four numbers had appeared but then launched
into a full scale attack on 6, 13, and 20 April, which ran in part:

> ... we are presented with a story, the incidents in which occur so
> recently as the year 1836, and these incidents are drawn from the very
> questionable source of a convict ship and its inmates, on their pas-
> sages to New South Wales. But, what is infinitely worse, the incidents
> are not in accordance with *fact*. They do not fulfil the condition im-
> posed upon writers, who treat of circumstances with which men are
> personally conversant, or which are only of recent occurrence.
> Destitute of all claim to the charms of *romance*, the greater reason is
> there that they should possess the recommendation of *reality*. But, not
> only are these incidents untrue—they are also devoid of the slightest
> approximation to probability. There is nothing whatever of
> verisimilitude about them ... who can foretell the effect of this
> exaggerated—this unfounded writing upon the public mind in

England? Who is *there* on the spot, to point out the falsities which stand recorded in almost every page of the work? Who is *there* to expose the ignorant, and therefore, offensive delineations of Colonial society, with which this publication abounds? Affording a fine field for detraction to the enemies of the Colony, the very reviewers who would undertake to notice it, are in the most complete ignorance of the real state and condition of New South Wales;—and, who is to say that, led away by the spirit of party, they will not gladly seize upon the statements put forth in this book, as so many facts to use for our disadvantage? Let not the writer suppose, that we have condescended to a notice of his book, because of its *literary* merits. Upon this plea, it is entitled to no footing in any critical court in Christendom. But, we shall not suffer its exaggerations, and its falsities, to go forth without contradiction, and without placing on record our solemn protest against them.

Much more reasonable and accurate reviews appeared in the *Australasian Chronicle* and the *Sydney Morning Herald* for 14 and 19 April respectively. The former, presumably by W.A. Duncan and showing his customary critical good sense, commenced with an amusing description of other reactions to *Legends of Australia*:

FROM the tone of criticism which some our contemporaries have adopted with respect to this publication, their readers must have adopted one or more of the following conclusions, namely: that the work is both illiterate and immoral, which we think untrue; or that literature is of such general cultivation, and grows with such luxuriousness among us, as to require much less of fostering care than of the critic's pruning knife, which we also disbelieve; or, finally, that the writer has given some deadly offence to the literary gods of the nation, for which they have determined to consign both him and his work to the other side of the Styx without appeal. For our own part, although we are well inclined to treat ignorant pretensions with severity, and writings of immoral tendency without mercy, we have seen nothing in the "Legends" hitherto to induce us to depart from the qualified approbation which we bestowed upon the first number, it being a principle with us that literature, if not *positively bad*, is *relatively good*, and therefore is deserving of encouragement; above all, in a country which as yet can boast of no native literature, but remains at the end of half a century a complete blank in the republic of letters. Now, the "Legend" just completed is not only free from an immoral tendency, but is expressly written, as the author informs us, to establish a moral principle, namely that *debt is one of the most powerful instigations to crime.* We do not mean to say that the tale is in this respect perfect, for the first chapter seems to furnish the sole proof of this proposition; but there are other good maxims and sentiments scattered over the work, which, taken as a whole is *not* objectionable in a moral point of view. In a literary point of view, much, no doubt could be said about the absence of anything like a plot, the want of *vraisemblance* in some of the incidents, and the negligence of the style in some places. But, with all these defects, the work, we maintain, does contain passages which promise greater things after the writer shall have matured his judgment and adopted a more equal style. It is easy to perceive that he is but "lately off the irons," but this is a motive for indulgence rather than severity. The writer succeeds best in his delineations of real character ...

It is by concentrating in one person the peculiarities of a class that Boz has succeeded so admirably in his imaginative career; and it is only when ... our author directs his efforts to the accomplishment of this, that he is successful. In his purely imaginary characters (among whom we must include even his hero) he fails; and, unless he can succeed in investing his new hero, Ned Nox, with something more like reality, we fear that the Legends will fall under the weight of the hypercriticism to which they have been, we think, unfairly subjected. A greater variety of eligible subjects than this colony presents no graphist could desire, and there are also abundant historical incidents of sufficient singularity to give a higher interest to his delineations. The success of the work under notice will depend entirely upon the manner in which the writer shall lay hold of the characteristics of the Cheerybles, Pickwicks, Squeerses, Fagins and Sykeses which are before him.

The *Herald* also praised Lang's pictures of colonial life, advising him in future numbers "to keep as much as possible to bush scenes which he depicts faithfully". But no further numbers appeared; Lang had departed for India on 17 April.[3]

The better known Australian fictional works of the 1840s, such as Charles Rowcroft's *Tales of the Colonies* (1843) and Thomas McCombie's *Arabin* (1845), were rarely reviewed locally, editors being content to print extracts and favourable notices from overseas. An exception was the *Sydney Morning Herald*'s review of *Tales of the Colonies* on 19 March 1844. In the manner of the day, this was mostly given over to extracts and plot summary, with a few critical comments:

We are too favourably disposed to those narrations which have truth for their basis to cavil much either at language or style ... True it is spun out to the orthodox number of volumes, (three to wit), and one might well have been spared us. There is an incidental love affair which makes it a novel, but just a novel; but there is much of valuable information to the colonist which renders the work worthy of far higher attention than that of mere novel readers.

Alexander Harris's *Settlers and Convicts* (1847) also received only one Australian review, though a perceptive one, printed in the *Atlas* on 16 October 1847:

> Without laying claim to any very great merit as a literary production, or as a systematic, comprehensive and acute enquiry into colonial affairs in general (indeed, the title of the work shows the humbleness of its pretensions in this latter particular), yet must we with pleasure confess that it is one of the most interesting works of the kind which we have as yet perused. The descriptions are very graphic; the narrative, natural and easy; and the particulars embodied are not only extremely interesting and amusing, but also illustrative of colonial manners, customs, and society. There is a Robinson Crusoe kind of character indeed about it.

The *Atlas*, particularly in its early years under Robert Lowe, was the only early Australian publication to give regular original review of overseas works. In the first issue of the *Atlas*, 4 November 1844, one also finds a rare, and sound, statement of critical principles:

> Discarding literary criticism as a mere business; applying it only when necessary to prevent sounding quacks from deceiving themselves and the public into the conceit that they are sages; and now and then, perhaps, using it in giving a friendly hint to a real artist, that he do not look so strenuously upward as to stumble on the stone at his feet—we shall reserve this department of our journal for things amusing, not frivolous—witty, not impertinent—pleasing, not insipid—soothing, not soperific—instructive, not tiresome.

Generally, as will have been seen from these examples of their practice, early Australian reviewers were content to leave critical theorising to such School of Arts lecturers as R.K. Ewing. Most were, however, more concerned with moral than aesthetic values. Nearly all believed the development of a strong literary culture essential for the moral well-being of colonial society, and so were inclined to treat local authors kindly, except when they offended personal or political prejudices. By the 1840s, indeed, some Australian writers seem to have come to expect freedom from criticism as their right—a disability allowance for labouring in such a benighted materialistic country. Thus "Z.", rather incongruously midway through a flowery eulogy on "England", in the *South Australian Odd Fellows' Magazine* for January 1845, complained of attacks on some earlier pieces:

... in the great cities of Europe, where the press is adorned by genius, and supported by wealth, the critic is called upon to interpose his dictum in the strife for preeminence, and to bar the transient success of pretenders ... But in a remote Colony the palm is not thus contested, and the voluntary effusions of the amateur should be mildly dealt with. It is never lawful to convert the office of a reviewer into that of a satirist ... His method of correction is only calculated to extinguish the flame of incipient ambition, and make our literary Chaos darker still.

It was to be many more years before the critic's reply, in the *South Australian Register* for 20 January, found general acceptance; "as to remote Colonies, we must remark that the laws of criticism have no sliding scale of leagues, they are the same in India, or Australia, as in Europe."

3

Towards Seeing Minor Poets Steadily and Whole

ELIZABETH PERKINS

The minor writer is always a problem. Critics, embarrassed at finding themselves busied with minor writers, try to assess them briskly and catalogue them neatly away. Other readers who have given time and thought to untangling the life and works of a minor writer, or who have unearthed some previously unknown document or literary remains, tend, for some time anyway, to over-value their protégé. And why not? There are students of literature enough and to spare, and a little posthumous care and attention are not too much to ask for the writer who has a lesser place in the development of our literature. The sheer amount of Australian writing is now so great, and our critical output so prolific, that there is no longer any danger of distorting the achievement of minor colonial writers. Indeed, to exaggerate the importance of a minor writer of the past is bad criticism, but the effect is not as harmful as exaggerating the importance of contemporary achievement. Not that, as our contemporary writers will say, there is much possibility of that. What the living writer wants from criticism is encouragement and the assurance that his best work is being read with pleasure and his worst with disappointment; but the service criticism can perform for our earlier writers is to place them in their relevant settings and see them in the fullest perspective. A minor writer of the past is recognized as minor, there is no need to assay how minor he is or how far he fell short of being a major writer. As a literature develops the minor writers who contribute to that development become less important as individual figures, and it is enough that they sometimes still give pleasure. Colonial writers, however, because they mark a beginning, and sometimes, although not always, have sociological importance, require a more thorough investigation.

The three colonial poets, Charles Harpur (1813—68), Henry Kendall (1839—82), and Adam Lindsay Gordon (1833—70) have each received a fair share of recent critical attention, although it cannot be said that justice may be seen to be done for Harpur until there is a complete edition of his poetry. It is not redundant, nevertheless, to make some observations about each of these poets which may help them to be seen more steadily and in a fuller perspective. There is little need to contradict anything that other and abler critics have written, but some additions may be made, and some variations in emphasis may be suggested.

Charles Harpur is the most difficult of our earlier poets to see in entirety, and this is not only because most of his work is still in manuscript.

The greatest difficulty encountered in finding a just reading of Harpur lies in understanding the personality of the man. His character emerges quite clearly. Intelligent, idealistic, high-principled, dogmatic, independent, vain, and conscious of being undervalued by his contemporaries, Harpur's character is a hallmark on all his writing, just as Wordsworth's character stamps his work. There is no doubt, certainly, that Marvell's work influenced "A Mid-Summer Noon in the Australian Forest" or that Dante and Shelley provided literary models for "The Scamper of Life", and all the longer poems of Harpur are fashioned from a patchwork of styles or modes. The gentler critic might call the patchwork a mosaic, and point out that it takes a craftsman to construct as impressive a mosaic as "A Storm in the Mountains". This is true enough, and the most successful of Harpur's poems are the result of a strongly intuited vision expressed competently through a synthesis of received poetic tradition and a highly individual character. But the personality of Harpur is the stumbling-block, and becomes so more and more as biographers and social historians present the reader with the "facts" of the poet's life and details of his political involvements. If the reader wishes to see Harpur's poetry clearly and steadily, it is wisest to read first all the poems themselves, and interpret them by whatever intrinsic help they themselves offer. From such a reading the simple explanation derives that the character and sensibility of the poet created all that is strongest and best in his work, and that his unhappy personality and his consciousness of himself as a "poet" worked assiduously to impede this excellence and strength. Keats would have admitted the simplicity of the explanation, for he wrote, in a letter to Richard Woodhouse, 27 October 1818, "A poet is the most unpoetical of any thing in existence; because he has no Identity—he is continually in for—and filling some other Body. The Sun, The Moon, The Sea and Men and Women who are creatures of impulse are poetical and have about them an unchangeable attribute—the poet has none; no identity—his is certainly the most unpoetical of all God's Creatures." Every good poet knows that Keats has exactly explained the most agonizingly simple of the poet's feats. Harpur very rarely managed to escape from his personality and allow himself to empathize with his eagles and his sea-birds. His poems are almost all blanketed by the personality of the poet telling us to look here, observe that, become indignant about this. It would be too easy to find blatant examples of this intrusion, and the point is better made by examining lines in which the weakening effect is more subtle and therefore more insidious. This passage, describing the night-scene in "The Bush Fire" is exciting in its intensity:

> Or down the flickery glades
> Cheerfully glaring, huge dry-mouldered gums
> Stood 'mid their living kin as barked throughout
> With eating fire expelling arrowy jets
> Of blue-lipt, intermitting, gaseous flame,
> Boles, branches,—all! Like vivid ghosts of trees,
> Frightful to see!—the immemorial Wood's
> First hoary Fathers wrapt in burning shrouds,
> Come from the past, within the Whiteman's pale,
> To typify their doom. Such was the prospect!
> Illuminated cities were but jests
> Compared with it for splendour.   (MS A87)[1]

The description is compressed and the experience was obviously gained at first-hand and registered by a keenly observant eye. But no sooner had the eye observed than Harpur as poet was busy verbaliz-

41

ing and finding similes and metaphors for his observation. He paints his picture and holds it up for viewing—"Such was the prospect!" The last two lines of the passage are explained by the fact that Harpur had recently read about, disapproved of and wrote a poem about the Easter illuminations of St Peter's, Rome, celebrating the return of Pius IX to the capital in April 1850. Harpur, as a patriot and nationalist, was indignant at the Austrian domination of Italy, and found the illuminations dimmed when compared with "one luminous deed / Evoked by Garibaldi's patriot creed". The more that is read of Harpur's verse, the more it becomes clear that its problems are not primarily matters of technique, but problems of an over-anxious, didactic personality, driven by a desire to justify itself. Here the didactic patriot bobs up in a description of a forest fire. The point can be made conclusively, if that is necessary, by looking at a brief passage from Harpur's "The Glen of the Whiteman's Grave" and comparing it with very similar lines from Coleridge's "The Lime-Tree Bower my Prison". Here is Harpur's eagle:

> And once a dusky Eagle came
> In solemn travel o'er the same—
> Steadily straight, as from afar
> Came over,—but the airy jar
> Of his huge wings in swift decrease,
> Soon faded, as with upward sweep
> They passed beyond the opponent steep,
> And all around was perfect peace.   (MS A97)

And here is Coleridge's rook:

> When the last rook
> Beat its straight path along the dusky air
> Homewards, I blest it! deeming its black wing
> (Now a dim speck, now vanishing in light)
> Had crossed the mighty Orb's dilated glory,
> While thou stoodst gazing.

The eagle is just a shade too long in passing, Harpur dwells too poetically on its passage. Coleridge's economy shows us the steady flight of the rook more clearly, but what separates the two extracts is Coleridge's dominant concern that *his friends*, not himself, are watching the bird's flight. And this is not a small matter.

"A Mid-Summer Noon in the Australian Forest", in spite of its apparent seventeenth century ancestry, or even because it implicitly aknowledges the tradition, deserves its popularity. In this poem we do not find the personality of the poet, but only his receptive and receiving sensibility. The details are precise:

> Tis the dragon-hornet—see!
> All bedaubed resplendently
> With yellow on a tawny ground—
> Each rich spot nor square nor round,
> But rudely heart-shaped, as it were
> The blurred and hasty impress there,
> Of a vermeil-crusted seal
> Dusted o'er with golden meal:

but there is no attempt to explain how these details make their impression on the poet. The perfect relaxation of the forest slumbering under the summer heat has imposed itself upon that anxious personality:

> Tired Summer, in her forest bower
> Turning with the noontide hour,
> Heaves a slumbrous breath, ere she
> Once more slumbers peacefully.   (MS A97)

Harpur, caught in the spell of emotion recollected in tranquillity, appears, like Summer, to rouse himself for the moment of writing his poem, and then to fall back into the drowsy contentment he has recreated, allowing the poem to do its work without him. This happens far too rarely in Harpur's verse.

The packed lines, careful supervision of the reader, and unwillingness to economize lest some poetic nuance be missed, make most of Harpur's descriptive verse difficult to read, although some of it is quite fine. Nevertheless the critic who accused Harpur of doubling up on the one effect, by killing two eagles by thunderbolts in "A Storm in the Mountains", is not quite in order.[2] At the end of part I of the poem, the eagle "Falls whizzing, stone-like, lifeless to the ground!" And in part II a giant mountain tree is destroyed:

> Now dimly seen through the tempestuous air,
> His form seems harrowed by a mad despair,
> As with his ponderous arms uplifted high,
> He wrestles with the Storm and threshes at the sky!
> But not for long. Up in the lurid air,
> A swift red bolt is heard to hurtle there—
> A dread crash follows—and the Peak is bare!   (MS A97)

Here it is not the personification of the tree, "the seeming Patriarch of the Wood" with "rock-encrusted roots", that troubles the reader, but the intrusion of the poet with his "seeming" and his "seems" betraying the observing presence. A great poet would retire into the background and allow the tree and the elements to fight it out alone.

But to continue the search for this mischievous, intrusive personality it is necessary to look at almost any of the sonnets. A sonnet may surely be a very personal piece, but this does not permit the personality of the poet to crowd out his subject, even if that subject happens to be his own emotions. And it is unpleasant to find Sonnet XXV of the "Rosa" sonnets reappearing almost unchanged in MS A87 under the title "Wordsworth's Poetry", with the effects formerly ascribed to the influence of Rosa's love on the poet now placed to the credit of Wordsworth's poetry. Still less attractive is it to discover that the sestet of a sonnet to Dr. Lang was used with some minor alterations as the sestet of a sonnet Harpur wrote about himself and his superiority to his critics. This thrift operates again when the sonnet "On the Repeal Movement in Ireland" (MS C376) reappears as "On the Wrongs of Poland" (MS C87), and a sonnet which originally commemorated the death of Harpur's brother, "How distant in a moment are the *dead*!" (MS A90) was later included in a group of poems written on the death of his son Charles (MS A87). These examples are *argumentum ad opera*, not *argumentum ad hominem*, and one appeals to the works in order to discover the man, not to biography in order to explain the work.

A reliance on biography and an incomplete knowledge of Harpur's work have led to some debatable conclusions about the meaning of certain poems. It has been asserted, for example, that Harpur rejected Christianity to become "a humanist with a thin wash of deism", an assertion perhaps based on the facts that Harpur neglected the Anglican church into which he was baptized, did not become a convert to Catholicism as did his brother Joseph, and fulminated against the papacy in the manner typical of the non-Catholic writers of the colony who were antagonistic to all forms of authority.[3] A careful reading of laboriously written poems like "Onward" (MS A87) and "The World and the Soul" (MS A87) will show that Harpur finally could not abandon the idea of a personal God and the individuality of the soul. Early in the history of Harpur criticism the name of Nietzsche—that *sine qua non* of the literary article—was mentioned, with the suggestion that Harpur's concept of the soul would be familiar to readers of Nietzsche.[4] Since Friedrich Nietzsche's first work, *The Birth of Tragedy*, did not appear until 1872, Harpur's ideas must be pre-Nietzschean, but the observation that they have something in common with the philosopher's is not entirely inaccurate. Harpur was profoundly affected by, although he modified and selected from the transcendental religious philosophy of Ralph Waldo Emerson, to whom Nietzsche also later acknowledged his indebtedness. Harpur was impressed by various aspects of William Channing's Unitarian teaching, but he was selective in these also, looking for principles rather than doctrine, and unlike Emerson, whose extreme limit of theological heresy appears to have been to deny the divinity of Christ, Harpur refers specifically to "the divine Jesus". Indeed, if Harpur's work is to be seen in true perspective, due weight must be given to the influence of the independence of Unitarian thought and the idealism of American romantic transcendentalism.

It is hardly just, however, to quote a bad poem by Henry Kendall in support of the notion that Harpur experienced a loss of religious faith. In one of Kendall's memorial poems to Harpur, he writes ("Charles Harpur", 1868):

> The burden of a perished faith
> Went sighing through his speech of sweetness,
> With human hints of Time and Death,
> And subtle notes of incompleteness.

Kendall probably had nothing very specific in mind when he evoked this impressionistic picture of Harpur's burden or refrain "sighing" through his speech. There is no evidence anywhere to suggest that Harpur could express himself with so little energy as to mute his voice to a sigh. Harpur's faith in the men around him certainly did perish, and Kendall would have evidence of this both in Harpur's poems and in the letters the two poets exchanged. More persuasive evidence that Harpur did *not* lose his faith in God is found in a poem he reprinted in 1867 which begins:

> Have faith in God! for surely He
> Is good as He is wise and great:
> Have Faith—for here or elsewhere, we
> Shall prove the harmony of Fate! (MS C384)

ELIZABETH PERKINS

At the time of his death he was preparing manuscripts, with the hope
of publication in England, in which he included the sonnet "Trust in
God". If the image in the last seven lines recalls the following lines
of Gerard Manley Hopkins (from sonnet 42, *Poems* 1876—89):

> O the mind, mind has mountains; cliffs of fall
> Frightful, sheer, no-man-fathomed. Hold them cheap
> may who ne'er hung there.

it is indicative that Harpur maintained his faith with the same tough
and recurrent struggle experienced later by the Jesuit poet:

> And when I've stood upon some hazardous steep
> Of speculation—heaving up its bare
> And rugged ridge high in the nebulous air
> Of endless change, and thence tremendously
> Throwing its shadow, like a blind man's stare,
> Out through the dread unknown—deep trust in Thee,
> O God! hath likewise been my refuge there.
>
> (from "Trust in God", 1883 edition)

Because Harpur makes no overt reference to the fact that both
his parents were transported for theft, critics have suggested that
either he was little affected by his family origins, or else too deeply
affected to come to grips with the experience and find some means of
expressing it. Some very substantial pieces among Harpur's work,
however, do indicate that he felt deeply the problems of guilt,
punishment, and atonement, and the discrepancy between divine
justice and man-made laws. These pieces are the five-act
melodrama, "Stalwart the Bushranger" (MS A94), the narrative
poems "The Spectre of the Cattle Flat" (MS A97), and "The
Murder of the Lamb" (MS A92), and "The Witch of Hebron" (MS
A87), "a Rabbinical Legend", a story about the transmigration of a
guilty soul through a series of living bodies, animal and human.
Until these poems are available to readers generally, Harpur's
achievement as a writer can hardly be justly estimated.

When Harpur's complete opus is known, it is unlikely that any
critical opinion will wish to claim him as a great writer of the
colonial period. But no reader will be able to contemplate the range
of his work without curiosity and some admiration. The long
dramatic monologue, "The Sorrows of Chatterton or Genius Lost"
(MS A87), was written while Alfred de Vigny was presenting in
Paris his melodrama called *Chatterton*. A comparison of the general

mood and background of the two pieces shows that the aristocratically minded Frenchman and the republican Australian shared the same concepts of later romanticism and through their differing sensibilities drew remarkably similar portraits of the youthful poetic spirit. The revisions through which the "Rosa" sonnet sequence (MS C383) was converted into a mid-Victorian study under the more fashionable name, "Nora" (MS C376), will indicate how much Harpur was influenced by progressive changes in reader expectations over several decades. Social historians, impressed by Harpur's use of verse as a political instrument, have quite rightly emphasized his role as a satirist and reformer in colonial society.[5] If the literary critic will now readjust the balance of emphasis it will be seen that Harpur reflected with surprising fidelity many of the chief European and American literary preoccupations of the mid-nineteenth century.

It is a worthwhile exercise to place both Kendall and Gordon in this perspective of nineteenth century literature unconfined by colonial conditions. Indeed, it is possible to assert that neither poet was selfconsciously an "Australian poet", and to set aside once and for all the old notion, applied also to Harpur, that the most important thing about these three poets was that their sensibilities, trained by European traditions and culture, could not happily or adequately interpret the Australian environment.[6] The sense of loneliness and displacement so much in evidence in the poems of Kendall and Gordon is another manifestation of the European malaise, usually summed up by Heinrich Heine's concept of *les enfants perdus* and Matthew Arnold's description of himself standing between two ages, one dead and the other powerless to be born. It must be admitted, nevertheless, that an emergent colonial society and a pioneer landscape add a new dimension to the European condition, even if one were not an exile like Gordon. On the one hand, a new country, and new social and political conditions suggest hope and energy to replace the exhaustion widely, though not constantly or ubiquitously, felt in Europe. On the other hand, the awareness in Australia that neither society nor physical environment was fully explored and comprehended also aggravated the tendency to spiritual bewilderment. These ideas are certainly not being stated here for the first time, but perhaps insufficient emphasis has been placed on this view of Kendall and Gordon as participants in the mid-nineteenth century malaise.

Kendall was the tougher of the two. In spite of the langour of much of Kendall's verse, and in spite of the greater physicality and energy of Gordon's "From the Wreck" compared with Kendall's lyrical ballads like "The Squatter's Song" and "The Song of the Cattle Hunters", the philosophical fibre of Kendall's verse was much stronger than Gordon's. This assertion may be demonstrated by tracing the actual thought content in a number of poems by either poet to its final resolution in each poem. For all the misty vagueness and idealism of Kendall's thought—and we have learnt to call his aspirations "mystic" rather than "misty"—it must be allowed that he was definitely and solidly in search of something that most readers will recognize as an ever-beckoning but never attainable goal.[7] And if this goal seems too maddeningly vague for sensible souls to worry about, at least even the sensible souls admit that apparently some unfortunates spend their lives in very real misery because they cannot reach it. There is nothing imprecise, logically or psychologically, when Kendall writes (in "After Many Years"):

> But in the night, and when the rain
>   The troubled torrent fills,
> I often think I see again
>   The river in the hills,
> And when the day is very near,
>   And birds are on the wing,
> My spirit fancies it can hear
>   The song I cannot sing.

The stanza may be read as a total emblem, with "night", "rain", "troubled torrent", "day", and "birds" as symbols of the poet's changing states of mind. "My spirit fancies it can hear / The song it cannot sing" is not, philosophically speaking, any different from Browning's "Ah, but a man's reach should exceed his grasp,/ Or what's a heaven for?" But Gordon was the poet who most obviously bears the superficial marks of Browning's influence. Gordon, however, lacked the mystic's strength to believe in a vision, and lacked Browning's toughness in admitting failure and making a virtue of it. Gordon denies the vision but cannot find a substitute for it. In "Wormwood and Nightshade", he catches Kendall halfway up the climb to the source of his river and suggests that all the time the aspiring mystic has been standing before a desert mirage.

> The restless throbbings and burnings
> That hope unsatisfied brings,
> The weary longings and yearnings
> For the mystical better things,
> Are the sands on which is reflected
> The pitiless moving lake,
> Where the wanderer falls dejected,
> By a thirst he never can slake.

Gordon of course is wrong. Restless throbbings and burnings and weary longings for mystical better things are very real and palpable experiences, and Kendall had the conviction and courage to make poetry from them, but Gordon despises them, denies their reality, and idealizes instead a dogged pessimism, insisting that life is a situation where everything must be endured and nothing can be done. Gordon's poems of action and his attempts at a vigorous gothic demonstrate that he was at least determined to endure with all the energy at his command.

Kendall's rhythms have been called "Swinburnian", but it should be remembered that Kendall published the following "Swinburnian" lines in 1862 (in the poem "The Muse of Australia"), three years before the publication of Swinburne's first volume, *Atalanta in Calydon*:

> Where the pines with the eagles are nestled in rifts,
> And the torrent leaps down to the surges,
> I have followed her, clambering over the clifts,
> By the chasms and moon-haunted verges.
> I know she is fair as the angels are fair,
> For have I not caught a faint glimpse of her there;
> A glimpse of her face and her glittering hair,
> And a hand with the harp of Australia?

Although Kendall (and Harpur) carefully labelled the harps of their muses with "made in Australia", it is difficult not to see that they were manufactured with some help from American transcendentalism. If the effort to see what Kendall looks like in this perspective seems worthwhile, the reader might turn to poems like Edgar Allan Poe's "Israfel" (1831), addressed to the angel poet of the Moslem paradise:

> The ecstasies above
> With thy burning measures suit—
> Thy grief, thy joy, thy hate, thy love,

> With the fervor of thy lute—
> Well may the stars be mute!
>
> Yes, Heaven is thine; but this
>   Is a world of sweets and sours;
>   Our flowers are merely—flowers,
> And the shadow of thy perfect bliss
>   Is the sunshine of ours.
>
> If I could dwell
> Where Israfel
>   Hath dwelt, and he where I,
> He might not sing so wildly well
>   A mortal melody,
> While a bolder note than this might swell
>   From my lyre within the sky.

Or to Emerson's "Ode to Beauty" (1843):

> I hear the lofty paeans
> Of the masters of the shell,
> Who heard the starry music
> And recount the numbers well;
> Olympian bards who sung
> Divine Ideas below,
> Which always find us young
> And always keep us so.
> Oft, in streets or humblest places,
> I detect far-wandered graces,
> Which, from Eden wide astray,
> In lowly homes have lost their way.

Tracing influences can be a profitless pursuit, and is exhausting when dealing with Kendall who apparently believed that imitation is the sincerest form of flattery and who wanted to flatter everyone. Kendall imitated with a naive ingenuousness which seems now to make irrelevant the outcries of those nineteenth century critics who condemned his plagiarism as morally reprehensible. He imitated Harpur with great zeal, taking up ideas and phrases rather than verse form, although much of his blank verse seems to be modelled upon Harpur's. His earliest verse form demonstrably owes much to Poe's metrical forms, refrains, and euphonious ululating names. With the well-known "Bell Birds" Kendall transposed some prose notes from Harpur's poem "The Kangaroo Hunt" into pleasing verse, but it is a mystery why he should have followed Harpur as closely as he did, for example, in the poem "Faith in God", which leans heavily on two poems written some twenty years earlier by Harpur, and mentioned in the preceding comments on Harpur. When surveying colonial verse as it appeared in newspapers and journals from about 1830 to 1880, the reader will be a little surprised at the amount of cross-fertilization and borrowing that is obvious among the poems. This occurred to an extent that would hardly be tolerated today, and it can only be surmised that the prevailing conventions permitted such imitation. The prospect of compiling an anthology of colonial verse of *very* minor writers is not especially inviting, but such an anthology would throw interesting light on the literary climate of the time and have some sociological value.

The consideration of literary interaction between colonial poets leads to a question raised by the death of Gordon who "was found dead in the heather near his home with a bullet from his own rifle in his brain".[8] His death occurred within a few days of the publication of *Bush Ballads and Galloping Rhymes*. Gordon had received just the morning before the bill from the publisher and was at the time quite unable to meet this expense. He apparently spent the day drinking with Marcus Clarke and Kendall, and the latter read Gordon the proof-sheets of a review of *Bush Ballads and Galloping Rhymes* which he had written for publication in the *Australasian* of 25 June 1870. Gordon's biographers express surprise that this review, which has been described as "highly favourable", did not sufficiently raise the spirits of the poet to prevent the tragedy which occurred on the following morning.[9] Kendall's review says much in praise of Gordon's poetry and its final comments are generous but controlled in a way that makes them more impressive than mere panegyric could be. The final assessment is grave and sincere:

> But after all has been said for and against him, the fact remains that he has laid Australia under a deep and lasting obligation. Amongst the few writers of imaginative literature that these colonies have produced, he certainly occupies no secondary position. He has contributed what we believe to be a durable addition to the treasure of the English language, and one that will be talked about, written of, read, and enjoyed long after this unquiet, unsettled generation has passed away.

In the review, however, Kendall points to a limitation in Gordon's achievement which he felt was circumscribed by the extreme despair that lay at the heart of Gordon's philosophy of life. It was suggested earlier that Kendall, for all his melancholy and tears, was a stronger man than Gordon. Kendall perceived that Gordon's pessimism was due not to a very deep reflection on life, but to an inability to penetrate below the surface level of the "tears of things". His comments are courteous, but clearly censuring:

> And now we come to what may be called his efforts in the domain of introspective verse. There, of course, the faculty for meditation is required; but of this our author like Swinburne, is singularly deficient. In plainer words, while his successes in other directions are always remarkable, his failures in the school of which Wordsworth is perhaps the great leader are complete and immediately evident. After taking the descriptive element out of such pieces as *Doubtful Dreams* and *The Swimmer*, and putting aside their exquisite versification, the reader will find little left to repay his attention.

Now this is not the kind of assessment which would deflect a sick and penniless man from the course of suicide. Praise for exquisite versification does not compensate for the suggestion that one's verses are otherwise worthless. What Kendall means about the singular deficiency in the faculty of meditation is illustrated by lines from the two poems which epitomize the "philosophy" which they express. Kendall's criticism implies that the sentiment—for to Kendall it was sentiment rather than Wordsworthian meditation—is worthless. This "worthless" sentiment, as all Gordon's biographers attest, was the prevailing creed of his life.

> A little season of love and laughter,
> Of light and life, and pleasure and pain,
> And a horror of outer darkness after,
> And dust returneth to dust again.
> Then the lesser life shall be the greater,
> And the lover of life shall join the hater,
> And the one thing cometh sooner or later,
> And no one knoweth the loss or gain.

(from "The Swimmer")

This is something far different from the melancholy of Kendall and it might even appear to be a stronger emotion than that of the man who could not with his "feeble feet" climb after his desire. And yet it is clear that while Gordon's sentiment is more passionately expressed than almost anything Kendall wrote, it stops short of the threshold of spiritual experience. It is a shallow meditation. Gordon referred to himself, and to the South Australian squattocracy, with whom he identified, as *les enfants perdus*, the *morituri*.[10] One may be reluctant to call Heine, Clough, or Baudelaire a shallow thinker, and they too claimed the status of *enfants perdus*; but although Gordon's verse suggests that he felt emotionally the same spiritual displacement as these men, it does not suggest that he struggled up and down quite the same spiritual paths as they traversed. Two stanzas from "Doubtful Dreams" should justify these assertions:

> Vain dreams! for our fathers cherish'd
> High hopes in the days that were;
> And these men wonder'd and perish'd,
> Nor better than these we fare;
> And our due at least is their due:
> They fought against odds and fell:
> '*En avant, les enfants perdus!*'
> We fight against odds as well.
>
> There is life in the blacken'd ember
> While a spark is smouldering yet;
> In a dream e'en now I remember
> That dream I had lief forget—
> I had lief forget, I had e'en lief
> That dream with *this* doubt should die—
> '*If we did these things in the green leaf,*
> *What shall be done in the dry?*'

What occurs in the poem is a fiercely pessimistic but vague questioning of the validity of certain dreams and high hopes, and Kendall is justified in implying that neither the dreams nor the high hopes that "our fathers cherish'd" were fully understood by Gordon who rejected them. Kendall did not question the sincerity of Gordon's meditative verses, but he felt that Gordon was deficient in "the faculty of meditation". Gordon wrote to a friend a month before his death that he had "no great opinion of Kendall's judgement" as a critic, but he admitted "He is *reckoned* the best critic of poetry here, and he is certainly the best poet."[11] Kendall's review perhaps did not weigh very heavily with him, but it is not exactly the "fascinating draught of criticism" that one biographer thought it to be.[12] If the meditative poems in *Bush Ballads and Galloping Rhymes* meant more to the author than others in the collection, Kendall's outspoken criticism of them must have affected Gordon to some extent in the circumstances in which he was struggling in the mid-winter of 1870.

It is regrettable that Gordon could not develop a more

philosophical perception of his emotional conviction that he belonged to a transitional generation existing in the no man's land between the end of one era and the beginning of the next. Australia herself at this period, the mid-sixties to the nineties, was feeling the transition from an early pastoral ascendancy to the beginnings of trade unionism, commercial and industrial power. Gordon's sense of exile and loss was a personal one, but it was also a national one, to which many factors contributed, political, economic, and social.

Marcus Clarke wrote an evocative and emotive account of the Australian landscape which was prompted partly by Gordon's poetry. It has often served as an introduction to Gordon's collected verse, and in it he says: "Australia has rightly been named the Land of the Dawning. Wrapped in the mist of early morning, her history looms vague and gigantic. The lonely horseman riding between the moonlight and the day, sees vast shadows creeping across the shelterless and silent plains ... "[13]

Like Sidney Nolan's Ned Kelly, Gordon's sick stockrider— and Gordon himself—are men dispossessed of one inheritance, and yet inseparably part of the landscape they inhabit. They wait in the mists between moonlight and day: between the past and the future.

It should be reiterated that this was also a European experience. Even Matthew Arnold, when he was still a poet, allowed the doubtful ambiguous moonlight to illumine much of his poetry. The effects of hot, bright sunlight and brilliant sunsets in Gordon's verse have been ably discussed, but even then the critic points out that Gordon's favourite view was that of a landscape softened or humanized by a haze of tobacco smoke.[14] Although this may well be "an emblem of contemplative peace" the sick stockrider who reminisces about it is, after all, about to die, or, as the classically minded Gordon would say, *moriturus*.

There is no one way of looking at these minor colonial poets which is in itself better than any other way, but their significance as social and literary phenomena is more fully understood if all relevant approaches are explored. Seeing a minor poet in a new perspective will not change him from a minor poet into a major one, but there are good reasons for trying to see minor poets steadily and whole: "For minor poets do achieve minor triumphs; but they often represent as well, in their untriumphant poems, certain twists, changes, dilemmas, problems, oddnesses, of the human spirit with peculiar candour because they are poetically naive and unoriginal enough to be more like our common selves than the great poets."[15]

4

English Publication of Australian Novels in the Nineteenth Century: The Case of *His Natural Life*

L. T. HERGENHAN

Until near the turn of last century novels written in or about Australia were first published, or if possible soon republished, in England, presumably because authors were otherwise faced with restricted readership and publishing opportunities. There has been some comment and speculation, but no detailed study, on the effects this orientation had on the content and quality of Australian fiction, for instance the widespread use of the stereotyped and retarding forms of "books of travel in disguise"[1] and of what Joseph Furphy scornfully called the "rose water" romance of bush life. But before we can attain a clear picture of such effects more needs to be known about the practicalities and economics of publishing—an author's agreements with his publishers, his earnings, the rights and distribution of his works. This publishing history is no doubt a story in itself.[2] The most famous and the best novel of the last century, Marcus Clarke's *For the Term of His Natural Life*, offers an interesting example, though here—as no doubt in other cases—only some of the evidence is presently available, and even this raises as many questions as it answers.

It has been reasonably assumed that Clarke's novel proceeded from serialization (*Australian Journal*, March 1870—June 1872) to revised, book publication in Australia (Melbourne: George

56

Robertson, 1874), then to publication abroad (3 vols., London: Bentley, 1875) in the normal way—as part of the natural life cycle of a novel of the times. But this history has some curious and unexpected aspects. The Melbourne publisher A.H. Massina told two stories about part of it, both of them generally accepted but open to question. They derive from a newspaper interview[3] in which his memory of much earlier years was unreliable at some points[4] and his comments are obviously coloured by hindsight and by his desire to make the most of his association with a famous work.

Massina recalled that when Clarke asked first for £50, then almost in the same breath for £100, advance on a serial (for the *Australian Journal*) he proposed to write up from the criminal records while on a visit to Tasmania, "we jumped at it".[5] To query the economic facts alone, such alacrity and generosity (for the times, as we shall see later), while it is not beyond probability, given Clarke's rising reputation in Melbourne and his previous association as one of Massina's authors,[6] does sound too glib—especially as the latter had introduced the story by presenting Clarke as being in the habit of bleeding him: "Oh you've had enough of me. What more do you want?"[7] Whether this was the real and total payment is not clear. By expanding the serial, or as seems more likely, letting it run away with him for better and worse, so that it lasted for two and a half years instead of the proposed one, Clarke could not *reasonably* expect more money as Brian Elliott has pointed out.[8] Certainly the usually impecunious Clarke would have had no scruples about asking for more, and Ronald Campbell has speculated about whether he received additional "refreshers".[9]

Massina's second story is similarly patronizing and self-important:

> A funny thing happened when Clarke brought in the last of his copy of *For the Term of His Natural Life*. He said, "There's the end of it," and I said, "Thank God." Clarke said, "Why?" and I said, "I don't want to hear the name of the blessed thing any more." "Will you give the story to me?" said Clarke. I did, there and then. He went right away with it and got £25 for it to start with from George Robertson. I could have made a lot of money out of it, but at the moment was glad to get rid of it.[10]

About this anecdote one thing is certain: subsequent events show that neither Massina nor any Australian publisher would have made a lot of money out of the first, or any early, book publications. Though Massina may not have known this at the time of the above incident (May 1872), he should have known it from his experiences as a publisher when he told the story in 1909. Even given Massina's understandable irritation and Clarke's mercurial nature the whole episode sounds too perfunctory, though it may have some sketchy truth. It cannot be assumed, for instance, that the rights of book publication were Massina's to give away, though he may have had first option as publisher of Clarke's previous novel *Long Odds*, and he did publish some later works. In the nineteenth century rights of serial and of book publication were often separate. Indeed, as Elliott comments, Massina "seems to have retained his sole rights over the posthumous republications of the serial, unrevised version", although when he reprinted it he unctuously pointed out that "the proprietors of the *Australian Journal* ... have taken pleasure in paying tribute to the genius of Australia's greatest prose writer by a donation to the fund for the maintenance and education of the children".[11]

Elliott nevertheless cautiously concludes that "the question of copyright [of the serial version] does not appear to be altogether clear", but his further comment that "Clarke's rights in the revision were never challenged",[12] is inaccurate, as Clarke's correspondence with Bentley reveals.

Not all of this correspondence appears to have survived but there is enough to throw new light on the English publication of *His Natural Life* and, indirectly, of Australian novels generally. In his *XIX Century Fiction: A Bibliographical Record* Michael Sadleir appends two letters[13] (the originals remain untraced) to his bibliographical description of the first Australian and English editions with the comment that the correspondence "throws an interesting light on the history of this famous novel". The first appears either to open negotiations, or at least, to have been written shortly after they began:

30 Dec. 1874

The Public Library
Melbourne
Victoria.

Dear Sirs,

I have received through Messrs Baillière of this city, London and Paris, an intimation from Mr Sterry [*sic*] (of Messrs Kelly & Co. Lincolns Inn) that your firm would publish my novel 'His Natural Life' and secure me the copyright, provided that certain alteration was made in the end of the story.

Mr Sterry informs me that it is your wish that the book ends happily, and suggests to me to correct the sheets accordingly. I have by this mail forwarded to Mr Sterry the last pages of the novel altered as he desires, and concluding with an ad litional chapter putting that pleasant construction upon events which I belive you think to be best suited to your purchasers.

The story—if you will recall it—originally ended in the death of the hero and the death of the woman whom he loves. Mr Sterry informs me that you object to that end. It would be monstrous to make the hero—a convict—*marry* his love, so I have given the woman a daughter and contrived that the hero shall rescue that daughter from death and see in her the mother whom he once loved.

As I have informed Mr Sterry by this mail, I desire *that the correction which I send him be the only correction in the novel.* Unless you can see your way to publish "His Natural Life" as I have written it (replacing the original end by the MS sent to Mr Sterry) and retaining the Appendices etc. I would rather not have it re-published at all. I hope however that the MS and this letter may arrive in time to prevent any correction by a strange hand.

Mr Sterry gives me—through Mr Baillière—to understand, that you give no price for the book, but publish an edition at your own cost, securing to *me* the copyright of future editions. I shall be glad to have a reply from you to this note.

I am, dear sirs, Yours faithfully,
Marcus Clarke.

The letter is worth discussion in detail. Later correspondence shows that the lawyers, Kelly & Co. (their correspondent was Skerry, not Sterry as Sadleir, or Clarke, mis-transcribes it) were acting for Clarke, as apparently was Baillière. F.F. Baillière "represented in Melbourne from the early 1860s a publishing and bookselling dynasty—still flourishing—that had already branched out from its native Paris to London, Madrid and New York".[14]

It is apparent from Clarke's letter that he had been asked to change the ending of the revised novel (already greatly changed from the serial version) to conform to the Victorian convention of a happy, "inoffensive" ending.* One wonders whether Clarke was willing,

---

*Since this article was written I have discovered two readers' reports commissioned by Bentley, one by Geraldine Jewsbury, 22 September 1874, the other by Charlotte Jackson, 11 September 1874 (Bentley Papers, British Museum, vols. CI and CII). Both reports were favourable for publication, but Jewsbury, the more influential and

if disinclined, to comply in order to achieve English publication. (There was also the fact, as will emerge later, that there was no copyright to the first publication outside Australia, though it would appear from this letter—the final paragraph—and the following one that neither Clarke nor George Robertson knew it at this stage.) Clarke's irony at the expense of the diluting conventions of Victorian fiction, determined by publishers and reading tastes, is urbanely lethal: "I have by this mail forwarded to Mr Sterry the last pages of the novel altered as he desires, and concluding with an additional chapter putting that pleasant construction upon events which I believe you think to be best suited to your purchasers." The continuation of this irony in the more specific comments on the ending is also a continuation of the novel's attack, sometimes subtle sometimes crude, but generally savage, on the rigid English class structure: "The story ... originally ended in the death of the hero and the death of the woman he loves. Mr Sterry informs me you object to that end. It would be monstrous to make the hero—a convict— *marry* his love, so I have given the woman a daughter and contrived that the hero shall rescue the daughter from death and see in her the woman he once loved." This has parallels in some of the novel's most poignant and bitter moments showing the helplessness of those trapped in the convict system and, both directly and by implication, of other social "systems". The concluding of the 1874 revised version with the deaths of Dawes and Sylvia develops the point to its utmost, for even if somewhat melodramatically handled, this ending is the "logical" outcome of the novel's concerns and is far superior to the alternative ending served up to please Bentley but in fact not in the end adopted, as Sadleir notes. Indeed, this alternative ending sounds almost identical (except for being much more condensed) with the original serial ending that Clarke had been at pains to change. It is ironical that the revised ending, which displeased Bentley, has been attacked by modern critics as simply a pandering to Victorian sentimentality![15]

experienced reader, while more strongly advising acceptance did so on one "essential" condition: that the painful ending of the hero's death be avoided by the addition of a chapter in which he survives the cyclone and uses his "fearful sufferings" and "knowledge [bought] at a fearful price" for the help of others; for "it is *too* bad to let him be drowned just as the tide is beginning to turn in his favour!" It would seem, then, that Bentley's request for a happy ending was prompted by this report which explicitly states that it reflects what "a reader" would feel.

Clarke's willingness to change the ending, and his stressing that it be "*the only correction*", suggests some anxiety of the author disadvantageously placed at the antipodes and hoping by a combination of compromise and firmness to overcome delays in communication and metropolitan high-handedness from "home". (As it turned out, however, the English edition did not appear until nine months later, at the end of September 1875.)[16] It was usual in Victorian times for a publisher to suggest changes to authors and the house of Bentley was not untypical in that "one of the duties of the publisher's reader was to revise manuscripts by authors who could not or would not meet the standards of the publisher or conform to his tastes".[17] This was usually done in consultation with the author, and in some cases, as happened with *His Natural Life*, the suggested alterations were not made.[18] Elliott does note that there are "minor revisionary differences" between the Robertson and Bentley editions,[19] but it is not clear whether these were Clarke's emendations or editorial changes. Mrs. Cashel Hoey,[20] along with her husband a friend of Clarke's friend Sir Charles Gavan Duffy, read the proofs of the London edition[21] and both she and Duffy may have helped to ensure that Clarke's text was in the main adhered to.

The financial details mentioned in Clarke's letter—Bentley to publish at his own cost and Clarke to have copyright but with no price (authorial payment) yet given for the book—receive more detailed attention in the second letter quoted by Sadleir:

21st April 1875

Dear Sirs,

This letter will be enclosed to you by Mr George Robertson the Melbourne publisher of my novel "His Natural Life".

Mr Sterry writes to say that you expressed yourself willing to print the work for library circulation in England in the customary 3 vols. on the following terms:

£50 on publication
£50 on sale of 750 copies
£50 for every other 250 copies sold

but that this offer being contingent upon the fact that Mr Robertson send *no* copies for sale in England.

I was ignorant of the condition and asked Mr Robertson to send home some copies for review. He sent home 250 which did not sell (one vol. 8vo. 488 pages *7/6d.*) nor did any English journal review the work. Mr Robertson will, however, withdraw the copies from the market if you will publish the book.

Will you oblige me by making terms with his London agent and bring out the book? I have authorised Mr Robertson to do the best he can with the book, and to receive any money paid for its republication.

Sir Charles Gavan Duffy, writes me by the mail to say that he had—through Mrs Cashel Hoey—communicated with you. I have written to him to tell him the arrangement I have made with Mr Robertson, and to ask him to see you himself.

I am, my dear sirs, faithfully yours
Marcus Clarke.

This letter reveals a little known fact about English publication arrangements that could be forced on Australian writers, and publishers: publication was "contingent" on "*no* copies" of the Melbourne edition being offered for sale in England. On the face of it, it is surprising that Robertson, the main wholesale agent (with a branch in London) for the Australian distribution of English books,[22] and the main publisher within Australia at the time, was ignorant of the conditions Bentley invoked—conditions quite legitimate, or legally justified, but amounting to a kind of Imperialist "protection" policy. The probable explanation is that international copyright at the time was obscure and perplexing, as we shall see later.[23] Though it is true that English writers could suffer from unauthorized publication in Australia,[24] the market there was much smaller, and whereas colonial Australians preferred English books, the English took little interest in Australian ones, or at least certainly less than in their own. In a letter to Henry Parkes, later in the same year as Clarke's above letter (1875), Robertson warned of the bleak prospect for English sales of his book:

> As for sale in England ... past experience with other Australian publications forbids me to hope much. There is a tendency on the part of the English press and the English trade to neglect or, if noticed, to snub anything Australian. My London office is for "buying" and not for "selling"; but through this office I can, if you desire it, place a supply of your book in the hands of Simpkin, Marshall & Co. or some other "commission" house. The regular publishers decline all books except such as they have the producing of it themselves.[25]

The copyright laws unfavourable to Australia, are not referred to in Clarke's letter. Perhaps Bentley had spelt them out because Clarke had assumed in his first communication that copyright would be his: " ... securing to *me* the copyright of future editions".

Clarke's comment, "I have asked Mr Robertson to do the best he can with the book, and to receive any money paid for its republication" sounds a less hopeful note than his first letter, and even suggests some early—and enforced—"cultural cringe". The change from Baillière to Robertson as negotiating London agent may have arisen because Robertson first published the novel. Other possible reasons were the latter's greater commercial importance for British sales in Australia, Clarke's being possibly in debt and indebted to Robertson over the Australian edition (though he was in debt to a lot of people including Baillière), and also the fact that Robertson had published works of Clarke and of his friend, Sir Charles Gavan Duffy. Duffy's was a name to be reckoned with in the English political, literary, and publishing worlds.[26] The letter shows that Clarke enlisted his personal intercession with Bentley, Duffy being conveniently in London at the time. Duffy's friendship and patronage had already been shown in Clarke's application to him for advice about the revision of the serial (including the ending) and in the dedication of the book to him, a dedication retained in many editions and no doubt included in Clarke's injunction in his first letter to Bentley that the retaining of the "Appendices *etc.*" [my italics] were a sticking point for authorizing publication.[27] (Duffy had narrowly missed being transported to Van Diemen's land—as an Irish political prisoner—along with Smith O'Brien and John Mitchel.)

The financial terms offered by Bentley—"£50 on publication, £50 on sale of 750 copies, £50 for every other 250 copies sold"—were reasonable and took one of the usual forms of agreement for the times and for a first novel by an "unknown" author.[28] Publishing agreements varied greatly both in form and in individual cases. Outright fees covering first and all subsequent editions were commonly and legitimately made and adhered to regardless of how successful a novel was or became. Under other arrangements the author's earnings could, after the advance, vary according to the costs of production (including advertising) and sales, as in Clarke's case. "The sale of copyright ... was neither so frequent nor so simple as is commonly assumed"[29] and it is not clear when the royalty agreement first came into use. "The first actual use of the system seems to have been in an agreement with Mrs Lynn Linton in 1885.'"[30] Some guide to how much Clarke was to earn (and hence the size of the edition), and some clarification of his dealings with

Bentley over the first and later English editions, is provided by later letters in the Bentley papers in the British Museum.[31]

In these papers Clarke's name is nowhere to be found in the "Agreements" records, and in the "Letters from Authors" there is a total gap from early 1874 until 1876 when, as we have seen, Clarke was negotiating with Bentley. (There were also no letters from Skerry, Baillière, or Robertson.) In the correspondence of the following years there are four letters relating to Clarke, one to him personally, one to Skerry, and seven written after his death. The first concerns the second English edition of *His Natural Life*:

11 December 1879.

To J.W. Skerry Esqre.,
51 Great Queen Street, W.C.

Dear Sir,

We are sorry that there should have been any appearance of delay in communication with you on the matter of the publication of "His Natural Life".

We have looked into the accounts and find that the proceeds of the 6/- edition [1878] are not favourable.

As we purchased the right of publication in this country we do not think under the circumstances of a new edition resulting *in a loss* that we can reconsider the amount paid for the work, as we might have been disposed to do if the publication had been a success.

We remain, dear Sir,
for Richard Bentley and Son,
B. Cousens.

This letter is best considered along with a later, summarizing one written after Clarke's death to John S. Woolcott, 82 Collins Street, Melbourne, presumably the lawyer of Clarke's widow (for he is listed as a solicitor of this address in Sands and McDougall's *Melbourne Directory*, 1881):

2 December 1881.

Dear Sir,

We were sorry to hear shortly before your letter arrived, of the death of Mr Marcus Clarke and beg that you will convey our expressions of regret to Mrs Clarke.

Mr Clarke's business relations with us were in brief as follows.

A few years ago a work entitled "For the Term of His Natural Life" was published in Australia[32] and strictly speaking there is and was no copyright protection to the work in this country, it having first appeared in Australia. Being struck by the power of the work we reprinted it in three volumes in this country, with the consent of the author, and forwarded to Mr Clarke in 1876 a cheque for £50.

Some time afterwards the work was reprinted in a 6/- form, but it did not meet with such popularity in that form as we had reason to anticipate and when an enquiry was made on the subject two years ago, we had then to report that the work had not even paid the expenses of its reprint.

This it has now done and as soon as our profits on the work have reduced the amount already paid to Mr Clake viz. £50 we shall be agreeable to divide any succeeding profits in equal proportion with Mrs Clarke. As the work is however a very slow selling one in this country Mrs Clarke should not count upon any large sum from this source. Last year Mr Clarke had another work in contemplation to be entitled 'Felix et Felicitas', the first chapter or two we saw and wrote to him in Nov. of 1880, that if he completed the work in the same style which it commenced we should probably publish it over here and in the event of so doing to have paid him £50. As this story has not, however, we believe been completed it would be impossible to publish it (in part) with any hope of success.

> We remain, dear Sir,
> Yours Faithfully,
> [signed] R. Bentley & Son

P.S. In reference to the memorial volume of Mr Clarke's life.[33] This work should we think be published in Australia where Mr Clarke was of course well known as over here it must necessarily meet with too limited a sale to pay the expenses of production

[Enclosed in this letter is a copy of an extract from the one to Clarke of 18/11/1880, quoted above: "I am unable ... not anticipate the decision."]

It is not clear what is meant in the 1879 letter by Bentley's claim that they had "purchased the right of publication in this country". The 1881 letter does spell out, after Clarke's death—though it may have been made clear to him at some stage in missing correspondence—what was in fact true: "strictly speaking there was no copyright protection in England of a work first published in Australia". Perhaps Bentley had "*purchased* [my italics] the right of publication" in the sense that the £50 advance on the first edition and an arrangement to pay more according to the extent of the sales of this and any later issues of it, had been accepted as an equitable "purchase" price though whether this was all made clear to Clarke—and Robertson—is uncertain. Bentley had nevertheless acted considerately in gaining "the consent of the author" and in his payments for what was apparently a small first edition and a slow-selling reprint. But although Bentley was a reputable publisher one may wonder if Clarke would have been less well treated without the personal intervention of influential friends.

Since in 1881 Bentley was waiting for "profits" on the second edition "to reduce the amount already paid [for the first] to Mr Clarke, viz. £50", before sharing any "succeeding profits in equal proportions with Mrs Clarke", it would appear that the first edition had in fact been published at Bentley's expense (as the 1874 letter indicated) and that it had made a financial loss, even though it had been well reviewed.[34] On the basis of the terms offered in the letter of 1875 this suggests that sales fell far short of 750 copies, at which point Clarke was to receive another £50.

One may wonder how George Robertson, publisher of the first Australian edition, was involved jointly with Bentley in the rights of later publications. Apparently for a time he retained, or shared in, the Australian rights.

The only clues to the nature of Robertson's involvement, apart from the far from conclusive Bentley letters which claim sole proprietorship of English rights, are the pieces of brief publishing information contained in the post-1875 editions. But before this is examined it is necessary to take into account the general state of copyright at the time—a state unclear and perplexing to publishers, authors, lawyers alike in respect to first publication within the colonies, let alone United Kingdom republication and distribution of colonial works. In 1869 the London *Athenaeum* drew attention to anomalies and injustices of a judgment of the House of Lords that had attempted to clarify imperial law regarding colonial copyright:

> The result of this opinion of the House of Lords is very disastrous, and justly creates great dissatisfaction in the Colonies and India; it has either destroyed all copyright property in the numerous works which, since 1842, have been first published there, or rendered such property comparatively worthless; and this hardship is increased by the fact that, since 1842, it has been and still is compulsory upon *all* publishers in the British dominions *gratuitously* to send one copy of every book published by them to the British Museum, and four to the Libraries of Oxford, Cambridge, &c.
>
> The anomaly and injustice of such a state of our copyright law become the more apparent when it is remembered that, under the

International Copyright Conventions entered into by England and France, and most of the other chief European states, works first published in France, &c. have long been, and may still be, protected from piracy in the United Kingdom or any other part of the British dominions.[35]

Not long afterwards, in 1877 and between the first and second English editions of *His Natural Life*, "the colonial problem" with regard to copyright seemed no nearer to solution, as Sir James Stephen pointed out in a digest annexed to the report of the royal commission of copyright:

> It is uncertain whether an author obtains copyright by publishing a book in the United Kingdom, after a previous publication thereof in parts of Her Majesty's dominions out of the United Kingdom.
> It is uncertain whether an author acquires copyright ... in any part of Her Majesty's dominions out of the United Kingdom (apart from any local law as to copyright which may be in force there) by the publication of a book in such part of Her Majesty's dominions.[36]

Given this context of the murky state of copyright law, the meagre publishing details to be found in the post-1875 editions of *His Natural Life* can but dimly suggest the possible nature of Robertson's involvement in its copyright. The 1878 edition (about which there is some confusion in Sadleir and the Bentley letter of 18-81),[37] appeared in two issues. One bore on its title page the double imprint: "A New Edition. Melbourne, George Robertson. London, Richard Bentley and Son"; Richard Bentley appeared on the spine and the edition was printed in England (by Hazell, Watson and Viney of Aylesbury). The other issue of the edition bore Bentley's imprint only (there is a copy in the British Museum), and this is the only 1878 edition listed by Morris Miller, and by Miller and Macartney.

The third English edition of 1885, the first with the longer title (although there is a very scarce edition dated 1884 of which the 1885 is probably a reissue), carries the double imprint (Bentley's coming first this time), and the verso of the title page notes: "This edition is especially issued by the Proprietors of the Copyright for circulation in the Australian colonies only". (The next, 1888 edition, carries a similar claim.) It would appear from this and from the 1878 "joint" issue that Bentley was sharing in the Australian copyright. The posthumous change in title—never satisfactorily explained, except for the assumption that it was thought to be more "catchy" and "clear"—may even have had something to do with copyright, for this is the first time "Proprietorship" is publicly stated with the suggestion of a claim being staked.

It is not clear, then, how George Robertson was associated as publisher with the colonial editions of 1885 and later.[38] Perhaps, like Clarke's literary heir, his wife, Robertson had some share in profits as well as in distribution. So far as I can discover the next Australian edition after that of 1874 was in 1897, published by Angus and Robertson (of Sydney, and distinct from the George Robertson Melbourne firm) with a preface by A.B. Paterson. By the turn of the century Bentley apparently disposed of or "lost" the rights, as there were a number of cheap editions by Macmillan (including "Colonial Editions") and Ward Lock.[39] An edition by the latter in 1911 states that it is "published under the terms of the Copyright Act, 1911, by special arrangement with Mrs Marcus Clarke, the owner of the copyright". (I have not attempted to pursue the copyright question beyond the 1890s.)

Although the evidence considered so far shows that the first English edition was virtually a financial failure in its early years and that the second (1878) sold slowly, letters in the Bentley Papers to Hamilton Mackinnon[40] corroborate Brian Elliott's comment that the novel enjoyed "a steady and increasing sale"[41] after Clarke's death in 1881. These letters suggest that profits derived mainly from cheap colonial editions for the Australian market and were regarded as satisfactory by Bentley, but the sales do not, however, appear to have brought much money to Clarke's widow, judging by her continued enquiries to Bentley through Mackinnon. Perhaps growing Australian nationalism in the 1880s and 1890s stimulated demand for a novel that was becoming an Australian classic, though the demand was catered for by English publishers until almost the turn of the century.

Another Bentley letter does suggest that the English reputation won by *His Natural Life* was nevertheless sufficient to gain Clarke the offer of ready consideration of another novel, the projected "Felix and Felicitas", though the mooted terms were not good—in fact not nearly as good as for the previous novel. A low fee, apparently "outright" but possibly an advance, was named pending completion and the quality being satisfactory:

8 New Burlington St,
London.

Nov. 10. 1880

To Marcus Clarke Esq.,
The Public Library, Melbourne.

Dear Sir,
I have safely received the few sheets of the book[42] you kindly sent to me.

I am unable without seeing the whole to speak definitively of the book, but as far as it goes I like it. If it makes as much [length] as your former work I will pay you Fifty Pounds for it, if you will first let me see the whole work. Send the whole to me, and I will telegraph to you "Yes" or "No". If "No" I will try to place it elsewhere for you in England, but I do not anticipate this decision.

I take it I should *reprint* in England, so don't work any copies for our market, and above all take care that none of your copies come over here except the one to me.

Yours truly,
George Bentley

Some of this information about "Felix" was repeated in the letter above to Mrs. Clarke. It is notable that here again, acceptance is conditional on reprinting in England, so that copyright can be acquired and safeguarded—though by whom is not mentioned.

"Felix" was never completed, and the faiture to obtain English publication for the posthumous collections of Clarke's shorter writings is anticipated and explained in another Bentley letter I have been able to discover as well as in the P.S. of the letter to Mrs. Clarke:

To Hamilton Mackinnon Esq. (Yorick Club, Melbourne)
[This is an extract from a letter written 19 April 1882]
... We do not think that you can count on much sale for a memorial volume in this country where Mr Clarke was comparatively little known. Should you feel disposed, however, nevertheless to test the feeling of the English market we should be very pleased to do what we can if you will send 50 or 100 copies over here when the work is complete, through the Robertson's agency. (The title page should, for this purpose bear our imprint) ... .

R. Bentley and Son
per B—[?]

The only copy of the *Marcus Clarke Memorial Volume* in the British Museum *Catalogue* bears the Cameron, Laing and Co. of Melbourne, imprint, and it may be that alternative arrangements for a small English distribution were made. Other works of Clarke, novels and collections of stories, were published later in England, but not by Bentley.

It is impossible to tell whether the disadvantages of English publication facing an author in colonial Australia affected the literary career of Clarke who had enough difficulties of a personal kind on his hands. His experience with his one considerable work must have been deeply disappointing, and with the poor terms suggested for "Felix", the novel he was struggling with at the end of his short life, his disappointment must have deepened. Still, literary achievement does not depend necessarily on recognition and commercial success, and if Clarke and other Australian novelists had been writing in England using English material they would by no means have been free from publishing problems and pressures to conform to popular taste. What is clearer is that Clarke's colonial experience suggests how the practicalities and economics of publication in England could increase the pressures on Australian writers to satisfy the market there. Writers in England were in a similar, but not quite the same, position. For a start they had the advantage of using recognizable, if not familiar, English material. In addition their difficulties were not exacerbated by the "tyranny of distance" that put them at a greater remove from their publishers as well as readers and by the tyranny of imperialism, or muddle that placed them at a disadvantage with regard to publishing rights. Clarke could have fared even less well than he did, and other colonial authors fared worse:

> Recent British novels might appear as local newspaper serials, with or without authority. The newspaper or magazine was the Australian author's most readily accessible forum, but he only obtained Australian and not United Kingdom copyright. An example is Thomas Alexander Browne, police magistrate of Albury, New South Wales: after *Robbery under Arms* (London, 1888) had made his fame as 'Rolf Boldrewood' one of his earlier serialized novels was promptly reprinted, legitimately but without his consent, in Britain. Kipling's earliest writings, published in Calcutta and Lahore, were unprotected elsewhere under palm and pine.[43]

A modern scholar, Simon Nowell-Smith, has further commented:

> By the latter part of the century copyright and publishing in the Empire had become matters not so much of complexity as of chaos. If I say I do not know what the law was at any particular date I must not be charged with lack of curiosity or application ... .[44]

It is fitting to end with a similar statement by Clarke himself, writing out of his perplexities and difficulties as an *Australian* author and with a customary fairness and wit which, though amongst his attractive qualities as man and writer, probably masked his increasing frustration and disappointment. Clarke's comment reveals that the copyright confusion was even more far-reaching than we have yet seen, for at times there could be no safeguarding of rights even between the several Australian colonies let alone within the far-flung Empire and the rest of the world. Clarke was writing[45] apropos of the "piracy" in Sydney of one of his plays (first performed in Melbourne and an adaptation of a novel):

> There is another point, though, in connexion with this petty piece of pilfering to which I would invite your attention. I sent instructions through a solicitor to see the lessee of the theatre in which my drama was played, and was advised in reply not to continue the action, as the "law of copyright is so uncertain." Surely, Sir, this uncertainty should be removed. Why should not copyright be at least intercolonial, instead of purely Victorian? Why should my drama be played in New Zealand and New South Wales (as it has been played repeatedly) without my being paid or being able to recover payment? It may be urged with equal force—why should I be able to dramatise Mr. Reade's novel *Foul Play* without paying him for the privilege? To which I reply—I am willing that the copyright law be altered, for Mr. Sefton Parry dramatised my novel, *Long Odds*, and played it for nearly a month in London without paying me for it. As Mr. Stephen Hartpool remarks (in a play called "Hard Times," dramatised from Dickens's novel of that name without his permission) "It's a muddle!"—Yours &c.,

April 4.   Marcus Clarke.

5

The Short Stories of Marcus Clarke

MICHAEL WILDING

The weight put on the "nationalist nineties" by the new nationalist critics of the 1930s, 40s, and 50s has produced its particular and predominant version of Australian literary history. Its negative results are obvious: firstly a devaluing of writers not actually born in Australia, even though their creative life was spent in Australia; and secondly, an assumption that anything before the 1890s is derivative writing, merely imitative of English modes, second-hand, second-rate, colonial. The more positive emphases of the myth are a stressing of those literary forms that found especial flowering in the 90s as representative, typical, and expressively Australian forms. So there is the nationalistic cult of the short story, with Henry Lawson as the particular native genius.

Marcus Clarke comes out especially badly from this version of Australian writing. Nettie Palmer voiced the new nationalists' complaint in her introduction to C. Hartley Grattan's *Australian Literature* in 1929. "The usual reviewers have persisted in regarding us as still 'colonials' of the nineteenth century. To them the interesting theme is that of an Englishman in wild Australia, and their attention has been concentrated on novels like *Geoffry Hamlyn* and *For The Term of His Natural Life* to the exclusion of more indigenous work."[1] As well as this downgrading of Clarke's great

72

novel, there was a total neglect of his short stories. The Australian story began with Lawson, the myth read; so anthology after anthology of Australian short stories was produced beginning with Lawson. It was forgotten that Clarke (or anyone else) even wrote short stories before Lawson. And this lapse of memory produced a distorted picture of the literary history of Australia. For what we see in Clarke's stories are at least three distinct strands of story writing. There are his realistic stories and sketches of Australian up-country life; there are his formula magazine stories, melodramatic, plotted, sensational; and there are his experimental, metaphysical, and fantasy stories.

With the emphasis on the Lawson tradition, the new nationalists implied there was only one sort of story worth writing; indeed, as far as any critical comment or anthologist's selection went, it seemed there was only one sort of story being written. These were the realistic, up-country, outback, bush stories. To look at Clarke's work in this area is to realize that Lawson was not starting with a complete *tabula rasa*; Clarke, and others, had been opening up this territory; indeed they had consciously seen it as "Australian" territory. This in no way reduces Lawson's achievement; for it was with Lawson that an appropriate voice was at last found. But the tradition was being established before Lawson: and Clarke was one of the pioneers.

The late reduction of the variety of the short story to this single strand of the outback story, a reduction fostered by the new nationalist critics, immensely damaged Australian writing. A single, narrow tradition took its increasingly barren way on; it became established, enshrined, protected, and the literary magazines gave it a home. While all the other things that could be done with short fiction were neglected; or at least, rarely saw the light of publication. Yet if we look back to the full range of Clarke's stories of the 1870s, we can see a plurality of form and traditions. Then there was an internationalism, an eclecticism, a richness of literary culture: which became reduced to the single, utilitarian, insular, aggressively anti-experimental, philistinely parochial "write Australian" line: something caused not so much by the nationalistic nineties writers, but by the new nationalist theorists, critics, and publishers' and magazine editors from the 1930s through the 1950s.

Although Clarke wrote a large number of stories, only two volumes were published in his lifetime. These were *Holiday Peak and Other Tales* (Melbourne: George Robertson, 1873) and *Four Stories High* (Melbourne: A.H. Massina, 1877). All the stories in these two volumes were originally published between 1869 and 1873, most of them in *The Australian*, but two in *The Colonial Monthly* which Clarke himself had been editing.

Clarke's journalism reflected his experience of Melbourne life. It dealt with the varieties of urban experience, in both its topical and its more enduring aspects. But Clarke had spent a couple of years in the Wimmera district of Western Victoria, between 1865 (he was then nineteen) and 1867. It was during those years that he first began publishing in *The Australian Monthly Magazine* which, under the new title of *The Colonial Monthly*, he was later to edit. Clarke was working on two sheep stations, Swinton and Ledcourt, near the small township of Glenorchy. Some of his experiences of those years found their way into his "Peripatetic Philosopher" column in *The Australasian*. He wrote, for instance, on swagmen very unromantically and unflatteringly, in accord, no doubt, with the political line and readership of the *Argus-Australasian* group, the voice of the conservative, landed squattocracy. To Clarke the swagmen were "hordes of vagabond 'loafers'" who shunned work but demanded lodging and food. "I have no desire to take away the character of these gentlemen travellers, but I may mention as a strange coincidence that, was the requested hospitality refused by any chance, a bush-fire invariably occurred somewhere on the run within twelve hours."[2] But for his full response to those years in the Wimmera, Clarke used not his journalism nor his novel writing, but the short story. The Lawson tradition of the Australian short story, that you take your material from the bush, the outback, up-country, had already been established by Clarke. The short story was seen as the appropriate form for those materials. With Clarke, however, the tradition was not a reductive one: to write about the country you turned to the short story, certainly; but to write a short story, you did not have to turn to the country. He also wrote urban melodramas, historical fantasies, speculative gothic stories, and naturalistic stories that were not set in the country; and these different settings and types were an important part of his short story output.

Yet when Clarke came to collect his first volume of stories,

Holiday Peak, he gathered together stories that were all, despite their very great variety in manner, set in the Australian up-country. A tradition was established.

Holiday Peak is a collection designed to show the range of Clarke's writing. The up-country setting provides an overall unity; but formally the pieces include fantasies (the title story, for instance), naturalistic stories, and sketches. He even includes one piece that was originally written as a "Peripatetic Philosopher" column, "Arcades Ambo".[3] An Addisonian essay, it portrays the changing nature and conditions of the squatters, contrasting a description of the old style squatter Robin Ruff with the new style young gentleman squatter leading an elegant, wealthy life, Dudley Smooth. The Latin title, the names denoting the types of the characters, indicate the English essay genre to which the piece belongs. And we are presented with the two antithetical types. Ruff "is six feet high, his hands are knotted and brown—mottled with sun and hardened with labour. His shoulders are broad, his head well set on, his eyes confident".[4] Whereas Dudley Smooth "was of a very different stamp. Mr. Smooth was a very young gentleman. His hands were brown but well-kept, and his whiskers were of a fine yellow floss-silk order, like the down on a duckling. He had but lately come down from his station, but was arrayed in the most fashionable of fashionable garments".[5] Yet these eighteenth century antitheses are seen, even as they are formulated, as belonging to the past. In this new world there are no static, permanent structures; the antitheses now are a dynamic dialectic from which a new force is emerging. Smooth

> has not arrived at the glory of his next neighbour, the Hon. Tom Holles, younger son of the Marquis of Portman-square, who was educated at Oxford and Cirencester, and has taken up squatting on scientific principles. The Hon. Tom washes his sheep in an American dip at the rate of 200 a minute, drafts cattle in lavender gloves, has nearly perfected a shearing machine, quotes Aeschylus to his overseer, prohibits all swearing, except on Sundays, and has named his bullocks after the most distinguished of the early Christians. The Hon. Tom belongs to a later phase of development, and Dudley is far behind *him* in civilisation, but he stands out in alarming contrast to poor honest, simple-minded Robin Ruff.[6]

The Peripatetic Philosopher's facetious note catches that eighteenth century contempt for enthusiasm, for faddish belief in progress; but at the same time the realities of scientific advances, of the technologies of that older New World of the United States have begun to intrude. The *Australasian* readers may have laughed at the Hon. Tom and admired the traditional antitheses of the Ruffs and the Smooths. But Clarke knew the Hon. Toms were on their way. And he had to look for a new literary tone to accommodate them.

There are two pieces in *Holiday Peak* that are sketches of a very different nature—far less formally stylized, essayistic pieces. These are "An Up-Country Township" and "Grumbler's Gully"; and they have a direct, nauralistic manner, a contemporary, immediate, documentary note. "An Up-Country Township" is a description of Bullocktown: Clarke used Bullocktown and its environs as the setting for practically all his up-country stories. Hamilton Mackinnon records that "'Bullocktown' is well known to be Glenorchy, the post-town of the Swinton Station, and all the characters in it are recognisable as life portraits presented with that peculiar glamor which his genius cast over all his literary work."[7] The Bullocktown setting provides something of a Balzacian unity for these separate yet interrelating stories; we finally assemble a topography and sociology of a representative Australian country area; though the enforced unification of setting creates some tensions when naturalistic stories and sketches, melodramas, and utter fantasies are yoked together.

"An Up-Country Township" itself, however, is in a strictly naturalistic mode—and that distinctively low-keyed, wry, dry, ironic, Australian naturalism.

> Bullocktown is situated, like all up-country townships, on the banks of something that is a flood in winter and a mud-hole in summer. For general purposes the inhabitants of the city called the something a river, and those intelligent land surveyors that mark "argicultural areas" on the tops of lofty mountains, had given the river a very grand name indeed.
>
> The Pollywog Creek, or as it was marked on the maps, the Great Glimmera, took its rise somewhere about Bowlby's Gap, and after constructing a natural sheepwash for Bowlby, terminated in a swamp, which was courteously termed Lake Landowne. No man had ever seen Lake Landowne, but once, and that was during a flood, but Lake Landowne the place was called, and Lake Landowne it remained; reeds, tussocks, and brindled bullocks' backs to the contrary notwithstanding.[8]

In "Arcades Ambo" Clarke was using the urbane essayist's tone, looking at characters out there, observing them with a knowing, worldly, distant attitude; sympathetically, certainly, but not with the sympathy of the participant in that world; the essayist is an urban man of letters with a good classical education. But in "An Up-Country Township" there is a marked difference; here the writer is expressing an identity of stance with the inhabitants of Bullocktown—laughing wryly at the city-based surveyors who know nothing of the actualities of the country they map. The Great Glimmera is known to the Bullocktonians as the Pollywog Creek, and it is as the Pollywog Creek that it is introduced, the distant, formal, official name added as a subordinate, secondary piece of information. Interestingly, what starts out as if it is a third person narration, evolves into a first person account—stressing even further the identity of the narrator's stance with the Bullocktonians. Here is somebody writing about the country with the values and assumptions of those living in the country: not as an urban, literary, pastoralizing intellectual. This is the sort of stance we so admire in Lawson's best writing. Clarke, however, differs in a major tonal aspect from Lawson here. Though Clarke is writing from the stance of the country inhabitant, he is not writing as a country worker. Lawson made that further move in vocabulary, rhythm, and tone. Clarke is still writing as the well educated countryman who can recognize a classical allusion. But importantly he does let the country worker speak, and he frequently puts his narratorial support behind the quoted speech of those workers; though making it clear that while he is used to mixing with people who talk in this colourful and lively way, and democratically happy to mix with them, he himself does not speak in his way. He will quote Wallaby Dick, but not imitate or simulate that manner for himself.

> There was a church in Bullocktown, and there were also three public-houses. It is not for me to make unpleasant comments, but I know for a fact that the minister vowed that the place wasn't worth buggy-hire, and that the publicans were making fortunes. Perhaps this was owing to the unsettled state of the district—in up-country townships most evils (including floods) are said to arise from this cause—and could in time have been remedied. I am afraid that religion, as an art, was not cultivated much in Bullocktown. The seed sown there was a little mixed in character. One week you had a Primitive Methodist, and the next a Hardshell Baptist, and the next an Irvingite or a Southcottian. To do the inhabitants justice, they endeavoured very hard to learn the ins and outs of the business, but I do not believe that they ever suc-

ceeded. As Wallaby Dick observed one day, "When you run a lot of paddocked sheep into a race, what's the good o' sticking half-a-dozen fellers at the gate? The poor beggars don't know which way to run."[9]

Drinking is a recurrent theme of the Bullocktown stories. Most of the sketch of "An Up-Country Township" revolves round the description of the three public houses there. Similarly, "Grumbler's Gully" describes a mining township twelve miles from Bullocktown, and consists mainly of a description of its hotels. And though Clarke departs from them in order to describe the main street, the gossip, the cemetery, and the religious sects, it is to the hotels he returns at the end of his piece. And what began as a genial, comic sketch of a mining township develops a suddenly bitter note. He describes the life of Daw, the editor of the local newspaper.

> Daw writes about four columns a day, and is paid £250 a year. His friends say he ought to be in Melbourne, but he is afraid to give up a certainty, so he stays, editing his paper and narrowing his mind, yearning for some intellectual intercourse with his fellow creatures. To those who have not lived in a mining township the utter dullness of Daw's life is incomprehensible. There is a complete lack of anything like cultivated mental companionship, and the three or four intellects who are above the dead level do their best to reduce their exuberant acuteness by excess of whisky-and-water. The club, the reading-room, the parliament, the audience that testifies approval and appreciation are all found in one place—the public-house bar. To obtain a criticism or a suggestion one is compelled to drink a nobbler of brandy.[10]

In most of the Bullocktown stories Clarke finds the hotels and public houses places of amusement, and the drinking part of the geniality of social interchange. In "Grumbler's Gully" it is a torment. "To sum up the jollity of Grumbler's Gully in two words—'What's yours?' "[11]

This powerful sketch was the only one of Clark's stories that also achieved publication outside Australia, appearing in *All the Year Round*, the journal edited by Charles Dickens, as "An Australian Mining Township".[12] Its bitter note gives an authenticity: this is not a glorification of outback life, but an insider's view of the destructive restraints and limitations that that sort of life produced. Because the image of Clarke's bohemian irresponsibility and spendthriftness was so firmly established (not least by himself), we expect to find his fiction and journalism extolling the virtues of alcohol. But generally the reverse is the case: it appears as something destructive, even if also inevitable and unavoidable. "The curse of the country", he called it in one of his *Humbug* pieces.[13] Yet his attitude is nonetheless very different from the prudish fervour of the crusading tea-totallers—they turn up as figures of absurdity in Clarke's stories and sketches. While the Reverend North is portrayed in *His Natural Life* with a deep sympathy—North fighting his addiction, yet losing the fight, inevitably drawn more and more hopelessly into alcoholism. In his pamphlet *The Future of the Australian Race* (an excerpt from which Hamilton Mackinnon included amongst the "Australian Tales and Sketches") Clarke, looking forward a hundred years with a degree of seriousness no commentators have ever been in agreement on, predicts:

> The Australians will be selfish, self-reliant, ready in resource, prone to wander, caring little for home ties. Mercenary marriage will be frequent, and the hotel system of America will be much favoured. The Australians will be large meat eaters, and meat eaters require more stimulants than vegetarians. The present custom of drinking alcohol to excess—favoured alike by dietary scale and carnivorous practices—will continue. All carnivora are rash, gloomy, given to violences. Vegetarians live at a lower level of health, but are calmer and happier.[14]

"How The Circus Came to Bullocktown" tells how alcoholic chaos ensues when two proseltyzing lecturers on teetotalism visit Bullocktown simultaneously with the absurd, tawdry "Buncombe's Imperial Yanko-American Circus". It is a comic story of no pretensions and some nice observations—the sideshows, for instance: "John Lambton Merryweather. Age fourteen and a half years, born in the County of Grant. He swallows knives, swords, and all sorts of old iron. He eats pebbles, and is passionately fond of chalk. Australians! Patronise Native Talent! Price 6d."[15] And the Bullocktonians create their own additional entertainment by cutting the tent ropes of the circus in mid-performance. "Squirming, struggling, gasping, fighting, there lay the best blood of the township, the human bottles that held what Daw, the editor of the *Quartzborough Gazette*, so euphoniously termed the 'vital fluid of the colonies'".[16] The culmination of the evening's merriment is the lacing of the two teetotaller lecturers' bitters and cordials with gin and brandy, and then guiding them in their drunkenness to the rooms of each other's wives. Slapstick as it is, the up-country humour captured makes an amusing tale.

H.G. Turner, who knew Clarke and was a fellow member of the

MICHAEL WILDING

Yorick Club and the Cave of Adullam, the two literary-bohemian
clubs Clarke was much involved in, wrote the first sustained critical
assessment of Clarke in the *Melbourne Review* of January 1882.
Discussing the *Holiday Peak* volume, he stressed the authenticity of
the material in the collection: and for Turner what was authentic was
"the daily dreary dullness of a small mining community, or decaying
bush hamlet". The isolation, the limitations, the dullness, the
monotony—these were the qualities of up-country life Turner saw
established by Clarke—and established well before Lawson.
Amongst the stories collected in *Holiday Peak*, Turner wrote,

> will be found some sketches that are most essentially and originally
> Australian. "Grumbler's Gully", "An Up-Country Township", and
> "How the Circus Came to Bullocktown", are as completely il-
> lustrative of the daily dreary dullness of a small mining community,
> or decaying bush hamlet, as are the graphic pictures of Bret Harte
> when describing the haunts of the Californian miner. Who that has
> travelled much in the bus could fail to recognize in the "Royal Cobb"
> the photograph of many a hostelry where he has passed the night; or
> in Flash Harry, Boss Corkison, or Wallaby Dick the types that he has
> found lounging under the verandah or in the bar?[17]

Turner's insights into the context of Clarke's work are generally
acute, and may well derive from conversations with Clarke about his
literary models and his intentions. The mention of Bret Harte here,
for instance, indicates a context that was clearly in Clarke's mind for
some of these stories. Writing to George Gordon McCrae to ask him
for a cover design for the volume, Clarke mentions a volume of Bret
Harte's:

> My dear McCrae: Robertson, who is publishing me a little book
> desires an illustrated cover, and has asked me to supply him with a
> design for the woodengraver. The cover is to be printed in two
> colours. He will pay for the design .. on paper merely ready to be
> copied by the engraver on to the block .. one guinea. Will you supply
> me with a design? The size of the book is the same as the small edition
> of Bret Harte. I send you a proof of the story which I think would il-
> lustrate best, with a mark at the spot which seems good for an il-
> lustration.[18]

In itself the reference might seem insignificant. But Clarke had
reviewed George Robertson's Australian edition of Bret Harte's *The
Luck of Roaring Camp* in *The Australian Journal* for March 1871
and had been immensely excited by it. It was to have an influence on

some of his own writing, and to some extent the *Holiday Peak* volume, in its contents and presentation, was an Australian response to the stimulus of Harte's work. Clarke's review had opened:

> We have always urged upon Australian writers of fiction the importance of delineating the Australian manners which they see around them every day, instead of dishing up the English customs which are current 20,000 miles away. The success with which Mr. Bret Harte—a San Franciscan, whose name we never heard until Mr. Robertson introduced it to us—has pictured the diggers of California, makes us regret that our advice has not been taken.
>
> The notion that, because a thing is common it is unclean, and that the ordinary daily life of our colony contains no poetry and no pathos, is, of all notions, the most foolish. In no condition of human society can poetry and pathos be wanting; for, to eliminate them from a record of human struggles, it would be necessary to annihilate human feeling. But in a new country, where the breaking down of social barriers, and the uprooting of social prejudices, tend to cultivate that incongruity which is, in reality, the very soul of pathos, there are opportunities for fresh and vigorous delineation of human character which the settled society of the old world does not offer ... Australia has strange and marked features in her young civilisation, which have never yet been touched upon by the writers of fiction. Some day, perhaps, some author as unknown as Mr. Harte was yesterday, will make use of the material that lies ready to his hand, and produce a work as admirable as Mr. Harte's. We hope that day will come soon.[19]

Harte excited Clarke because here was a writer successfully doing what Clarke had been advocating; Harte was showing the way for a new literature for a new country. "Any old Australian can call to mind stories as pathetic as the 'Luck of Roaring Camp', or 'Tennessee's Partner', but it never occurred to him that any wholesome lesson might be told in such stories, or that such stories would be worth the writing."[20]

The influence of Harte is apparent in Clarke's story "Poor Jo", which first appeared in *The Australasian*, 15 April 1871. It is a tear-jerking melodrama of the dumb, mental defective Jo who lays down his own life to save the lives of the young lady he adores, and her lover, from a flood. "They found his little weak body four days afterwards, battered and bruised almost out of recognition; but his great brave soul had gone on to Judgment."[21] Clarke captures the Harte formula of the combination of tragic self-sacrifice, of dumb devotion, of a great spirit in a deformed earthly body that can find no socially conventional way to express itself (here Jo is literally mute), of the spirituality and goodness that are latent in the primitive, crude, outback community. And however sentimental and melodramatic we may find the mixture, however routinely formulaic it may seem to us now, Clarke has undeniably learnt the skill of Bret Harte's new formula for making the reader—despite his jaded senses and his literary sophistication—sniff back a tear.

Returning to Clarke in an article in *Once a Month* in October 1885, H.G. Turner again discussed these stories, and amplified his comments on them and their relationship to Bret Harte.

> In the more humorous sketches, where he deals so realistically with the eccentric humankind that animated the deadly dullness of "Bullocktown", his style bears a strong resemblance to that of Bret Harte. In no sense, however, can he be said to have copied that entertaining writer, for the humour is essentially and radically Australian, and the characteristics delineated are as racy of our own soil, as the creations of his American prototype are distinctively Californian. "How the Circus Came to Bullocktown", "Grumbler's Gully", "Poor Jo", and "An Idyll of Bullocktown" are all of them so redolent of a phase of life that has now quite passed away in Victoria, and are so clearly sharply outlined, that they may be said to serve a similar purpose to that of a photograph of some whilom important building that the march of progress has ordained to destruction.[22]

Yet it was just this comparison with Harte that Arthur Patchett Martin had challenged in his article on Clarke in the London *Temple Bar* of May 1884.

> These little stories show that their author could easily distance all local competitors. Even the slightest of them has some grace of expression or delicacy of treatment that elevates it above the commonplace novelette of colonial journals. But I must part company with those local critics who maintain that Clarke's sketches are to be placed side by side with Bret Harte's immortal pictures of early Californian days. At best, the Melbourne *littérateur*, when he attempts to portray the rough scenes of "up-country" life as in "Grumbler's Gully", or "How the Circus came to Bullock Town," is but an imitator of the author of "The Outcasts of Poker Flat," and he moreover lacked that great gift of artistic sympathy which gives to the pages of the American story-teller the "one touch of nature" without which we cannot feel kinship with those creations of fiction that are so entirely outside the range of our own experience.[23]

The criticism that Clarke lacked artistic sympathy, humanity, feeling, is one that, originating with Arthur Patchett Martin, is reiterated by Francis Adams, A.G. Stephens, and Vance Palmer. The story "Pretty Dick" is a focus of disagreement in this issue. It is a slightly earlier story than the others collected in *Holiday Peak* and it appeared originally in Clarke's own *Colonial Monthly* in April 1869.[24] It is the story of a child lost in the bush—a theme that has had recurrent treatment in fiction and in painting. Clarke originally made the child twelve years old in the magazine story, but after some criticism involving the sturdiness and self-reliance of twelve year old bush children, he dropped the age to seven for the book. This five year reduction in Pretty Dick's years makes the remorseless emphasis on his little hands, little feet, little tearstained face more justifiable though no more palatable. A work very much of its time, "Pretty Dick" has a much more English "literary" tone as a model than Harte's mining tales.

> The night wore on—with strange sounds far away in the cruel bush, with screamings of strange birds, with gloomy noises, as of the tramplings of many cattle, with movements of leaves and snappings of branches, with unknown whirrings as of wings, with ripplings and pat-terings as of waterfalls, with a strange heavy pulsation in the air, as though the multitudinous life in the forest was breathing around him. He was dimly conscious that any moment some strange beast—some impossible monster, enormous and irresistible, might rise up out of the gloom of the gullies and fall upon him;—that the whole horror of the bush was about to take some tangible shape and appear silently from behind the awful rocks which shut out all safety and succour. His little soul was weighed down by the nameless terror of a solitude which was no solitude,—but a silence teeming with monsters.[25]

The grinding pathos leads inevitably to the shameless piety of the final line: "God had taken him home."[26] The following year Clarke himself remarked on the cloying genre he was working in, in his obituary of Dickens. "Unfortunately the success of the 'dying children' urged Dickens to extremes. Every book must have a dying child, and the trick became wearisome."[27] Yet Oliver Wendell Holmes replied to Clarke, who had sent a copy of the story to him in Boston, that he "sat down almost at once and read the story. It in-terested me deeply, and I felt as much like crying over the fate of 'Pretty Dick' as I did when I was a child and read the *Babes in the Wood*. I *did* cry then—I will *not* say whether I cried over 'Pretty Dick' or not. But I *will* say it is a *very* touching story, *very* well told."[28] Holmes's reaction must have pleased Clarke, and he dedicated the *Holiday Peak* volume to him. And Holmes's judgment was shared. Turner found "Pretty Dick" "probably the most perfect of his minor stories".

> Apart from the charming grace and touching pathos of the narrative, the artistically graphic finish of his picture of a hot day on the plains and in the ranges is a model of lucid word-painting.[29]

And he went on to remark

> The gem of the little volume, as before mentioned, is undoubtedly "Pretty Dick", the most perfect little idyll he ever wrote, and distinguished from anything else by its refined pathos and almost reverential delicacy of treatment.[30]

Arthur Patchett Martin found similar qualities in the story—qualities that he felt Clarke's other work too often lacked.

> The most pathetic of these colonial stories is "Pretty Dick", which describes with great power the terrible agonies of a little child lost in the bush. Such incidents were at one time no uncommon feature of Australian country life, and such a true story as that of the Duff children whose bodies were discovered locked in a last embrace, when it was seen that the little girl with gentle motherly instinct had divested herself of her dress to wrap her brother from the bitter cold of that fatal night—are even more pathetic than the novelist's fiction. Yet "Pretty Dick" is a beautifully told story, and stands out amongst its author's writings as a piece of pure pathos, and an exceptional tale whose attraction is owing neither to its ghastly horrors nor to its flippant wit.[31]

But a reaction soon set in. Francis Adams wrote in the *Sydney Quarterly Magazine* in June 1887, "There is no tale of Clarke's so popular as 'Pretty Dick' and it is poor stuff enough." He found it "indeed an excellent example of the determinedly pathetic"—but that was no longer something that was admired.

> When I read "Pretty Dick" I seem to hear the kind edificatory voice of a thoughtful Sunday-school teacher, dispensing literary provender at home to her nephews and nieces ...
>   I hear the pseudo-humorous cadence of the good creature's voice and the gentle pseudo-laughter of the nephews and nieces seated around. But O the poetry of some of the passages, the poetry and the unspeakable pathos![32]

Adams called "Pretty Dick" and "Poor Jo" examples of "laboured affectation"; "Pretty Dick" he saw as an "edificatory little puppet" and "Poor Jo" a "label put round the throat of a tear-bottle. But tear-bottles have gone out of fashion now".[33] And Adams repeated his judgments in *The Fortnightly Review* for 1 September 1892—in an article he incorporated the following year in his book *The Australians*.

> In one of his short tales ("Pretty Dick") he sat down, deliberately and of malice prepense, to make a special "study" of the bush scenery.
> Unhappily he also made it a special "study" of the pseudo-pathos of Dickens.
> The results were, as we have seen, terrible; for Mr. O.W. Holmes praised them as highly as he knew how.[34]

And A.G. Stephens condemned the story with similar enthusiasm. He repeated Martin's charge of Clarke's lack of humanity; this, Martin found, vitiated even *His Natural Life*: only "Pretty Dick" was exonerated. Stephens, however, found *His Natural Life* was the sole exception; while "Pretty Dick" demonstrated how Clarke artificially and unfeelingly tried to work up "feeling": the children's suicide in *His Natural Life* had for Stephens

> a true, natural pathos which Clarke must have felt keenly; and throughout the novel there is ever and again a glow of genuine humanity. But Clarke's other work, with rare exceptions, has no humanity whatever. He writes as cleverly as Thackeray, and often in Thackeray's vein, but there is seldom a glimpse of Thackeray's heart. Clarke was usually content to pile epithet and epigram upon the surface of things, without attempting to sound the human depths. And when, perhaps understanding his deficiencies, he deliberately tried to move his readers by pathetic arts, he failed more dismally than Dickens at his most mawkish moments. For Dickens at least was sincere, though in the attempt to reach "effects" corresponding with his emotion he strained his art to breaking-point, and his work was false. Dickens has tried to cheat his readers, but it is nearly certain that he also cheated himself. In that grotesque and laboured sketch of "Pretty Dick", which almost moves his dull editor to tears, Clarke has never cheated himself. The anti-climax shrieks throughout; and he was far too good a workman not to have heard it. It is the story of a child lost in the bush, elaborated with portentous art, as if the writer were saying, "Now I will write a pathetic tale. I will wring out your tears, and play upon your emotions; your entrails shall be rent with compassion, and you will say, 'Oh, the fine writer! the great writer!'" And always the tale is mechanical; the psychology unnatural. From the Dickensy beginning ... to the careful ending—such an ending from the Clarke of the Moorhouse controversy! ... all is hard-ground artificiality. Clarke *must* have known his failure. And he sent it for

print, with his tongue in his cheek at the dull audience of Mackin-nons![35]

When all of Clarke's other stories had been forgotten, "Pretty Dick" still remained in the critical mind as a touchstone of excess, of bad taste. It was the only story H.M. Green mentioned in his *An Outline of Australian Literature* (1930) and he found it "extremely sentimental. It is hard to judge such work in an age in which sentimentality is, at least officially and among the educated, anathema. But Clarke was always an extremist, who loved to 'pile on the agony' and to squeeze out the last drops of pathos, and he does this here. It would be interesting to know how much of his own work he himself took quite seriously".[36] Green's doubts about the story are clear enough, though he has enough historical sense to realize the way literary taste changes. But Vance Palmer uses the story simply as a stick with which to beat Clarke: "how could a man with that clear, sceptical mind be so uncritical of what he wrote as to send a story like 'Pretty Dick' ('they always felt they had their Sunday clothes on in his presence') to the author he most admired, Oliver Wendell Holmes?"[37] Palmer forgets—as H.M. Green does not—that Holmes *liked* the story.

"Pretty Dick" has one paragraph, however, that is worth remarking for other reasons. It is an unemphasized, unheralded account of an out-of-body experience, something so unusual and distinctive that Clarke must have experienced this in order to describe it; yet his use of it here so casually suggests that he was probably unaware of the comparative rarity of the phenomenon. Pretty Dick classically wakes at dawn to find himself looking down at his body.

> By-and-by it dawned. The birds twittered, and the dew sparkled, and the mists came up and wreathed themselves all about the trees, and Pretty Dick was up in the pure cool sky, looking down upon a little figure that lay on an open space among the heather. Presently, slowly at first, and then more quickly, he found out that this little figure was himself, and that he was in pain, and then it all came back, with one terrible shock, and he was Lost again.[38]

Clarke was always interested in the phenomena of different states of consciousness. There is the story he wrote under hashish, "Cannabis Indica"; there is his claim to have smoked opium;[39] there are his fantasy stories. But this brief paragraph touches on the fringes of the transcendental more surely than his contrived fantasies ever do.

There are two fantasy stories in *Holiday Peak*. One is simply a literary clubman's joke; though the latin tags remembered from "a sound English and classical education at a high-class private school"[40] are swapped here not from leather arm chairs over the port, but over "eggs, bacon, and whiskey, at Coppinger's"[41]—the Royal Cobb Hotel in Bullocktown. The stranger who walks into the hotel and engages in a learned literary discussion about plagiarism from the works of Horace turns out to be none other than old Quintus Horatius Flaccus himself, redivivus. "Holiday Peak", the title story, is fantasy of a different order. Its heightened, gothicized and Egyptianized description of the Australian bush is a fine excursion into the macabre.

> There is an indescribable ghastliness about the mountain bush at night which has affected most imaginative people. The grotesque and distorted trees, huddled here and there together in the gloom like whispering conspirators. The little open flats encircled by boulders which seem the forgotten altars of some unholy worship. The white, bare, and ghostly gums gleaming momentarily amid the deeper shades of the forest. The lonely pools begirt with shivering reeds, and haunted by the melancholy bittern only. The rifted and draggled creek-bed, which seems violently gouged out of the lacerated earth by some savage convulsion of nature. The silent and solitary places where a few blasted trees crouch together like withered witches, who, brooding on some deed of blood, have suddenly been stricken horror-stiff.[42]

Gradually the writing departs from any reality as the narrator begins to speculate on the human sacrifices, "mystic worship", "gloomy glamour of ancient barbarism" performed on the plateau he approaches, citing Mithra, Isis, Osiris, Tammuz, and the religions of Mexico, Africa, the Himalayas, and Central Asia. The Egyptian imagery recurrently used to describe the Australian landscape at this time, Brian Elliott has suggested, is in part a response to the charge that Australia has no antiquities:[43] geographically this young country was older than Europe—a paradox that fascinated Clarke. Elliott sees Clarke's source in Adam Lindsay Gordon. And certainly it was Gordon who made that marvellous rhyme of trunks Eucalyptian with weird columns Egyptian.[44] But the human sacrifices are more of a speciality of Clarke himself—Gabbett's cannibalism in *His Natural Life* the supreme example, and there are glancing allusions in "The Romance of Lively Creek" and in "A Modern

Eldorado". "What initially rose up out of the deep imagination of Europeans, released from imageless repression by the news of savages consuming each other in the Antipodes, was a buried longing for the taste of human flesh—not quite sublimated even by the symbolic eating of the Christian Man-God in the Mass."[45] Clarke's lack of interest in or knowledge of the Australian Aborigines is nowhere better evidenced. He draws not on Aboriginal religions or rites, but on the gothic imaginings of the European yearning for the primitive; his inspiration is not anthropological or observational, but literary; as is quite appropriate for the way the story evolves when he arrives at Holiday Peak, also known as Mount Might-ha-been. For what ensues is an extraordinary set of might have beens from history and from fiction, from life and from art. Charles Kingsley plays cards with Dr. Newman and Swinburne, the Count of Monte Christo has sold his island to an Australian wine grower, Thackeray, attended by Dr. Lydgate from *Middlemarch*, has recovered, completed *Dennis Duval*, and become good friends with Dickens.

Amongst all this occur what seem to be gloomy reminiscences and unfulfilled hopes from Clarke's own life. In the land of Might-ha-been the narrator, Marston, has become "an author whose readers are counted by millions and to whom Chapman and Hall give £5,000 a volume."[46] Marston recalls how as a youth a certain Mostyn

> ... used to take me up from Aldershot in the baggage-train and introduce to my schoolboy eyesight the wonders of London at midnight. Pray, are the Armida-gardens still existent?"
> "I don't know what you mean. Mostyn never took you to London with him. You never were in the Armida-gardens in all your life."
> "Thank Goodness, Gerard! Are you sure?"
> "Quite certain. You *might have* wasted your youth in such places, and got into no end of mischief, had not your father kept such a strict and friendly eye upon you."[47]

Clarke gives expression, in a way that his journalism did not reveal, to his wish that he had never had to leave England for Australia. Though he speculated on returning to England in his letters to Cyril Hopkins, in his journalism his base was firmly Australia; he wrote as someone committed to be there, not as a visitor or tourist or unwilling exile, not as the stock fictional figure come out to make a fortune to be able to return home and buy back the family estate. But in

"Holiday Peak" the doubts are allowed to emerge. Gerard tells Marston that he is famous.

> "You jest. A poor devil banished to Bush Land, tied neck and heels in debt, soon slips out of the memory even of his friends."
> "So you persist in that dream about Australia! Surely you know that your fortune was recovered; that your year of poverty but served to correct your boyish extravagances, and that in easy circumstances you banished Poins and Pistol, and settled down to the career you chose!"[48]

Alas, that all remained might have been. However, what happened to Gerard on Holiday Peak corresponded with what was to happen to him in reality.

> Passing by an old house which stood back from the others in the terrace, my attention was caught by a crimson scarf trailing from one of the upper windows. "An artist lives there," was my first thought, for nowhere in the world but in the pictures of Prout do we see bits of colour floating about in that fashion. "Yes, you are right," said a young man emerging from the well-dressed crowd which throngs in Spring the steps of the Academy.
> It was Gerard! Gerard, my boy friend, who fled from Oxford to Stonyhurst, and embraced the discipline of Loyola. "Gerard, what means this?"
> "Dear old fellow," said he, putting his arm round my neck in the fond old schoolboy fashion, "it means that I thought better of my resolve, and followed out the natural bent of my talents. My picture, the 'Death of Alkibiades', is the talk of the year. I shall soon be as famous as you."[49]

Clarke was never to know that though Gerard Manley Hopkins did become a Jesuit priest, he did not give up his artistic ambitions; though his fame was to be in poetry, not in the painting of his schooldays.[50]

Clarke had returned to the Wimmera for Christmas and New Year 1872—73. He had been overworking as ever, was struggling with the revision of the serial version of *His Natural Life* into book form, and his financial difficulties were increasing. His marriage was unhappy and he was involved in some sort of relationship with Rose, his wife's sister, also unhappily married; they speculated on running away together to Europe, America, anywhere, but in the end the difficulties seemed too great.[51] The gloom he took with him to the Wimmera issued in stories rather different from the gloom of the "daily dreary dullness"[52] of the up-country. He had been thrown back to thinking about his childhood and adolescence. to the circumstances surrounding his ever coming to Australia. "Holiday Peak" first appeared in *The Australasian* for 18 and 25 January 1873. It was followed there on 8 February by another story that looked back even more substantially to the period of Clarke's last years in England, and that has a similarly sombre note: "La Béguine". But whereas "Holiday Peak" is set in Australia, with reference back to England, the events of "La Béguine" are set totally in England and France.

Clarke collected "La Béguine" in *Four Stories High* in 1877. The "wasted youth" amidst "the wonders of London at midnight" referred to in "Holiday Peak" is a motif that recurs.[53] In the land of Might-ha-been, the narrator's father kept "a strict and friendly eye" on his son: the implication is that Clarke's father did not, and in "La Béguine" the implication is spelled out. The narrator, Marston again, records that "My holidays, passed in my father's widowed house, were enlivened by the coming and going" of cousins Tom, Dick, and Harry and a host of friends "for as long as he was undisturbed, the head of the house rather liked to see his rooms occupied by the relatives of people with whom he was intimate". "So, a wild-eyed and eager schoolboy, I strayed into Bohemia, and acquired in that strange land an assurance and experience ill suited to my age and temperament."[54] And Marston tells how as a sixteen year old schoolboy he encounters a nineteen year old girl who has just been abandoned by her wealthy lover. Marston and the girl go off to Paris and spend all the money the lover has left the girl; then Marston returns to school and La Béguine to a richer and more distinguished lover than the previous one—moving from man to man till her tragic death.

Balzac was Clarke's favourite author. One of his earliest published essays was on "Balzac and Modern French Literature", and he returns to him in other critical discussions of French novels in his essays and journalism.[55] La Béguine might have stepped out of the world of Balzac's *Splendeurs et Misères des Courtisanes*: so too might another heroine in *Four Stories High*—Pauline Christoval, the tragic adventuress of "The Romance of Lively Creek". A station owner's son falls in love with her when she tours the outback in a seedy theatrical troupe. But Captain Sporboy recognizes her, torments her with her past, and drives her away without the station owner's son: though Sporboy receives his own come-uppance from a poisoned dart he has presented to the local museum. Sporboy is a marvellous creation:

> Sporboy, the newly-arrived, Sporboy, the adventurer, Sporboy the oracle of tap-rooms, Sporboy the donor of curiosities to our Museum, Sporboy the shareholder in the Great Daylight, Sporboy the traveller, the narrator, the hot whisky swiller;—honest Jack Sporboy, the richest man, the hugest drunkard, and the biggest liar in all Lively Creek.[56]

And his dialogue lives up to his description.

> I've eaten brain soup and *basi* in Ilocos, my boy. *Human* brains! Devilish good, too. Ha! ha! ...
> The Palanese had just achieved a victory over the Guinanès, and seventy-five heads were served up in my honour. Gad, gentlemen, the fellows cracked 'em like cocoanuts, and whipped out the brains in less time than you would disembowel a crayfish![57]

But the story's concern is with the destruction of Madamoiselle Christoval. The comic note is only incidental, as indeed it is to the whole volume of *Four Stories High*. "King Billy's Breeches" is a satire on bureaucratic red-tapeism—the endless correspondence ensuing upon a fruitless attempt to issue the king of the Great Glimmera blacks with trousers instead of the govenmentally ordained blanket. (The focus is, of course, on the bureaucratic correspondence, not on the Aborigine it concerns.) But none of the other stories is comic. "The Poor Artist" deals with the hopeless aspirations of an utterly untalented painter who finally dies of tuberculosis. It is a chilling theme; for, as Clarke makes us realize, the sufferings and commitment of the talentless artist are as real as those of the genius; and it touches on that anxiety that every artist represses—that perhaps his work is worthless, that his commitment is the delusion of a madman, that the support of his friends and his family is uncritical, unintelligent.

"A sad tale's best for Winter"; and Clarke may have thought the sombre note appropriate for this volume for the Christmas trade. But Christmas in the antipodes is in Summer. Perhaps he forgot, perhaps he no longer cared. The volume appeared in 1877—but it consisted of stories all written between 1870 and 1873.[58] Was he conscious of scraping the barrel? Or was he simply taking the opportunity of collecting earlier stories into book form, when such an opportunity arose? Clarke did write a new surround for the stories; the volume opens with a discussion between four characters—Marston, Falx, Tallowfat, and the anonymous narrator. Each of them tells a story and each story is linked by a brief continuation of the four-sided dialogue; and then the narrator rounds off the volume by telling his son a bedtime story, making a fifth, untitled, unacknowledged story. It concerns a sparrow that emigrates to Australia, has a generally rough time, but finally brings joy to a dying old woman by reminding her of the chirping of sparrows in her youth in England. As "The Acclimatised Sparrow" Clarke had first published the story in *The Colonial Monthly* in January 1870. Then it was used on two further occasions as a substitution for original copy from Clarke. It replaced the usual "Peripatetic Philosopher" column in *The Australasian* for 29 January 1870 when Clarke, just returned from his visit to Tasmania, presumably had found no time to write his column. The following January, 1871, it was used when Clarke, "overwhelmed with work" and unwell, sent only one chapter of *His Natural Life* to *The Australian Journal* instead of the usual two—and the story made up the deficiency again. It is strange that Clarke incorporates the story here untitled, as a fifth story to a volume proclaiming only four. Had it come to represent an inability to deliver the goods; so that Clarke included it here as a way of saying he could not write a new Christmas volume but was simply collecting old material? Or did Clarke feel, having twice cheated his readers by its unheralded substitution in the past, he would throw it in as a bonus to this volume?

Holiday Peak derived its unity as a collection from the up-country setting of its stories. *Four Stories High* derives its unity from the clubman's Canterbury Tales device of the four characters each telling a story. The stories told involve events and characters and references ranging through England, France, Asia, and Australia, through city and country, through tribal societies and cosmopolitan sophistication. There is none of the exploration of a milieu, of "Bullocktown", that there is in *Holiday Peak*. But there is an exploration of a mood, of a sense of loss, of despair, of exile.

The naturalistic sketches and the formula magazine melodramas are well represented in these two volumes of stories—though there are other examples of his work in those genres that he never collected. But the third major group of his short stories, the speculative and metaphysical fantasies, were only collected into volume form after his death. This genre of story has come back into fashion now with the North American and European discovery of the work of Jorge Luis Borges and other Latin American writers. Borges, of course, acknowledges his admiration for the work of such turn of the century English writers as Stevenson and Chesterton, who were writing in this English fantasy tradition. It was a major strand of the short story in English—but its lack of distinctively "Australian" materials has prevented its recognition as a component of an Australian fictional tradition.

Clarke's *The Mystery of Major Molineux and Human Repetends* (Melbourne: Cameron Laing, 1881) is a posthumous volume collecting two of his stories in this area. One of them, "Human Repetends", first published in *The Australasian*, 14 September 1872, looked back to his life in England and the circumstances surrounding his coming to Australia. It shares some of the materials, and the same sombre note, of "Holiday Peak" and "La Béguine". The narrator, Hugh Pontifex emigrates to Australia and ends up writing for *The Argus*. But the interest of the story lies not so much in these autobiographical motifs, as in the theme of what De Quincey called "unutterable and self-repeating infinities". The story belongs to a formula that has emigrated from English writing but that is alive and well and living in Argentina: Jorge Luis Borges's "Theme of the Traitor and Hero" is one recent version of it—appropriately, unending versions of it crop up in different centuries in different continents. "There are in decimal arithmetic repeated 'coincidences' called *repetends*. Continue the generation of numbers through all time, and you have these repetends for ever recurring."[59]

Pontifex has to sell all his belongings; but he retains a fifteenth century engraving signed Finiguerra of an unknown, beautiful woman with whose image he is infatuated. One day he sees her in Melbourne. He spends the next three days looking for her after that brief glimpse—only to discover she was murdered by drowning in the Yarra the night he saw her. At the inquest of the girl, whose name was Jenny Gay, he meets Warrend who also has a copy of the engraving, and who knows the story attached to it.

Jehanne La Gaillarde was a woman whose romantic amours had electrified the Paris of Louis XI. She was murdered by being thrown into the Seine. "All attempts to discover the murderer were vain, but, at length, a young man named Hugues Grandprête, who, though he had never seen the celebrated beauty, had fallen in love with her picture, persuaded himself that the murderer was none other than Sieur De la Forêt ... followed De la Forêt to Padua, and killed him."[60]

Pontifex remembers that the man he saw Jenny Gay with was called Forrester. All the names fit: Sieur De la Foret/Forrester; Grandprete/Pontifex; Finiguerra/Warrender; Jehanne la Gaillarde/Jenny Gay. The whole pattern is repeating itself, inexorably. The narrator waits to fulfil his unwilling part in the inevitable design. "I live here in Melbourne at the seat of his crime because it seems the least likely place again to behold him ... But I *shall* meet him one day, and then my doom will be upon me, and I shall kill him as I killed him in Padua 400 years ago!"[61]

"The Mystery of Major Molineux", one of the last things Clarke wrote, is a fine piece of Tasmanian Gothic. It has a Major who never appears on Thursdays, his toothless, glassy-eyed housekeeper Mary Pennithorne, and his surly, animal-like ex-convict manservant, Bagally. They inhabit the "Wuthering Heights" style forbidding house, Castle Stuart, where visitors are accommodated only grudgingly and where a ghostly face appears at a window on a storm-wracked night. Amongst all this broods the hint of some sexual evil. There is the grave of the transported forger Arthur Savary who suicided, it seems, when he discovered his wife was having an affair with the Major's brother-in-law; there was the mysterious death of beautiful young Agnes Tremayne after she discovered what happened to the Major on Thursdays; and then there is beautiful young Beatrice Rochford, recovering from concussion after a horse fall, found dead with an expression of extreme horror on her face after a brief visit from the Major—who promptly commits suicide. We never know what the horror is, what form the possession by devils that the Major says he suffers, takes. The narrator, who is in love with Beatrice, though she is young enough to be his daughter, spends a Thursday night of horror with the Major, but never reveals what happens. This unexplained mystery creates the suggestive suspense, but finally the story is unsatisfactory just because too much is missing when so much of the rest of the story is circumstantially detailed.

Fantasy, mystery, metaphysical speculation—these were all in-

terests of Clarke's, though anecdotes of his expression of his specula-
tions generally involve some ironic distancing that he protects
himself with. He proclaimed a belief in reincarnation but substan-
tiated by claiming that two cab horses driving him were Plato and
Pythagoras; on another occasion he tried to persuade a barmaid that
she was a reincarnation of Cleopatra.[62] L.H. Allen has remarked
that

> The dream-element in his nature accounts for some of his reading. He
> knew Poe, and mentions "Marie Roget". "The Mind-Reader's
> Curse" suggests Dupin, though alas! it is written more in the style of
> Monk Lewis than of Poe. In that sketch he mentions Count Saint-
> Germain and Cagliostro. This may have influenced his creation of the
> alchemist in the serial [of *His Natural Life*]. He mentions de Quincey
> in "Cannabis Indica", an adventure into the eerie which may have
> been prompted by *The Opium Eater*.[63]

"The Mind-Reader's Curse" is one of the four stories collected
in the posthumous volume *Sensational Tales* (1886),[64] together with
"Human Repetends" (retitled "The Mysterious Coincidence"), and
two stories that Francis Adams thought well of. Generally Adams
did not like Clarke's stories: "In nowhere more than in his tales does
the literary journalistic vice of Clarke appear in all its
detestableness. So many of them bear the stamp of haste, of haste
weary or clever".[65] But of these he wrote: "Clarke also did some
short stories in the style of Edgar Allan Poe, and, at least, two of
them, 'The Dual Existence' and 'The Golden Island', are worthy of a
more permanent preservation".[66]

"The Dual Existence" (originally called "The Doppleganger"
in *The Colonial Monthly*)[67] is another version of that "Human
Repetends" theme of re-enactment in a later generation; it also contains another sort of out of body experience, not like "Pretty Dick",
but a human splitting into two of himself as a result of a curse, one
part watching what the other is doing with a variation of the mind
reader's second sight: and these three fantasy motifs are united by a
detective story plot. In "A Modern Eldorado" (originally called,
"Gipsies of the sea, or The Island of Gold" when it appeared in *The
Melbourne Herald*)[68] we pay a quick visit to a kingdom run by an
English expatriate who has found isolation and happiness in un-
limited gold, a beautiful mistress, and a pact with the sophisticated,
human-sacrificing civilization adjoining his own territory in that last
unknown, New Guinea: "It was a dream from the Thousand and

One Tales. It was the vision of an opium eater."[69] While "The Mind-Reader's Curse" (originally published as "The Curious Experience of Anthony Venn" in *The Australasian*)[70] is an extravaganza set in the convict settlement of Sydney in 1803, which involves the hideousness of being able to read other people's minds: and it certainly is a hideousness in a community whose members live a melodramatic gallimaufrey of theft, murder, adultery, illegitimacy, and incest. At the story's end it emerges that the entire experience has taken place in a mesmeric trance—the protagonist mesmerized into believing he has these mind-reading powers. Yet perhaps, while under the trance, he does have them ...

I have surveyed here those stories of Clarke's published in volume form, hoping to give some indication of the range and significance of them, and to encourage some further exploration amongst them. There has been no full collection of Clarke's stories. They are scattered through *The Australasian Monthly Magazine*, *The Colonial Monthly*, *The Australasian* (where sometimes they appeared as part of his "Noah's Ark" column), and *The Australasian Sketcher*. Others appear in various Christmas annuals published by W.H. Williams (1868) and Cameron, Laing and Co. (1878, 1880, 1882). Hamilton Mackinnon collected a few into his *Marcus Clarke Memorial Volume* (Melbourne: Cameron Laing, 1884). But the most comprehensive collection is in Hamilton Mackinnon's *The Austral Edition of the Selected Works of Marcus Clarke* (Melbourne: Fergusson and Mitchell, 1890) in which they are often given new titles, and are grouped into two categories.

One category is called "Australian Tales and Sketches" and comprised Part II of *The Austral Edition*. It contains all the *Holiday Peak* stories, three from *Four Stories High*, two further Bullocktown melodramas of betrayed love and tragic devotion ("Gentleman George's Bride" and "A Romance of Bullocktown"), plus three non-fictional pieces: Clarke's autobiographical sketch "Learning Colonial Experience" (originally called "In a Bark Hut"), and excerpts from the preface to Adam Lindsay Gordon's poems, and *The Future of the Australian Race*. This Part II of *The Austral Edition* in its entirety, together with Mackinnon's biographical introduction to *The Austral Edition*, was issued as a separate volume in 1896 as *Australian Tales* (Melbourne: A & W

Bruce), and again in 1897 as *Australian Tales of the Bush* (Melbourne: George Robertson). The original title of the part, "Australian Tales and Sketches", is preserved in the running title of these volumes.

Mackinnon's other category of stories was "Stories— Imaginative and Fanciful" and comprised Part III of the *Austral Edition*. It incorporated the four stories from *Sensational Tales*, together with "A Hashish Trance" (originally "Cannabis Indica"), "The Author Haunted by His Own Creations", and "A Sad Christmas Eve Retrospect".

But there are still numerous stories that have never been reprinted and that can be found only in their original magazine or newspaper publication.

6

A. G. Stephens,
The Bulletin, and the 1890s

LEON CANTRELL

One of the most ineluctable of Australian myths is that the period of the 1890s represented something like a golden age in our national life and literature. Though numerous writers have suggested modifications to the legend, it still appears, in various guises, in such recent works as Ian Turner's *The Australian Dream* (1968) and Geoffrey Serle's *From Deserts the Prophets Come* (1973). Who first circulated the misconception, and when and why, is not easy to ascertain. Professor G.A. Wilkes, in his lecture to the Sydney University Arts Association in 1958,[1] put forward George Taylor's wistfully yet emphatically titled *Those Were the Days* (1918) as perhaps the source, though the tone of Taylor's book suggests a sermon to the converted and uncontrite. And even Wilkes, concerned to offer strong qualifications to the legend of the nineties, ended up positing redirections rather than reinterpretations. What has been ignored up till now is a singular and highly relevant fact: that nowhere, as far as I know, do we find the writers of the 1890s proclaiming the literary millennium in the here and now. On the contrary: the literary autobiography and theorizing of the period is marked by alienation and discontent at one end of the scale and by a merely tentative and speculative sense of achievement at the other. We need not go beyond Lawson's ironically titled "'Pursuing

Literature' in Australia" published in the *Bulletin* in 1899 or A.G.
Stephens's equally well-known reply to see the implications of such
attitudes. Lawson was preparing to leave Australia at the time and
his account of the local writer's life is full of the bitterness of experience:

> My two books published by Angus and Robertson, *In the Days When
> the World was Wide* and *While the Billy Boils*, are advertised as in
> their seventh thousand and eighth thousand respectively. The former
> is sold to the public at 5s; the latter has been sold in various editions at
> from 5s to 2s 6d. My total receipts from these books have been
> something over £200; and I have sold the entire rights. The books
> represent the cream of twelve years' literary work. I estimate my
> whole literary earnings during that period at £700.
>
> There are, perhaps, a score of Australian writers known to the
> *Bulletin*, and most of them little more than lads, who could write bet-
> ter stuff than has been appearing in the shoal of popular English
> magazines lately (no offence intended); but they have no scope, and,
> as far as I can see, no hope of future material encouragement from the
> "great" and wealthy Australasian weeklies and dailies, only one or
> two of which (excepting the *Sunday Times*) that I know of have, up to
> date, offered even the most niggardly assistance to purely Australian
> writers, and this only after the *Bulletin* had introduced them and es-
> tablished their Australian reputations. Many papers, notably in
> Maoriland, clip their racy Australian sketches from the *Bulletin*, and
> in at least one of these offices that I know, and have a hearty con-
> tempt for, it would be thought an act of charity to offer a hard-up *Bul-
> letin* writer 5s per col.; while in another it would be a mark of special
> favour to offer him a chair.
>
> My advice to any young Australian writer whose talents have
> been recognized, would be to go steerage, stow away, swim, and seek
> London, Yankeeland, or Timbuctoo—rather than stay in Australia
> till his genius turned to gall, or beer. Or, failing this—and still in the
> interests of human nature and literature—to study elementary
> anatomy, especially as applies to the cranium, and then shoot himself
> carefully with the aid of a looking-glass.[2]

Stephens published this blast on his Red Page and then, a few
weeks later, offered the rejoinder that whatever Australia might
have done to Lawson, the man's literary as opposed to financial success was inextricable connected with his own country. The value of
Lawson's verses and sketches, he said, is largely an Australian value.

> We are moved by them so much because we breathe their at-
> mosphere, are familiar with their persons and scenes—our minds go
> half-way to meet them. The same truth, sympathy, graphic strength,

might be put into a series of South American pictures, and leave us much less impressed. That is, Lawson's pre-eminent Australian appeal lessens the force of his universal appeal. He is splendidly parochial. That increases his claim upon his country, but decreases his claim upon literature.

Doubtless, Lawson is the most characteristic literary product that Australia has yet achieved. So far as he knows our country, he has scrutinised it with a microscope. His work is crowded with intimate detail. But as Art it lacks perspective: Lawson is always too close to his subject. It results that his work is minutely vivid, but also scrappy, detached, solitary. This objection is not at all concerned with the omission or inclusion of any items in his sketch-series; as Lawson seems to think. Were the whole of the Mitchell or Steelman sketches printed together, they would still remain flat silhouettes. In Australia, given the foreground of his picture, we can invent the middle distance and the background for ourselves. But it is not so elsewhere.[3]

Events proved Stephens right and Lawson was back in Australia by mid 1902, his tail between his legs and his literary career behind him. But the striking thing about the earlier exchange is neither the accuracy of Stephens's predictions nor the vehemence of Lawson's claims. It is, rather, the common ground on which they both recognized the difficulties under which the writer in Australia had to labour. Lawson, naturally enough, saw it largely in terms of bread and butter. To Stephens, it was a question of educating both authors and readers into an awareness of the nature of literature and of literary achievement. Both men saw the Australian situation as their greatest stumbling block; but whereas to Lawson this was a crying shame, to Stephens it was a fact of life.

Another observation which seems relevant to any discussion of our literature of the nineties is that as one reads through the poems, stories, and novels written during this time, one is increasingly struck by two major themes. On the one hand, many writers speak of a golden age which has passed and which can only be recreated though the memory of the lives and deeds of yesteryear. Two of the most popular poems of the period, "The Man From Snowy River" and "In the Days When the World Was Wide", romantically celebrate a way of life and an age which have passed; a time when it seemed possible to perform great and noble deeds in Australia. The popularity of poems such as these can only be understood in terms of their conscious myth-making, their celebration not of the nineties but of the eighties and the decades before:

And down by Kosciusko, where the pine-clad ridges raise
Their torn and rugged battlements on high,
Where the air is clear as crystal, and the white stars fairly
   blaze
At midnight in the cold and frosty sky,
And where around the Overflow the reed-beds sweep and sway
To the breezes, and the rolling plains are wide,
The Man from Snowy River is a household word today,
And the stockmen tell the story of his ride.[4]

When Lawson and Paterson and their fellow writers speak of the present, in pieces such as "Faces in the Street" or "Clancy of the Overflow", it is with a sense of disillusionment and betrayal.

On the other hand, running parallel to this romanticizing of the past, the nineties produced a substantial body of work which prophesied the coming Australian civilization when the golden age would again be at hand. Lawson and Paterson are again prominent here, and even the work of a man as consciously and euphorically Australia as Bernard O'Dowd exhibits this dual vision, not of living in a great age, but of recognizing it in the recent past and of anticipating it in the near future. His sonnet "Australia" bears the nineties' hall-mark in its curious mixture of unease and prophecy:

Are you for Light, and trimmed, with oil in place,
Or but a Will o' Wisp on marshy guest?
A new demesne for Mammon to infest?
Or lurks millennial Eden 'neath your face?

The cenotaphs of species dead elsewhere
That in your limits leap and swim and fly,
Or trail uncanny harp-strings from your trees,
Mix omens with the auguries that dare
To plant the Cross upon your forehead sky,
A virgin helpmate Ocean at your knees.[5]

In 1903 the *Bulletin* published O'Dowd's hymn of praise "to young democracy" in Australia. It was entitled *Dawnward?*—not with a tone of assertion as was the title of Taylor's book of 1918, but with a question mark. William Lane's novel, *The Workingman's Paradise* (1892), another characteristic piece and one written out of bitter political experience, was less equivocal in its turning away from the harsh realities of the present to predict the socialist utopia of the future.

To move from these works to those from the nineties which grapple with the here and now is to journey, like Bunyan's pilgrim, down from the heights where one can look backwards and forwards into the valley of shadow and the slough of despond. Of course there are exceptions and even within the one work passages can be found which tell of a glowing future side by side with those which decry the harshness of the present. Furphy's *Such is Life*, one of the finest products of the nineties, exhibits a forcefully jaundiced view of many of the values we regard as integral to the myth of the democratic tradition, and does so in conjunction with an almost apocalyptic concept of the new Australia:

> It is not in our cities or townships, it is not in our agricultural or min-ing areas, that the Australian attains full consciousness of his own nationality; it is in places like this, and as clearly there as at the centre of the continent. To me the monotonous variety of this interminable scrub has a charm of its own; so grave, subdued, self-centre; so alien to the genial appeal of more winsome landscape, or the assertive grandeur of mountain and gorge. To me this wayward diversity of spontaneous plant life bespeaks an unconfined, ungauged potentiality of resource; it unveils an ideographic prophecy, painted by Nature in her Impressionist mood, to be deciphered aright only by those willing to discern through the crudeness of dawn a promise of majestic day.[6]

But the prevailing tone of the novel, its picture of life, is much more in the direction of loneliness, betrayal, physical and mental suffer-ing, and injustice than has generally been suggested. Put in the con-text I am suggesting, it is "offensively Australian" in a sense which has not been sufficiently emphasized. The sense of the present as a denial of that which men rightly and properly anticipated is a power-ful uniting force in much of our literature of the period. Lawson's sense of betrayal at the hands of middle class capital, so obvious in his exchange with Stephens, is given the edge of moral outrage in his lament for the passing of the "roaring days":

> But golden days are vanished,
>   And altered is the scene;
> The diggings are deserted,
>   The camping-grounds are green;
> The flaunting flag of progress
>   Is in the West unfurled,
> The mighty bush with iron rails
>   Is tethered to the world.[7]

The best short stories of the nineties too, such as Lawson's "Union Buries its Dead" and Joe Wilson sequence or Barbara Baynton's *Bush Studies*, present a world of deeply felt alienation and despair, much more attuned to Brennan's poetry, especially "The Wanderer", than the legend has ever allowed. Lawson, casting himself as Humphrey Bogart at the unionist's funeral, achieves such a degree of existential alienation that he is able to destroy even those hoary remnants of the past which so frequently provided solace elsewhere:

> Our grave-digger was not altogether bowelless, and, out of respect for that human quality described as "feelin's", he scraped up some light and dusty soil and threw it down to deaden the fall of the clay lumps on the coffin. He also tried to steer the first few shovelfuls gently down against the end of the grave with the back of the shovel turned outwards, but the hard dry Darling River clods rebounded and knocked all the same. It didn't matter much—nothing does. The fall of lumps of clay on a stranger's coffin doesn't sound any different from the fall of the same things on an ordinary wooden box—at least I didn't notice anything awesome or unusual in the sound; but, perhaps, one of us—the most sensitive—might have been impressed by being reminded of a burial long ago, when the thump of every sod jolted his heart.
>
> I have left out the wattle—because it wasn't there. I have also neglected to mention the heart-broken old mate, with his grizzled head bowed and great drops streaming down his rugged cheeks. He was absent—he was probably "Out Back". For similar reasons I have omitted reference to the suspicious moisture in the eyes of a bearded bush ruffian named Bill. Bill failed to turn up, and the only moisture was that which was induced by the heat. I have left out the "sad Australian sunset", because the sun was not going down at the time. The burial took place exactly at midday.[8]

My version of the literature of the nineties then, is far removed from the traditional picture of a burgeoning national greatness. It may well be though, you could argue, that I have confused the issue by denying that a golden age can exist even if those living and creating it do so blissfully unaware. It is certainly true that the writers I have considered spoke of the greatness of the past and forecast that of the future in a way which has ensured their permanency; but if this is the most we can grant, the legend requires an even more wholesale reinterpretation than I have so far suggested, for one of its integral platforms has always been the notion of literary selfconsciousness, of the awareness of the writers of the nineties of the myth they were ostensibly creating. Even Wilkes, in the lecture I referred to, conceded that "the writers of the nineties ... set out to exploit indigenous material, to produce a literature that [should] be defiantly Australian ... [and their work reflects] the egalitarian and utopian visions of the day". The crucial, unstated point is that insofar as it is a literature of the present, it is a literature of despair.

The case I wish to advance here is one which sees the nineties in a much more crudely chronological way than has been usual. The nineties came, to state the obvious for a moment, between the eighties and the nineteen-hundreds, and we shall do more justice to our sense of the past if we retain at least that degree of perspective for it was one of which the period itself was acutely aware. No doubt it has been tempting for social and literary historians to close the first full century of Australia's history with something of an air of summation, of genuine consolidating achievement, as if literary ideas and effort somehow gathered momentum with the years, aiming for a climactic display at the century's end, rather like the massive display of fireworks on Sydney Harbour which heralded the chimes at midnight on 31 December 1900.

And that date, the end of the colonial age in Australia, has presented a further temptation to see the immediately preceding decade as the fruition of earlier seeds. In a political sense such an hypothesis may well be true, but it is surely axiomatic that the Federation of the states in 1901 was not a literary act. It represented the culmination of a decade or more of political horse-trading and wheeler-dealing in which literary men, for better or worse, had played a negligible role. It impinged upon the world of literature barely more than did the death of Queen Victoria three weeks later. George Essex Evans, growing vegetables in Queensland, wrote commemorations of both events, but has anybody read them?

The principal barrier to an adequate assessment of the nineties, however, has been our concept of the Sydney *Bulletin*. The notion that this magazine spearheaded a decade of nationalism, democracy, and literary achievement has long occupied a seemingly unassailable position in Australian social and literary history. Its image as a repository of radicalism, fervent idealism, and the genesis of a national literature, first propagated by social and political historians, has been echoed by their literary counterparts. Russel

Ward's thesis of an Australian legend sees the *Bulletin* in the nineties as the culmination of a century of democratic progress[9] and few have been disposed to differ. And if we turn the pages of Archibald's paper it is certainly true that its unique brand of irreverent vitality has, at first, an overwhelming sense of conviction. We cannot deny, for instance, that the *Bulletin*'s consistent anti-monarchism and anti-imperialism sounds a healthy note, any more than we can ignore the impressive quantity of versifying and story-telling contained within its familiar pink covers. Equally, we cannot miss the paper's consistently strident assertions of support for some aspects of political behaviour we have come to regard as imperative. One man, one vote is an obvious example, as is the paper's support for payment for members of parliament. But just as obvious, it seems to me, is the realization that the *Bulletin*'s so-called radicalism is composed of just such small-l liberal gestures as these. Its platform, published week after week inside the front cover, aimed at a number of constitutional and administrative changes but left unscathed the basic social and economic structures of society. If we attempt to pin the *Bulletin* down to a specific, political stance, I suggest, it is essentially one of liberal, bourgeois reform, constrained by a hefty dose of sectarian bigotry, racism, and xenophobic nationalism. Its claim, in 1893, to be "the only well-established Australian journal which, throughout its career, has been consistently Radical", is deliberately ambiguous and makes sense only if our image of radicalism is sufficiently broad to encompass a persistent and vitriolic campaign against Jews and Asians and an equally persistent campaign in favour of such pillars of middle-class society as protection and the ballot box. The cliche that we receive the politicians we deserve is at least as true of our newspapers and perhaps it is a salutory comment on the *Bulletin*'s admittedly enormous circulation in the 1890s to observe that the only present-day magazine to achieve a comparable penetration is the *Australian Women's Weekly*. "The more equitable distibution of wealth is a good thing", the paper conceded in 1901, "but unless it is first made certain that the country has a reasonable amount of wealth of its own to distribute more equitably, it is not so good as it looks. 'Socialism in our Time' has its advantages, but 'solvency in our Time' needs to come first."[10] Indeed Archibald, a millionaire magnate by today's standards, saw his editorial achievement retrospectively almost in the terms of a con-

LEON CANTRELL

ventional Victorian moralist. Writing in 1907 of Sydney at the time
the *Bulletin* began, he said:

> It was a Cant-ridden community. Cant—the offensive, horrible
> Cant of the badly-reformed sinner—reigned everywhere. There was
> no health in the public spirit. Socially, politically, all was a mean sub-
> servience to a Spirit of snobbery and dependency. What was most
> Australian in spirit had been lost by the secessions first of Victoria
> and then of Queensland. Sydney, socially, limped in apish imitation
> after London ideas, habits, and manners. Politically and industrially,
> it was the same. And over all brooded in law courts, press, and Parlia-
> ment, the desolating cruelty inherited from "The System". Sydney in-
> vited revolt from existing conditions, and *The Bulletin* was the organ
> of that revolt. It was to stand for more humanity in the laws, more
> freedom in the Parliaments, more healthy independence in the press.[11]

Other papers of the time, such as the *Daily Telegraph* and *The
Sydney Morning Herald*, may not have pursued such a campaign so
vigorously, but they were not antagonistic to its aims. The *Bulletin*'s
means, like Archibald himself, were often garrulously offensive, but
its ends contained little to disturb the complacent prosperity of
honest burghers.

Like the labour parties which shared so many of its views, the
Bulletin failed to reform society in any other than a narrowly liberal-
bourgeois sense principally because it lacked any coherent
ideological basis. The doctrines of scientific socialism, widely disseminated in Europe by this time, were virtually unknown in
Australia, and the *Bulletin*'s arrogant dislike of self-analysis and
criticism, also shared with the labour parties, rendered it peculiarly
insensitive to any discussions of a theoretical kind. Its principal
political concern was for the preservation and furtherance of middle-
class self-help and capital. Its reputation as a radical, democratic
weekly can only be understood in the context of a singularly un-
democratic and un-radical society. If it was the "Bushman's Bible"
we may have found one reason why today's bushman invariably
votes for the Country Party.

The most offensive part of the *Bulletin*'s bourgeois vision,
however, was its xenophobia. Its most obvious form was the crude
racism which insisted on Australia as a bastion of white supremacy,
though, as B.R. Wise pointed out in the London *Times* of 1903, John
Bull-Cohen would also be unlikely to find a place in the *Bulletin*'s
land of the future.[12] More subtly, however, Archibald's policies rob-

106

bed the paper and its readers of any active interest in the outside world by a virtual embargo on any other than the most cursory or peripheral overseas news and commentary. The sense of Australia as a closed community, white, anglo-saxon, and preferably protestant, which lay at the heart of *Bulletin* editorial policy, was thus actively reinforced by the sense of the selfcontained world its pages offered. A concert in Geelong was more important to Australia's national weekly than a revolution in Europe or a famine almost anywhere.

If our traditional picture of the *Bulletin* as an organ of radical, democratic opinion needs to be revised in this way, what of our notion of its role in our literature which has so frequently been seen in similar terms? Wilkes was prepared to grant the quantity of *Bulletin* material, though he had strong reservations about its quality. More recent writers have drawn attention to the work of other papers of the time in soliciting and publishing Australian material: The *Australian Journal*, the *Sydney Mail*, and the *Town and Country Journal* were all active in this regard before the *Bulletin*, even if, as Lawson claimed, they did not pay very well. But it does seem undeniable that the *Bulletin*'s willingness to listen to and encourage even the beginners in literature attracted to its pages a substantial proportion of Australian writing of the bush ballad-short sketch kind. A glance through its files or through the pages of the *Bulletin Reciter* or the *Bulletin Story Book* reveals a great range of names and talents; something approaching a cross-section of the most popular Australian literature of the time. And while it is futile to speculate that much that has happened in Australian politics since the 1890s could have been different if a paper with the circulation and influence of the *Bulletin* had been more concerned with social and economic restructuring, it is fruitful to suggest the manner in which its rabid nationalism had a significant effect upon Australian literature.

Archibald's early reprinting of English serials and fiction soon gave way to an insistence on Australian material and by March 1892 his famous literary principles were clearly formed:

> "Every man can write at least one book", every man with brains has at least one good story to tell; every man with or without brains moves in a different circle and knows things unknown to any other man. Write carefully and plainly on one side of the paper only, obliterating every unnecessary word; then mail your work to *The Bulletin* which pays for accepted matter ... Short stories, or ballads, especially on

bush, mining, sporting, social, or dramatic themes, are preferred by *The Bulletin*; 1360 words go to a column. If you can possibly keep your story within a column all the better. Don't write a column on any subject if a half-column will do; don't write half-a-column where a mere paragraph is enough. "Boil it down."[13]

As principles these do not add up to much. They have that same degree of pragmatism and self-interest already noted in Archibald's social views. Poems and stories, as much as politics and news, had to accord with *Bulletin* preconceptions before finding a place in its pages. One is reminded of George Bentley, the Victorian publisher's prescriptive definition of a novel: a book of 920 pages with 21½ lines on each page and 9½ words in each line![14] In George Gissing's partly autobiographical novel *New Grub Street*, published in 1891, we see the debilitating effect such prescriptions could have on a writer's talent and one wonders how many would-be story-tellers of the period counted out their thoughts in units of 1360 words. Certainly A.G. Stephens, during his period as literary editor of the *Bulletin*, was aware of the need to see beyond these arbitrarily imposed patterns of authorship. If Edgar Allan Poe were to submit "The Fall of the House of Usher" to us for publication, he mused in 1896, he would reject it with the injunction: cut by half and omit the introduction![15] And in his introduction to the 1901 *Bulletin Story Book*, far from puffing and praising his material, as the *Bulletin* itself frequently did, he saw its accomplishments and limitations quite objectively:

> In collating these stories and literary sketches from the files of the *Bulletin*, the aim has been to make an interesting book. It has not been attemped to choose the best examples of literary style. Judged by a high canon, our most talented story-writers are still only clever students of the art of writing. A mere two or three have been able to earn a living by the profession of literature, and even these have been obliged to make the perilous compromise with journalism. So the stories and sketches which follow are usually the literary dreams of men of action, or the literary realization of things seen by wanderers. Usually they are objective, episodic, detached—branches torn from the Tree of Life, trimmed and dressed with whatever skill the writers possess (which often is not inconsiderable). In most of them still throbs the keen vitality of the parent stem: many are absolute transcripts of the Fact, copied as faithfully as the resources of language will permit. Hence many of them, remaining level with Nature, remain on the lower plane of Art—which at its highest is not imitative, but creative—making anew the whole world in terms of its

subject. What is desiderated is that these isolated impressions should be fused in consciousness, and re-visualized, re-presented with their universal reference made clear—yes! with the despised Moral, but with a moral which shines forth as an essence, is not stated as an afterthought. In other words, the branch should be shown growing upon the Tree, not severed from it: the Part should imply the Whole, and in a sense contain it, defying mathematics. Every story of a man or a woman should be a microcosm of humanity; every vision of Nature should hold an imagination of the Universe. These be counsels of perfection which it is easier to teach than to practise, though many writers in other lands have practised them. So we take the good the gods provide, and are properly grateful, while striving for better and best.

Such critical analysis struck a new note in Australian writing and is an accurate measure of the gulf which separated Stephens's literary awareness from that of his *Bulletin* employers. The traditional picture, related by Vance Palmer in more than one place, of Stephens being summoned from his position in London to implement and expand Archibald's literary ambitions will simply not do; any more than will Stuart Lee's concept of him as providing Archibald with a "literary soul"[16] or John Barnes's version of Stephens as integral to the *Bulletin*'s programme of encouraging nationalism.[17] It is important to establish AGS as a figure outside of this *Bulletin* world with which he is usually identified. His famous Red Page, begun towards the end of 1894 and continued till 1906, represented a radical turning away from the principles of literary nationalism and a strong qualification of Archibald's view of the world. Stephens's own retrospective account of "an empire within an empire" is true in a way which has never been sufficiently realized. My earlier contention that the most effective denial of the legend of the nineties comes from the writing of the period itself is nowhere better demonstrated than in Stephens's work.

His diverse background peculiarly fitted him for this role. Born in Toowoomba in 1865, he had lived and worked in Sydney, Brisbane, Gympie, and Cairns, as well as in the United States, England, and Europe before his appointment to the *Bulletin* in 1894. He had published several books on Queensland politics as well as a collection of travel essays and had read widely in English and classical literature as well as that of America and the Continent. Archibald's offer, while "too flattering to refuse", to use Stephens's words, was seen by him as an opportunity to further his polemical and literary interests without the imposition of too onerous a workload. His unpublished diary, now in the University of Queensland library, makes it clear that he regarded his *Bulletin* post as a stepping-stone to more amenable positions. His most fervent ambition was to produce a literary journal of genuinely international scope. From his early days he had been a regular reader of such magazines as *Blackwoods* and *Scribners* and had indeed produced a weekly column of gleanings for the Brisbane *Boomerang* in 1891, providing his northern readers with an up to the month account of literary developments in England and America. By 1896, with the Red Page barely under way, he was busy applying for other jobs, such as the New South Wales government printership, which he hoped would help further his long-term plans; and in October of that year he was proclaiming in the pages of the *Bulletin* itself that what Australia needed most was a literary magazine of broader and more substantial scope than anything yet offered. He persuaded Archibald, and the even more sceptical business manager, William Macleod, to establish a regular publishing company, with himself as editor; not just to give permanence to *Bulletin* authors, but to produce those works which neither the *Bulletin* nor any other local magazine could contain. Furphy's *Such is Life* was his most significant title.

In 1899 his first magazine, *The Bookfellow*, appeared under *Bulletin* auspices and its five slim numbers contain an astonishing range of material—a range which only *Meanjin Quarterly*, within Australia, has been able to emulate. Conrad, Hardy, Yeats, and Beardsley were the subjects of articles and Brennan was persuaded to contribute his now well-known accounts of the French symbolist poets. On the Red Page itself discussions and printings of Australian literature ran side by side with reviews of Stephen Crane, Kipling, Mark Twain, Gorki, Oscar Wilde, Olive Schreiner, Bernard Shaw, D'Annunzio, Henry James, and many others. More to the point, there was a good deal of comparative exegesis and presentation, with Stephens never allowing his readers to lose sight of the world context within which local writers must be judged. A discussion of the stories of Louis Becke and Alex Montgomery, for instance, led naturally to an account of Maupassant, who was cited as the master from whom the Australians must learn.[18] Many English, American, and European poems were printed and Stephens was delighted with the success of his policies, demonstrated by the regular reader who wrote that her favourite Australian poet was T.B. Aldrich. If we turn through the Red Pages of this period it is noteworthy that something like half the literary articles and reviews were concerned with non-Australian books and authors. Considered in relation to the isolationist ethic of the rest of the paper, it is clear that the Red Page was a unique as well as a valuable window on the world.

Stephens, though, was aware of the fact that he was constantly swimming against the tide. "It is hard in Australia to get even a nodding acquaintance with recent foreign literature other than British", he lamented in 1897.

> Is there a single Australian who could pass an examination in Huysmans, Maeterlinck, or Verhaeren?—to say nothing of Verlaine or Baudelaire, or others comparatively far-back. Yet Maeterlinck seems probably quite as notable as Tolstoi, and Verhaeren and Verlaine have far more poetical significance than the rabbits of the English warren, like Kipling or Watson, of whom every local body with a smattering of letters can appraise the merits. And what, generally speaking, do we know of Russian literature, beyond the well-advertised names—or of German, or of Scandinavian? Really, if somebody would establish a cosmopolitan bookshop, and keep the Southern Cross abreast of the northern lights, it would be a Boon.[19]

When Stephens left the *Bulletin* in 1906, he did just that.

In giving this account of his work, however, I do not want to suggest that he was operating outside the mainstream of Australian literature, for clearly this was not the case. But I do want to insist that the nationalist ethic of the *Bulletin*, and the legend of the nineties to which it has given rise, was directly antithetical to Stephens's critical awareness of the state and function of our literature and of the literature being read and written elsewhere in the world. Yet so much has been made of him as a nationalist critic that it is worthwhile considering the point in some detail.

In the *Review of Reviews* for April 1896 E.E. Morris, professor of English at Melbourne University, published a review of Lawson's first book of verse, *In the Days When the World was Wide.* More offensive than incompetent, his patronizing strictures aroused Stephens's latent antipathy towards university men. "The Literary Fish", which appeared on the Red Page the following month, was his savage reply. Undoubtedly both men made their points, though Stephens made his better. He conceded that Lawson was no great poet; indeed "second-rate ... with gleams, gleams. But he is Australian—and one likes to have a little land-plot and a literary poetry-plot to call one's own". Stated thus baldly, Stephens's case sounds dangerously like a plea for the dreaded "double standard", a recurrent concern in Australian literary criticism since the middle of the nineteenth century. But his main point lay elsewhere. Lawson's Australian qualities, he argued, were simply the focal point, the locus of his more general concerns:

> The ring of "The Star of Australasia" ... is the ring of the pulse that throbbed in the ears of Leonidas's Spartans, of Cromwell's Puritans, of the Texans who fell at the Alamo. Does Prof. Morris hear that note, this ring—Prof. Morris, the Literary Fish? Not he; he thinks "The Star of Australasia" is "a fine, vigorous poem", and argues gravely against its ethics. "The drawback is the uncertainty who is to be Australasia's foe". Oh, Oh![20]

Professor Morris, Stephens contended, was so caught up in his academic realization that Lawson was not Wordsworth or Milton that he could not see beyond the Australian's immediate imagery and setting. As a local writer Lawson obviously meant more to local readers than to others, though ultimately he must be judged by the standards of those others. But equally, his status as a local writer did not preclude him from their company, as Morris had implied.

Stephens here achieved an important balance which had far-reaching implications, not just for the Red Page, but for Australian literature as a whole. He was perhaps the first critic to see beyond the immediate reality of Lawson's literary world to the larger context into which Brian Matthews has only recently placed the best of the stories.[21] And in doing this he compromised nothing of Lawson's local appeal or of his own literary standards.

A few months before Morris's review Stephens himself had reviewed *In the Days When the World Was Wide*, and had been quite prepared to concede Lawson's shortcomings:

> His mental scope is narrow; he is comparatively uncultured; he iterates the same notes, and rarely improves his thought by elaboration; he wants harmony and variety of metre; his work is burdened with many weak lines and careless tags. But how graphic, how natural, how true, how strong! How he feels and makes his readers feel, in poems like "Out Back!" when phrase by phrase is painted an imperishable bush picture.[22]

And in an article three years later, already referred to, he wrote of Lawson's stories and verse as having "largely an Australian value": "Lawson's pre-eminent Australian appeal lessens the force of his universal appeal. He is splendidly parochial. That increases his claim upon his country, but decreases his claim upon literature".[23] There is no double standard here but the recognition of a vitally important truth: literature which is "splendidly parochial" can have a cultural and historical significance of the highest importance without necessarily needing to be great literature. By the highest standards of literary criticism Lawson fails. By the highest standards of the Australian experience his "shortcomings ... are as nothing beside his merits". The spirit which moves criticism such as this might be patriotic, as Brian Kiernan has recently pointed out, but it is far removed from the xenophobic nationalism which had the imprimatur of the *Bulletin.*[24]

A.G. Stephens is a central figure in the nineties in a quite different manner to that which has gained wide acceptance. If we accept Professor Wilkes's contention that the legend of the period is in part at least based upon the legend of AGS, we are forced back upon the critic as

the Blender of the pure
Australian Brand of Literature

whom Victor Daley saw.[25] Instead, we need to emphasize the manner in which that mixture of the recognition of failure with the hope of prophecy in the greatest creative writers of the period, was mirrored in Stephens's own work. He saw the writing of his time, neither as part of the unique achievement of a decade nor as the culmination of a century, but as continuous hesitant steps in the formation of a body of work which could continue across the years to be one day called Australian Literature. To him, the isolationist impulses of the *Bulletin* were the very thing most likely to destroy that literature by removing it from the only context in which it could genuinely flourish and flower. His own image I cited earlier, of a branch lopped from a tree, applies equally to his awareness of the dangers facing Australian writing. It must be the function of criticism in this country, he insisted, to cultivate both the branch and the tree. If we ignore the latter, then the former will surely wither and die.

7

The Structure of Brennan's
The Wanderer

TERRY STURM

The wrecks of systems which philosophy has scattered over the earth in her monstrous infatuation for that spectre, the Absolute, are almost innumerable: they have been refuted and wrecked by the simple human process of getting past them.

Christopher Brennan[1]

The fourteen poems of Brennan's sequence *The Wanderer* have always been regarded—by anthologists and critics of Brennan's poetry—as among his most accessible work. Unfortunately, however, belief in the "accessibility" of the poetry has not made for close or detailed attention to it.[2] Impressionistic assertion— particularly of the sort which lifts encapsulating phrases at random from the poem, without consideration of context—seems to be endemic to criticism of *The Wanderer*. The assumption is that what is true of one poem (or even one line) is true of the whole: that the structure of *The Wanderer* is essentially static, each poem simply illustrating or restating ideas and attitudes announced, presumably, at the poem's beginning and informing the whole sequence as a kind of "given" centre.

Perhaps the notion that *The Wanderer* was a spontaneous outburst has something to do with implications—contained in so much comment on the poem—that it lacks, for better or worse, the kind of

114

systematic planning that went into the making of *Towards the Source* and *The Forest of Night*. Such evidence as there is, however, suggests that although the idea for *The Wanderer* did not occur until relatively late in the planning of *Poems* (1913), and possibly suddenly, the actual writing and rethinking were just as careful as for other phases of *Poems* (1913). Eight poems appeared in *Hermes* in 1902;[3] yet additional poems were still being written and contemplated in 1906; and a letter to Bertram Stevens, discussing his intentions for the whole poem, refers to "*The Wanderer*, with additions (all allowed for, and sketched out at the beginning) say 15—20 pieces."[4] The six poems eventually added to the eight published in *Hermes* were not simply tacked on at the end, as if the overall ordering of the poems did not matter, but carefully inserted at different points in the original sequence.

Such evidence ought to make us wary of generalizing from phrases like "foredoom'd disastrous" (no. 13) and "no ending of the way, no home, no goals" (no. 14) to the so-called "pessimism" of the whole; or of an argument like the following, about the movement between *The Forest of Night* and *The Wanderer*: "We have passed through night to dawn again, only this time it will be the restless, horrible dawn of 'The Wanderer'."[5] The phrase "horrible dawn", picked up from the concluding lines of the first poem of *The Wanderer* and applied to the whole, is *not*, however, a description of anything that actually occurs in the poem, but a question ("O, what horrible dawn will bare me the way ... ?"). And the force of the question, cutting abruptly across the comfortable reverie in which the Wanderer has been absorbed in the earlier part of the poem, focusses our attention on his emotional state: his horror at the prospect of being cast adrift from what is secure and habitual in his past life into a world without identifiable landmarks (only "crude lumps of hills"), a landscape devoid of any refuge from the restless forces associated with the sea, and conceived of, at this early stage of *The Wanderer*'s development, as wholly threatening and destructive.

The dawn which eventually does break, in the final poem of the sequence, is very different from the horrible dawn anticipated fearfully in the first poem: neither a dawn of unmitigated bleakness nor, as in traditional religious and secular typology, an instant Utopia. Instead, it is now "clear gray day". Surrounded by the remnants of a battlestrewn landscape ("the wrecks of systems which philosophy has scattered over the earth in her monstrous infatuation for that spectre, the Absolute"), the Wanderer, for the first time in the poem, asserts his identity ("I am the wanderer of many years ... ") and feels, momentarily, in the heart of the winds, not the sense of alienation predicted in the first poem, but a sense of release. The effect—in this shift from the mood of the first poem to that of the final poem—is of a transformation in the Wanderer's consciousness.

My aim in this chapter is to suggest that a key to the understanding of *The Wanderer* lies in grasping the essentially dynamic structure in which this transformation in the Wanderer's consciousness is enacted: it is a dramatic sequence, in which the protagonist's feelings and attitudes are tested, discarded, or reformulated in a progressive movement employing irony as its fundamental structural method. The Wanderer's tendencies to self-pity, self-dramatization, sentimentality, and vaticination—which are often seen as symptomatic of a failure in the poetry itself[5]—are in fact conscious preoccupations of the poet, and are eventually revealed, in the ironic structuring of the sequence, as illusions which the Wanderer must cast off if he is to understand and accept the full implications of his role as a Wanderer. The mode of the poem, as I have outlined it here, is thus the *same* as that of the two earlier phases of *Poems* (1913), *Towards the Source*, and *The Forest of Night*. The Wanderer's recognition and acceptance of his role is not reached until the final poem of the sequence, the poem from which the sequence gets its title, and the only poem in which the phrase "the wanderer" is used.

The theme of the nature of "wandering", as Brennan's important background article "Philosophy and Art" shows, is primarily philosophical in orientation, and its ramifications in the context of Romantic theory have been discussed in detail by G.A. Wilkes in his article "*The Wanderer*: A Progressive Romanticism?", and in relation to specific cultural traditions in Australia by John Docker in his *Australian Cultural Elites: Intellectual Traditions in Sydney and Melbourne* (1974). Brennan's poetic approach to these issues, in *The Wanderer*, is to focus on the consciousness of the Wanderer himself—the poem's landscape is primarily an interior one, an emotional and mental landscape—and on the drama of his transformation of consciousness. In this dramatic movement fixed habits, beliefs, and prejudices—particularly, belief in some absolute or

116

transcendent order of existence—have to be uprooted and replaced by the consciousness that all systems of thought laying claim to final or absolute truth are human constructions rooted in the flux of time and history. Yet this very recognition is a means of releasing from the past, petrified and closed off in belief-systems no longer available to man, the *human* truths which underlie them, an alternative history in which man is seen as involved in a continuing struggle to humanize his environment and understand his own nature. The Wanderer's recognition of his identity at the end of the sequence represents both a release from the nightmare of history expressed in *The Labour of Night* and from the torments of his own time-obsessiveness, and a making available of the past (one meaning of "the ways of all the worlds" he is now free to explore) in quite new ways. The position of the 1908 "Epilogue", for example, in which Brennan returns to his personal history in a mood free of the tormenting anxieties expressed in earlier poems in *Poems* (1913), might be seen, I think, as indicating a new awareness made possible by the recognitions of *The Wanderer*.

Dramatic tension in *The Wanderer* is felt primarily, however, in the protagonist's *resistance* to the challenge of being a wanderer, in the full sense that the role has attained by the end of the poem. In the first movement his resistance is mainly emotional, an interior struggle in which he is tormented by the desire to cling nostalgically to sentimental feelings and beliefs, romanticizing his past, in the face of the increasingly remorseless uprooting forces of wind and rain and the disturbing challenge of the unknown symbolized by a sea whose violent rhythms seem to invade the very centre of his being, in dream and nightmare. *The Wanderer* structures this dramatic movement very carefully. The opening poem establishes a mood of apparently concentrated, luminous reverie, presenting a protagonist rather complacently self-absorbed in personal memories, only to have this mood shattered by a sudden, horrified fear of what the dawn will bring. It is a poem which establishes in a tense, dramatic way, the mood of resistance to possibilities of change. In the remaining six poems which complete the first movement of *The Wanderer* (the two movements of the sequence—each of seven poems—clearly separated by a blank page in the original text), the mood of self-absorption is maintained, each poem concentrating on a different aspect of his resistance, until a nadir is reached in the seventh and final poem ("I sorrow for youth—ah, not for its wildness (would that were dead!)"). There is an increasing intensity in the Wanderer's despairing attempts either to cling to a past seen more and more through the falsifying lenses of self-pity and idealization, or to escape, in consoling fantasies, from the forces of wind, rain, and sea; and these, interrupting at the end of each poem the various moods established at the beginning, assume an increasingly imperious, threatening character.

The first three poems in effect constitute a minor sequence within the first movement. The sudden sense of horror which ends the first poem is replaced, in the second poem, by what looks like an acceptance of wind and rain. Envying the passengers returning to their home port after a long sea voyage, he thinks of the winds and the sea as cleansing, vitalizing forces, and attempts to draw an analogy with his own situation:

> ... if I might, some day, landing I reck not where
> have heart to find a welcome and perchance a rest,
> I would spread the sail to any wandering wind of the air
> this night, when waves are hard and rain blots out the land.

However the conditions which he proposes here, before he is willing to accept the hardships of wandering—that there be the prospect of an end or term to them—misconceive a central fact of wandering ("no ending of the way, no home, no goal"). And in the third poem, wind and rain assert their implacable, inevitable character, in a choric climax which mocks the protagonist's despairing acknowledgment ("I am driven everywhere from a clinging home") that a permanent home—even the prospect of one—is an illusion:

> You shall find neither home nor rest; for ever you roam
> with stars as they drift and wilful fates of the sky!

This choric assertion of the wind, at the end of the third poem, completes an opening movement in which the protagonist is progressively reduced to helpless passivity, a progression emphasized by the shifting tense of each poem. The sense of active choice in the Wanderer's physical movements and in his initiation of a contemplative mood in the first poem ("I rose and left ... I stopt, remembering ... ") is replaced by the more tentative conditional tense in which the false resolution of the second poem is conceived ("if I might ... I would ... "), and in the third poem by a simple passive tense ("I am driven ... my heart is shaken and fill'd ... "). And this sense of helplessness is emphasized also in the imagery used by the wind itself, positing a universe in which man is subject to forces of random chance ("stars as they drift") and to possibly hostile agencies over which he has no control ("wilful fates").

By the end of the third poem, then, the Wanderer recognizes that he is irrevocably cast adrift, and in the remaining four poems of the first movement the sense of hopelessness is intensified as the effects of this new condition of exposure and loss are described, and the Wanderer's personality gradually fragmented and dissolved. The fourth poem ("O tame heart, and why are you weary and cannot rest"), is deceptively complex, ending on a note of defeatism carried over from the previous poem. Taking up the recognition of the previous poem—that his heart is "shaken" out of its familiar, sustaining routines (its 'tameness")—he interrogates the source of its restlessness, imagining initially that it might be the positive manifestation of a latent heroic impulse, a dream of abandoning the conformist impulses of the hearth and confronting life in the youthful spirit of challenge and defiance which he had once possessed. The poem ends, however, on a note of bitter irony, denying that the Wanderer has that kind of heroic past to look back to in order to bolster his present dream. His heart has *always* been "tame"; the challenge of "manhood" and of the "perilous joy of the bold" has never been accepted (not simply "gone", but "forgone"). The notion entertained earlier, that his heart's restlessness might have some positive implication for him, is thus dismissed; its "real" meaning, conveyed in the message of the "ancient rain", reinforces his despair, reminding him perpetually of opportunities never accepted and now irretrievably past.

The failure of the heroic impulse to provide any purposeful direction to the Wanderer's sense of meaningless drift is followed by a feeling of the mind's fragmentation in the fifth poem ("Once I could sit by the fire hourlong when the dripping eaves"), a relatively simple poem in which the Wanderer is pictured among the domestic comforts of hearth and home longing nostalgically for the certainties of past knowledge even though he recognizes (as his "mind drifts wide") that they are illusory, and that there are vast, unexplored and uncharted regions whose reality, if it were known, might challenge the simple certainties he longs for. And in the sixth poem ("How old is my heart, how old, how old is my heart"), the self-pity and nostalgia of the fourth and fifth poems are concentrated on the Wanderer's sense of emotional insecurity and loss. A potential realization (that he has travelled "many ways" and had "many homes") is swallowed up in the sentimental desire to dwell on what has been lost, or left behind, with each new beginning, and in the Wanderer's emphasis on its scarring, eroding effects on a heart desiring peace and security. His apparent submissiveness to the "ancient winds", at the end of this poem, has an unmistakeable quality of self-regard in it, as he muses over "mine own heart" and indulges in "regret, and a memory".

The development traced in *The Wanderer* thus far has two aspects: an increasing urgency and imperiousness in the assertions of wind and rain, and a corresponding inward-turned momentum—a regression—in the patterning of the Wanderer's responses to them, as he attempts, continually, to resist the implications of his exposure, and escape into consolations of the past, only to find these avenues of escape blocked off. The seventh poem of the sequence—the final poem of the first movement—represents a nadir in this regressive momentum. The symbolic forces of storm disappear, and the Wanderer, turning specifically to idealized personal memories of his wife ("O her eyes in the rosy face that bent over our first babe!") and mother ("to whom we ran with our childish joy") yearns, in the morbid fantasy of the poem's conclusion, for a retreat into a dream world of his childhood. In this difficult poem the time-obsessiveness underlying the Wanderer's earlier resistance to the forces of wind and rain—which he sees as destroying all the permanences he wishes to retain—reaches an intolerable pitch. The poem's first half establishes the Wanderer's anguished sense of precious moments from the past ("soft nests of time") enshrined in his memory—anguished, because they *are* only memories, rapidly fading, like the brief moments they recall. Yet the preciousness of these moments (conveyed, throughout the poem, in the peculiarly *fin de siecle* image of the Madonna-like expression in a mother's eyes) is somehow bound up with the pain which the prospect of their inevitable loss causes, and the Wanderer turns to the more repellent and pathological forms of *fin de siecle* religiosity. His escapist impulses, in the second half of the poem, take the fantasy-form of a yearning for a "deathless heart" (the Immaculate Heart of Mary?) in which his suffering might be "haven'd", find consolation and peace, without the inevitable sense of loss accompanying his personal memories of such moments, in his marriage and childhood. The association of the child's feeling of being protected and loved with the mother's knowledge of its inevitable exposure to suffering is implicit in the Madonna-Christ imagery that the Wanderer invokes, and made morbidly explicit in his literal focus on the brothers' spilt hearts' blood (a more specific metaphor of the heart's fragmentation into "portions" in the previous poem) in the poem's concluding lines:

> O brother! if such there were and each of us might lead each
> to lean above the little pools where all our heart
> lies spilt and clear and shining along the dusky way,
> and dream of one that could save it all and salve our ache!

The brotherhood-in-suffering yearned for here, as the brothers gaze languidly into the "little pools", "shining and clear", and *"dream* of one that *could* save it all and salve our ache!", contains specific elements of narcissism and masochism. The Wanderer's desire is not, in fact, for any actual resolution to his suffering which might result from his merging with a "deathless heart", since this is acknowledged as impossible ("Ay", in the eighth line, having the force of "once") even as the wish for it is being formulated. His desire is for the pleasurable consolation of the *dream* of a "deathless heart", a dream which, as long as it remains unrealized, might enable him to enjoy, and even prolong, his suffering. The Wanderer has reached a point here, after the blocking off of previous avenues of escape, of literally embracing fantasy as a means of coping with the disorientation of his world.

At this low point in the sequence, marked by a blank page in the text, the regressive momentum exhausts itself. A counter-movement begins, and a shift occurs in the Wanderer's attitudes, as a new, increasingly confident mood emerges. Its immediate manifestation, in the three poems (nos. 8, 9, and 10) which begin the second movement, is a turning away from self-preoccupied moods to a consideration of the destiny of the folk. The nature of this transition between the first and second movements—which may seem, on the surface, to be sudden, and even arbitrary—is conditioned by the dramatic patterning of the relationship between the Wanderer and the forces of storm in the first movement. The regressive momentum, which is accompanied by feelings of desperation and anguish in the Wanderer, exhausts itself because its object—the retention of an old self—reaches so attenuated a point, in the fantasy-impulse concluding the first movement, that the self has no further way of sustaining an identity, and *must* collapse. But the collapse is itself a sign that, despite the Wanderer's emotional resistance to them, the apparently destructive forces of wind and rain have in fact been creatively at work throughout, scouring the Wanderer's consciousness and dissolving his old personality, as a necessary phase in the process of transforming and remaking his self. The blank white page which provides a visual turning point for the poem, on each side of which its two movements are balanced, can be seen as representing both the death of the Wanderer's old self, and the potentiality of a new self, whose making is to provide the dramatic momentum of the second movement, culminating in an assertion of identity in the final poem of the whole.

The movement out of self-absorption initiated in the first poem of the second movement ("You, at whose table I have sat, some distant eve"), as the Wanderer turns to the folk, is accompanied by a repeated claim to be the possessor of new knowledge, the message conveyed by the winds to him and uncomprehended by the folk. However, the apparent casting off of self-pity in the poem's opening lines—as he spurns the ignorance on which the folk's pity for him is based—and his attempt to redirect that pity back to the folk in the poem's conclusion, are tinged throughout by a slightly arrogant and contemptuous insistence on his own, isolated possession of knowledge. There is a quality of self-dramatization in the stance—a dwelling on his own isolation—which ironically qualifies the new note of confidence released into the sequence. And the form which his expression of pity for the folk takes ("and pity you, if you should come to know"—i.e. "if you should gain the kind of self-knowledge which only I possess at present") reveals an undercurrent of self-pity persisting from the first movement of the poem.

The Wanderer's attitude to the folk is progressively revalued, however, in the course of the next two poems (nos. 9 and 10), the three "folk-poems" in effect constituting a minor series parallel to the three poems initiating the first movement. In his changing relationship to the folk the Wanderer gains release from the self-preoccupied inner torments of the first movement by coming to realize that the experience he has been through is not some special property of his own, but part of a general experience to which all are subjected. In the course of the three folk-poems, the Wanderer's stance shifts from that of a proud, aloof exile, preferring that the folk remain inarticulate (no. 8), to that of a historian, analyzing their condition, identifying in it the pattern of his own experience and predicting a similar, inevitable upheaval of their world (no. 9), to that of a prophet, angrily denouncing, as servile and conformist, their conservative hearth-consciousness, and exhorting them to accept the challenge of the unknown in a spirit of stoicism and defiance (no. 10). His analysis of the folk's condition recapitulates his own experience, so that in these three poems images, motifs, and attitudes from the first movement recur: the destruction of hearth and home by storm; resistance to change; the onset of disorienting awarenesses of "the uncared wastes" (compare with no. 5), and of subconscious fears ("a cry and a parting in your sleep"); exposure to the nightmare of history (the "worthless drift of the dead"), and the dissolution of certainties into the apparently meaningless drift of the present.

The servility of the folk, which attracts them to the illusory dream of "some master that holds the winds in leash" (an escapist impulse recalling the Wanderer's personal fantasy of "one who could save it all and salve our ache" in the first movement), has to be replaced by an acceptance of the "hard doom" implied in an alternative dream:

> For this is the hard doom that is laid on all of you,
> to be that whereof ye dream, dreaming against your will.

This dream, forcing its way unwilled into the consciousness of the folk, is the "instinct which whispers that man is a wanderer from his birth", and has, here, "no continuing city".[7] It has its source in the same restlessness as that which rendered the Wanderer dissatisfied with the "tameness" of his heart in the fourth poem in the first movement, even as he resisted and rationalized its implications. By turning to the folk, he is now able to see it as a universal instinct, a source of energies and possibilities which need to be tapped and released. At this point, the rhetorical crescendo building up through the ninth and tenth poems reaches a climax. The Wanderer assumes a strident, oracular tone, as he takes on the mantle of prophet and delivers an exhortation to the folk in a choric voice reminiscent of the voice of the wind itself at the conclusion of the third poem of the first movement:

> Go: tho' ye find it bitter, yet must ye be bare
> to the wind and the sea and the night and the wail of
>   birds in the sky;
>   go: tho' the going be hard and the goal blinded with rain
>   yet the staying is a death that is never soften'd with sleep.

The stridency of tone—the tenth poem is the most declamatory in the whole sequence—carries its own suggestion of a loss of control—as if the *person* of the Wanderer is absorbed too completely into the role of the prophet.[8] The way of "disembodied"or pure knowledge which the Wanderer sees himself as representing—as an oracle from "the outer night", the voice of the winds themselves—has its pitfalls no less than the regression into self in the first movement. The Wanderer, as prophet, is still far from an identification in feeling with his role as Wanderer. He still conceives the necessity of wandering as a "hard doom", and despite the important new stress on possibilities (ending the "ancient feud" of man's division from nature and himself, "housing" the cry of the waves, and satisfying the hunger of wind and rain for "some heart's warmth") the poem's final line contains a sense, not of acceptance and release, but of escape from the worse alternative—"yet the staying is a death that is never soften'd with sleep".

The next three poems, as if testing the implications of this note of stridency, turn once more to the Wanderer's introspective processes and to sources of inner conflict, undercutting the mood of apparently limitless confidence and challenge. The Wanderer now deals directly with his personal experience of wandering, the three poems focussing successively on his mind, subconscious, and heart in a movement which reconstitutes his personality, thus preparing for his claim to identity in the poem's conclusion. It is a more chastened and subdued Wanderer, in the eleventh poem, who reflects on the new knowledge of the world which his waking consciousness of so many dawns has given him. By contrast with the "romantic" dawn dwelt on in the fifth poem, in which he imagines, from the comfort of the fireside, a nature refreshed and vitalized by the storm outside, the dawns of this poem do not possess the sustaining quality of newness and freshness; nor do they provide sudden revelations of any "miracle of night". The poem's sober renunciation of such a miracle, in the context of its recapitulation of woodland imagery derived from *The Forest of Night*, represents a final shedding of the Lilith-quest for the Absolute. The chill light of recurrent dawns exposes to the conscious mind its timebound condition, its alienation, and (acknowledged by the Wanderer for the first time in the sequence) the visible presence of evil. In the twelfth poem ("What is there with you and me, that I may not forget") the oblivion-impulse to which the Wanderer now turns is shattered by nightmare; the sea invades his sleep in the form of ghostly shapes with "a thousand beckoning hands", summoning him to take up into his conscious mind the unknown subconscious forces they represent, and to break the cycle of frenzied confrontation and retreat powerfully imaged in the delirium of the sea itself, in the ceaseless alternation of yawning trough and breaking crest. These two poems, with their suggestions of mental and emotional exhaustion, present necessary aspects of the experience of being a Wanderer different from the expression of despair—born of resistance to the prospect of wandering—in the first movement. In their personal emphasis, also, they both illustrate the generalizations which the Wanderer makes, in the folk-poems, about the necessary "bitterness" and "hard going" of wandering, and qualify the rhetorical flourish, verging on triumphant assertion, with which he enunciates his "truths".

In the penultimate poem ("O desolate eves along the way, how oft") the Wanderer's subject is, once again, his heart, as he takes up and redefines the heroic role which he had rejected in despair in the fourth poem of the first movement, in an attempt to reassess his past and come to terms with the desolation he feels. He now explicitly rejects the idea that the "warmth" of his heart—a sense of inner purpose and stability—had its source in the life of the hearth and the memories it provided, and identifies it instead as the warmth of heroic quest ("the solitary unquenchable fire that burns / a flameless heat"). In a passage of increasing intensity, drawing its imagery from the Gotterdammerung and the legend of Roland, he sees his past life as a continuing confrontation, imbued with a spirit of defiance and challenge, with absolute forces, an attempt to make them yield, "in some last fight", if not victory, then the "last hope of a glory won in defeat".

The poem's concluding lines, however, contain a significant qualification of the terms of heroic questing:

> whence, knowing not sure if such high grace befall
> at the end, yet I draw courage to front the way.

The Wanderer draws from his sense of his past life as heroic, a courage which sustains him in his current mood of desolation; but the lines also contain a note of scepticism about ends which is carried to its conclusion in the opening lines of the final poem. The Wanderer's identification, eventually, is with what he sees as a universal human truth underlying heroic questing in the past—its example of human courage and aspiration—not with the now untenable structure of absolute beliefs about the nature of the universe, in terms of which such questing was once conceived. In the final poem the phrase "glory won in defeat" is ironically reformulated as "defeated glory", underscoring the Wanderer's scepticism. The opening lines of the final poem provide, in fact, a parody of the heroic quest. The apocalyptic landscape of a "last fight", a Gotterdammerung, evoked in the previous poem, becomes a ghostly nightscape, a limbo (the image of limbo carefully chosen, I think, to exclude the "absolute" poles of heaven and hell). A kind of apocalypse-in-reverse has occurred: not ushering in a new, absolute order of things, but ushering it out. Man emerges here not as a king, in a universe whose structure is preordained and permanently fixed, but as a wanderer whose nature it is to be uncertain of his own nature. Released from his dreams of kingship, the Wanderer sees himself as freed, as if for the first time, to explore the worlds within and around him in a search whose goals are unknown, and possibly limitless.

There *is* a tension in this poem, as numerous critics have pointed out, but what is climactic, here, is the Wanderer's capacity to *state*, in the way he does, that he is "the wanderer of the ways of all the worlds ... ", feeling momentarily that the pressures of what he has had to cast off—symbolized by the wreck-filled landscape, and the "phantom" night which has tormented him with a promise of miracle always withheld—are now balanced by new possibilities of quest and a felt promise of peace. The Wanderer is able to absorb conflicting impulses into his personality without the sense of fragmentation felt earlier in the sequence. Brennan is implying, I think, that there is a sense in which the Wanderer's capacity to state that he has an identity *demonstrates* that he has one. But the limitations of *merely* stating are implied in the fragile, but controlled, verbal paradoxes conveying the assertion that tensions are resolved: "clear grey day", the peace falling in the "the heart of the winds", the "clear dusk" settling. The Wanderer's feeling of peace is also conditional on his "saying this to myself as a simple thing"; and both the verbal paradoxes and his "saying" imply a world and a self whose complexity can never be totally grasped by language—this is one of the conditions of "wandering" itself. But the sense of identity and the feeling accompanying it are not for that reason negligible, overshadowed by a "pessimism" often attributed to such lines as "no ending of the way, no home, no goal" (as if the Wanderer were offering an absolute statement about the universe, when in fact he is speaking of the provisional state of human knowledge of the universe, and remaining silent about the possibility, or otherwise of absolute dimensions). The poem does, I think give full weight to the "simplicity" of the Wanderer's utterance (particularly through its rhythms, and its dramatic placing as a conclusion to the sequence) without implying its finality. One could say, perhaps, that it is an achieved moment in an on-going process, implied by the absence of a terminal date in the poem's subtitle: *The Wanderer*, 1902—.

Reduced to schematic form, the main outlines of *The Wanderer*, as I see it, are as follows:

FIRST MOVEMENT

Theme:　Resistance to wandering; inward regression
Key word:　Heart

1.	The onset of fear	
2.	Resistance to goalless wandering	Resistance to the necessity of wandering
3.	The necessity of wandering	
4.	The failure of the heroic impulse	
5.	The fragmentation of mind	Dissolution of personality
6.	The fragmentation of heart	
7.	Retreat into dream	

SECOND MOVEMENT

Theme:　The challenge of wandering; the gaining of knowledge
Key word:　Know

8.	Wanderer as exile from the folk	
9.	Wanderer as historian of the folk	Emergence from self; the appeal to knowledge
10.	Wanderer as prophet to the folk	

127

11.	Waking consciousness of evil	
12.	Nightmare vision	Reconstitution of personality; the conscious mind, the sub-conscious, the heart
13.	The heroic impulse redefined	
14.	The assertion of identity	Resolution: synthesis of heart and intellect

The ironic progression underlying this development in *The Wanderer* indicates, I think, that its relationship to *The Forest of Night* is not that of a simple or sudden shift in direction or poetic method. The ending of *The Forest of Night* records the failure of a quest for the transcendent, casting its protagonist adrift among, as the epigraph to *The Wanderer* puts it, "the stars of this revelation". At the centre of *The Wanderer* is Brennan's attempt to discover a meaning in that failure; its dramatic movement is concerned with the Wanderer's need to become fully aware that he *is* cast adrift, with his emotional resistance to it, and with his gradual discovery of a meaning in it, a recognition not of failure but of release into new possibilities.

One sense in which *The Wanderer* is simpler of access than *The Forest of Night* is that it lacks the obscurity of mythic reference and literary allusion in the latter. But this is not say that it lacks *any* mythic dimension. In fact, Brennan's basic myth in *The Wanderer*— of a universe "builded upon the winds, and under them upon the storm"—has, as Brennan's prose writings have identified it, an extremely obscure origin in mediaeval Kabbalistic traditions. Its elements, however, are much simpler than those of Lilith in *The Forest of Night*, providing Brennan with a landscape of primal forces— wind, rain storm, and sea—in terms of which the Wanderer's drama of ideas and passions is enacted. More importantly, its simplicity is part of a *poetic* strategy to convey a revaluation of the meaning of myth itself in the shift from *The Forest of Night* to *The Wanderer*. In *The Forest of Night* myth is exhaustively interrogated for its capacity to provide revelations of the absolute and timeless, and to aid man in an escape from the timebound, the contingent and the imperfect. Its failure to provide such a revelation and escape, in the climactic encounter with Lilith in *The Forest of Night*, appears, at the end of that sequence, to have shattered the very idea of myth.

The Wanderer's redefinition of heroic questing provides an example of the way in which myth is eventually reincorporated into his understanding of himself and of his relationship to nature. It is to be explored and used, not for any access it might offer to the Absolute, but for the insights it provides into the nature of man and of his relationship to the world. In effect, myth, in *The Wanderer*, is secularized: deprived of their absolute dimensions, myths are released into a human history now able to be seen in dynamic terms, available to the present for the human truths they embody about man's struggle to humanize his environment and understand himself; and the Wanderer himself becomes an archetype of man in history, questing for human knowledge within the limits of the finite and timebound. The primary symbolism of wind, rain, and sea, contrasting so strongly with the esoteric elements in the myths of *The Forest of Night*, is one of the most powerful poetic means *The Wanderer* employs to convey this redefinition of the significance of myth.

The same kind of qualification needs to be made about the simplicity of Brennan's language in *The Wanderer*, and his manipulation of rhythm. Although there *is* a general shift, in *The Wanderer*, to a more simplified vocabulary and syntax, and a reliance, often, on quite simple repetitive effects to create cadences and rhythms suggesting primal or universal responses, what needs to be emphasized, I think, is both Brennan's conscious control of language and rhythm, and the range of effects he achieves within the general movement towards simplification.

The Wanderer contains, for example, more lines built up entirely of monosyllabic words than any other poem of comparable length that I know (twenty-two lines, or ten per cent of the poem); and if the incidence of lines in which only one word is not monosyllabic is included, the proportion is greatly increased, to well over a third of the whole poem. Such a pattern is especially significant (suggesting a conscious aiming at effects derived from the simplicity of the poem's vocabulary), because of the long line which *The Wanderer* employs, based on a pattern of five or six stresses, in which the actual number of syllables can vary enormously. (Compare, for example: "to the wind and the sea and the night and the wail of birds in the sky;" (no. 10), which has six stresses and seventeen syllables, with: "the ever-restless, ever-complaining sea?" (no. 1), which has five stresses and eleven syllables.   The figure does not take into account, either, lines in which there is a counterpointing of multisyllabic and monosyllabic words, as in the following: "[nor shall ye know] whither the yesterdays have fled, or if they were" (no. 9), where the folk's experience of being unwillingly caught up in the passing of time, only to lose their bearings completely, is enacted in the contracting rhythms within the line.

Not surprisingly, the poem which emerges as the most significant in this rather arithmetical calculation is the final poem of the sequence: three lines consisting wholly of monosyllables and another eight in which only one word is not monosyllabic. The general aim, here, is to emphasize, in the effects of vocabulary and rhythm, the Wanderer's "saying this to myself as a simple thing". Even so, the three lines built wholly of monosyllabic words give some idea of the variety of rhythmical effects Brennan is able to achieve in order to convey the "simplicity" of his utterance.

Line 1   The land I came thro' last was dumb with night,
Line 8   now it is clear grey day and the road is plain,
Line 20   I feel a peace fall in the heart of the winds

The first line is almost (except for a half stress needed on "thro'") a perfectly regular iambic pentameter, and its rhythmical force, in a poem almost totally devoid of iambic pentameter, is derived from its contrast, as sober statement, with the heroic mood which had increasingly dominated the previous poem until its final two lines. (Significantly, the previous poem, no. 13, contains no lines consisting wholly of monosyllabic words at all; in its evocation of a heroic mood, the poem goes back to the style—the rhythm, language, and complicated syntax and epithet ("foredoom'd disastrous")—of the "hero-mood" poems of The Forest of Night, thus making for a general contrast with the final poem of The Wanderer.) The eighth line requires six full stresses, and builds into its rhythm a tone of simple but emphatic assertion; produced by the opening stress on "now", the three consecutive stresses on "clear grey day", and the hint of a caesura after "day", which reinforces the syntactical parallelism of the two halves of the line and the assonance of "grey day" and "plain". In the twentieth line the rhythmical effects are different again, particularly in the arrangement of sound and stress to isolate the word "fall", momentarily, and enforce a brief pause before and after it, thus enacting, rhythmically, the sense of the line. It prepares for the more emphatic pauses, emphasized by punctuation as well as stress, as that momentary "pause" in the winds is absorbed into the Wanderer's personality:

> I feel a peace fall in the heart of the winds
> and a clear dusk settle, somewhere, far in me.

Brennan's letter to Richard Pennington[9] on the scansion of poems in *The Wanderer* gives some idea of the careful thinking which went into the blank verse measures he used; a full scale analysis of rhythm in *The Wanderer* would, I think, be especially revealing of the poetic force of the language in the poem, and suggest much about its structure. Structural considerations also have a bearing on Brennan's use of archaisms, syntactical inversions, and the stylistic mannerisms and imagery of the Celtic Twilight, at different points in the sequence. There is a significant pattern in their use, suggesting that—far from merely "dating" the poem in the nineties—Brennan's use of this language is quite self-aware, and consciously related to his purposes at each stage of *The Wanderer*'s development. I mentioned, earlier, his repeated use of the archaism "ye" in two of the folk-poems (nos. 9 and 10), as a way of establishing a distinctive rhetorical tone. These are poems in which archaisms recalling the language of the Old Testament prophets—phrases like "ye have built you ... ", "where of old ye went", "ye shall stand at amaze, beholding ... ", "full oft ere all be done", and such words as "winterward", "riven", "whither", "yonder", "nay", and "anhunger'd"—are deliberately employed to establish the Wanderer, at this stage of the poem, as the conscious artificer of a prophetic role.

This kind of language might be contrasted with the Celtic Twilight mannerisms, similarly "placed", which recur particularly in the poems of the first movement, associated with the Wanderer's moods of inexplicable yearning, sentimental regret, and world-weariness. The fourth poem, with its Celtic Twilight subject of the "tame heart", and its use of the archaisms "fain" and "ween", is an obvious example. Particularly noticeable, in the construction of this poem, is a characteristic Celtic Twilight cadence in which "and" is used as a device to suggest world weary questioning and longing. Except for the final two lines, with their bitter, ironic twist, Brennan's

TERRY STURM

poem is built on this device: "and why are you weary ... and were you
not fain ... and is your dream now ... and you ween you are back in
your life of old ... ". A variation of this mood is provided by the
opening lines of the sixth poem:

> How old is my heart, how old, how old is my heart,
> and did I ever go forth with song when the morn was new?
> I seem to have trod on many ways: I seem to have left
> I know not how many homes; and to leave each
> was still to leave a portion of mine own heart,
> of my old heart whose life I had spent to make that home
> and all I had was regret, and a memory.

Here, the emotion of nostalgia is evoked through repetitive effects of
a special sort, announced in the opening lines, each cadence or syntactical unit taking up and repeating, in a slightly different form, the
language and syntax of the clause it follows. In the third line the syntax of "I seem to have trod" is repeated in "I seem to have left"; in
the fourth line the *idea* of departure from a home is caught up and
repeated in a different syntactical form—"and to leave each" referring back to "I seem to have left" and "homes"; in the fifth line a
simple repetition of "to leave" ("to leave each / was still to leave ...
") introduces a new idea in which departure from a home is equated
with the abandonment of "a portion of mine own heart"; and in the
sixth line it is the shape and cadence of the phrase which is repeated
("of mine own heart, / of my old heart ... ") only to have the new
idea which follows (the spending of the heart's life) circle back, at the
end of the line to the obsession with having a permanent home, expressed two lines earlier. The effectiveness of Brennan's evocation of
the Wanderer's nostalgia, in a passage like this, flows primarily
from his manipulation of a syntax which has the Wanderer lingering
over words, cadences, rhythms, at the same time as he is being
propelled, as if unwillingly, into new forms of expression.

What these examples suggest is that in the poems of *The
Wanderer* Brennan draws consciously on a variety of dictions, whose
function is to contribute to the progressive unfolding of its structure;
the criterion governing the choice of language, in particular poems,
is that of its *dramatic* appropriateness. The diction of the Celtic
Twilight present in the poems of the first movement, and the
rhetorical diction of the folk-poems, identify the Wanderer's sensibility in different ways, and are thus "placed" in the ironic pattern-

ing of the whole poem. The eleventh and thirteenth poems, in which impulses and ideas from *The Forest of Night* are reassessed, incorporate the stylistic features of the "haunted forest" and "hero mood" poems of the earlier sequence: especially their syntactically dense patterns of thought, and their jagged, often awkward rhythms. The twelfth poem, coming between these poems, employs by contrast a much more straightforward diction and syntax, free of inversions and archaisms, its intensity deriving, in part, from this directness. And the final poem, after an opening in which one of the Lilith-styles flickers briefly before exhausting itself on the deliberately archaic note of "glimmer'd at whiles"—signalling a final collapse of the Lilith quest itself—ushers in a conclusion whose main stylistic feature, creating a tone different from anything else in the sequence, is its special, consciously announced claim to simplicity.

A similar complexity is present in Brennan's patterning of repetitive effects throughout *The Wanderer*. A number of examples have been given already. Repetitive effects in *The Wanderer* are sometimes very localized—as in the syntax of the opening lines of the sixth poem ("How old is my heart, how old, how old is my heart"); or in the repetition, three times, of the key word "remembering", in the opening section of the first poem, in order to emphasize the active movement into a mood of reverie; or in the association of the words "regret" and "memory" in the sixth, seventh, and eighth poems successively; or in the ironic shift from the phrase "glory in defeat" in the thirteenth poem, to the phrase "defeated glory" in the final poem. More pervasive, however, in the structuring of the poem as a whole, is its broad contrasting of two clusters of symbols. A passive, conformist, past-oriented consciousness is symbolized by a humanized landscape at the centre of which are the domestic comforts of hearth and home, and by an associated imagery of dreaming, of hibernation during the winter, and of being protectively clothed against the cold. Opposed to this consciousness is that symbolized by the "way" itself (perhaps the commonest word in the sequence), implying an active exposure to the non-human landscape of wind and rain and to the rhythms of the sea, and reinforced by the many active verbs suggesting physical movement: going, coming, leaving, walking, treading, passing, fronting the way, travelling, riding away, roaming, spreading sail.

But there are, I think, two words in particular in *The Wanderer* whose repetition and contrast provide a key to the structuring of the poem: these are the words "heart" and "know". The heart, as a key word, dominates the first movement of *The Wanderer*, appearing as a significant point of reference in all but one of the poems, and providing the immediate subject of the fourth and sixth poems. In a sense the Wanderer's heart might be seen as the subject of the first movement itself, the gradual collapse of his personality traced through the shifting contexts in which it occurs: from the illusion of fulfillment which his "deep awake heart" gives him in the first poem, to the heart "shaken" out of that illusion in the third poem, to the phases of disintegration marked out by the sentimental questionings of his heart's weariness and nostalgia in the fourth and sixth poems, and finally, to the Wanderer's retreat into the dream of a "deathless heart" in the seventh poem. In this movement the heart is the symbolic focus of the Wanderer's inner life (just as the hearth symbolizes a social context and attitude) seen increasingly by him as a refuge of all the feelings, moods, and impulses to which he attaches himself in his efforts to resist the forces of wind and rain.

However, in the second movement of the poem, in which counter-impulses lead the Wanderer to a revised, and ultimately transformed consciousness of himself, the poetic contexts of the heart change, and a revaluation takes place. Its immediate manifestation, in the first five poems of the second movement, is that references to the Wanderer's heart, with its multiple associations of feelings and sentiments focussed on the past, disappear completely (except for a reference, in the tenth poem, to "the winds that roam anhunger'd for some heart's warmth", anticipating the resolution of the final poem, when the Wanderer recognizes for the first time, in "the heart of the winds", the possibility of an alternative identity to that associated with the hearth in the first movement). In the opening poems of the second movement—the three folk-poems and the poem following them ("Dawns of the world, how have I known you all")—the new concept which supplants the earlier emphasis on the heart is *knowledge*. "Know", as a key word identifying the Wanderer in the new role of spokesman for the meaning of the winds, dominates these poems (forcefully announced by its repetition, five times, in the opening poem of the second movement) as the heart had provided a focus for the poems of the first movement.

134

However, *The Wanderer* does not come to rest at this point where the claims of the intellect appear to have triumphed over the feelings of the heart. In the penultimate poem the Wanderer's heart once again provides the subject, and a movement is begun in which the association of heart and hearth is explicitly rejected, and the claims of the heart reincorporated into the Wanderer's consciousness. Heart and intellect, feeling and knowing, are revealed, finally, as the terms of an antithesis whose synthesis is momentarily achieved in the Wanderer's assertion of his new identity:

> I know I am
> the wanderer of the ways of all the worlds ...
>
> I feel a peace fall in the heart of the winds
> and a clear dusk settle, somewhere, far in me.

8

"Cyrus Brown of Sydney Town": Christopher Brennan and Dowell O'Reilly

H. P. HESELTINE

On 30 June 1900 there appeared on the Red Page of the *Bulletin* the following poem:

"The Symbolist"

Come! Let us rail at Cyrus Brown,
The Poet pale of Sydney Town;
His form is frail, his curls hang down,
His hat suggests a matyr's crown,
He must not fail to win renown—
     As a Symbolist!

He writes of a "rose," but it means—in brief—
Sweet scents for his nose, and thorns for his grief;
Red sunsets—and glows—and blood—and beef.
One phrase (in his hand) will expand to a sheaf,
And a forest he grows from a single leaf,
     Does this wrinkling Symbolist!

His mind is sure—his purpose planned,
To purge and purify the land
Of poetry we understand.
"For the world is curled in a grain of sand,
And poetical homeopathy's grand,"
     Sings the tinkling Cymbalist.

                               D.

136

The identity of the subject of these verses could scarcely have been in doubt to any Sydney reader of the *Bulletin* even remotely acquainted with local literary affairs: the conjunction of the initials "C.B." with a Blakean allusion and the Symbolist aesthetic could have pointed only to Christopher Brennan. The initial "D", on the other hand, may have had some success in cloaking the authorship of the pasquinade, although many members of the literary community must have recognized it as a pseudonym often used by Dowell O'Reilly.

Among those who were certainly privy to the authorship of "The Symbolist" was Brennan himself. Even before its publication he had been shown a copy by A.G. Stephens, in 1900 still the editor of the Red Page. Any reservations Stephens may have felt about printing the piece must have been settled by a verse letter he received from Brennan, writing in the character of "Cyrus Brown", and dated 13 June 1900:[1]

> *Nihil Obstat*
>   Dom X.Y.Z.—Censor
> Imprimatur
>   C.J. Card B
> Once with this young man's tardy brains
> I gave myself a heap of pains
> while as he sat before my feet,
> His education's not complete:
> else had he hearken'd what I said
> & held his Blake in rightful dread
> nor stol'n his 'grain of sand', nor set
> after the noun its epithet,
> nor writ—I read with eyes a-twinkling—
> so strange an adjective as 'wrinkling',
> so homeopathetical
> with meaning tighten'd to a ball.
> He's coming on tho', I admit:
> His second stave gives proof of it;
> he reads some meaning in a rose
> by eyesight—let him trust his nose
> and he'll find more. His genius too
> can pierce the veil of matter thro':
> what tho' my form assign'd by fate
> speak to the gross of cakes and ale,
> *he* sees me hung with 'curls' and 'frail',
> ideal, rapt, poetic—'pale'.
> You see, he doesn't merely 'rail'.
> So print him: pay him nothing less
> than ten-&-six & he will bless.

In commenting on these lines, Terry Sturm understandably spoke of Brennan's being "sufficiently detached to enjoy the caricature of himself which O'Reilly published anonymously in the *Bulletin*."[2] If Brennan managed to maintain his equanimity before the event, however, his behaviour after the appearance of "The Symbolist" indicates that he did so only by the exercise of a very considerable self-control. The sustained intensity of his anger at O'Reilly's squib indeed suggests that far more was involved on both sides than a good-natured and passing joke, that the publication of "The Symbolist" merely brought to a head profound and increasingly exacerbated differences in a friendship that went back the better part of a decade.

Thus, almost ten months after the appearance of the poem, its insult was still rankling in Brennan's memory. On 18 March 1901 he devoted a considerable part of a letter to F.S. Delmer ("an Australian", as A.R. Chisholm reports, "then lecturing in English at the University of Koenigsberg")[3] to the "Cyrus Brown" affair:

> I can't send your feelings to O'Reilly: an estrangement arose, owing to O'Reilly's having published a satire on me in the Bulletin. It was so strong that the editor submitted it to me before publishing. I wouldn't spoil any man's fun: so in it went. Then I began to worry O'Reilly with Blake-quotations bearing on it. He thinking I merely suspected him, lay low—as he thought. Finally, when the quotations became too direct, he came out with a confession & an apology—which was really a scream of triumph at having—"deeply wounded" me & forced me to come "down from my pedestal" to look for the man who had shot me in the back. Having got the confession—all I wanted—I spoke to him directly, & told him the facts of the case & what I had a right to think concerning it—carefully acquitting him of any malicious intention. Whether out of stupid pride, or childish pique at seeing a childish trick miscarry—for real regret would have led him to an answer as frank as mine—he has been silent for six months: & it's not my part to wake him up.[4]

Neither Brennan's disgruntled tone here nor his pleasure in his revenge is a usual symptom of "detached amusement". That the cat-and-mouse game that he had been playing with O'Reilly, however, had been successful seems clear enough. In a letter to J. Le Gay Brereton, a friend of both parties in the dispute, O'Reilly set down his version of the incident. The letter is almost certainly to be dated in September 1900:

Dear Jack,

    I wish you were here to lend me your ears—and sides—you remember the Cyrus Brown comedy in several acts—it was a comedy only, then. I saw Brennan a week or so after you remember? he was serenely oblivious of anything that had happened to disturb the very pleasant relations that had always existed between the creature and its creator. We met several times—drank—eat—wrangled together—but never a word Hal never a word—had I but known!

  The storm burst about 3 weeks ago and it has been hailing ever since—cats and dogs—Valas—Albions—Jerusalem Spectres (any quantity) "grains of sand"—Ha! "wrinkles" blue lead pencil—red—black—fire and horror shot with equal rage!

  To the first few [four?] sheet lightnings I returned a spluttering reply which he returned endorsed as follows

    spelling good
    writing poor
    composition so-so

but of course I was "serenely oblivious" to that—for a time! The third and—he says—the last Euroclydon arrived two or three days ago.

  Now do you think I have [scored?] Standing mid-way on the balance do you not see that—in noticing Cyrus Brown at all—his dignity has kicked the beam! He has deserted his Senlac Hill—fled from his kopje—but these are unworthy similes (?) The cloud capped mountain has come to the false prophet! Think how solemnly it would have fallen on me had I gone to it. Three months the dear old [—] has ogled me, wishing me to smirk for his sentiments on the accursed thing, and now—he has delivered himself into my hands. I write to him tonight telling him that it was only when his third budget of manuscript arrived that I realized that my friendly (if philistinic) verses had so deeply wounded him—that I had foolishly taken him at his word and thought him indifferent [to] public opinion—indeed that he need not take so black a view of the result, as the verses must have gained him a certain notoriety—however small—which is the first step to recognition as a popular favorite. I enclose him the following lines and ask him if I shall send them to the Red Page as a reply, signing them C.B. Can I do anything else in atonement? I think that ought to draw a few more pages from the highlands.

    O let me not be mad sweet Self
    But all my powerful labours crown
    By shrouding in his narrow shelf
    The thing that railed on Cyrus Brown

    False palsy grip the caitiff hand
    And strike the simian forehead down
    That spawned throughout the croaking land
    The legend false of Cyrus Brown

139

I—I am Cyrus Brown! for long
In silence deep I sought to drown
The writhing agony of wrong
That stung the heart of Cyrus Brown

Serpent and frog! with foetid dash
Of ape that mows the grinning town
DIE—in this four fold lightning flash
From out the brain of Cyrus Brown.

Vala for sure shall steadfast stand
Jerusalem nor tumble down
While CYRUS triumphs through the land
For he is green and I am BROWN[5]

If there was satisfaction in Brennan's letter to Delmer at the discomfiture of O'Reilly, there was equally in O'Reilly's letter to Brereton a slightly sour note of envy in his attitude towards Brennan. The cause of these feelings, generated by what should have been a trivial public confrontation, must be sought in the very beginnings of the friendship between the two men. It is uncertain when they first met, but it cannot have been much later than Brennan's return from Germany in August 1894, and conceivably was before his departure in June 1892. The agent of their meeting, again, cannot be identified with absolute surety, but it was very likely A.B. Piddington, who had lectured on English literature to the undergraduate Brennan and had corresponded with him while he was teaching at Goulburn in 1891. Piddington, whose major career was in the law, married Marion O'Reilly, Dowell's sister.

In 1894 the balance of the new friendship must have been weighted towards O'Reilly. Born in 1865, he was five years Brennan's senior. He was already a twice published poet: *Australian Poems* had appeared in 1884, and *Pedlar's Pack* in 1888. After 1895 he was a married man, and in 1894, being elected to the New South Wales Parliament for the seat of Parramatta, he became a figure of some public eminence. He was, further, in a position to be of financial assistance to a Brennan desperately in need of funds to conduct a long distance courtship with Anna Werth in Berlin. An undated letter of the period demonstrates both the measure of Brennan's financial need and the intimacy of his relationship with O'Reilly which could permit him openly to ask for money:

I have become a most shameless beggar (in all senses of the word) but as a man whose love-affairs want setting to rights always is. It has become necessary for me to send another telegram to Berlin. Pid whom I struck for 50/- for the last one is no longer "available". I don't know how you stand monetarily; if you possess such a sum I don't make the slightest bones about robbing you of it. Failing you— is there any mutual friend who has that much, or any number of mutual friends who could make it up between them.

Yrs
C.B.[6]

Age and social circumstances probably combined to establish O'Reilly's primacy at the outset of the friendship; the glamour of re-cent overseas travel, superior education, and simple force of per-sonality, however, must soon have enabled Brennan to make of the intimacy a relationship between peers. And, of course, they were drawn together not only through mutual acquaintances like Pid-dington but by shared interests and allegiances. Brennan, thus, probably concurred in O'Reilly's Labor politics. They both felt the strength of their inherited Irishry: Brennan's sense of his ancestry coloured his whole life and career, while in "Ireland"[7] O'Reilly had written a poem sufficiently anti-English to satisfy any antipodean son of Erin. But what brought the two young men most forcibly together and cemented their regard for each other was their concern for poetry. Such evidence as survives suggests that poetry—its theory, its craft, its making—was the principal stuff of their conver-sation. Between 1894 and 1902 Brennan composed the bulk of the verse which would later constitute *Poems 1913*, and often seems to have used O'Reilly as a sounding board against which to test his latest work. Certainly, up until the turn of the century he was in the habit of sending his friend manuscript copies of his poems, often quite soon after they had been written. On 2 June 1896, thus, he copied out the pieces then entitled "Cities" and "Imogen", inscrib-ing the manuscript "C.B. for D. O'R."[8] On 28 July 1897 he wrote out "What of the Battles I Would Win,", this time with the inscrip-tion "To the Poet Dowell O'Reilly."[9] On 7 August 1899 he sent off a text of "Red Autumn in Valvins," addressed from the "Lilith-manufactory."[10] O'Reilly, too, was the recipient of ephemeral pieces which did not find their way into the design of the *livre com-posée*. Even these have their interest in revealing Brennan's current preoccupations. In several he adopts the Hamlet pose that he found especially congenial in 1895-96:

Conceive me if you can
one of no Julian clan
who calls him Hamlet-kind
kick'd hard behind

when pride & spirit had fail'd
ridiculously assail'd
& driven ass upon
his Rubicon[11]

In another piece from the same humorous sequence ("The Shadow of the Black Diamond") he parodies Emerson's "Brahma":

If the O'Reilly think me dark
or if my owner think me plain
they know not well the subtle lark
I play and cut & come again[12]

Alongside the genuine affection and regard which prompted such communications, however, there existed fundamental differences of opinion between the two men about the art of poetry, and how it should be practised in Australia. One basic disagreement was over the issue of a conscious Australianism in local verse. By no means a nationalist of the bush ballad school, O'Reilly nevertheless took the view that poems written in Australia should have a discernible Australian content—a theory which, in his mild and somewhat derivative way, he had put into effect in both his published books of verse. *Australian Poems*, indeed, announces in its very title the bias of its author's attitudes. Brennan's bias was, of course, quite the reverse. Local phenomena certainly do appear in his lines, but most usually at the prompting of inner need. On the rare occasions that he could be goaded into writing, immediately and overtly, about Australian data, he was likely to adopt a tone of sardonic mockery. On one occasion, thus he prefaced a holograph text of the sonnet, "Fire in the Heavens", with the words, "NOON: YE JAMIESON VALLEY AT KATOOMBA: SOMETHING AUSTRALIAN FOR BRERETON: NOT FOR YE IST TIME COPIED OUT."[13] In similar vein he addressed the piece known as "Eucalypti" to O'Reilly in the following terms: "SOMETHING AUSTRALIAN, PATRIOTIC, for O'REILLY, M.P., the *Bulletin* and the PUBLIC generally."[14]

The aesthetic arguments between Brennan and O'Reilly, however, went beyond disagreement about local content in verse.

They centred and (as Terry Sturm has shown) split on the theories of art expressed by James McNeill Whistler, whose work Brennan had enthusiastically discovered while he was abroad. The key poem in this regard is the piece entitled "Simple Addition", written by Brennan to refute O'Reilly's "claim that Whistler's aesthetic was 'a caveman's idea of a picture' ".[15] For all their humour, Brennan's stanzas seriously assert his doctrine of the proper relation between art and nature, of the artist's need and right to filter sense phenomena through the fine mesh of his own consciousness. The caveman's view of art (directly opposite, of course, to Brennan's) is stated thus:

> so don't go flattening Nature out
> suppressing detail at your will
> he who would offer her this flout
> his general effect is nil.[16]

This primitive prescription has unfortunately commanded a following right down to modern times. The last stanza of "Simple Addition" deplores the continuing vitality of the caveman tradition:

> His children flourish'd like the bay
> uncircumcis'd, they linger on
> & to the very Judgment Day
> shall live—in Gath and Ascalon.

Lest O'Reilly should fail to take the point, Brennan spelt out its local pertinence in a marginal comment to the final line: "or Parramatta &c."

In practice, the debate resolved itself into prolonged and often vehement arguments about what O'Reilly alleged to be the "obscurity" of Brennan's verse and what Brennan defended as the necessary means of expressing his complex intellectual and emotional themes; at the same time Brennan rejected O'Reilly's plea for "naturalness" in poetry, which he dismissed as merely a too cheap and easy appeal to a popular audience. In the event—perhaps swayed by Brennan's intellectual force in discussion, almost certainly influenced by his more powerful personality—O'Reilly seems, in some measure at least, to have accepted Brennan's position. By 1898, indeed, he was willing to express some admiration for Brennan's French master, Mallarmé. On 5 November 1898, barely two months after Mallarmé's death, he published this obituary tribute on the Red Page of the *Bulletin:*

"The Butterfly of Night"
A Symbolist Poem, written to commemorate Mallarmé's 56th Birthday

[For the Bulletin]
The Chrysalis is free!
No more the spun cocoon of yellow and white
Subtly inwoven with threads of rarer light
Crumples wide wings from infinite liberty.
Unfolded now, their trembling tips
Darken the confines of the last eclipse.
One odorous plume upslanting flings
In eddying rings
The ashes of celestial things.
The nether dips
Along sealed eyes and ever-silent lips
As, on eternal flight,
Floats out the phantom Butterfly of Night.

D.

The O'Reilly who could compose those lines had come a long way from *Australian Poems* and *Pedlar's Pack*. Yet not even in 1898 (or at any other time in his life) was he willing completely to submit to Brennan's intellectual dominance. His admiration for his friend's great abilities and achievements could never quite overcome his suspicion (even resentment) of what he took to be Brennan's élitist attitude towards art. The publication of "The Symbolist" was in part O'Reilly's intellectual rebellion against the view of poetry of which Brennan was the most conspicuous local representative.

It was also, to be sure, a rebellion of a rather more personal and emotional nature. The early years of the friendship appear to have been characterized by a quite genuine sense of camaraderie, typified in these lines written by Brennan and dated 30 August 1896:

Beneath the midnight's Low'ring murk
a sleepy rhymer tramped and curst
from Redfern O the weary work
and up the hill of Darlinghurst

and shadowless beneath no star
his brain mechanic whirl'd his thought
O had I found in some bazaar
what he who sold his shadow bought

but that my pain be not unshared
upon O'Reilly be this curse

who in his climbing well hath fared
to loose this tightened knot of verse.[17]

On 14 May 1897 Brennan, still a bachelor, sent, in what must have
been one of many such notes, an invitation to O'Reilly and Julian
Ashton to dine with him in five days' time at the Paris House.[18] On 6
October of the same year he issued a prospectus for an enlarged edition of *Towards the Source*, naming O'Reilly as patron of the
enterprise.[19] It was in December 1897, however, that Brennan married Anna Werth. Thereafter (at least for a few years) his habits were
perforce more domestic; it is from about the time of his marriage
that his relationship with O'Reilly seems to have become more distant, to have become tinged even with a certain dislike.

By mid 1899, Brennan's correspondence makes clear, he was
suffering increasing impatience with O'Reilly and his circle of
literary acquaintances. On 30 June 1899 he wrote to Brereton,
"O'Reilly was up here on Monday night, ate plentifully of
sauerkraut for the first time in his life, borrow'd my umbrella, &
went to see Irvine."[20] Irvine, along with Brennan, Brereton, and
O'Reilly, was involved in the production of the short- lived journal,
The Australian Magazine. Brennan was apparently dubious about
both the venture itself and some of his associates in it, as his letter to
Brereton makes clear:

> not knowing whither he [O'Reilly] tended he fell in among the "New
> Boys", couldn't do any business & carried away an ineffaceable
> memory of Adams showing his white teeth perpetually—like Catullus
> Ignatius. (who polished his teeth with his own p)—& Beattie looking
> deeply inspired and Adams telling simperingly how somebody said
> that Beattie ought to get a large brooch made with the name chelab on
> it & wear it on his binjie—Ha Ha cavernously from Beattie who
> began to tell simperingly what somebody had said of Adams—et
> patati et patata. And thus is literature made ...

Brennan's sense of estrangement from much that constituted
the local community of letters is here all too apparent. That O'Reilly
himself was to be included among those who outraged his imagination is hinted at as early as September 1898, in another letter to
Brereton. "This is the kind of doggerel", Brennan wrote, "I used to
send to O'Reilly."[21] The air of dwindling intimacy hangs heavy over
another letter of the period, this time to O'Reilly himself:

> Herewith I send this month's due—with revise of last month's

sending. You, of course, instead of following suit, keeping your word, & doing some decent work, will only endeavour to "get off" some smart remarks on mine—the result being cheap, nasty, impertinent (in all senses) with nothing more original in it than the remark that I am "obscure."

—*These* remarks of mine are not merely the outcome of personal smart, or anger at the way in which you break your promises. They arise from sheer *disgust* at the spectacle you present. Here you are, "getting off" with the greatest self-satisfaction possible, glib washinesses about Impressionism (which you don't understand) verse latent in prose (& you won't write either!) & God-knows-what other *rot* compared with which your very hustings speeches are jeweller's windows—when you might have been &— yet might be ... who knows what? Has the Pedlar died since '88? '88! nearly ten years off! ... — where is he? & what are you? For ...'s sake, if you won't speak *as you can*, shut up! &— I don't want to see you shut up.

Ponder all this ...

Yours ever
Chris: Brennan[22]

After such an outburst, it is hardly surprising to discover the harsh explicitness of Brennan's remark to Brereton in 1899: "O'Reilly visited me on Tuesday night. Isn't he altogether too child*ish*? (German distinction between child*ish* & child*like*—is it English?)."[23]

By the end of the decade of the nineties, then, a friendship which had started out with shared hopes, energy, and aspirations of young manhood was being corroded by bitterness, hostility, and sometimes blank misunderstanding of an alternative point of view. O'Reilly, for his part, must have been galled by Brennan's increasing psychological ascendancy and what (with some justice) he took to be his intellectual arrogance. Brennan, on his side, found O'Reilly's aesthetic theory and practice altogether too simplistic and limiting, his involvement in trivial local affairs both time wasting and imaginatively debilitating. In this worsening situation, O'Reilly seems to have channelled all his sense of grievance into continuous complaints about Brennan's cavalier attitude towards his audience, the reading public. Brennan summed up the grounds of his alienation in a verse letter to Brereton of 1 August 1899:

The editors that long for public pence
whom I had set with back against the fence
& charged to print or not the rotten trifles
or nought of what my bosom's captive stifles
have chosen the latter, wisely, since not song

but greasy pence is all for which they long:
O'Reilly frothing fragrantly & free
turns loose his weltering monster-haunted sea
& mad mirage of misfit metaphors;
his democratic mind of course abhors
my supercilious hermitry, because
(say I) I irk his sloth with praise of Laws
(says he) I write but for the bloated 'few';
he teaches me my English ('tis not new)—
I only hope his boys don't take it down—
he excommunicates me from renown;
says 'artful aid' he never has abused,
then lays him back 'complacently amused'
...[24]

Under the circumstances, O'Reilly's publication of "The Symbolist" less than a year after Brennan had penned his rhymed epistle to Brereton must be regarded as the well-nigh inevitable outcome to which the whole course of the friendship had been tending since it began nearly a decade earlier. The "Cyrus Brown" episode, however, does more than sum up the personal differences of opinion and temperament between a major poet and a minor. Even a preliminary scrutiny of the facts in the case suggests that it has a profoundly exemplary value for understanding the whole literary climate of Sydney in the 1890s. A more prolonged acquaintance with its nuances and shadings may well enforce the judgment that, quite as much as the already celebrated debate between Lawson and Paterson in the pages of the *Bulletin* during 1892, it stands as a paradigm for the status of the poetic imagination during one of the crucial periods of our literary history.

The friendship between Brennan and O'Reilly did not, of course, come to a full stop with the appearance of "The Symbolist", though it was never again resumed with quite the old trust and candour. There is, however, evidence that by the end of 1901 O'Reilly had made some effort to repair the breach between them. On 2 November 1901 there appeared in the Sydney University magazine, *Hermes*, a sonnet printed over O'Reilly's characteristic signature, "D", and simply entitled "C.B.":

Green twilight trembles in the Autumn skies
 Translucent shadows lap and overflow
The garden, and the glimmering poplar-row,
 And battlemented hill. The planets rise

As he pursues his solitary emprise
  Against the sword of Cherubim, to know
The perfect beauty of the flowers that blow
  Deep in the mist that dreams of Paradise:

— And the rich guerdon of his steadfast eyes,
    And rare desires that through his passion glow,
  And crystal light with which the stars bestrow
    The soul that through the empyrean flies,

  And consecrated to the god who lies
    Asleep, by the broad lake of Fontainebleau.[25]

Whether O'Reilly made any other gestures of reconciliation is not known, but that Brennan responded favourably to his approaches is indicated by the fact that on 2 March 1902 he transcribed a copy of "Twice now the lucid fiction of the pane", and inscribed it "For D. O'R./C.B."[26] Thereafter for some four years the record is largely silent about their relationship. About 1906, however, the old enmities and tensions seem to have flared up again. A letter from O'Reilly to Brereton of 30 March 1906 contains a wry allusion to Brennan as "the oracle of the Public Library."[27] Later in the same year (probably October) O'Reilly, again writing to Brereton, reverts with some irony and animus to his theme of Brennan's intellectual arrogance, his scorn of popular approval:

> You and [Brennan] taught me all I know of technical verses—you handle words as a girl handles flowers—he bullies them into submission as old Frederic bullied his giant guards. I like your freedom and grace—I like his reserve and concentration. But his contemptuous attitude that doesn't please himself but does please others well able to understand is mere egoism gone mad. I admire and try to live up to his ideal of trying to do your best work solely to please your best self—a mere platitude in Art of course—but his corollary that whatsoever pleases thousands must ipso facto be bad is merely stupid. He divides the world into two classes:
> 1. ME
> 2. The Philistines
> I think the artist may as well recognize three classes:
> 1. ME
> 2. The large class that can appreciate the beauties of the Bible and Shakespeare
> 3. The Philistines
> And if, in endeavouring to satisfy Class I (always the first consideration) we incidentally please class 2 we should feel pleasure and frankly admit it.

Brennan doesn't care a damn for the Public (i.e. everybody) — and *Publishes* his works—with eccentric frills too, to attract the stupid curiosity of the Public he derides! He scorns the *Public*—but sees that "Poppies" (especially adapted to public intelligence) is published in a "Popular" Anthology. What of it! Brennan has a perfect right to be himself! Of course he has; but the danger is that with a man of great virtues and vices, only the lower half is visible to those who look up ...

I said all I have said to you to him; only much better—I addressed him from the balcony—he was amused—so was I.

Yours ever
Dowell O'Reilly[28]

Early in the following year (13 February 1907) O'Reilly was complaining to Brereton, "I see Brennan seldom, and when I ask him to criticize he merely blows continuously through his lips or some other part of his volcanic personality."[29] It was in 1907, too, that both O'Reilly and Brennan, through the good offices of Bertram Stevens, became members of the Casuals Club, an informal literary and artistic society that met fortnightly in a variety of hotels and restaurants around Sydney.[30] The simultaneous presence of the two poets at a meeting of the Casuals was not always calculated to engender that good fellowship and *bonhomie* that the club aimed at. Indeed, on 4 September 1908, O'Reilly wrote to Brereton about events at a recent meeting of the group;

I am really troubled about Brennan. It never occurred to me, until last Tuesday, that he could possible "go under", but his extraordinary outburst sets one thinking.

I wrote to him when I got home—expressing the regret I felt that I should ever have wounded him—a flag of truce a gentlemanly Civil Servant would have assuredly answered promptly—or was it a red rag to an infuriated Centaur—I don't know what it was—or which it is—but the answer has not arrived.

I owe a lot to Brennan—just as the battered traveller owed a lot to the thieves as well as to the good Samaritan—working together, they enlarged his knowledge of life immensely ...

And now I begin to feel that, while the eclipse of his great shadow was good for me, I am passing out of it and may as well twinkle as best I can no matter what he thinks. Hitherto, I have always thought him a *big* man, as well as a big mind—his tipsy-petulant allusion to "Silas [*sic*] Brown" was at once sad and exhilarating (Do I amuse you?—I amuse myself—most of all, when most serious—God help me!—a pregnant thought strikes my heart—my emotions labour—it leaps into words—a squealing bloody joke) Sad—because I had never thought he could be so little—Exhilarating, because I wondered whether his vitriolic contempt for my work might not be partly his vitriolic contempt for "Silas Brown".[31]

Brereton, cast as he so often was in the role of peacemaker, did his best to reassure O'Reilly. His reply is dated 4 September 1908:

... You are taking Silas Brown to [sic] seriously; only one need do that. You know Brennan's defect of mental vision, surely—his confusion of perspective. Something is preying on his mind and has been for a good while. I have felt your apprehensions for his safety, and have been seriously alarmed at his violence; but he still has to wrestle for himself, and none of us can help him. But if he ever does go under there may be others in the plunge: did that strike you too? I wish I could do something—attempt it and be flicked off as a worrying fly! ...[32]

Whether or not through Brereton's intervention, once again a *détente* was effected, for on 18 September 1908 O'Reilly sent this letter to Brereton:

What a large—in fact immense night that was! "Brennanus Rex" was really royal in his amende.

I feel I owe it to him—and myself—to withdraw and apologize for my fraternal doubts breathed in your ear. I told you I wrote to him: he took me aside and in that glowing sincerity that is in him at his best, he told me my letter "had touched him to the heart"—that his resurrection of the smelly Silas Brown was inexcusable—that whom the Lord loveth He abuseth, and he had been annoyed at my not working for some years past, and finally he said (while I threw a record chest) "Brereton—and—you have got what I have not—you do naturally what I do by har-r-d wor-r-k" ...[33]

The happy outcome of the incident speaks eloquently of Brennan's reserves of Irish charm, yet the quarrel itself seems unhappily symptomatic of dangerously destructive tendencies at work within him. That in a moment of drunken anger he chose to revive a piece of trivial name-calling now eight years in the past (and even then could not get the name right) surely confirms Brereton's diagnosis that something was preying on his mind. A large part of his difficulty was, to be sure, centred in his family life. Yet some other elements of his dis-ease were also surely responsible for this seemingly haphazard revival of the "Cyrus Brown" episode. O'Reilly sensed something of the truth when he told Brereton that Brennan's rage was probably directed inward, against himself; equally, Brennan was sidestepping the same truth when he blamed O'Reilly's creative silence for his own intemperate behaviour. If Brennan had some justification for feeling wounded by the original publication of "The Symbolist" in 1900, his irrational rage over the same incident in 1908 can point to nothing but self-destructive frustration at his own imaginative sterility.

The year 1908 saw the composition of "The droning tram swings westward", the last major piece to be incorporated in *Poems 1913*. Thereafter Brennan was never able fully to recapture his creative powers, which had waned indeed almost to extinction by 1903. Nor did he ever again clash with O'Reilly with the vehemence that characterized the encounters of 1900 and 1908—perhaps for the very reason that he felt his imagination to be so paralyzed as to be unresponsive even to threat. The latter end of the relationship, in fact, is a tale of subdued but comparatively settled amity broken only occasionally by a flicker of the old animosities. On 12 April 1911, thus, Brennan subscribed a cordial note to O'Reilly, "Yours /C.B./(no connexion with any C.B. you ever knew)."[34] Two years later he appealed to O'Reilly for assistance in obtaining a clerkship for his brother in the Harbour Trust.[35] In November 1913, however, some incident caused O'Reilly to write two letters to Brereton in which he "complains very bitterly about Brennan's conduct towards him."[36] In August 1914 the weight of a quarter century's friendship pressed in on Brennan when he learned of the death of O'Reilly's wife, moving him to send a heartfelt letter of condolence. For the rest of the war years, as attested by some pleasant but unimportant notes, the relationship remained harmonious if a little distant, warmed now by nostalgia for past years.

During 1920 Brennan, anxiously hoping for an appointment as an Associate Professor at Sydney University and again hard pressed for funds, made successful application to O'Reilly, as he had done so long ago, for a loan.[37] It was, however, in 1921 that the opportunity was offered to O'Reilly to perform the most extraordinary service he might have carried out for Brennan or any other Australian writer of his generation. On 29 September 1921 he received a letter from a friend, the minor poetess Alys Hungerford:

> My dear Dowell,—do not for a moment think I am trying to drag you into a heated correspondence; nor even that this is to thank you for your kind and charming letter—that would take longer than my impatience to tell you what I am going to tell, will allow.—This is it:—

Mrs Dale is going to write to you, or your wife, or both, to ask you to some lunch or tea, or something of a hospitable nature. DO, DO, go,—if you possibly can. Firstly, you will meet a very nice woman of whom possibly Lady M[acmillan] has told you,—and she will meet you, and be nice to her.—But though I put the word "FIRSTLY" up on the above line, I scorn to deceive you: I meant secondly. The firstly is that you can, if you go, perhaps do a good turn to your friend Brennan. She, the nice woman, the Swede, has something to do with the Swedish Government. She very greatly admires both the poetry and the lecturing and the personality of Brennan and thinks that possibly she could get him the NOBEL Prize.

Of course, his poetry, in the more difficult portions, is a little beyond her English; and my thoughts at once flew to you as a Being who could, if he would, help her; I am writing this very humbly, so do not think I am dictating in any way.—I feel I am not up to a level from whence I could explain Brennan: but you are. Do be a lamb, and do so. She is dying to meet Brennan also; but he might not see fit to explain himself or his poems. But I should like him to receive the Nobel Prize ...

Yours sincerely
Alys Hungerford

P.S. Do not say I mentioned the Nobel Prize, when you meet the ladies mentioned farther back.[38]

Whether O'Reilly ever received or accepted Mrs. Dale's invitation to "something of a hospitable nature" is not certain. It is certain that Brennan was not awarded the Nobel Prize. In 1921 it went to Anatole France, and in 1922 to the Spanish dramatist, Benavente Y. Martinez. In 1923 Dowell O'Reilly died, having been granted no further chance to assist his friend of thirty years. There is, however, a rather touching piquancy in this closing episode in a long and often ambivalent relationship. There was probably no real chance of Brennan's being awarded the Nobel Prize, nor perhaps would he have desired it. Yet that Dowell O'Reilly, the maligned champion of the poet's public responsibilities should have been even marginally concerned in any effort to bring him this highest of international honours involved an irony that Brennan above all would have recognized and enjoyed.

9

Such is Life and the Observant Reader

JOHN BARNES

At the beginning of *Such is Life* Tom Collins remarks that his proposed plan of selecting and amplifying certain diary entries "will afford to the observant reader a fair picture of Life, as that engaging problem has presented itself to me". Like so many of Collins's remarks about himself, this has an ironical edge, which is apparent only after one has read—and re-read—the whole work. The "observant reader" comes to see that *Such is Life* does show *how* life has "presented itself" to a very observant and exact chronicler (which is what Tom Collins claims to be), who does not always grasp the significance of what he is chronicling. Thus the reader is implicitly invited to assume part of the responsibility normally carried by the narrator in a work of prose fiction. Furphy intends that the reader should discover the inadequacies of the nominal narrator as an interpreter of the circumstances he records, and so experience directly the "problem" which fascinates Collins through the book—the problem of making sense of what happens in life. That, at any rate, is what I take to have been Furphy's intention in *Such is Life* as he originally wrote it.

Once alerted to the tendency of the narrator to misinterpret happenings, the reader finds himself pitting his wits against those of Tom Collins; and this intellectual challenge to the reader is obviously part of the enjoyment which the novel offers—to the "observant reader". A simple and amusing example of Collins's being unable to see what is obvious to the reader is his bewilderment at the "almost comically Scottish" appearance of Mrs. Sollicker's child. "The coming Australian is a problem", he declares, with a sidelong glance at theories about the future Australian. All the relevant facts about the Sollicker marriage have been revealed in the conversation of the preceding pages, and Collins's identification of the national characteristics of the husband and wife ought to be enough to ensure that the reader will arrive at the right conclusion—which apparently never occurs to the bemused Collins.

A recent commentator, Professor Barry Argyle, has suggested a parallel between this incident and the earlier visit which Collins makes to the O'Hallorans. He writes:

> The situation recalls the earlier one concerning Collins's Irish Catholic new-chum friend, Rory O'Halloran, also a boundary-rider, married and with one child, Mary. Unlike Mrs Sollicker, Mrs O'Halloran angrily answers Collins's same waggish question about the child's age with a Protestant Irish concern for truth's simplicity. Even to the obtuse Collins, Rory and his wife appear unhappily wed. Mary, her father's single love, is the only reason for the marriage, Mrs O'Halloran having been formerly something of a shanty queen whom marriage appears merely to have embittered. Her nature and her past are sufficient to indicate that she was Warrigal Alf's adulterous wife.[1]

On first reading this I was brought up with a jolt. It's true that Collins asks his question about the child's age on both occasions. Mrs. Sollicker's reply is one of the pieces of evidence which point to the inescapable conclusion that the child's father is not Sollicker but his Scottish employer, M'Intyre, after whom the child is in fact named. She is naively delighted at Collins's pretended incredulity when she tells him the child's age. By contrast, Mrs. O'Halloran curtly rebuffs Collins's attempt to flatter her through the child. The exchange does reveal her to be embittered, as Professor Argyle suggests; but does it point to some deeper significance, some closer parallel with Mrs. Sollicker, whom M'Intyre has married off to a servile employee? The connection between Mrs. O'Halloran and Warrigal Alf had never occurred to me, but here it was assumed with a confidence worthy of Tom Collins himself.

Reviewing the book in which the above passage appears, Brian

Kiernan complained that Professor Argyle lightly tossed off "a discovery that has eluded generations of readers", and observed tartly that "because of the lack of explanation or reference, it is impossible for the plodding reader to follow the tracks that led the mercurial author to this 'discovery'".[2] While we do not know how Professor Argyle arrived at this conclusion, we can appeal to the text itself. What evidence is there that the story of the O'Hallorans is connected with the central "love story" of Alf Morris and Molly Cooper in a way we have not previously recognized? Have readers up till now missed one of what Frank Dalby Davison called Furphy's "secret intentions"?[3]

Warrigal Alf's wife is known to us only through the stories told by Cooper and by Warrigal Alf himself. In chapter I Cooper gives a summary of what happened after Alf (whom he does not once name) jilted the disfigured Molly.

> Then he begun to stop away altogether; an' by-'n'-by ne suddenly got married to a girl out o' the lowest pub. for ten mile round; an' his father—real decent ole bloke he was—he told him never to show his face about the place agen. (P. 27.) *

Alf is helped by an uncle who arranges for him to take over a sawmill:

> ... an' I believe he got on splendid for a couple or three year; an' his wife had one picaninny—so we come to hear—an suddenly he balled her out with some other feller. I on'y got hearsay for it, mind, but I know it's true; for it's just what ought to happen. Anyhow, the hand of God was on him, an' he got it hot an' heavy. Accordin' to accounts, he sold out, an' give her the bulk o' the cash, an' then he travelled. Last year, out on the Namoi, a man told me he seen him bullock drivin' in the Bland country seven year ago. It might be him, or it might n't. (P. 27.)

That is all Cooper has to tell about Alf and his wife. In chapter IV Warrigal Alf, ill and remorseful, insists on telling Collins four stories of unfaithful wives and how their husbands behaved on discovering the truth. The fourth story is about a saw-mill owner:

> He had been married a couple of years, and had one child. I could n't say that he actually loved his wife; in fact, she was n't a woman to inspire love, though she was certainly good-looking. At her very best, there was nothing in her; at her worst, she was ignorant, and vain, and utterly unprincipled—no, not exactly unprincipled, but nonprincipled.

* Page references are to the 1944 Angus and Robertson edition of *Such is Life*.

155

> She was essentially low—if you understand my meaning—low in her
> tastes and aspirations, low in her likes and dislikes, low in her
> thoughts and her language, low in everything. She may not have been
> what is called a bad woman, but—that miserable want of self-
> reverence—I can't understand how— (P. 186.)

Alf's manner of talking about the unfaithful wife clearly suggests a
personal relevance that the other stories do not hold for him. His account confirms what Cooper reports as hearsay, and carries the
story futher: Alf has continued to support his wife, though their little
boy has died. Here we have the explanation of Alf's poverty in spite
of his success as a bullocky, and also the explanation of his mis-
anthropic outlook. As Alf later tells Collins, he believes that his wife
"was divinely assigned to me as a punishment". (P. 189.)

What of Mrs. O'Halloran? Before he actually meets her, Collins has heard that Rory has married "a red hot Protestant, from the
same part of the globe as himself" (p. 69). During the night he spends
in their hut he finds a Bible inscribed to her by the Anglican
clergyman on the occasion of her leaving Northern Ireland for
Australia eight years earlier. It would be tedious—and, I hope,
unnecessary—to go over all the details of place and chronology in
order to prove that this "stern-looking woman of thirty-odd" with
the heavy Irish accent and rigid moral notions could not be the good-
looking barmaid—the "essentially low" woman—whom Alf married and continues to support.

I have quoted this instance of a reader jumping to the wrong
conclusion in order to focus attention on certain aspects of Furphy's
art which seem to me to be worth more discussion than they have
received. Professor Argyle appears to assume that there is more to
the unhappy marriage of the O'Hallorans than "the obtuse Collins"
is capable of discerning. This description of Collins fits well enough
with the general impression we form of him as a result of his failures
to interpret situations rightly; and in the light of the rest of the novel,
it would not be surprising to find that the O'Halloran story was
closely connected with that of Alf and Molly. Questions of identity
are raised in the novel, Rory himself being one of those who has acquired another name, and, as it were, another identity in the
Riverina. But what Professor Argyle has missed, I think, is that in
describing his visit to the O'Hallorans Tom Collins is a reliable narrator, and that in his presentation of the O'Halloran story Furphy's
whole strategy is different from that of the rest of the novel.

What I want to argue is that in chapters II and V—in which the O'Halloran story is contained—Furphy has altered the relationship between the narrator and the reader, with important consequences for the novel as a whole. These two chapters were written in 1901, five years after Furphy completed the first version of *Such is Life*, and replaced the two much longer chapters, which were afterwards rewritten as *Rigby's Romance* and *The Buln-buln and the Brolga*.[4] In *Such is Life* as he originally designed it, Furphy undertook the immensely difficult task of writing a narrative which made clear to the "observant reader" what was hidden from the narrator. The failure of the narrator to recognize the patterns in his own narrative was the philosophic point. In Tom Collins's misreading of the book of his own life Furphy was showing how the human mind is defeated by the tangle of circumstances. However, in the new chapters he grasped his central theme of the "ageless enigma" of life in a subtly different way, which avoided the difficulties inherent in his original conception, and significantly altered the emphasis of the total work.

In the nomadic community of *Such is Life* Tom Collins's sympathies are with the bullockies; but although he is a former bullocky, he is not regarded by them as one of themselves. Mosey's description of him as "My lord Billy-be-damned", and Dixon's suspicious comment—"Too thick with the (adj.) squatters for my fancy. A man never knows what game that bloke's up to"—indicate the reservations felt by the bullockies, despite their friendliness. Collins does not strike the bullockies or his other acquaintances like the squatter Stewart, as being obtuse or foolish. Quite the reverse. Beside the other bushmen Collins appears as the superior intelligence, and for all his pedantry he has a breadth of real knowledge and a capacity for reasoned argument beyond that of his companions. Recording the talk around the camp fire he observes justly: "A metaphysical question keeps slipping away from the grasp of the bullock driver's mind like a wet melon-seed" (p. 37). It's a mark of his intellectual difference from his fellows that we cannot imagine any of them capable of such an observation.

And, of course, the style (or, more accurately, styles) in which the book is written establishes Collins as being able to see more than any other individual within the world of the novel, and preserves a kind of distance between him and that world. There are dead pas-

JOHN BARNES

sages where the prose becomes still and inert, but the characteristic note is a lively, almost self-mocking verbal awareness. Collins can write plainly, but his usual manner is an amalgam of literary allusion and colloquial speech, which impresses upon us his relish for life in all its incongruity.

Not only is Collins a witty, reflective—and sometimes verbose—commentator, who moves in thought far beyond the mental bounds of his companions, he is also, on most occasions, a shrewd and precise observer of men and manners. At the beginning of the novel he appears as the presenter of the bush company, introducing the bullockies with neat thumbnail sketches which must give us confidence in his judgment. And nowhere in the novel do we have cause to doubt Collins's assessments of the characters of the people he meets, except for Alf Morris and Molly Cooper. Whatever his faults, they are not serious moral faults: he is throughout the exponent of the humane values that the novel affirms.

All this might lead us to expect Collins to be a wholly reliable narrator. He is observant, he gives us exact details of scene and incident, he is unquestionably knowledgeable about bush life; and as an author he explicitly rejects the conventions of romantic fiction. This is another way of saying that in most respects Tom Collins is Furphy's *alter ego*. But in his failures as an interpreter Collins is to be sharply distinguished from Furphy. At the end of *Such is Life* Collins is unaware of "the patchwork web of life" that he has displayed to us. Furphy's irony is finally working against his narrator and his illusion that he understands what has been happening.

In the course of the novel Collins's love of theory and speculation—of philosophizing, as he would call it—distorts his sense of fact. He can size up Sollicker accurately and exploit his vanity, but he cannot put two and two together when it comes to explaining the physical characteristics of Sollicker's child: "And, as I looked at the child, I drifted into a labyrinth of insoluble enigmas and perplexing hypotheses—no new thing with me, as the sympathetic reader is by this time well aware". (P. 179.) Here is the reason for Collins's missing the obvious. Instead of using his common-sense (of which he shows plenty at other times) he indulges his liking for abstract reasoning. At crucial moments in the narrative Collins's philosophizing makes him obtuse: he stops using his intelligence, as it were, and constructs a version of reality which is at odds with the reader's perceptions.

158

There are occasions in the novel when Collins is consciously pretending to be what he is not. He assumes a false personality, for instance, when he encounters Sollicker, and chameleon-like, a completely different and equally false personality when he encounters Terrible Tommy. Running through the whole of *Such is Life* is an interest in the way we are forced to play different parts in our relationships with others. Collins acts a number of roles, which involve varying degrees of pretence, and he is always very quick to draw our attention to the sort of figure he is cutting in a particular situation. There is always a hint of amusement, a sly self-deprecating note, in his descriptions of his own mental processes; but his "Hamlet mood" is not a pretence. He points out his "besetting sin" with a complacency that should be familiar to all of us. It would be easy to accept that Tom Collins was pretending to be obtuse about the Sollickers' child, but the novel asks us to believe that he was lost in a labyrinth of thought. When Collins is "afflicted" in this way he ceases to be a reliable narrator, and the observant reader must become his own interpreter.

This conception of Tom Collins owes a great deal, I think, to Furphy's reading of *Tristram Shandy*, an influence that was more apparent in the first verson of *Such is Life*. Furphy was amused by the notion that man's intellectual powers can blind him to reality. The spectacle of the bookish man unable to tell what is happening in front of his nose has always been good for a laugh. Though Collins is clownish, he is much more than a comic type. As I have been suggesting, he is a man who is ordinarily very alert, quick-witted—even at the time when he is speculating about ethnology, he is deceiving Sollicker. His "low comedy acting", as Stewart calls it, is an expression of Collins's lively understanding of the men he is dealing with. Yet, at crucial moments in the narrative he must stop being wide-awake, and drift into a "philosophic mood". Furphy's manipulation of his narrator at this point does create some strain in the novel, most severely in the description of the visit to Nosey Alf.

There would be pretty general agreement among readers, I think, that the story of Alf Jones and Molly Cooper, the most elaborate of the hidden narratives, is something of a disappointment. It has been called novelettish, and the criticism doesn't seem unfair. What is disturbing in a novel which draws attention to the conventions of romantic fiction only to mock them is the unrecognized conventionality of the lovers. Molly was modelled on a real person whom Furphy had known,[5] but the character is sentimentally conceived. Like Kate Vanderdecken in *Rigby's Romance*, Molly is the ever-faithful martyr of love; and Alf is the betrayer, plagued with remorse. While another novelist might have explored the motives and feelings of these two characters, Furphy's energies are concentrated on making plausible the narrator's failure to recognize the relationship of the two Alfs and his own part in their story.

Furphy intends that the reader should see the connections between Cooper's camp-fire yarn in chapter I and Warrigal Alf's incomplete confession in chapter IV, and spot the identity of Nosey Alf. There are various clues—such as the name of Molly—which should lead the reader in the right direction. Furphy's handling of the story reveals him to be a cunning artificer. In chapter I, for instance, he introduces Warrigal Alf, but contrives that he won't meet Cooper, who is a stranger to the region. Later, when Cooper has asked his companions not to use the name of Alf ("I got reason to hate that name"), they actually discuss Warrigal Alf without once mentioning his name. At this time there is no reason for Collins to associate the young man of Cooper's narrative with the morose bullock-driver whom he knows as Warrigal Alf. And in chapter IV, four months later, it is hardly surprising that Collins doesn't make the connection. When Alf asks him which of the four cuckolded husbands, whose stories Alf has told, acted correctly Collins sees himself as humouring a sick man, and begins to lecture him on Shakespearean examples of jealousy. Alf insists on an answer, and Collins approves of the man who separated from his wife but continued to support her. Much relieved by this answer, Alf is now ready to confide in Collins, but Collins is only half-listening; the sound of the bells on Alf's team indicates that they are being driven away, and Collins hurries off in pursuit. He carries with him a mental image of Alf's wife—"a tawny-haired tigress, with slumbrous dark eyes"—which comes straight out of the Ouida romance he was re-reading earlier in the day. In his own mind he constructs a sentimental romance around a dead wife, and convinces himself that he has divined the secret of Alf's unhappiness. Later he repeats to Stewart this wholly imaginary version of Alf's life, "obtained by an intransmissible power of induction, rare in our times" (p. 212). Tom Collins has unconsciously demonstrated to us the seductive power of romantic fiction.

This version of Alf's past is firmly fixed in Collins's mind when, two months later, he talks about him to Molly, whom he knows only as Alf Jones or Nosey Alf. Collins never realizes that he is misrepresenting Warrigal Alf's situation, or that he is influencing the future course of Molly. In this episode Furphy has set himself a very difficult task: as chronicler, Collins must so describe what happens that the reader sees through Molly's disguise; and, at the same time as he is drawing our attention to the feminine characteristics of Nosey Alf and his fascination with the other Alf, Collins must fail to arrive at the right interpretation. Collins describes Nosey Alf's appearance very fully, noting how apart from the disfigured nose, the boundary rider's face is "More beautiful, otherwise, than a man's face is justified in being ... " (p.304), and how unmasculine he is in build; but the possibility that Nosey Alf is a woman in disguise simply doesn't occur to him. And the reason for this is that he has a ready-made explanation for anything odd in Nosey Alf's behaviour: "Ah! years of solitary life, with the haunting consciousness of frightful disfigurement, had told on his mind. Moriarty was right. And I remembered that the moon was approaching the full." (P. 308.) As a result of talking with Moriarty, the storekeeper on Runnymede, Collins expects Nosey Alf to be "cranky", and so he blunders on amiably, until Alf breaks down and weeps. "It's pure effeminacy to brood over such things ... " (p.322) he tells Nosey Alf, who has referred to his facial disfigurement, and quotes the proverb that "A woman's first duty is to be beautiful". He is quite unaware of the pain he is giving, and makes a joke about Nosey Alf's reaction: "The boundary rider laid down his pipe, rested his forehead on his arm upon the table, and for a minute or two sobbed like a child. It was dreadful to see him. He was worse than Ida, in an argument with Mrs Beaudesart; he was as bad as an Australian judge, passing mitigated sentence on some well-connected criminal." (P. 323.) Collins's good-humoured account of the episode is, by design, insensitive, and inevitably the reader's attitude towards Collins is affected.

During the night Collins wakes, and on going outside sees Nosey Alf kneeling at the fence weeping, as he faces the setting moon:

> Thou art in a parlous state, shepherd, thought I; and it then occurred to me that my own acute, philosophic temperament was one of the

things I ought to be thankful for. But I couldn't feel thankful; I could only feel powerless and half-resentful in the presence of a distress which seemed proof against palliative, let alone antidote. At length the moon disappeared; then the boundary man's forehead sank on his arms, a calm came over him, and I knew that his shapeless vagaries had taken form in prayer. So I withdrew to my possum-rug, speculating on the mysterious effect of a ray of lunar light on grey matter protected by various plies of apparently well-arranged natural armour (P. 325.)

The effect of a passage like this is rather curious. The sight of the grieving figure stirs Collins to speculate on the relationship between the moon and insanity. What we are meant to find touching, he sees only as a specimen of insane behaviour. Yet the "reality" which he does not comprehend is on the level of romantic melodrama. Because Furphy has cast Collins in the role of the uncomprehending narrator, he cannot use him to register directly any insights into this love story. Indeed, in the actual narrative of Collins's night at Nosey Alf's hut the real focus of interest is Collins himself.

Throughout *Such is Life* Collins prides himself on his ability to sum people up, and he is naturally intrigued by Nosey Alf. He imagines that Alf will reveal himself through the songs he sings:

Here was my opportunity. I was interested in this boundary man, and resolved to know his history. Rejecting Alf Jones as an assumed name, Nomenology would be at fault here; yet knowing already, by a kind of incommunicable intuition, that he was a Sydney-sider, and had been in some way connected with the drapery-business, I expected to have my knowledge so supplemented by the character of his songs, that—counting reasonably on a little further information, to be gathered before my departure—I should be able to work-out his biography at least as correctly as biographies are generally worked-out. (P. 321.)

This is carefully calculated to show Collins drawing the wrong conclusions from what he has observed. Alf's singing convinces him that Alf is suffering because of a hopeless love (which is, in one sense, true). That Collins, like everyone else, should accept Nosey Alf as a man on meeting isn't surprising. But as the narrative proceeds it is increasingly difficult to accept that Collins could be as obtuse as he is made to appear. The passage I have just quoted is intended to represent Collins's private thoughts about his strange companion, and it makes him seem absurd and unintelligent. The prose is quite unable to suggest the working of the human consciousness—if it was seriously intended to—and it has the effect of reducing Collins to a kind of comic oddity, almost a buffoon. He is manipulated by Furphy in a way that disturbs our sense of him as a person. The long and tedious disgression on music is a serious miscalculation on Furphy's part, but perhaps not as open to objection as the account of Collins lecturing Nosey Alf on ideals of womanly beauty as he undresses. Because Collins appears to be lacking in any tact, any fineness of feeling, in his dealings with the disfigured boundary rider, his status as a character is diminished. This seems to me to be the unintended consequence of Furphy's determination to exploit what he took to be the comic possibilities of the situation.

Another consequence of Collins's obtuseness here is that the reader gets no real insight into Molly Cooper's thoughts and feelings. In a sense, Tom Collins blocks our view of Molly: his authorial commentary is the opposite of illuminating. In this chapter of *Such is Life* Furphy allows himself to be dominated by an idea at the expense of character. Repeated readings of the chapter leave me admiring the ingenuity with which Furphy planted clues and accounted for Collins's failure to spot them; and at the same time feeling that such is not life.

As a small example of how Furphy works in this chapter I want to look again at the passage quoted above. Collins tells us that he knew "by a kind of incommunicable intuition" that Nosey Alf "had been in some way connected with the drapery business ... " Nosey Alf, we recall, corrected him on the subject of dress-materials. But why should he jump to the conclusion that this boundary rider had once been a draper? The explanation is to be found in the description of Collins's adventures in search of trousers in chapter III. When in the darkness he attempts to debag a man, his victim screeches, and "the thought flashed through my mind that he was one of those De Lacy Evanses we often read of in novels".[6] As the newspaper report quoted at the beginning of the chapter makes clear, Collins's intended victim was not a woman in disguise but a drapery assistant. Later during the same adventure, "Jim" Quarterman, riding a horse "*à la* clothes-peg", turns out to be Jemina. This happened three months before the visit to Nosey Alf, and one might well have expected that Nosey Alf's physical appearance and attitudes would have at least stirred suspicion in Collins's mind about the sex of the boundary rider. Collins's "intuition" that Nosey Alf had been a draper's assistant is left as something he can't explain. One would like to suggest that Collins's subconscious is at work, but the text will hardly support such a reading. Furphy is having a sly joke with the "observant reader".

The other major concealed narrative—that involving the deaf swagman, Andy Glover—is managed less factitiously. The moment of strain comes when Collins—himself disguised in borrowed clothes—meets Tom Armstrong and Andy Glover. He succeeds in persuading the Scotsman that he is not the Tam M'Callum whose company Armstrong had so enjoyed. And he is nagged by the thought that he has met Glover on some previous occasion: "Confused identity seems to be in the air. Had I seen that weary-looking figure, and that weather-worn face, before? I couldn't determine; and I can't determine now—but the question has nothing to do with this record." (P. 364.) The last remark is, of course, an incitement to the observant reader to find the answer to the question. The swagmen's story of how he was wrongly accused of burning a haystack and imprisoned for three months, jogs our memories of how Collins set fire to a haystack, but it doesn't have the same effect upon Collins. Instead of searching his memory, he constructs possible hypotheses to explain what he takes to be his illusion of having met Glover before:

> By this time, I had provisionally accounted for my vaguely-fancied recognition of the man. With the circumspection of a seasoned speculatist, I had bracketed two independent hypotheses, either of which would supply a satisfactory solution. One of these simply attributed the whole matter to unconscious cerebration. But here a question arose: If one half of my brain had been more alert than its duplicate when the object first presented itself—so that the observation of the vigilant half instantaneously appeared as an intangible memory to the judgment of the apathetic half—it still remained to be determined which of the halves might be said to be in a normal condition. Was one half unduly and wastefully excited?—or was the other half unhealthily dormant? The thing would have to be seen into, at some fitting time.
>
> But this hypothesis of unconscious cerebration seemed scarcely as satisfactory as the other—namely, that, having at a former time heard Terrible Tommy mention the name of Andrew Glover, my educated instinct of Nomenology, rising to the very acme of efficiency, had accurately, though unconsciously, snap-shotted a corresponding apparition on the retina of my mind's eye. (Fp. 369—70.)

This burlesque of the thinking process might lead one to think that Collins is pulling our leg. Brian Kiernan suggests that Collins "refuses to admit to himself his implication in Glover's false imprisonment", but this reading implies a kind of moral and psychological complexity in the characterization of Collins for which the text gives no warrant. It is the final example of how Furphy attempts to represent man's difficulty in comprehending what he calls "the Order of Things". Unfortunately, Furphy's method of accounting for Collins's unawareness of the real situation and his part in it involves a degree of exaggeration and that makes Collins seem hardly life-like.

Collins is wholly unaware of his responsibility for Glover's suffering. Not only did he commit the act for which Glover was jailed, but he contributed to the illusion of circumstantial evidence against Glover by the ambiguous answers he gave to the questions of Mr. Quarterman. And his warnings about the dangers of criminal prosecution have also rebounded on Glover, as Mr. Quarterman presses a minor charge which is dealt with by his fellow magistrates, instead of a more serious charge which would have had to go to a higher court and would be hard to sustain. Collins's interview with Mr. Quarterman is one of those occasions—like the interviews with Sollicker and Tom Armstrong—where we relish his role-playing; but Collins's cleverness has quite unforeseen consequences, as I've just mentioned. Basically, the situation is a very familiar one in comedy—talking at cross purposes. Both Collins and the Justice of the Peace are secretly congratulating themselves on their shrewdness. We of course get Collins's version: he leaves imagining that he has disuaded Mr. Quarterman from taking any action, and it is only when we hear Glover's story, over four months later, that we recognize the irony of what results from Collins's cleverness. This scene is perhaps the most stylized piece of writing in the whole novel. Furphy's reading of Fielding and Dickens seems to have been put to good purpose here.

The interview with Mr. Quarterman is one of the most entertaining episodes in *Such is Life*, giving full rein to Collins's genial self-mockery. Considered in the total context of the novel, it expresses perfectly Furphy's sense that life is unpredictable, that no man can fully comprehend the patterns that his own actions help to form. Tom Collins remains ignorant of how his actions have affected Andy

Glover, just as he remains unaware of how he has influenced the future of Alf Morris and Molly Cooper. We don't know what the end of that story will be, though we do know that Collins has enabled Molly to find Alf but added confusion by telling her that Alf is a widower.

In the two narratives we have considered there is a discrepancy between what Tom Collins understands and what the observant reader understands. However, in the other major narrative—that concerning the O'Hallorans—there is no such gap. In relation to the O'Hallorans Collins fulfils the traditional role of a narrator, and his extended philosophizing on cause and effect has a direct and obvious bearing on the events he describes. The notion of the obtuse narrator, so bemused by his theories that he is unable to see what is in front of him, has no part in the narration of the story of the O'Hallorans.

The mistake which Collins makes in not stopping to speak to the swagman he sees near Rory's hut is the sort of mistake any bushman might have made. Thinking that George Murdoch is just another sundowner, he allows himself to be ruled by his "instinctive sense of bush etiquette", and in his ignorance of the man's plight he makes the apparently trivial decision which means the difference between life and death. No one could be blamed for reacting as Tom Collins did.

This decision of Collins's is a link in a chain of circumstances that raises most movingly and interestingly the question of man's ability to comprehend the meaning of his own actions. Three months later Collins hears Thompson tell how Mary was lost in the bush and died just before she could be found. He is uneasy and disturbed by the thought that he unwittingly contributed to her death: "Soon a disquietude from another source set my mind at work in troubled calculation of probabilities. At last I said: 'Would you suppose, Steve, that the finding of George Murdoch's body was a necessary incitement among the causes that led to the little girl's getting lost?'" (P. 247.) Thompson is asleep, and anyway there can be no answer to the question. The whole train of circumstances seems to point to man's profound ignorance of the shape of things.

The central concern of Collins's philosophizing throughout the novel is how to account for the way in which things happen. He introduces his chronicle with a summary of the two fundamental hypotheses which men have arrived at to explain how events come to pass. A theme running through the camp-fire discussion in chapter I is how to account for the disasters that have occurred in the lives of the bullockies, who interpret circumstances in differing ways according to their particular superstitions. Thompson believes that he has a curse on him for not paying a debt in full to a dead man. Cooper believes that he is cursed for swearing and sabbath-breaking, and by way of illustration tells the story of Molly as far as he knows it. When Cooper's wagon capsizes the next morning, there is a discussion about the "esoteric cause of the capsize", with Cooper blaming it on his having begun a trip on a Friday, and Thompson putting it down to travelling on a Sunday. To Collins the bullockies appear as "grown-up children" in their superstition.

As far as we can tell from the manuscript and typescript which has survived, Collins's exposition of the "controlling alternative" was not in the original version of *Such is Life*. Its inclusion in the new chapter II reflects a shift in Furphy's attitude towards Collins. The reflections given to Collins in this chapter are serious in tone and relate directly to the narrative. They strike me as representing hard thought on Furphy's part. Collins's theory of the "controlling alternative" is an attempt at a positive statement about life in which free-will and determinism are reconciled in a theory of choice:

> ... each alternative brings into immediate play a flash of Free-will, pure and simple, which instantly gives place—as far as that particular section of life is concerned—to the dominion of what we call Destiny. The two should never be confounded. "Who can control his fate?" asks the ruined Othello. No one, indeed. But every one controls his option, chooses his alternative. (Pp. 85—86.)

Beyond this Collins cannot go: his thinking is agnostic:

> Such momentous alternatives are simply the voluntary rough-hewing of our own ends. Whether there's a Divinity that afterwards shapes them, is a question which each inquirer may decide for himself. (P. 86.)

The very solemnity of the prose with its Shakespearean borrowings and illustrations, and the elaborate railway analogy, all suggest that this piece of theorizing is meant to carry considerable weight. And Collins directs our attention to the bearing of his "afterthoughts" on "my own apparently insignificant decision not to disturb the masterly inactivity of that sundowner under the wilga" (p. 88).

This piece of theorizing is presented as one of the fruits of Collins's experience of life. It is outside the fictional world of the novel, the result of his reflections on the experiences he has chronicled. As it happens, the swagman episode does not illustrate the theory very well. The examples which Collins draws from Shakespeare and his own analogies all involve a person making choices which affect *his* future. Collins's choice—his decision not to speak to the swagman—does not affect his future but that of the swagman—and ultimately that of Rory's daughter. The episode haunts one's memory, not because of the theorizing attached to it, but because it so poignantly expresses the vulnerability of men in the bush. In choosing to do what he thinks is a kindness, Collins has actually sealed the man's fate, as he afterwards realizes. And as the novel unfolds, this particular irony becomes part of the larger irony of circumstance, which prompts comparison with Hardy's fiction.

For most readers of *Such is Life* the O'Halloran story is the most memorable strand in the closely woven pattern, and this, I suggest, is partly because of the role played by Tom Collins. During his visit to Rory's hut he is perceptive and sympathetic, quickly recognizing the unhappiness there. His stature is increased by comparison with Rory, who has made pathetic efforts at authorship, and at the same time one feels his affection for Rory. In chapter V when he hears the story of Mary's death, he comes as close as he ever does to expressing depth of emotion. Throughout Thompson's telling of the search for Mary, Tom Collins and the reader are in the position of listeners for whom the search has a significance it does not have for the story-teller and the other listeners. Quite apart from the skill with which Thompson tells the story—it is Furphy's most extended and successful piece of yarning—the events mean more because the feelings of the reader (and the narrator) are involved. The account of the O'Hallorans is the most intimate view we get of a family in *Such is Life*, and though Furphy exhibits a notable lack of sympathetic insight into Mrs. O'Halloran the account rings true.

The Tom Collins who narrates the story of the O'Hallorans—who appears in chapters II and V, in fact—is not required to become obtuse at critical moments to sustain Furphy's design. He is less of a comic figure, more a conduit of feeling than he is elsewhere in the novel. We feel with him the "ageless enigma" of life as it is expressed in the death of a child.

Furphy's art is at its most creative here, where Tom Collins comes closest to being a direct expression of his own personality. I doubt that *Such is Life* in its original form would have meant as much to us as the version we now have.

10

Henry Lawson's Fictional World

BRIAN MATTHEWS

The aim of every artist is to arrest motion, which is life, by artificial means and hold it fixed so that 100 years later when a stranger looks at it, it moves again since it is life.

I discovered that my own little postage stamp of native soil was worth writing about and that I could never live long enough to exhaust it, and by sublimating the actual into the apocryphal I would have complete liberty to use whatever talent I might have to its absolute top. It opened up a goldmine of other peoples, so I created a cosmos of my own. I can move these people around like God, not only in space but in time too. The fact that I have moved my characters around in time successfully, at least in my own estimation, proves to me my own theory that time is a fluid condition which has no existence except in the momentary avatars of individual people. There is no such thing as *was*—only is.
William Faulkner, Interview with Jean Stein Vanden Heuvel, *The Paris Review*, Spring, 1956

... these people I invent and after that I just run along and put down what they say and do. I don't know always what they are going to develop into myself.
William Faulkner, *Faulkner in the University*, (New York: Random House, 1959), p. 141.

Henry Lawson's *While the Billy Boils* is so clearly established in our minds as a classic of Australian literature[1] that it comes as something of a surprise to be reminded that its initial reception, though undeniably enthusiastic, was also at times grudging and beset with numerous heavy qualifications. There were complaints about his various limitations: "There is not a horse in the book", one reviewer notes incredulously, "from title page to imprint—not one horse!";[2] complaints about his sombreness: "His landscapes are graphic ... but depressing ... blankly monotonous ... dreary places where the poor tortured earth shows its wounds all bare ... ";[3] and perhaps above all, worries about the fragmentary, piecemeal nature of the book: Price Warung, in a positively favourable review, regrets that "There is too much here of the merely ephemeral or the paltry—of the odd scrap written with the urgent need for the guinea ... ",[4] but the most stringent and the most famous objection along these lines was made, of course, by A.G. Stephens.

> Certainly no complaint has to be made on the score of quantity; there is some as to quality, and a good deal as to arrangement. Many of Lawson's sketches are written in series: there is a "Mitchell" sequence, a "Steelman" sequence, a bush sequence, a city sequence, and so on. The obvious way of dealing with these was the best way. They should have been classified and put in sections, so that continuity might be broken and the characters might gain force and distinctness from the massing of impressions. Exactly the opposite course has been followed. The book is like a bad cook's ragout. You get here a mouthful of salt, there one of pepper, the next is meat uncondimented. Not only is power lost, but the haphazard mixture jolts the mind like an unexpected bottom step.
>
> The pity of it is greater because with the best arrangement the matter would seem scrappy and disconnected. Written for occasional publication, these detached sketches have no unity of idea or treatment. Their appeal was bound to be diffused and vague: the least that could be done was to concentrate the interest as far as the slight skeins of similarity permitted, and instead of half-a-hundred taps to strike half-a-dozen blows. It was not done.[5]

Stephens characteristically has isolated the essential problem: it is true that there are, ostensibly, curiosities and irritants in the arrangement of the stories and that numbers of them appear ephemeral and dispensable; candidates for the wastepaper basket as Price Warung observed. Yet if Stephens has identified the right problem, he has, in my opinion, fixed upon the wrong answer.

Returning to *While the Billy Boils* and reading through both series at a sitting, I have been struck not only by a sense of the *newness*, the continuing relevance of this work with which I had fancied myself so thoroughly acquainted, but also by the impression of a greater unity, a more intriguing inter-relatedness, than is usually attributed to these fifty-two diverse stories. The disconnections and the apparent haphazardness which so irritated Stephens are certainly there on the surface; the very form and "look" of *While the Billy Boils* work against notions of interconnection and interdependence of stories, as does the quite justifiable tendency on the part of most readers and critics to single out for special attention those pre-eminent stories which give the book its distinctive flavour and which contribute so heavily to its greatness: for example, "The Union Buries Its Dead", "The Drover's Wife", "The Bush Undertaker". Nevertheless, the impact of that reading-at-a-sitting which I have mentioned, persuades me that there is a unity in *While the Billy Boils* which Stephens entirely missed, and that it is a kind of unity so essentially *modern* that it probably helps to explain why the book seems continually to renew itself, why, "when we turn back to it we are surprised and delighted".[6]

Obviously, the question of the arrangement of the stories compels immediate attention before much else can be said about them with any confidence. Despite Stephens's onslaught, at least one voice was raised in defence of the book as it stood; but the argument, well begun, peters out rather lamely:

> Exception has been taken to the arrangement of the fifty-two sketches ... It is objected that those which deal with one character ... should have been brought together in sequence. But, whatever may be argued in favour of such an arbitrary and rather inartistic grouping, there is much, both in the shape of artistic precedent and principle, to be arrayed upon the other side. As for precedent there are the collected short stories of Kipling ... And such treatment seems the most natural and proper ... If a man talked round the camp fire all Mitchell and all Steelman for a stretch his mate on the track would grow very weary and would probably cut the series short with an expressive, "Blarst yer, stow it." Readers would feel very much the same, whereas now if they are sorry to leave Mitchell, their regret only increases the pleasure with which they come up with him again.[7]

There is something in what he says; indeed, it is a brave try. But the argument scarcely begins to cope with Stephens's battery of charges. Lawson's own contribution to the debate is, in a way, unenlightening. In a letter to George Robertson from Perth a week or so after the Stephens review appeared, he advises:

> Don't take any notice of Stephens' complaints in *Bulletin* review. *It was I who suggested to him the order of selection which he now suggests as his own.* He and the *Bulletin* know that we had to abandon our original plan of selection because the *Bulletin held the sketches which were to complete series and would not put them through.*[8]

About two years later, in January 1899, he returns to the subject in his famous letter to the *Bulletin* on his literary career in Australia:

> While the publication of *While the Billy Boils* was being arranged for the *Bulletin* held some stories and sketches which were to complete the "Steelman" and "Mitchell" series; and as the *Bulletin* could not rush them through, an idea of having them arranged with an eye to sequence had to be abandoned. Which explains the apparently haphazard appearance of the order of the stories and sketches in that volume, and will be responsible for the same thing in my next prose volume ... [9]

I find some of this difficult to fathom: there are fifty-two stories in *While the Billy Boils* and, presumably, despite the many obstructions and delays that undoubtedly plagued the operation, there came a time when Angus and Robertson knew that these fifty-two at least were finally accessible to them and available to be made into a book. Why could not a sequential grouping have been organized at that point? Why could not the *existing* Mitchell and Steelman stories, along with any others that would group naturally, have been placed together in the book? The notion of "completing" the Mitchell and Steelman pieces is also a curious one since, even if one does group, say, the Mitchell stories from this book there is no sense of their moving towards completion, towards a final story, as it were. The character of Mitchell himself develops in certain ways of course, but as the sketches stand, their incompletion—that is their refusal to trace Mitchell through *all* the events of a major part of his life—is one of their strengths. It is in the nature of these sketches that we do not look for a completing or final one, either in this volume or elsewhere in Lawson. In short, Lawson's defence against attacks upon the ordering of his material seems unconvincing on one or two points.

Some of the answers to these questions are to be found, I think, in the fact that Lawson was extremely sensitive to adverse criticism. His response to Stephens's 1896 review provides strong evidence of this sensitivity and throws some light on the issue of the book's internal arrangement. One of the features of this letter to Robertson, from which I have already quoted, is Lawson's obvious concern to boost Robertson's spirits, to bolster him up against unfavourable reviews and the like. Clearly, he doesn't want Robertson to lose confidence in him—a perfectly reasonable and human fear—yet his exhortations show him as peculiarly vulnerable, badly lacking in confidence and a sense of proportion about the real import of adverse comment, even from Stephens's pen: "Don't take any notice of Stephens' complaints ... Don't take any notice of S. or his kind of literary old women. Keep on as you are going and let me keep on as I'm going ... "[10] Just how much notice Lawson himself was taking is shown in the same letter and stands in contradiction of his own urgings to Robertson. The last sentence of Stephens's review reads: "Not the best, but the most promising, are those which tell 'An Unfinished Love Story'. Here, for the first time, Lawson ceases to describe characteristics and starts to create characters." "An Unfinished Love Story" is competent enough but scarcely warrants being distinguished as something in which Lawson was striking an important new note. Yet Lawson, despite his angry dismissals of Stephens, concludes his letter to Robertson with this assurance: "Mind you I think Stevens's [sic] idea, or rather mine, of a novel, or something connected, is right, and I can do it ... I'm at work on a story—an autobiography really—of selection diggings and vagabond life. There will be a lot of that 'Unfinished Love Story' style in it." Thus, almost despite himself, it seems, Lawson offers to Robertson an encouragement which is largely in terms of and based on Stephens's views. The degree to which he has suppressed his own judgment can be gauged not only by the element of desperation in the promise—the "Unfinished Love Story" style would, after all, sit uneasily upon a story of "selection diggings and vagabond life"—but also by his rather wearied reversal of a few months later:

> You mustn't take notice of the drivel to the effect that I should write a long novel—anything in fact save what I *have* written. That was originally one man's idea ... My line is writing short stories and sketches in prose and verse. I'm not a novelist. You will find a man to

write you an Australian novel soon enough. If you were a builder, would you set the painters to do the carpentering?"[11]

It is interesting to note that, once he has unequivocally rejected the notion of writing a novel, it reverts to being Stephens's original idea, not his own! All of this has important implications for the argument about the arrangement of the stories. I have already suggested that there are some practical problems associated with accepting Lawson's explanation about the breaking up of story sequences. To these must be added, I think, considerable evidence of sensitivity to criticism, a tendency to precipitate and ill-considered reply[12] and yet, as well, a painful need to *please* the critics, to disarm criticism. Against this total background, Lawson's response to Stephens makes it appear increasingly likely that he simply laid his hand to the first available retaliatory weapon that seemed viable in order to soften the impact of a tough and damaging judgment ("with the best arrangement the matter would seem scrappy and disconnected"). My own speculation is that Lawson was happy with the arrangement of *While the Billy Boils* until Stephens assailed it so savagely; and that, as far as "An Unfinished Love Story" was concerned, it had not occurred to him to see it as a stylistic departure until Stephens implied that it was. Lawson's own judgment—conscious or half-intuitive—was right in both cases: he capitulated on both points because he did not have the confidence to do otherwise. Whatever the truth of the matter, the reference to abandoning "our original plan" sketchily suggests that some sort of substitute *plan* and not a random confusion, operated in the end. *While the Billy Boils* does have an order of a kind and it is an order which Lawson must have controlled. He said himself, "I selected, revised, and condensed the material for *While the Billy Boils*"[13] and in any case, his remarks already quoted and his manifest and enduring concern with the publishing details and presentation of other, later books, all attest to his care in these matters. But recognizing the precise nature of that order, which is sufficiently understated to have eluded Stephens and other contemporary reviewers, remains a difficult and tantalizing task. There are several obvious ways in which the work might have been arranged: one is the thematic organization, about which Stephens was so trenchant and which was rejected for whatever reason, and the next most obvious is arrangement in the chronological order in which the stories were written. Not only has this *not* been done, it seems to have been as thoroughly disregarded as the thematic method. For example: "The Bush Undertaker" and "The Drover's Wife", which are among the earliest stories, are placed in the second half of the book—the former about half way through; "His Father's Mate", Lawson's first published story, is one of the last few stories of the first section; other relatively early stories—such as "The Union Buries Its Dead", "Baldy Thompson"—are similarly distributed through the book, the last mentioned being placed second last though published in 1894. In short, the chronological order of publication has been so totally ignored that it is clear that the sequence of the stories is either random or is governed by some other set of rules.

At least two recent critics have had something to say about the coherence or otherwise of Lawson's body of work. Stephen Murray-Smith suggests that:

> the apparent untidiness of Lawson is to some extent illusory. His stories all fit loosely together, philosophically and thematically, despite the fact that none of them is designed to. He was, in fact, writing of a world peopled by his characters: a world completely consistent and coherent in itself. He was not writing a series of disconnected studies; in one sense he spent his whole life writing one book.[14]

And Chris Wallace-Crabbe, writing specifically of *While the Billy Boils*, draws attention to the book's incipient, unasserted coherence:

> Many of the stories ... fall into strings or clusters, marked by the recurrence of names, places and even fragments of plot. The book is not arranged to enforce these connections and they often have little importance beyond telling us something about Lawson's habits of composition.[15]

These important comments both throw their weight behind notions of organization in the stories and against randomness; they recognize "connections" (though with differing degrees of emphasis) yet at the same time remain aware of the elusiveness of these connections. But above all, it seems to me that both Murray-Smith and Wallace-Crabbe are looking in the right place for clues to the coherence of Lawson's stories (especially as far as *While the Billy Boils* is concerned). The book holds together by virtue of an inner logic which is chronological in terms of the people it presents—though with some important qualifications and exceptions even in that—and consistent only in so far as those people themselves are consistent. The way in which the stories are connected thus has to do with the fact that it is possible to follow what happens to a particular character over a period of time and a number of stories; but these connections remain loose and elusive because, for various reasons, there are enormous gaps in individuals' experiences as they emerge and there are apparent inconsistencies and seemingly needless obscurities constantly upsetting otherwise neat interdependencies between stories. In the rest of this essay I should like to examine the nature of the book's "inner logic" and explore some of the issues that such an examination raises.

One good example of how these connections work while remaining curiously beyond one's certain grasp, and of how they nevertheless become strangely powerful if all the details can be held in tension at once, is to be found in the pattern of inter-relations running through "Drifted Back", "An Echo from the Old Bark School", "Brummy Usen", and "The Bush Undertaker". In "Drifted Back" a stranger returns to a small bush town "with the air of one who had come back after many years to see someone who would be glad to see him". But he has taken too little account of the passing of time and he learns with increasing distress that both people and their circumstances have changed so much that he is truly a stranger and can expect no warm, personal welcome. Among the people he enquires after are Jimmy Nowlett, but the storekeeper has never heard of him ("Before my time, perhaps."), and, with significant hesitation, Mary Wild:

> "Mary?" said the grocer, smilingly. "That was my wife's maiden name. Would you like to see her?"
> "No, no! She mightn't remember me!"
> He reached hastily for his swag and shouldered it.

The stranger has already established that his own family connections with the town, by implication once considerable, are now apparently nonexistent (" ... I don't s'pose I remind you of anyone you know around here?" "N-no! ... I can't say you do."); there is nothing to keep him and the sketch ends with his departure: "He drifted out and away along the Sunset Track." Several stories later in the sequence, some of these characters recur in "An Echo From the Old Bark School". James Nowlett is on the school roll but is absent—possibly "wagging it" like William Atkins; the headmaster is quite certain about Atkins's delinquency but no comment is made on

Nowlett. We don't know whether this is the youthful version of that same Jimmy Nowlett whom the stranger asked after in "Drifted Back" or whether perhaps it is the next generation, but the atmosphere of the Old Bark School together with its very name and the reality that the name conjures up, all suggest that it is the original generation we are dealing with. In any case, there is something attractively persuasive in the fact that Nowlett is absent on *both* occasions, without explanation or the slightest clue to his whereabouts, so absent, as it were, that he might as well be dead. The Nowlett who crops up again in "Brummy Usen" is a bullock-driver, just as the Stranger had described him in "Drifted Back", and *again*, it is a story of absence: Nowlett

> used to carry from the railway terminus to the stations up-country. One time he went up with a load and was not heard of for such a long time that his missus got mighty uneasy.

Eventually she hears that he is dead and for some time she

> struggled along and managed without her husband as she had always struggled along and managed with him—a little better perhaps

until what was in fact a case of mistaken identity is cleared up by Nowlett's sudden return. It is somehow appropriate that the Nowlett we have come to know subliminally amongst the many faces and names crowding through the world of *While the Billy Boils* should again be distinguished by his absences, be actually reported dead and remain as difficult an identity for us to pin down as he was when merely a name on the school roll. But Nowlett's non-story does not end there, nor is it as neat as I have implied; for, of course, the Nowlett in "Brummy Usen" is called "Billy" by the swagman-narrator. There is no indication whatsoever (as indeed there need not be) whether "Billy" should really be "Jimmy", whether they were brothers or merely chance namesakes. It may be no more than a Lawsonian inconsistency. Yet the recurrence of the name, together with the consistent details surrounding it remains persuasive and becomes more potent when it is realized that in "Brummy Usen" itself the swagman's main anecdote—the one that gives the sketch its title—is providing very good reason why we should not look to him for accuracy of detail. For if it *is* Brummy Usen himself who is telling the story—and the surprise in the last few sentences suggests that it is—then we realize from his own tale that he has been known as weak and ineffectual ("he hadn't spunk enough to be a bushranger") and from his listeners' slow-dawning reaction, which we have to endorse, that certain aspects of his account show him to be "an awful old liar". So that an inconsistency about Nowlett's name could be due as much to the intransigence of the teller as to any other reason. It is consistent with what we know of him that Brummy should die alone and on the track, and though we have not seen him drinking, it comes as no real surprise, on reflection, that "the rum ... was the death of" him. This at any rate is the conclusion of the hatter shepherd who discovers Brummy's sun-blackened body in a story appearing later in the series, "The Bush Undertaker". Brummy's second name is never mentioned by the old man; it seems probable that it is Brummy Usen for the name is distinctive, and, as I have said, this fate seems to fit details of his life, marginally indicated, and the character which close attention to detail within stories and the connections between them has allowed us to attribute to him. Brummy and Nowlett thus emerge as background characters who nevertheless are not mere recurring names but are actually *growing*, both in the author's conception and in the reader's view.

To return to "An Echo from the Old Bark School": the point of that story is that, in calling the roll, the master unwittingly calls the name of a pupil who has died.

> A solemn hush fell upon the school, and presently Janet Wild threw her arms out on the desk before her, let her face fall on them, and sobbed heart-brokenly. The master saw his mistake too late; he gave his head a little half-affirmative, half-negative movement, in that pathetic old way of his; rested his head on one hand, gazed sadly at the name, and sighed. But the galoot of the school spoilt the pathos of it all, for, during the awed silence which followed the calling of the girl's name, he suddenly brightened up—the first time he was ever observed to do so during school hours—and said briskly and cheerfully: "Dead, sir!"

The dead girl's name is Mary Wild. Again, one can't tell *which* Mary Wild; presumably, it is that same girl after whom the stranger enquired in "Drifted Back" only to find she had married the storekeeper to whom he was talking. In which case, there would seem to be a large and worrying inconsistency to deal with, or at best, a confusion engendered by an austere paucity of information (she *might* be some other Mary Wild in which case why foster the confusion?) But the questions raised really have more to do with the whole sketch, "An Echo from the Old Bark School", than with individuals.

I have said that *While the Billy Boils* unfolds in a more or less, though not tightly chronological sequence. If chronology is to mean anything, this sketch is clearly out of place; moreover, if it is wrongly placed, the remedy is, and presumably was, obvious: it belongs somewhere very near the beginning of the series, if not at *the* beginning, and the misplacement, if such it is, is pretty glaring. Such a transposition would not mend the apparent inconsistency concerning Mary Wild—she would die in the first sketch and be resurrected later—but it would put Arvie Aspinall and James Nowlett back into sequence, as it were: we would meet them first as schoolboys, which is not the case as the series stand. The point is that it would have been so easy to recognize this particular misplacement and to repair it that it seems to me obvious that "An Echo from the Old Bark School" is just about where it should be and where Lawson wanted it. For it is indeed an embodied echo—a reverberation down the years and across the landscapes of which *While the Billy Boils* is the record. When Arvie Aspinall answers his name on the roll, we have already seen his pathetic and needless death; it is only later, in "A Visit of Condolence" that we understand how he came to end his short life at a place like Grinder Brothers. Similarly with James Nowlett: when he does not answer his name he does not remain a cipher; we have already encountered him, at least by rumour and we know that he is to become a bullock driver. "An Echo from the Old Bark School" thus stands, in a way at the centre of the life of one part of the series, echoing back into the past and forward into the future lives of some of the protagonists. Both its placement and what we already know or later learn of some of the children named in it, suggest that Lawson's main interest is not chronological consistency in its usually accepted sense: it is a world in which characters do change in ways that a reader might find either initially or permanently puzzling, a world in which Mary Wild, though apparently grown up and married, can be considered, as a result of a subsequent, or simply *another*, authorial decision, better off dead before she grows beyond girlhood.

There are numerous other examples of this sort of thing, all distinguished by a reticence as to detail, a refusal to tighten the connection beyond the stage of bare intimation or to dispel doubts and obscurities which crowd about some of the possible inter-relations and which, it would seem, could be so easily dispelled. In "The Man

Who Forgot", the sixth story of the book, Tom Marshall (the "Oracle") and Mitchell are confronted with a strange "case"—a man who has forgotten everything. He was:

> a wretchedly forlorn-looking specimen of the swag-carrying clan whom a boundary rider had found wandering about the adjacent plain ... He was a small, scraggy man, painfully fair, and with a big, baby-like head, vacant watery eyes, long thin hairy hands, that felt like pieces of damp seaweed, and an apologetic cringe-and-look-up-at-you manner.

The outcast doesn't even know his own name, a fact which greatly disturbs him but which Mitchell considers to be of little note:

> ... as for a name, that's nothing. I don't know mine, and I've had eight. There's plenty good names knocking round. I knew a man named Jim Smith that died. Take his name, it just suits you, and he ain't likely to call round for it; if he does you can say you was born with it.

So Smith he becomes and he remains with the shed until he is sacked for forgetting to turn up to work one morning. When it is established however, as a result of Mitchell's ambiguous musings, that not only did Smith not forget to collect his cheque but that he also did not "forget" to remove all the shearers' valuables before departing, the Oracle goes after him and "stirs up" his recollections. Much later in the series, having already met Steelman and learned that he is a "a hard case", we encounter Steelman's pupil, Smith, thought by many to be a harder case than his "master". Smith is described as:

> ... small and weedy, of the sneak variety; he had a whining tone and a cringing manner. He seemed to be always so afraid you were going to hit him that he would make you *want* to hit him on that account alone.
>
> Steelman "had" you in a fashion that would make your friends laugh. Smith would "have" you in a way which made you feel mad at the bare recollection.

By appearance and manner, it is surely the same Smith, but the identification is not only unenforced, it is not even mentioned. Yet it is one of the ironies of "Steelman's Pupil" that there are strong indications, not evident to Steelman, that the pupil is a shiftier and altogether more slippery proposition that the master, and that irony suffuses the story the more thoroughly if we keep in mind the man who forgot. Even within the limits of the story, "Steelman's Pupil", it comes as no great surprise that Smith triumphs in the end; but the memory of what appears almost certainly to have been on earlier Smith escapade in "The Man Who Forgot" endows the last sentence of "Steelman's Pupil" with much greater ironic resonance and makes Steelman's own under-estimation of Smith the more delightful.

> "Look here, Steely, old man. Listen to the rain! I'll get wringing wet going home. You might as well lend me your overcoat tonight. You won't want it, and I won't hurt it."
> And, Steelman's heart being warmed by his successes, he lent the overcoat.
> Smith went and pawned it, got glorious on the proceeds, and took the pawn-ticket to Steelman next day. Smith had reformed.

It is consistent with what we have learned of Smith in the earlier story that he should be constantly on the move, that he should meet up with, separate from, and later rejoin a fellow bush nomad and confidence man like Steelman, and that he should turn out to be, behind his unimpressive exterior, more than a match for his flamboyantly dissembling "master". To revert momentarily to an earlier point, it is the same kind of inherent, unstated consistency that grows—paradoxically amidst rumour, lies, tall tales, and ambiguity—about the figures of Nowlett, who may be "Jimmy", "Billy" or both and who is always absent, and Brummy Usen/the tramp, whose own demonstrated fecklessness may well be at the root of all these confusions both about Nowlett's name and the identity of "Brummy Usen". But it is also consistent that, while we feel strongly persuaded on the basis of the available evidence, we cannot be *completely* sure about the identities and activities of "Smith", "Nowlett", or "Brummy Usen": in the world that is evolving in the pages of *While the Billy Boils* change, rumour, distance, mistakes, and misrepresentations make a mockery of most "certainties".

Macquarie is another, minor, elusively recurring yet "growing" character. In "That There Dog of Mine" he is down and out, he has been beaten up in a drunken brawl at a shanty and, from what he says to the doctor who is to treat him, it appears that drunkenness, tramping, and desperation have been the pattern of his life for the past ten years or so. Yet for all that, Macquarie has a fine streak in him; the dog is all he has, it is his only loyal companion, and when the doctor refuses to have the dog on the premises Macquarie, despite his injuries, prepares to leave. His parting shot is a speech "to the hospital staff in general" in which there is a moving, rough dignity and an intimation that, defeated and almost destroyed though he is, there is that in him which will ensure that he survives:

> ... he drew in his breath, shut his teeth hard, shouldered his swag, stepped into the doorway, and faced round again. The dog limped out of the corner and looked up anxiously. "That there dog," said Macquarie ... "is a better dog than I'm a man—or you too, it seems— and a better Christian. He's been a better mate to me than I ever was to any man—or any man to me. He's watched over me; kep' me from getting robbed many a time; fought for me; saved my life and took drunken kicks and curses for thanks—and forgave me. He's been a true, straight, honest and faithful mate to me—and I ain't going to desert him now.

We next meet "Macquarie the shearer" very briefly: he is travelling across a "hot, lonely, cotton-bush plain" with two mates, one "a little man ... known as Sunlight", the other "a tall, thin, young jackeroo whom they call Milky". The three shearers are intent on reaching "a certain shed next day" but they are distracted by the sudden, distant, and incongruous spectacle of two men fighting in the middle of the plain. Macquarie, who as we know, has seen so many fights and brawls, characteristically suggests that they "Hurry up and see the fun!" But the "fight" turns out to be old Rats fighting with his swag; Rats follows this altercation with a spell of "fishing" in the hot dusty track, landing "several cod and a bream". He borrows "about a pound of meat for baits" and Sunlight gives him half a crown, whereupon the shearers take up their journey again and when they last see Rats, receding in the distance behind them, he has resumed his vendetta with his swag. It is a curious incident, very funny, yet also intriguing in that our initial certain conviction of Rats's madness is uneasily weakened by the peculiar inner logic of his actions and his own matter-of-factness (in the same way that the Bush Undertaker is logical and matter-of-fact.) Apart from the implications of their kindly tolerance towards Rats, the effect of all this on the shearers is not recorded. Of subsidiary interest, and available in minimal, unemphasized detail, are some facts about Macquarie: he has a couple of mates and a job to go to and he retains some zest and a sense of fun. Temporarily, things are going better for him.

Macquarie's final appearance is in the third last story of the book, "Macquarie's Mate". In this story, a number of men "in the bar of Stiffner's shanty" were talking about Macquarie, an absent shearer—"who seemed, from their conversation, to be better known than liked by them". An old drunken down-and-out, known as Awful Example, defends Macquarie against their slanders, the defence including the information that Macquarie is dead. But the abuse continues (some of the men don't believe Macquarie is dead, others, though believing, are unimpressed) and Awful Example prepares, pathetically, to fight in defence of his old mate's name. But "a tall, gaunt, determined-looking bushman, with square features and haggard grey eyes", who had come in unnoticed and had been watching the situation deteriorate, restrains him and reduces the bar crowd to embarrassed silence. It is Macquarie himself.

This story seems to me to be an unusually good example of how a recognition of the understated inter-relations threaded and patterned through *While the Billy Boils* can greatly enrich, even alter, one's opinion of a particular story. The sketch, as it stands, is neither especially distinguished nor noticeably poor, though the ending has a distinctly melodramatic flavour. But seen as a few more strokes added to the portrait of a never more than minimally depicted background figure, "Macquarie's Mate" becomes irresistably moving. Macquarie, we recall, knows what it is like to be down and out, "drugged and poisoned at the cursed shanties"—to be an awful example, in short; he knows the value of loyalty, the importance of having a good mate and of sticking by him. At his very nadir, in "That There Dog ... ", Macquarie seemed to have in him some potential for resurgence. At least *some* better times ensued, as we know from that briefest of encounters on the cottonbush plain, but he is now gaunt and haggard-eyed suggesting that he has endured many years and many vicissitudes since that day he laughed at Rats fighting his swag. We are left to imagine what may have befallen him, but it is not difficult to fill in, not only because we know something of Macquarie himself, mostly from "That There Dog ...", but also because we know from other stories and sketches the nature of the world in which these events and characters are located. So that Macquarie's timely arrival, viewed against the bare, sparse detail built up over the series and the imagined details we supply to fill the huge, silent gaps in his life story, appears not melodramatic but proper—one more in a whole life time of random encounters and arrivals, descents and resurgences, returns, separations, and "resurrections", a lifetime in which the loyalty of a mate through all these vagaries has been and remains now, the one saving grace.

The so-called city stories, which might seem, on the face of it, out of place in a collection called *While the Billy Boils*, are in fact intimately connected with the outback world that Lawson is evoking in the series as a whole. In "An Unfinished Love Story", which bridges the worlds of city and selection and which, as we have seen, Stephens so admired, Brook has returned to the selection environment which he had left fifteen years before to live in the city. Like the stranger in "Drifted Back", he returns to a spiritual emptiness: "His father was dead; his other relations had moved away, leaving a tenant on the old selection." His very name suggests his isolation and irrelevance—it has no counterpart or echo anywhere in the entire book. The Brooks have faded from this land. After amusing himself for a few days with Lizzie, the tenant's niece, Brook abandons her and returns to the city, leaving her apparently heart-broken. The sketch intimates, with some sensitivity and reticence, the emotional flatness and impoverishment which "hungry, wretched selection existence" inflicts upon outback dwellers, especially women. So that when Brook's assiduous but essentially self-regarding attentions awake genuine, profound emotion in Lizzie, it is not only an experience with which she cannot even begin to cope (we sense this though we are not told it), but also such emotion seems positively alien to her personality: "He looked back ... and was just in time to see her bury her face in her hands with a passionate gesture which did not seem natural to her." But it is the citified man who is alien, un-attuned to the understated and submerged level at which emotional development, personal communication, and spiritual growth must proceed, in an environment which encourages none of them.

Where the outback world of *While the Billy Boils* is crowded (and confused) with names, characters, movement and places, the city to which Brook returns (staggering "'after hours' ... in through a side entrance to the lighted parlour of a private bar") is a place of anonymities and is peculiarly static. In the very next sketch, "Board and Residence", the narrator tells of the Orwellian plight of the boarder—the embarrassments and frustrations of poverty, the deadening despair of genteel boarding house life, the shifts and stratagems and endless boredom. "You *wish* you could get away up-country. You also wish that you were dead." "This is the sort of life that gives a man a God-Almighty longing to break away and take to the bush." All Lawson's city characters in this book—whether it is the amiably desperate "I" of "Going Blind" or the thoroughly desperate Mr. Careless of "Board and Residence"—are in touch with the bush in some way: they have either come from it or they are longing to get back to it, or both. Lawson's carefully observed, documentary, and passionate attack on certain city conditions reveals the city life as inhumane, even unnatural, yet his faceless city characters never see the bush as a panacea but only as another alternative. If anything, it is a horribly daunting alternative, but it *does* emerge as a place of growth for the ordinary man who can survive, whereas the city stultifies, cramps and constricts. Lawson's city characters thus look to the bush not for relief, but at least for *space*, spiritual, psychological, and physical. But there is little romanticizing about the price at which all this may be bought: "up-country", you have to devote yourself to survival, above all. It is in the various stages and phases of surviving that personal growth might occur.

The Aspinall stories—artistically among the book's weakest offerings—not only further underline aspects of Lawson's method that I have been discussing here, but also emphasize the notion of the city as a kind of living death. The first of these stories, "Arvie Aspinall's Alarm Clock", concerns itself almost exclusively with Arvie's death as a result of overwork and fatigue—a victim of "Grinder Bros". There is a little background information in Mrs. Aspinall's memories of past trials and difficulties, memories which she reviews while watching over Arvie sleeping, as the Drover's Wife does in a different situation. But the central concern of the story is to tell of the circumstances, causes, and actual occurrence of Arvie's death. Lawson returns to Arvie, however, much later in the book, in "An Echo from the Old Bark School"; we have gone back in time and Arvie, whose name is first on the roll, is there to answer "'Es Sir". Despite the weaknesses of "Arvie Aspinall's Alarm Clock", this moment's flashback—with its unstated suggestions of very young boyhood and fresh, though vulnerable, promise—impresses retrospectively the waste and pathos of Arvie's death more movingly than the over-wrought, melodramatic-tending descriptions of the first Aspinall story. The tragedy of child-death is further enforced moments later when Mary Wild fails to answer the roll.

Typically, this "echo" both clarifies and obscures our grasp and imaginative reconstruction of what Arvie's life has been like: we know where he grew up and we know where he died but we are left to guess why the journey that began in the old Bark School ended in a Sydney slum. "A Visit of Condolence"—many pages further on—begins the task of explanation. In terms of the stories' own time scheme, "A Visit of Condolence" resumes not months or years or an indeterminate time later, as is so often the case in this book, but within a few hours of Arvie's death. As Bill, the twelve-year-old, gently sympathetic urchin, and Mrs. Aspinall converse, we learn the context of all their lives, of how Arvie was driven to the grave, of the Aspinalls' migration from the bush five years before, of their many misfortunes, of Bill's own family and of his idea, typical of Lawson's city-dwellers, of "gittin' a billet up-country". "Jones' Alley", one of the last half-dozen or so stories in the book, finds Mrs. Aspinall in similar, though, if anything, worse straits, at least two but perhaps five or six years later; and an older-sounding yet essentially unchanged Bill offering to help her. The emphasis again is on recapitulation of what has happened in the past. There is a happy ending of a limited, inconclusive kind, in that Bill and his "push" help Mrs. Aspinall to move out of the neighbourhood of Jones' Alley; but it is a victory over circumstances of the same order as the Drover's Wife's conquest of the snake: there will be many more trials, many more heart aches.

These Aspinall stories *are* inferior, for several reasons: Lawson's anger at such inhumanities as he records here is too great, unmastered; his compassion is genuine and profound but too stagily dramatized, too insistently urged. But more than this, the inter-relations between these stories, leaving aside the role played by "An Echo from the Old Bark School", are not much more than recurrence of names and places. That sense of understated, barely perceptible growth and change in characters over a long period and as a result of experiences in diverse and widely separated places—the sort of development exemplified in Smith, Macquarie, Nowlett *et al*—is lacking in the city stories. And it seems to be lacking because, while Lawson may see the outback as a place mostly of human destruction, destruction itself is process, is energy, and there is paradoxically something creating and shaping in knowing, recording, and experiencing how man is unmade. Lawson's city environment slowly strangles, and its victims are static, never finally destroyed but always suppressed and with no metaphoric or physical room to move. His imagination responds to the exquisitely detailed and varied ways in which the outback reduces and destroys and to the distances a man may cover and the new starts and new selves he may essay before nemesis finally catches up with him. Thus, the city stories may lack the capacity of the rest, but they belong, nevertheless: there is a submerged, scarcely articulated but energetic dynamism in Lawson's portrait of outback life, even at its most destructive, which is absent from his city scenes, and if this discrepancy is due partly to the author's failure to respond imaginatively to the city, it is also a comment on that city. Life in Lawson's outback may often seem inhumanly cruel but there are grounds for thinking his city is *anti*-human. A quite explicit version of this city-outback opposition is found in the documentary piece, "'Dossing Out' and 'Camping'". (This is one of several occasions—"Stragglers" is another—on which a largely documentary sketch parallels and supplies atmosphere and detail for more imaginative evocations elsewhere in the series.) The plight of the "dosser-out" in the city is seen as unnatural and degrading— "And so Australian workmen lay at two o'clock in the morning in the streets of Sydney, and tried to get a little sleep before the traffic came along and took their bed."—but the bushman, even if unemployed and alone, has real compensations and is in tune with his surroundings: " ... in the bush you can ... whistle and sing by the campfire, and make poetry, and breathe fresh air and watch the everlasting stars that keep the mateless traveller from going mad ... " The examples I have given here of creative inter-relation in *While the Billy Boils* seem to me representative, but there are, of course, many others. There is the formidable Mitchell, whose sporadically intimated views and experiences allow, indeed force, the reader to build in his imagination a complex, attractive yet essentially puzzling personality as much from what has been left unsaid as from manifest evidence. Again, there is a whole array of narrators through whose varying tones and inferences are posed, re-posed, and counter-posed perspectives on the outback as different as those found in "Remailed" and "The Union Buries Its Dead". It is in short a whole world that emerges, various and crowded, and I have tried to indicate some of the mechanics, as it were, of that world, the ways in which the whole undeniably loose undertaking can be regarded as hanging together. But it is worth looking more closely at the exact nature of the world that thus emerges.

While the Billy Boils in fact evokes several "worlds".[16] At one level, it is documentary, depicting the Australian outback, in many of its appearances, with a genuinely breathtaking felicity and sharpness. Lawson's contemporaries valued the book very largely because they could recognize the world it presented, they could accept it as true, and they forgave its author what they considered were serious deficiencies in the work because of this overriding strength. The book "gives us Australia", says Price Warung,

> in a hundred phases of character, of episode and of scenery, and notwithstanding that there is more than an occasional recurrence of type, and a monotony of tone not always agreeable, taking the volume as a transcript of things Australian, there is scarcely a passage of ten consecutive lines which I should like to see expunged.[17]

Even A.G. Stephens makes much the same point:

> ... ordinary minds with pleasure recognize his own [i.e. Lawson's] impressions. "Why these are our thoughts; these scenes and places are the scenes and places we have known for all our lives."[18]

All this is true and important; it is one of Lawson's great achievements that he has captured and chronicled, in a way that no one else has equalled, a time and a place in our past. But that time and that world have gone and if that capturing and chronicling were all that *While the Billy Boils* had to offer, it would still be read with interest but with a good deal less excitement and wonder. There is a dynamic quality in this book which does not emanate from its factual and documentary accuracy, crucial though these are to the work's general impact, but from some other level of its evocations. One such level—another of the "worlds" that coexist interdependently in the pages of the book—is that which Lawson sets going in the reader's imagination.

In his review of *While the Billy Boils* in August 1896, David G. Ferguson notes, in what is almost a throw-away line, that "you must look for Lawson's comment not in what the author says, but in what he leaves out."[19] Though he is speaking exclusively of Lawson's point of view rather than generally about his artistic method, it is a potent observation and Ferguson, as far as I can see, was alone in making it. Its considerable significance as a contribution to our understanding of how Lawson's prose works is clarified and enforced by Chris Wallace-Crabbe who speaks of Lawson's "great imaginative tactic: *leaving out*."[20] But this is true not only of the method of individual stories, but also of the book as a whole. As I have already suggested, *While the Billy Boils* presents us with a diversity of characters and follows them more or less chronologically—that is, we meet them mostly at progressively later stages of their lives as we move through the book. But there are vast and arbitrary gaps in these individual lives: Macquarie turns up at Stiffner's shanty haggard and gaunt—an aged version of the shearer who encountered "Rats", and, in a vaguely implied way, a tragic figure, quietened-down and reduced in comparison with the Macquarie of "That There Dog ... " who, though in straitened circumstances, has an energy and a vigour about him, as well as an essential "straightness". The reader, on encountering Macquarie the second time, begins filling in the gaps, begins shaping a conception of Macquarie as a person and of the nature of his life, a few brief but evocative incidents in which he has been allowed to glimpse. He might conjecture also about why Macquarie is so badly thought of when he has emerged from each incident with some dignity, however minimal and unemphasized. It is because these kinds of questions, puzzles, alterations, possible inconsistencies, and silent unyielding gaps in the run of the years affect our engagement with so many of the characters in this book that there is forced upon the reader a growing and continual process of imaginative completion: he supplies detail where it is withheld, background where it has been totally omitted, evidence where there is doubt. I have given several examples of this process taking place, or rather, of its being enjoined upon the reader; and there are many others. Lawson is able to enlist the reader in this way not only because he has so thoroughly mastered the "tactic" of leaving out, but also because of his almost invariably unerring tact in knowing what to put in: such spare detail and context as is supplied at any one time for any given character is beautifully evocative—resonant, as it were, and responding to the barest tremors and actuations that unobtrusively and unpredictably occur in subsequent sketches and stories. *While the Billy Boils* thus stands as more than documentary. Lawson does not merely present an observed, static world, he compels the reader to set it in motion.

But there is a third level of evocation in *While the Billy Boils*, a third "world", and it is in my view the most important, on balance, and the one that most ensures the book's continued liveliness, its self-renewing quality. It is Lawson's fictional world—a country of the imagination, based firmly in observed reality, of the same order as Faulkner's Yoknapatawpha County.

This fictional world has some peculiarities. To begin with, it is not "completely consistent and coherent in itself".[21] I have already pointed out that it contains some strange *inconsistencies* which in several cases would seem to have been avoidable by dint of even the most routine editorial scrutiny. The truth is, I think, that Lawson's outback was not only the real life and terrain of western New South Wales in the nineties, not only that evolving world in which the reader finds himself participating creatively, but also and above all a world in Lawson's head and in his imagination, dynamic and organic, constantly growing in one detail or another, altering in some particular or other as he more surely understood it and its inhabitants. The Macquarie of "Macquarie's Mate" has grown haggard and gaunt not in the pages of *While the Billy Boils*, for he is only glimpsed there, but in the constantly growing and revised world of the author's imagination. The man who forgot enters upon this scene literally nameless, totally undistinguished, but with, it transpires, a certain native cunning; he reappears as a fully-fledged "hard case", more than a match for the redoubtable Steelman: like so many of the other characters, he has entered the author's imagination from the real world and grown there. Whenever he re-emerges ("Steelman's Pupil", "The Geological Spieler") we experience not just a recurrent name but a sense of a living and developing person. Again, Mary Wild is married to the storekeeper in a nameless town ("Drifted Back") but, in that chronological dislocation involved in taking several characters back to their childhood at the old Bark School, her life is cancelled. In the fictional world of *While the Billy Boils* it is possible to hold these two facts in tension: it is a world in which, as we know, "a name is ... nothing". There are plenty of Smiths, there may be several Mary Wilds. But in these circumstances the death of the child "Mary Wild" takes on an eerie quality and reflects back oddly on "Drifted Back" with its nameless stranger in a nameless town learning from a nameless storekeeper that no one there knows him at all.

191

This process of growth and constant revision; of moving backwards and forwards over lives and individuals' time spans revising or abruptly altering; of suggesting inter-relationships yet casting doubt on them by means as simple as a changed name or as complex as dual or overlaid chronologies—all this is not only a fictional method, it is also in the very nature of the fictional world projected. It is a world of constant change, of fluidity, a world in which things are rarely certain, rarely known for sure. The realities that entered Lawson's consciousness and imagination have been transmuted there into a vision of the world as one of uncertainty and innumerable degrees of changeability. One of the ways in which Lawson intimates this vision is in his use of names. The outback reality, in which names were often assumed, altered, conveniently forgotten or deliberately overlooked, becomes in Lawson's fictional world a veritable crescendo of identity confusion, misapprehension, or concealment. Names change slightly as with "Lally"/"Sally" Thompson, "Jimmy"/"Billy" Nowlett—yet other identifying details remain consistent so that one is torn between conviction that it is the same character and nagging suspicion that it might not be. Names are repeated where it appears impossible that the same person could be meant ("Mary Wild") or, on the other hand, where one feels the same person *must* be meant yet final certainty is withheld ("Smith"). Some like Mitchell's mate, Tom "Something", go by first names; some like Steelman, go by second names only; some go nameless, some have only pseudonyms ("Awful Example", "Mr. Careless", "Chinny"). It is a measure of the uncertainty of identity in this world of Lawson's that even Mitchell confesses to not knowing his real name: " ... as for a name, that's nothing. I don't know mine, and I've had eight. There's plenty good names knocking round." It is not that we should necessarily believe this; it is just that Lawson perceived at that point that Mitchell is the kind of character who might well have an alias, or several, or who might simply feel it appropriate to pretend he has. We can't be sure—*the author himself isn't sure*, for Mitchell inhabits this fictional world on the same terms as everyone else, that is, in a state of growth. But for a person of Mitchell's stature in the book to cast this kind of doubt on his own identity somehow intensifies our sense of the fluidity and uncertainty which is the element in which these characters live. Not only names but events and activities suffer this invasion of uncertainty: rather than being given, as it were, a narrated fact, we are left with a set of possibilities—a mixture of rumour, possible truth, likelihood; the event, whatever it is, remains living, fluid, creating and strikes us that way every time we return to it. And this is partly because the author is withholding artistically, but also partly because he is telling us *as much as he knows* at that stage. It is a dynamic, not a static world and its possibilities and outcomes can never all be known. Thus: when Bogg of Geebung dies, it is reported in the *Geebung Times*.

> "A well-known character named Bogg was found drowned in the river on Sunday last, his hat and coat being found on the bank. At a late hour on Saturday night a member of our staff saw a man walking slowly along the river bank, but it was too dark to identify the person."

The slight uncertainty in the circumstances of death is added to by the narrator in terms which exactly duplicate a reader's reaction to the elusive echoes, tenuous inter-connections, and half-certain relationships which form part of the experience of *While the Billy Boils*: "We suppose it was Bogg whom the *Times* reported, *but of course we cannot be sure.* The chances are that it was Bogg." (My emphasis.) Again, in "Hungerford", the narrator attempts to summarize the legal situation in a town straddling a state border, but it turns out that he has not so much observed the situation as heard about it, which forces him to conclude as follows:

> At least, I believe that's how it is, though the man who told me might have been a liar. Another man said he was liar, but then *he* might have been a liar himself—a third person said he was one. I heard that there was a fight over it, but the man who told me about the fight might not have been telling the truth.

Or, when Brooke abandons Lizzie: It is quite clear what her reaction must have been—the story has laid the necessary groundwork more than adequately—but the conclusion withdraws from what appears to be a certainty, conceding ground to what little doubt there is, leaving the episode living on, as rumour or fact or strong possibility in the world of *While the Billy Boils*: "They say that Lizzie broke her heart that year, but then, the world does not believe in such things nowadays." Or again, in "Some Day" where, in Mitchell's embittered speculation on what *might* have happened to himself and his mate, the fact of their death becomes lost in uncertainty and vague carelessness: "Who cares? If we hadn't found the track yesterday we might have lain and rotted in that lignum, and no one been any the wiser—or sorrier—who knows? Somebody might have found us in the end, but it mightn't have been worth his while to go out of his way and report us." There are many more examples.

One of the conditions in Lawson's world which helps to perpetuate and ramify uncertainties and enrich and elaborate rumours, is the huge distance over which people and their life episodes are spread. Distance and long separation also sharpen the impact of change in people and places. Travellers return to find no one knows them, or set out on a particular journey but become sidetracked into endless trampings, or fail to return when expected, or are misrepresented in rumour, or go mad in isolation. But above all, the rumour and the reality which stalks through Lawson's fictional world with almost medieval intensity and obsessiveness is Death. Death is at home in this country, it pervades the book—not always sadly or heavily—and actually plays some part or is mentioned in at least half the stories. But Death is *both* rumour and reality because, on innumerable occasions, characters are only thought to be dead or rumoured to be dead or assumed dead; very often, they turn up again, very much alive. Sometimes they "die" several times over. The great paradox about Death in Lawson's world is that, because it is enrolled in and always somehow suffused by the general uncertainty, because, indeed, it often turns out to be not death at all, it often actually asserts the dynamic and organic quality of the book. When people like Macquarie, Nowlett, Joe Swallow, and a whole range of lesser characters who are only yarned about, return from the dead, setting up reverberations and echoes through the several stories in which we have already met them, however briefly, the sensation that this is a living world—one which is constantly growing, being revised, better understood, in the author's imagination—is sharply and dramatically re-enforced.

Death's persistent and pervasive inhabitation of the world of *While the Billy Boils* is not difficult to exemplify. Smith gets his name from one "Jim Smith that died". "Take his name," advises Mitchell, "it just suits you, and he ain't likely to call round for it; if he does," says Mitchell, typically mindful of bush "resurrections", "you can say you was born with it." Mitchell returns home after eight years only to find that "a blundering fool of a fellow that got down the day before me told the old folks that he'd heard I was dead". Joe Swallow is rumoured dead and his ghost has even been seen, but "Joe himself turned up ... ". The tramp who may or may not be Brummy Usen has "been dead a few times"; Macquarie is reported dead, but turns up opportunely; Mitchell imagines his own unreported, unconfirmed death; the Drover's wife has not seen her husband for six months and is "anxious" about him. And so on. Then, there are the actual deaths: Tom Drew, Arvie Aspinall, Isley and Tom Mason, Mary Wild, "James Tyson", the Drover's Wife's child, Brummy, Mitchell's father, Malachi, "James" Bogg .... And the "background" deaths: Arvie Aspinall's father, Bill Anderson's father, Mitchell's mate Tom "Something", Tom Mason's wife and brother, old Ben Hake, the M'Lachlans, old Malachi Duggan ... As well, numerous narrating voices and characters talk about death, attempting to accommodate it, understand it, specify it, deny it, escape it: thus, in "The Union Buries Its Dead", the narrator's friend, having pointed out that the drover they had chatted with the day before was now the corpse they were following in procession, remarks with obscure awe,

> "You'd have taken more notice if you'd known that he was doomed to die in the hour, and that those were the last words he would say to any man in this world."
> "To be sure," said a full voice from the rear. "If ye'd known that, ye'd have prolonged the conversation."

At the other extreme, Sally Thompson in "Macquarie's Mate", riled by Awful Example's conscience-pricking, bursts out:

> "There's a blessed lot of tommy-rot about dead people in this world—a lot of damned old-woman nonsense. There's more sympathy wasted over dead and rotten skunks than there is justice done to straight, honest-livin' chaps. I don't b'lieve in this gory sentiment about the dead at the expense of the livin'. I b'lieve in justice for the livin'—and the dead too, for that matter—but justice for the livin'. Macquarie was a bad egg, and it don't alter the case if he was dead a thousand times."

For the narrator of "In a Dry Season" "Death is about the only cheerful thing in the bush" while, in its presence, the Bush Undertaker, who deals so matter-of-factly with anonymous bones and bodies, feels a great solemnity, a mysterious sense of obligation:

> "Theer oughter be somethin' sed ... 'tain't right to put 'im under like a

dog. Theer oughter be some sort o' sarmin." ... He removed his hat, placed it carefully on the grass, held his hands out from his sides and a little to the front, drew a long deep breath, and said with a solemnity that greatly disturbed Five Bob: "Hashes ter hashes, dus ter dus, Brummy—an'—an' in hopes of a great an' gerlorious rassaraction!"

Out from this crowded hinterland of Death's appearances and machinations, stand the great set-pieces of Death and separation in the world of *While the Billy Boils*: "The Union Buries Its Dead", "The Drover's Wife", and "The Bush Undertaker". All the themes and obsessions of the book—death and separation, distance, rumour and anonymity, profound loneliness—are gathered into these three stories and treated with a sort of ritual attention to detail, atmosphere, and elaboration, in contrast to the often minimal (though still powerful) suggestion and intimation of the "surrounding" sketches. As I have already noted, these stories are frequently, and for good reasons, taken out of their context and focussed upon as major achievements in the two series. It is only when they are returned to and firmly placed in the fictional world of *While the Billy Boils* that one notices their ritual character. "The Union Buries Its Dead" is governed by the movement of the funeral: it is a travesty but most of the story's revelations are made within and through the ragged, funereal and undignified process that begins "at a corner pub" and ends as the "hard, dry Darling River clods rebounded" on the coffin. "The Drover's Wife" is dominated by and derives its rhythm from the passing of twin time—the long night of watching, and the woman's flashback recollections. And "The Bush Undertaker" takes its movement from the funeral march of the shepherd and Brummy and the subsequent, oddly ritualistic burial. The sense of ritual is strengthened *in context* (it is not of course ever entirely absent) because so much that has been fleeting, yarned about, rumoured or barely sketched becomes elaborated in these three stories in terms of a definite incident: death, burial, and anonymity in "The Union ... "; death-like separation and horrifying isolation in "The Drover's Wife"; death's awesomeness, lonely madness, the insecure nature of identity in "The Bush Undertaker". They are the organizing stories of the series, the great syntheses dominating yet dependent on the less evolved sketches and brief vignettes that make up the context. Change, of which Death is an ultimate form, and separation, which can be like Death—these are the governing forces in Lawson's fictional world. From their basis in the observed reality of the Australian outback of the nineties, where they were emphatically present but, even at the worst, balanced and mitigated by other facets that the human condition invariably exhibits, they entered Lawson's consciousness and imagination and became intensified and nourished there. In so far as the outback became for him a metaphor for life and the world generally, it revealed to him a state of chronic insecurity, with people in stages of radical loneliness, cut off from each other by chance, distance, long, necessary or unpredictable separation, and death, real or rumoured. The whole series of stories in which this world emerges, with these emphases, is framed by images of change and decay: in the first story, "An Old Mate of Your Father's", two old men recall a previous generation which is passing away and the narrator—one of "the rising generation"—concludes:

> These old mates of our father's are getting few and far between, and only happen along once in a way to keep the old man's memory fresh, as it were. We met one today, and had a yarn with him, and afterwards we got thinking, and somehow began to wonder whether those ancient friends of ours were, or were not, better and kinder to their mates than we of the rising generation are to our fathers; and the doubt is painfully on the wrong side.

And the book closes with "For Auld Lang Syne", in which presumably the same narrator records, with the same quality of quiet sadness, the breaking up of his own world: "And one by one and two by two they have gone from the wharf since then."

The three worlds of *While the Billy Boils*, obviously enough, are inseparable in the life of the book; I have tried to distinguish them to a certain extent here in order to demonstrate what I have called levels of evocation. Above all, it is important to reiterate that we would not have the book at all were it not for Lawson's sharp perception of and humane response to the scenes of his childhood and his travels; but he was no mere documenter: he was a writer, or trying to be, and what he saw became not "A Record of Some Travels in the West of New South Wales and Elsewhere" or "With Pen and Rail Ticket into the Wilderness" in the best tradition of nineteenth century adventurers, but the Lawson country, growing—once conceived and born—almost in spite of its author, running ahead of him, living and dynamic. Lawson's preoccupation with this world as a living entity, something developing continuously in his imagination and which he was progressively understanding more closely and intimately, occasionally reveals itself in his letters. In a letter dated 7 May 1899, he is speaking of Steelman and goes on to explain various matters about he and Smith and their affairs, as if the characters were real people and their activities actual:

> He, [i.e. Steelman] by the way, has been, unknown to Smith, keeping a wife and two children in comfort all the time. She thinks he is a commercial traveller. He dies to save a Maori woman and half-caste child from a treacherous little snow-fed Maori river. *I know the river, and the incidents would be practically facts*.[22] [My emphasis]

This is not only a fine example of the continuing evolution of his characters and of their world in his imagination, but it is equally a unique indication, from his own pen, of how observed reality retains its authority while nevertheless being enlisted into the fictional world. In the same letter, he refers to a deliberately arranged name-recurrence:

> Original name, Peter Mackenzie; name of original character, "Peter McIntosh", which last name I'll use now in sketch, as Peter McIntosh is a leading character in my new long story "Last Days at Specimen Flat".

There are other, similar references in the letters—testimony, if any were needed beyond the evidence of *While the Billy Boils* itself, to the continuing presence and importance of this fictional world to its inventor.

I have argued that the many things we don't know about these characters, the many links left out, and the chronological and other kinds of obscurities, are not only a part of Lawson's method—applications of "his great imaginative tactic"—but also a condition of his characters' lives and of his fictional world. When we are not sure, as readers, what has transpired or who precisely is involved or what links exist or what the truth is, it is because the characters themselves live in that chronic state of uncertainty and because their author may also not know; his knowledge of them is still evolving. We are thus sharing in the developing and fluid conditions of a living fictional world, not being excluded from vital facts or having them manipulated for us by an omniscient authorial figure.

Lawson's creation of the kind of fictional world which I have tried to distinguish and discuss here has considerable importance for his presence in our literature as a proletarian writer. A.A. Phillips pointed out long ago that "the Australian proletarian writer" was faced with a problem of finding "simpler patterns of form to suit his homespun material", and he went on to develop the argument that "Lawson's prose form at its best is not only admirably conceived—it is his own invention".[23] So, to a large extent, is his fictional world and it is, among other things, another important weapon in his bid to cope with certain intractable features of his material. One of the remarkable things about *While the Billy Boils* is that it is a book virtually without heroes: with the possible exception of Mitchell and, even more arguably, Steelman, there is not a character in the book who could be called a hero in any traditional, fictional sense. On the contrary all the characters are, as it were, background people, peculiarly submerged in their life styles and in their communication with others. Some of them are genuinely rough and tough; many are of limited education, sensitive, doing the best they can in circumstances physically and emotionally abrasive; some are in work and grateful for it, others seek work at the end of a long journey "humping bluey", others again tramp just as far to avoid it; some are ineradicably lonely, gradually losing what powers of human communication they ever had in months and years of enforced solitude; a few are buried anonymously in the city; others are down and out; some are insane. They are *submerged* people—in fictional terms, nonentities: the kind of people who inhabit the shadowy backgrounds of the middle class novel, deemed necessary to the total picture but rarely understood. Above all, they are relatively inarticulate—unable to make their insights clear or to verbalize the nature of their pain or joy. The writer who seeks to capture with honesty, dignity, and sympathy this world of the labouring, the unemployed, the under-privileged, the down-and-out, thus faces extraordinarily formidable artistic problems. He must depict lives which, because socially and economically repressed, are often tedious and boring, yet his depiction must not in itself be tedious and boring; he must communicate, somehow, the psychological and spiritual intricacies of people who cannot themselves articulate them; he must bring to the centre of his own fictional stage people whom social injustice has in reality banished permanently to the wings and he must engineer the transition without either distortion of emphasis or loss of authenticity in atmosphere and milieu. These are some of the reasons why there is not much "proletarian literature" of real consequence. The author of *The Ragged Trousered Philanthropists* triumphed over these difficulties and his own literary inadequacies by the sheer intensity and commitment with which he recorded, from within, experiences which few previous writers had noticed in any depth or detail, let alone essayed. But that sort of achievement against the odds is rare. Lawson's own triumph owes much less to luck: in *While the Billy Boils* it is not only the famous prose style in individual stories but also the evolution over the whole work of a dynamic fictional world that enables Lawson to intimate the nature of the lives and the extent of the growth of inarticulate people. As characters emerge, disappear, return, in different stories and different circumstances; as links are suggested between events and people only to be obscured by rumour, human error, confusion; as the same individual is characterized at various times by assorted people in conflicting terms; as some characters develop startlingly and others drop out of sight ... as all this gathers momentum, we sense both a whole world and particular individuals growing, changing. Lawson implies the growth and something of the inner life of his inarticulate, reticent, or submerged characters by placing them in an organic world which is the mirror of their own condition, by having them inhabit and grow in that world continuously—in his imagination—and not only when they surface, as it were, into print, and by leaving the reader to infer the nature and the state of growth which, with respect to any particular character, may have taken place in any of the book's many vast, undocumented, silent "gaps". In this way, without large slabs of narration or lengthy explanatory description, yet also without betraying his characters' true natures by putting into their mouths detailed verbal self-appraisals and introspections, Lawson succeeds in indicating movingly and compassionately the full humanity of "proletarian" characters.

To return, by way of conclusion, to the influential A.G. Stephens review with which I began. For all Stephens's urging and Lawson's own wavering on the matter, *While the Billy Boils* would not have been improved by being arranged in its sequences. On the contrary: it would have lost much of that dynamism and organic character which reside in its very fragmentariness and embodied sprawl and in its halting, inconclusive, and half-known lives. The chronological complexities of the book would be set aside in any sequential grouping and the tremors of resonance between disparate stories, characters, and events would disappear. Story "blocks" take on their own authority: thus arranged, *While the Billy Boils* would cease to exist as a living, fluid, and evolving world and become a mere collection. Sketches which, as they stand, are already dangerously ephemeral or slight, would lose much of their point disjoined from the context which supports and sustains them. The city-bush opposition running through the book would be blunted ... And so on. It is a peculiarly Victorian impulse to require what is in appearance ragged, unordered, disturbing—though perhaps unpalatably truthful—to be brought into line with unexamined notions of what is *normal* and acceptable, even though, in the process, the edge of truth, the peculiar insight, is lost. And it is a specially modern tendency to eschew the claims of say, fictional chronology and other ordering mechanisms—such as plenitude of linking and explanatory detail—in the attempt to embody experience in its raw, unmanageable, and finally unknowable turmoil. Lawson, alone among his contemporaries and consequently often misunderstood by them,[24] adopted a method both in individual stories and in the series *While the Billy Boils* as a whole, which is an application of this latter tendency. It was not in the nature of his work that it could be effectively organized along conventional lines.

Such, as I see it, is Lawson's fictional world in *While the Billy Boils*. It is a world which, as we know, spilled beyond the confines of that book. Mrs. Spicer of "Water Them Geraniums" for example, *seems* to be the Drover's Wife emerged from the shadow, turning a darkened profile to the light; as ever, we cannot be absolutely sure but the available evidence including even such trivial but memorable incidents as that with the torn handkerchief—strongly suggests the identification. It is a classic case not of Lawson's careless randomness in the use and re-use of characters,[25] but, on the contrary, of his deliberate return to certain characters when he understood them more profoundly. Lawson was well aware of the commanding "presence" of the Drover's Wife in *While the Billy Boils*,[26] but it was only later that he was able to supply that same woman with the psychological reality which the earlier story starkly and hauntingly hinted at. It is not surprising that such a vital world should have grown beyond its original formal bounds and tragic that the imagination in which it was fostered should have, for whatever reason, failed to sustain it. But in its flowering it projected a vision of human life as submerged, anonymous, and quickly forgotten; existing and striving in a vast disturbance of change, uncertainty and death; fleetingly ennobled, more often sad and desperate; and always on a long, devious but inexorable journey to defeat. It is no doubt the vision of a man innately tragic, deaf, introspective, adrift frighteningly in his own inner silences, but much of what Lawson saw in the outback endorsed his perspective, and it was, in any case, his unique achievement not only to capture that world, to "fix it", but then to set it free again, living and dynamic, as much in motion half a century later as when he saw, transmuted, and recorded it. I have tried in this essay to distinguish and explain how that feat was managed.

11

Lawson the Poet

COLIN RODERICK

More than half a century has passed since leader writers throughout Australia paid tribute in obituary notices to Henry Lawson. With few exceptions they referred to him as "the poet Lawson"; but paradoxically enough, few of them maintained that his name would live by his "poetry"—by which they meant his verse. Few looked at his work in verse and prose as complementary. Yet any mutually exclusive identification of Lawson the poet with his verse or of Lawson the short story writer with his prose results in a partial view that obscures the total significance of his work. The superior merit of Lawson's short stories has led, by a kind of comparative assessment, to undue depreciation of his verse: it has of late even been dismissed as of no account, despite its perennial popularity.

This latter-day denunciation of Lawson's verse is characterized by a vehemence that reminds one of the suffragette's condemnation of St. Paul. It seems to me to echo the detractor's anxiety to convince himself as well as his readers that Lawson was no poet. The passionate energy, the surging vitality that inform Lawson's verse seem to unbalance those critics who find it unaccountable that so many people should after so many years find satisfaction in his portraits of the human condition.

That these portraits are rough-hewn matters less to men than that they offer insight into the human heart. Lawson himself had little interest in the subtleties of technique. He sought no greater mastery of prosody than he needed to express his emotion forcefully and memorably. His verse has in it too many of the elements of satire for prepossession with the artifices of lyricism. He made no erudite study of poetic technique: what he knew he had learned in childhood experience from Irish folk tunes and the old border ballads, both adapted to bush songs; in boyhood application to the popular poets of the nineteenth century; and in adolescent study of such widely varying models as Bret Harte, Kipling, Campbell, Tennyson, Byron—and G.R. Sims.

The creative urge that impelled Lawson very early to utter songs of so-called social protest—they are in fact songs of moral protest—was not harnessed by long discipline in the craft of poetry. His early verses were "clever and telling"—as John Farrell said of them—and it was not in Lawson's personality to hold his hand. His power of self-criticism was extremely slight. Nor were the circumstances of his life such as to favour that protracted apprenticeship without which there cannot be thoroughly grounded, steady technical development. There was no Horton to which he could retire to refine his views on the way of God and man.

Lawson's portraits of the human condition reflect his baffling personality, superficially unstable, yet fundamentally consistent. Here was a man with a deeply felt moral ideal of human brotherhood and social responsibility, the first singer of that ideal ethic which I have elsewhere called social humanism. Alas, it was a man haunted by an equally deep-seated sense of insecurity, a man without the educational experience that might have enabled him to formulate and communicate it in closer conformity with convention. To make the tragedy more complete it was a man cursed at the same time with a fear of insanity—not without reason—and driven by conflicting compulsions into alcoholism and its degrading aftermath. Poverty dogged him throughout his life—self-induced, as he well knew, and therefore all the more potent in its influence on his moral attitudes.

The essence of everything that is poetic in Lawson's verse rests in its essentially personal quality: whatever Lawson's mind approaches is brought into the focus of its relationship to his complex personality. And this applies to the simplest of his poetry. I have heard his rhetorical question,

> O who would paint a goldfield
> And paint the picture right?

spoken by a man who knew the goldfields; and his manner of saying the words suggested that between him and Lawson there was a secret shared. Perhaps he, too, had seen, as Lawson compels us to see, "in early morning's light",

> The yellow mounds of mullock
>   With spots of red and white,
> The scattered quartz that glistened
>   Like diamonds in light;
>
> The azure line of ridges,
>   The bush of darkest green,
> The little homes of calico
>   That dotted all the scene.

The knowledge that Lawson had been stone-deaf for eight years before he composed "The Roaring Days" enhances the merit of his imagery in the musical stanza that follows as he revives his emotional reaction to the goldfield when he viewed it at the age of seven:

> I hear the fall of timber
>   From distant flats and fells,
> The pealing of the anvils
>   As clear as little bells,
> The rattle of the cradle,
>   The clack of windlass-boles,
> The flutter of the crimson flags
>   Above the golden holes.

"Poetry? Y-e-s-s. But simple, crude, and narrow!" Perhaps. But I still hear another speaker say, (in "Men Who Came Behind "), with all the ironic weight that the words are capable of bearing, "There's a class of men (and women) who are always on their guard"—and the truth of Lawson's trenchant words leaps out from the line. Simple, crude, narrow? Well, "we'll leave *that* to be hackneyed by the fellow in the rear."

The late Miles Franklin looked on "Middleton's Rouseabout" as an epigram on the squattocracy: the shift of pastoral fortunes in the nineteenth century has never been more succinctly represented:

> Swiftly the years went over,
>   Liquor and drought prevailed;
> Middleton went as a drover
>   After his station had failed.

> Type of a careless nation,
>   Men who are soon played out,
> Middleton was:——and his station
>   Was bought by the Rouseabout.

Cecil Hadgraft held that "The Teams" had fixed the image of a bullock-team in the Australian consciousness: certainly no clearer image of it exists in literature.

> With eyes half-shut to the blinding dust,
>   And necks to the yokes bent low,
> The beasts are pulling as bullocks must;
> And the shining tires might almost rust
>   While the spokes are turning slow.

About this poem I have only one complaint to make: that whoever persuaded Lawson to amend the fourth line to what it reads as quoted did not know the bush, or the long double file of twenty bullocks or more pulling their weary way along a level dusty road with several tons of huge logs packed high on the waggon, or, what is more to the point, that the brakes of most bullock-waggons worked from the rear when the bullocky's offsider revolved a wheel with a handle to turn a long worm, forcing wooden pads to apply a gradually increasing steady pressure to the even-surfaced rims of the steel tires rather than to the uneven pitted surface of the tire itself. A knowledge of the amount of pressure required demanded experience and skill, first, lest the tire be buckled, but more importantly, to offset accurately the force of gravity. Lawson had seen the brakes working that way as a boy, as I myself often did, and the accuracy of his image is besmirched by the emendation. Put what he wrote when he composed "The Teams", and the picture is true: "Till the shining rims of the tire-rings rust". The tire rims shone from almost continuous application of the brake to retard the descent of the waggon down the mountain slopes and sidings, for the nature of the bullock is such that he continues to pull "as bullock's must": just as steadily and doggedly downhill as on the level. Once on the level road, snaking along through rain, mud, and dust, the steel tire-rims lost their gleaming brightness, dulled, tarnished, rusted.

To pass from the vignette of the teams to a longer sustained narrative poem, it is hard to find a genuine ballad of the bush that has been written in Australia since 1889 to compare with "Brighten's Sister-in-Law, or, The Carrier's Story", so long immured in the *Town and Country Journal*. The composition of the 200-line ballad in 1889, setting aside its unfailing linguistic consistency, becomes of some significance when related to the short story bearing the first half of the title, written between 1897 and 1900. The import of the ballad is almost identical with that of the prose story; but belonging, as it does, to Lawson's bachelor days in Sydney, the action emerges as an imaginative construction owing nothing to the experiences of his married life. The short story, which Lawson fathered on Joe Wilson in 1900, was composed quite separately from the Joe Wilson sequence as it appeared in 1901 and owes its present place in the sequence to William Blackwood's encouragement. But that is another story. The significance of the ballad is twofold: first, it reveals that as an artist Lawson was as capable of discerning and skilfully realizing the objective correlative as Goethe or Burger, and secondly, that it reveals a correlation between his verse and his prose that cannot be disregarded in any debate on whether or not Lawson was essentially a poet.

"Brighten's Sister-in-Law" was written in the tight double rhyming ballad stanza, a form which I venture to say suits the tone and movement of the ballad. When he came to tell another story in verse that demanded the swifter movement of conflict, he adopted the looser form of the fourteener, and his use of the long swinging couplets produces a stirring rendering of the riot at Ballarat.

Many *Bulletin*, *Truth*, and *Worker* rhymesters tried their hands at representations of bush and out-back; but too many are no more than photographs: they do not go beyond the fact. Today, for example, there is only one "Shanty on the Rise"—one that captures the (romantic) shantiness of all shanties, despite the obliteration of the original refrain that concluded each stanza. To illustrate one tint of the spectrum of Lawson's verse, I allow myself the luxury of quoting the final stanza as Lawson wrote it, premising by way of justification, or apology, that the solo and chorus arouse personal recollections of such festivities with the belles of Broweena forty years ago in

COLIN RODERICK

the parlour of the decaying coach-change inn at Musket Flat on the
old Cobb & Co. route to Kingaroy. May their eyes light upon these
lines!

> There is little real pleasure in the city where I am—
> There's a swarry round the corner with its mockery and sham;
> But a fellow can be happy when around the room he whirls
> In a party Up-the-Country with the jolly country girls.
> Why, at times I almost fancied I was dancing on the skies
> When I danced with Mary Carey in the Shanty on the Rise.

> CHORUS: O, at times I almost fancied I was dancing on the skies
>   When I danced with Mary Carey in the Shanty on the
>   Rise,
>   In the Shanty on the Rise,
>   In the Shanty on the Rise;
>   When I danced with Mary Carey in the Shanty on the
>   Rise.

Plus ça change, plus c'est la même chose. And for a witness, I go
back to a paragon of theorists, Sir Philip Sidney in his *Defence of
Poesy*:

> In Wales, the true remnant of the ancient Britons, as there are good
> authorities to show, the long time they had poets, which they called
> bards, so through all the conquests of Romans, Saxons, Danes, and
> Normans, some of whom did seek to ruin all memory of learning
> from among them, yet do their poets, even to this day, last; ... [and]
> certainly, I must confess my own barbarousness, I never heard the old
> song of Percy and Douglas that I found not my heart moved more
> than with a trumpet; and yet it is sung by some blind crowder, with no
> rougher voice than rude style ...

Likewise, only one singer of the shearer's joys and woes has
stood the test of time. His name, too, happens to be Henry Lawson!

> No church-bell rings them from the Track,
>   No pulpit lights their blindness—
> 'Tis hardship, drought and homelessness
>   That teach these Bushmen kindness;

And of what does that "kindness" consist?

> The mateship born of barren lands,
>   Of toil and thirst and danger—
> The camp-fare for the stranger set,
>   The first place to the stranger.

People who have lost contact with the simple ethic of the Nazarene—"which was neighbour to him that fell among the thieves?"—may shrug a sophisticated shoulder at Lawson's homely image; but I declare myself a believer, as John Le Gay Brereton and my lamented friend John Barrie were believers, in the gospel of Lawson's ethic of social humanism as expressed in his simple, concrete, sensuous language.

As for the city, its despair has been painted with such passionate insight in "Faces in the Street" that everyone immediately associates the idea with Lawson's words. "The Watch on the Kerb" may mirror circumstances that have perhaps passed with time—in Sydney; but they are still with us elsewhere. And the brutality of the low life of the city has never been depicted more ruthlessly than in "The Captain of the Push": substitute bikies for larrikins, and the idea remains.

Is there any verse, outside Shelley's and Ebenezer Elliott's, that can match "For'ard" and "The Triumph of the People" as a generous forecast of the victory of the all-encompassing democratic ideal?

> Not the victory of Churches, nor of Punishment, and Wrath
> Not the triumph of the sceptic, throwing shadows on the path,
> But of Christ and love and mercy o'er the Monarch and the Rod,
> For the harvest of the Saviour is the aftermath of God.

What other verses have scourged the betrayal of that ideal so mercilessly as "Rise Ye! Rise Ye!"?

> Rise ye! rise ye! noble toilers! rise! behold, revenge is near;
> See the leaders of the people! come an' 'ave a pint o' beer!

Not Byron himself could have been more scathing of the political life of New South Wales in 1891! Have things changed all that much since 1891? And where?

The sly echoes of Tennyson in "The Ballad of Mabel Clare" bring another dimension, that of irony, into Lawson's attack on the extravagant distortion of the democratic ideal that has merely worsened since his time. A sprig of the nobility—and the blue blood of England, be it said, flows in the veins of many a Queenslander—woos the daughter of a hard old cockatoo, a crimson Anarchist who

> Preached that ev'ry man was free,
>   And also "ekal born".

His lordship learns to love that radiant Mabel Clare while,

> Strolling through a moonlit gorge,
>   She chatted all the while
> Of Ingersoll, and Henry George,
>   And Bradlaugh, and Carlyle.

Things go on swimmingly

> Until he said he was an Earl,
>   And asked her to be his.

Confusion! For Mabel is a democrat and cannot "wed a swell". In vain he assures her that

> A simple lord can love as well
>   As any rouseabout!

He promises to drop the title, and Mabel Clare elopes with him, to the fluent fury of the cockatoo, whose command of curses arouses the admiration of the Western bullockies. But the old man's ire and Mabel's sorrow over her desertion of the people's cause to join the upper crust evaporate when her husband confesses that he had adopted the disguise of an earl merely to prove that Mabel's love for him was genuine and that he was in truth—a rouseabout.

> He pawned his togs, and home he took
>   His bride in all her charms;
> The proud old cockatoo received
>   The pair with open arms.
> And long they lived, the faithful bride,
>   The noble rouseabout—
> And if she wasn't satisfied,
>   She never let it out.

Turning from this, the only parody of a stock motif in Victorian verse that has endured, to a sombre note, Lawson captures magnificently the everlasting form and feature of the Western landscape in the lightning-swift pen portraits of "The Great Grey Plain":

> No break in its awful horizon,
>   No blur in the dazzling haze,
> Save where by the bordering timber
>   The fierce, white heat-waves blaze;
> And out where the tank-heap rises
>   Or looms when the long days wane,
> Till it seems like a distant mountain
>   Low down on the Great Grey Plain.

Modern readers, victims of the desecration of the word "aw- ful", unacquainted with the reality of the "dazzling" haze out back or with the universal reaction to the tank-heap that is enshrined in Lawson's image of it, may well miss the permanence of the idea ex- pressed in such poetry. He who has not seen what Lawson portrays here may be assured that it goes to the heart of the matter—in lines that evoke the vast, challenging, fascinating, terrifying idea of dis- tance that lives in the mind through experience of the out-back. It is indeed awful—"awe-full", in the pristine purity of the word, as Lawson meant it to be—immense, frightening, awe-inspiring. If the city reader's mind is insensitive to the poetry of these lines, is it the fault of the poetry?

Lawson's "Never-Never Land" survives to grip the imagination with the mystery of its symbolism:

> It lies beyond the farming belt,
>   Wide wastes of scrub and plain,
> A blazing desert in the drought,
>   A lake-land after rain;
> To the skyline sweeps the waving grass,
>   Or whirls the scorching sand—
> A phantom land, a mystic land!
>   The Never-Never Land.

Lawson's vision is not photographic; it is ideal. Yet how true it is to the probability that men forget—until the waters of the Gulf extend 200 miles into the inland wastes of North Queensland in irresistible flood. Lawson's "Never-Never Land" is a visionary land, a land where men and women of heroic stature alone can survive. This is his desert from which the prophets come. His vision of it transcends the limitations of time.

I confess that I feel the breath of Sweeney's ghost over my shoulder whenever the poem that he inhabits floats into my mind. "There, but for the grace of God, goes John Bradford." Bradford would have understood Sweeney—"And I wonder why he haunts me more than any other ghost." Perhaps the answer is in the belief that it is not because of any acquired characteristic that the fortunately endowed among us do not in actuality, but only vicariously, share the prophetic shudder that passed through the poet's frame with the recollection of his model:

> And, perhaps, his face forewarned me of a face that I might see
> From a bitter cup reflected in the wretched days to be.

It is a hard, nay, a cruel, thing to say; but *we* are the richer for Lawson's poverty, for his alcoholism, and for the manic-depressive temperament that excited it. The spiritual solitude that he suffered after the failure of his marriage led to the fragmentation of his personality, to a deep sense of failure, to the slough of Darlinghurst Gaol and into still deeper isolation and despair. Yet just as Coleridge's misery could awaken the artist in him, so the poet in Lawson could lift him out of the darkness of the pit, above the havoc of his personal disaster, to write the most moving prison poem in the language. I quote from the tattered fragments of manuscript, not from versions improved by *Bulletin* editors, by David McKee Wright, and other meddlers:

> The High Church service swells and swells where the tinted Christ looks down—
> It is easy to see who is weary and faint and weareth the thorny crown.
> There are swift-made signs that are not to God, and they march us hellward then,
> It is hard to believe that we knelt as boys to "for ever and ever, Amen".

Again, had his marriage not failed, had not his wife come to embody for him all that was evil in mankind—slander, deceit, faithlessness, dishonesty, treachery—it is unlikely that he would have substituted for her a ghostly image that enshrined his ideal of the graces of womanhood. That ideal inspired him to compose several poems in which it takes shape in the figure of Hannah Thorburn. It is of the essence of poetry that his ideal should have improved upon the model, and that his portrait of the ideal should have become one with Petrarch's Laura or Dante's Beatrice. Like Dante, he looks up to the ideal for guidance through the hell of his existence until death should unite their spiritual essences, and he puts his plea into the simple yet profound, the concrete yet ethereal and suprasensual lines "To Hannah":

> Spirit girl, the good is in me,
>   But the flesh you know is weak,
> And with no pure soul to win me,
>   I might miss the path I seek;
> Lead me by the love you bore me
>   When you trod the earth with me,
> Till the light is clear before me
>   And my spirit too is free.

It is significant that he could not finish "Ruth" until he had conceived this figure, and the Ruth must die to redeem Jack Drew, as the spirit of Hannah would redeem Lawson's own soul: the idea is not new, but it loses nothing of its poetry in Lawson's hands.

One might cite half a dozen poems in which Lawson moves from the particular to the general in depicting the tide of sorrow that washes over mankind. I venture to suggest that together they yield a composite impression of the sadness of stricken humanity. Let anyone who doubts it turn to the poetry of Lawson's years of suffering and ask himself if these poems apply only to Lawson.

In his essay, "Saint Henry—Our Apostle of Mateship" (*Quadrant*, vol. 5, no. 1, 1960), Professor Harry Heseltine makes the point that mateship as an ethic rarely, if ever, stirs Lawson's imagination: the assertion may be accepted, if, as Heseltine does, the critic confines himself to the short stories, but not if he takes Lawson's verse into account as well. To my mind, the most significant observation made by Heseltine is that Lawson's "idea of the highest masculine virtues lies in the nature of his principal figures ... the solitaries, the bearers of some secret sorrow, some thought that lies too deep for tears". In truth no other Australian poet save Brennan has explored the theme of the solitary wanderer more sympathetically than Lawson. He understands the inward compulsion of the lonely wanderer:

> For my ways are strange ways and new ways and old ways,
> And deep ways and steep ways and high ways and low;
> I'm at home and at ease on a track that I know not,
> And restless and lost on a road that I know.

It is unfortunate that Leon Cantrell should, in his review of *Henry Lawson Criticism : 1894-1971 (Australian Literary Studies*, vol. 6, no. 1, 1973), adopt such a stance as makes it necessary for me to repeat what has already been said in the introduction to that volume.

It is but one step, and that a short one, from the creation of a ghostly guide to the realization of the significance of the solitary. The superficial glance may take in the figure of the swagman on the track and dismiss it as an outmoded symbol of an Australian way of life that is past. Fallacy! Lawson's solitaries are permanent. They are in the long line that reaches back to the earliest literature in English. The lines I have already quoted struck St. John Adcock in

1919 as atavistic. Could it be that Adcock saw deeper into the poetic nature of Lawson's mind than Mr. Cantrell does? Saw deeper into the nature of man also, perhaps. So, too, perhaps did Emile Saillens in 1909, who had Alfred de Vigny before him for a comparison. So, it seems, also, did Adele Fuchs, in 1914, for whom Lawson's solitary was paralleled by Goethe's: it is the solitary who sees God, or the New Jerusalem, call it what you will, the solitary cursed with the compulsion of *Freiheitsdrang* and *Wandertrieb*. It is true that Lawson's verse does not spell out his vision : that took shape in his short stories. The verse proclaims the Idea, the short stories give it body and form: in one or two poems Lawson introduces a supporting symbol. With Matthew Arnold for warrant, perhaps Mr. Cantrell will permit me the luxury of quoting from my Introduction to *Henry Lawson Criticism : 1894-1971*. "His solitary rider, his lone wanderer, are only two of the manifestations of the poetic mind that evolves them as prophetic and symbolic warning figures whose appearance coincides with"—I might perhaps more truly have written "represents"—"a decline in social ethics amounting to a betrayal of his Idea of moral perfection." To put it in another way, they represent a facet of the search for a lost perfection, like the countless tribe of European wanderers represented in countless poems composed since the Anglo-Saxon scop first sang "The Wanderer": "Waraỗ hine wraeclast nales wunden gold." Richard II belongs to this tribe, as Mitchell and Voss do, as Brennan's "Wanderer" does.

Contemplating the type, Lawson had a vision of an ideal republic—a vision, like the visions of moral perfection vouchsafed to many poets, never to be realized—and it is this vision, expressed in poems like "The Never-Never Land" and "Above Crow's Nest", that converts many of his short stories to vignettes portraying its form and feature.

In "Above Crow's Nest" Lawson came as near to being explicit in his definition of the solitary as any Zoilus is entitled to expect:

> Is he—and who shall know it?—
>   The spectre of a scout?
> The spirit of a poet,
>   Whose truths were met with doubt?

Viewed in the mystic light that lights all poetry, such poems assume depth and breadth, become pregnant with moral significance. They make the claim that none of Lawson's verse is poetry manifest-

ly untenable. A substantial enough amount of it emerges as poetry of
no mean order, even if the greater part is inferior in quality, as many
another poet's is, to his best work. In spite of that, how little of it all
is dull! The verse that is technically conventional still has something
new to say, sometimes to the social historian, sometimes to the student of cultural attitudes.

And Lawson remains much more than a mere painter of social
and cultural attitudes. What distinguishes him from the social
protestants in our literature is the moral energy embodied in his vision of social humanism triumphant. His vision, as I say, is unat-
tainable, for the motives of fallible man are rooted in selfish instincts
and prejudices. Such passionate early poems as "A Song of the
Republic", "The Triumph of the People", and "In the Days When
the World Was Wide" predict his ideal republic of the mind, an ideal
moral state, not a political programme; but his moral programme
has been obvious enough to all receptive to it since first he wrote.
As time went on he drew it plain in his short stories and touched on
its finer features in such poems as "The Dons of Spain", "The
Stranger's Friend", "The Little Czar", "Who'll Wear the Beaten
Colours?", "Break o' Day", and, to mention one that always calls to
my mind Goethe's identically named poem, "New Life, New Love".

> The breezes blow on the river below,
> And the fleecy clouds float high,
> And I mark how the dark green gum trees match
> The bright blue dome of the sky.
> The rain has been and the grass is green,
> Where the slopes were bare and brown,
> And I see the things that I used to see
> In the days ere my head went down.

Goethe's way of putting the notion of regeneration through
renewed love is not so very different, despite the superficial differences of mood and tone. And speaking of Goethe and Burger, is
there no significance in the occurrence of the narrators' visions in
"Erlkönig" and "Brighten's Sister-in-Law" (both verse and prose
versions), to say nothing of "Lenore", again despite the variations in
their import? Those desperate night rides, the visions, the wordless
communication between apparition and horseman: are these of no
account?

The verse in which this personal vision found expression is
related to many of his short stories: they may be regarded as illustra-

tions of his deeply felt moral convictions—ballads in prose some of them; some of them, as I have shown, repetitions of earlier verse ballads.

Speaking for myself—and who shall arbitrate?—I would not willingly part with anything that he wrote, even the worst, for even that helps to measure his best; I would not wish anyone to be deprived on any of it. One may feel of Lawson the poet, as David McKee Wright did, that "the axemarks show in his work everywhere"; but one's own prejudices are no warrant for using a smoothing-plane on it, or endeavouring to force it into a preconceived political mould. It is fitting that the axemarks should show, for Lawson's Australia was hewn into shape with the axe, and for many the axe, as it was for Lawson, is still as proud a symbol of the shaping of man's destiny as the hammer.

We do not look, say, in *Hudibras* for subtle rhythms and cunning vowel music. We enjoy the comic looseness of *Don Juan*. We do not ask any satirist or social critic to embellish his verse with the trappings of Keatsian fancy. The eloquence we ask of poets in whom the critical faculty is the persuasive element places them in a different order. So does that for which we may justly look in Lawson. His eloquence is the eloquence of the inspired, indignant tribune of the plebs. If we fail to perceive that he wears a poet's robe, the fault may not be in him, but in those of us who take too narrow or too perverse a view of poetry. For poetry wears more than one robe: it is not always purple. Lawson's robe is of homespun stuff; and the significant thing about it is that it carries complementary colours on either side. Inside his verse, outside his prose. Lawson's verse is not to be read in isolated poems. Related where it may be to his prose, it carries its modest reward within it, for the divine finger touched this man—even if but lightly.

Of all Australian writers none has been more wronged by the restricted application of the English word "poet" to the writer of verse. Rhyme, blank verse, free verse—call it what you will—all is mere convention. The Germans are wiser in their universal use of *Dichter* to describe the imaginative writer, still wiser in their use of *Erlebnisdichter* for such an artist as Lawson, the whole body of whose work, it seems to me, is at the very least a late Victorian colonial *Dichtung und Wahrheit*.

One stubborn fact remains: more than four generations of

Australians have evinced unswerving fidelity to Lawson as poet. His continuing annual sales suggest that the general public still regards his work more highly than that of any other Australian. Academic fashions change, and with them the reputations of writers wax and wane. The devotee of today is the infidel of tomorrow. In the face of Lawson's popular survival and of the disappearance from the bookshelves of those below whom the contemporary exclusivists of poetic theory grade him, is not the onus on the infidel to prove that what Lawson writes is not poetry?

12

The Daunting Doubts of
William Hay

P. D. EDWARDS

Recent argument about William Hay's classic costume romance, *The Escape of the Notorious Sir William Heans*, has centred on two sets of questions: the extent to which the convict-hero feels, and ought to feel, that the sin for which he was transported, and perhaps some of his subsequent sins as well, require contrition and expiation; and the character and motivation of his chief enemy, Mr. Daunt. Without recapitulating previous contributions to the debate, or recording in detail the respects in which my own views agree or disagree with those of other critics, I hope in this paper to throw some new light on the questions at issue. There appear to me to be two sources of illumination, apart from the novel itself, that have not yet been adequately tapped: Hay's other novels, and his debts to certain of his predecessors in the field of romance.

Published in 1918, *The Escape of the Notorious Sir William Heans (and the Mystery of Mr. Daunt); a Romance of Tasmania* was the fourth of Hay's six novels. It had been preceded by *Stifled Laughter; a Melodrama (Time 1834)*, published in 1901, *Herridge of Reality Swamp* (1907), and *Captain Quadring* (1912). The two novels that followed it were *Strabane of the Mulberry Hills; the Story of a Tasmanian Lake in 1841* (1929) and *The Mystery of*

Alfred Doubt; Being the Adventure of a Retired Statesman (1937). *Sir William Heans* thus came midway through Hay's writing career. It also represents the peak of his achievement, the longest, most elaborate, and certainly the most adult of his novels and the culmination of a steady process of development. The two tales that appeared later seem to me clearly and revealingly inferior, not only to it but to *Herridge* and *Captain Quadring*.

Certain motifs recur in all six of the novels. The hero, often both the hero and the heroine, are always pursued and persecuted by malicious agencies. Even when the persecution is overt its means and motives are partly concealed from the victim(s). The persecuting agency is always identified with a particular individual or group of individuals, but except in one novel (*Strabane*) it derives its power from a system, a legal authority. Again with only one exception (*Stifled Laughter*), the victim of persecution is a gentleman, a person of refinement and proud self-respect, and the persecutor's malice includes a strong tincture of class-envy. An equally invariable part of the pattern is the heroine who, from love of the hero, natural kindness, and hatred of evil, bravely interposes herself between the victim and his persecutor. Except in *Alfred Doubt*, however, there are always in addition one or more weak or malevolent women who betray the hero; indeed in two of the novels, *Herridge* and *Strabane*, women are his worst persecutors: Hay's women tend to be either angels or devils. In all of the novels except *Stifled Laughter* the hero in effect escapes his oppressors towards the end by a hazardous flight in which he is pitted against inhospitable nature and in which his courage, stamina, and resourcefulness are tested.

Within this broadly uniform pattern there are of course important differences of detail, and in one major respect—the character of the main agent of persecution—*Sir William Heans* and *Captain Quadring* almost break out of the pattern. But some features of the pattern which are more or less common to all the novels, and which may throw light on matters that have worried commentators on *Sir William Heans*, can be noted at this stage. In particular it may be significant that while all but one of the heroes are convicts, or commit crimes rendering them liable to imprisonment, none is so morally flawed as to merit the punishments he suffers. Sir William Heans, it will be recalled, is transported for abducting a married woman and apparently threatening to rape her. Hay felt that he had to "find a crime that I could bear in a man for a hero",[1] and he implies his own lenient judgment of Heans's crime by recounting it only in an aside, an interpolated "note" (pp.86—87).* The abducted woman, he suggests, must have had some inkling of Heans's lustful designs and may even have been a party to them, though in the end, when alone with him, she created an uproar either because she belatedly took fright or because she had planned all along to embroil him in a scandal. Whatever the extenuating circumstances, Hay admits, Heans's "sin remains indelible", but this stern pronouncement is somewhat undercut by the concluding sentence of the "note": "It is a fair comment on the case that the lady was in after life again in the Courts." Critics who see Heans's sin as one that calls for penance and atonement take the view that he almost repeats it, perhaps more reprehensibly, when he tries to persuade Matilda Shaxton, who has helped him in his first plan of escape and who is a married woman, to fly with him. According to this line of argument it is only when he forfeits his second chance to escape by going to the aid of another woman, Abelia, who is in the clutches of a would-be rapist—a grim caricature of his unredeemed self—that he expiates his sin and earns the right to freedom.[2]

There is considerable evidence in the novel to support this line of argument, but none of it is unambiguous. There is also corroborative external evidence, such as Hay's intense uxoriousness, his commitment to Christianity, and his fondness for writers like Dickens, Marcus Clarke, and, I suspect, Victor Hugo in whom the message of redemption through suffering and humiliation bulks large. But if we look at Hay's work as a whole, if we take account of certain idiosyncratic aspects of the vision of life it expresses, it becomes harder to believe that Heans's punishment can be meant to be judged as condign and commensurate to his sins. His gallantry, his evident lack of reverence for the marriage-tie, may be unchristian; but for Hay it is clearly part of the aristocratic nature which is the source of all his "fineness" as well as of his blemishes. In this connexion it is notable that his heroes, in general, are not poor men or men of lowly position battling the oppressive power of money and rank, like Godwin's Caleb Williams, Hugo's Valjean (initially), or Nicholas Nickleby and his family. Nor are they men like Rufus Dawes who can forget or lay aside their pride of rank. On the con-

* All my references are to the Melbourne University Press reprint (1955). For all the other novels, my references are to the first editions.

trary they are nearly all self-conscious aristocrats, men of conspicuous and elaborate courtliness, especially towards women.[3] But although none of them, except possibly Heans, ever intentionally maltreats a woman, all are brought to bay by misjudgments of women, stemming in the main from aristocratic pride and self-sufficiency and from a gallantry that usually includes a large measure of quixotism: indeed nearly all of them (and also Jim Dust, the lowborn convict-hero of *Stifled Laughter*) are betrayed by women, some subtly, some with brutal directness.

Jim Dust learns that his wife had married him only to put herself in a better position to help her former lover, but he magnanimously forgives her when he recognizes that she now loves him and merely pities the other man. In *Herridge* the hero's clerical career in England is ruined when the girl he had loved blames him for her own faithlessness and lapse into vice, making him an object of execration. Later, as the wife of a convict-commandant in Manalia (New South Wales), she continues her vendetta against him and, through her husband, is instrumental in having him unjustly convicted. And not only is a woman his principal persecutor, but two other women—daughters of the army officer to whom he is assigned as a servant—are among the cruellest and most gratuitous of his tormentors. Yet Herridge had submitted to disgrace rather than defend his own good name by besmirching that of a base woman. In *Captain Quadring*, Sir Andrew Fairservice's betrothed transfers her affections to his brother and, by so doing, uproots both the brothers from their ancestral estate and causes a deadly feud between them. In *Strabane*, the hero believes that his young wife had deserted him, many years before, partly because of his unkindness to her—in a situation that sorely tried his forbearance—and partly because of her own fickleness. To atone for his fault and to fill her place he adopts two young nieces, but they, as they grow up, treat him with a derisive malevolence that culminates in a bizarre plot to poison him. He is rendered pathetically vulnerable by his chivalrous attitude to women, which prevents him from conceiving the intensity of his nieces' gratuitous hatred. One of the leading minor characters in *Strabane*, the bushranger Martin Cash, is presented as a man with a great faith in women whose life has been blasted by their treachery to him, but who remains at their service whatever the risk to his own safety.[4]

The persistence of this pattern of a too gentlemanly, too idealistic faith in women, which the women in question fail to live up to, makes it unlikely that Hay would have asked sympathy for a hero capable of abduction and rape. In Hay's parlance such a man would have to be "cynical", a man who had lost faith in the supremacy of good over evil in human nature and human life. Unlike Alfred Doubt, and all of the other heroes, he would be excluded from the category of the "looking-for-good sort of man" (*Alfred Doubt*, p.301). He would in all likelihood be not a gentleman but a "vulgarian", for, as the chief narrator of *Strabane* rhetorically demands, "can any but a vulgarian be ruthless?" (*Strabane*, p.170.) In lying to a woman for lascivious ends he would have been guilty of grossly and unmistakably betraying his own honour as a gentleman; he would have been the "libertine" that the novel almost expressly says he is not (p.19). What seems much more likely, if we bring the evidence of the other novels to bear on the complex evidence of *Sir William Heans* itself, is that the charge of abduction and rape against Heans was groundless, that the lady framed him for some malevolent purpose not fully intelligible to herself and not at all to him, and that his gentlemanly honour made it impossible for him to exculpate himself by blaming her.

But if this was the case, it will naturally be asked, why doesn't Heans, or Hay, ever tell us so in private? At any rate why are we not given more definite hints? The answer to the first question is that Heans, in his own person, tells us hardly anything, that the novel is simply a version of his story pieced together by a friend, Charles Scarning, partly from Heans's "private album", but chiefly, it appears, from letters he later wrote to Scarning. As "editor", Scarning comments at one point (p.205) on Heans's "reticence"—even in his private album—and Heans was evidently so reticent about the affair that led to his being transported that our information about it comes in a note interpolated, presumably, by Scarning himself. However, less than two chapters after the note occurs a scene which is scarcely comprehensible except on the assumption that Heans feels he has been trifled with and savagely betrayed by some lustful woman, some Salome. The scene is that of his arrival at the Shaxtons' country property on the day before his first attempt at escape, so that it takes place *after* Matilda has shown him how kindly and devotedly a woman can serve a man:

> Sir William in a pair of exquisite duck breeches, with white leather straps, a high-shouldered clawhammer, and a "pudding cravat" of blue satin, held his grey hat and cane by the door. A few women placed pale eyes on him; a few looked coldly; a few stared evilly. How shocking is evil in a woman! The men—benevolent, courtly,

diplomatic, grizzled, grave, jocose—treated the appearance of the newcomer after their several ways: some—of those that knew him—simulating surprise; others concealing discomfort; one or two speaking suddenly to him, as they passed, of the weather, this or that.

His eyeglassed eye passed slowly round ...

Here and there were grim heads, poised like decapitated John the Baptists, on chargers of satin cravat, and offered up to some epicure Herodias in a wreathing of social smiles, which Heans had seen in situations less gentle. The transmigration, if convincing, did not seem to reassure the absconder, whose eyes, if indifferent, had a chilled look when resting on them. (p.93)

The point of view here is explicitly identified as Heans's own, and the extreme bitterness that flavours it—as well as some of his conversations about women with Jarvis Carnt—appears quite disproportionate to the immediate occasion for it. It strongly suggests that Heans must have been, or felt that he had been, grievously misused by some woman—a suggestion that would account also for other puzzling allusions to female villainy such as the editorial aside on page 40, "Surely life holds few contrasting facts so confusing as its vulgar-minded woman—than [*sic*] which no man can be so little or so base—and its angel, rich or poor."

The supposition that Heans was tricked by an evil woman who played upon his chivalrous impulses is supported by the fact that he at no stage reveals any outward sign of guilty conscience, though in general he is not good at dissembling his feelings. His one more or less overt reference to the episode with the woman—in his exchange with O'Crone just after his arrival at the Shaxtons' country property (pp.96—97)—is marked by a defensive irony which might conceal shame but which certainly doesn't strike O'Crone that way. There is an earlier scene in which it would appear that any secret qualms he might have must come to the surface; and none do. This is his long conversation with the governor, Sir John Franklin, in book 1, chapter 12. Franklin, because of his feats as an explorer and naval commander, is an acknowledged hero. He is also a fervent Christian "whose love of man was such that [his lips] were incapable of forming the word 'beast'", and a gentleman of a precise oldfashioned type, with a "great and feeling heart", at whom "we, who, in our own time, with our wild equalizing of human temperaments, are threatened with a drab end of formlessness", may feel we can afford to laugh. But Heans, who shares Matilda's enthusiasm for "the brave fellows" of the queen's navy (pp.17—19), and who in a homesick moment has christened a picture of ships in line of battle that hangs on his wall "England and the English" (p.16), is certainly not disposed to laugh at such a man. Franklin's nominal purpose is to warn Heans against "drifting" further into bad company, letting his gentlemanly standards slide; indirectly, he perhaps hopes to persuade him to abandon any thoughts of escape, but when he urges Heans to pursue "an honoured life" where he is, Heans bridles:

> "Your Excellency said 'honoured life'," said Heans, dropping his glass, with a wild, little bow. "Is there such a thing? And will you find it, sir—great traveller as you are—for a convict in this town? I put little value on existence. My dignity and honour none of your laws can touch. If I lose them, I shall cry out to no one. When they are gone, the more vulgar officials can use no worse methods against me than have been used hitherto. Do not fear for me, kind sir. I am grown too old and grim" (with a bow) "with the grey side of difficulty to play with the young ladies. The worth of a man's life—what is it? I pray you credit me with a certain happiness in my own way of it."

The touchiness about his "honour" that Heans displays here must be sheer hypocrisy, or at best crass moral obtuseness, if he has in truth betrayed it by lying to a woman for violent and lustful ends. For his remark about "the young ladies" makes it clear that he is aware of the public cloud hanging over his honour but believes that his intrinsic "dignity and honour" remain intact despite this and despite the degradation of his present "existence". Franklin, failing to perceive Heans's irony, takes his words for half-desperate bravado and anxiously warns him of his continuing responsibilities—to others if not to himself:

> "You talk of honour. Hush!" he went on, deeply moved; "I will give you my idea of it in a man. It is that he should not wound his friends by his falling. If a man have bravery and not compunction, he is no gentleman. What to him becomes mere life, must be to his friends a perpetual tragedy. If you must go your own way, Sir William Heans, see that you wound as little as need be that gentle woman who has tended you in your distress—by some unthinkable bravery."
>   ... Sir William Heans took up his glass, as he stood staring out (at the grey-clad prisoners in their black hats, at the wet town, and vastly above, the splendid frown of Old Storm Mountain ...), and put it carefully in his eye. Then he turned and bowed quickly and gravely.
>   Franklin swung round to the table, and, fingering for a second among some papers, lifted his hands towards a brass touch-bell. "I am waiting for your word to ring, sir," he said.

> Sir William Heans said, after a moment's hesitation, "Pray be good enough to ring, your Excellency."

Heans's decisive rejection of the moral cap which Franklin is trying to fit upon him, the cap of a man with "bravery" but without "compunction", is all the more convincing if we bear in mind that in general his emotions, and especially his nervous fears, do show. His blank stare, his "careful" manipulation of his eyeglass, his "grave" bow (in contrast to his earlier "wild" one) argue strongly that, at this moment of crisis, face to face with a man he must reverence, his conscience and his "honour" are clear.

Yet he apparently can reconcile it with his ideas of honour and compunction to attempt, only a day or two later, to steal another man's wife from him. This, it has been commonly asserted, shows how unregenerate he still is. But the novel hardly invites us to view it as a very dark blot on his escutcheon. The author-editor is content to observe mildly that he "would have been better had he loved the woman *just so little* more that he could have seen no reason to regret leaving her" (p.94; my italics). Matilda herself, while sharply resisting his proposition and clearly understanding that it asperses her own honour as a married woman, harbours no resentment. They part with loving kindness, and the feeling between them is described as "*their* erring love", not simply his (p.94). Even Matilda's husband, who overhears Heans's proposal, evinces no strong animus against him subsequently. Had Heans continued to urge his plea after Matilda had given the only answer compatible with her honour, he would no doubt have forfeited Shaxton's goodwill completely, perhaps also Matilda's and the reader's. But as it is Heans declares his love with such delicate self-restraint, yet such plangency, as virtually to belie (rather than validate) his notorious reputation.

Doubts may persist, nevertheless, about his apparent selfishness and lack of "compunction" in using Matilda, in taking advantage of her sympathy to secure her assistance, even at the risk of injuring her reputation. Similar doubts arise later about his failure to stop Abelia from jeopardizing her own safety in her efforts to distract Spafield's attention from Heans to herself, and about his rather brutal hectoring of the girl, on the night of his second attempt to escape, when urging her to persuade her father to give him a pass; despite her fears he has no compunction, either, in using her to carry the vital lavender pad back to Matilda. In these matters, however, the attitude we take to Heans may again be modified by what we learn from Hay's other novels about his idea of the nature and role of women.

Compared to the angel-women in some of the other novels, both Matilda and Abelia get off lightly. In *Herridge*, for example, the supposedly feebleminded Ellen, whom Herridge first meets as a little girl, and who becomes the light of his life ever after (as he of hers), disguises herself as a male convict in order that she may share his sufferings and if possible relieve them. (Even in disguise her angelic woman's nature exerts a marvellous softening influence over the enchained men.) In *Captain Quadring* the lapse of Ann, the girl who blighted the hero's life and caused his bitter feud with his younger brother, is compensated for by the "kindness", bravery, and truth of Elizabeth, who begins to soften the "iron" in his soul when he sees her for the first time as a girl of fourteen, and who eventually brings about a reconciliation between the brothers. She finds a way to "exercise the hardier elements within her woman's nature" (p.141) by driving a wagon through a quarry swarming with rebellious convicts in an effort to save the hero and his property. (The convicts, however, are again charmed by her influence, no less than is the scapegrace younger brother, who hails her as "sweet miracle" and credits her with having "brought a candle into the dim, wild nursery of life", pp.256, 258). In *Strabane* the wicked sisters who vent their derision and homicidal malice on the long-suffering hero (and who are carbon-copies of the quaintly named sisters Tea and Coffee who were among Herridge's cruellest taunters), are set against the belatedly disclosed nobility of his lost wife, which evokes from the chivalrous bushranger Martin Cash—who has been betrayed by women all his life—a notable rhapsody beginning, "These poor angels ... seem connected in a different manner with Heaven than we men; their compacts with us are, I firmly believe, more dreadly to be accounted for to Almighty God." (p.213) In *Alfred Doubt* the hero, who has tapestries on the subject of Jephtha's daughter all over his walls, is buoyed up by the instant and gushing sympathy of the heroine at a time when he is under dire threat from her three brothers; later, when they try to detain him, she shows him the way to escape.

Even the least adventurous of Hay's heroines, such as Matilda and Abelia, are more active and intrepid than the little madonnas who win the hearts and purify the souls of Sidney Carton, Jean Valjean, and Rufus Dawes. They belong, certainly, to the same romantic family, but to a more Teutonic branch of it, a branch that includes Beethoven's Leonore and the scaled-down Brunhildes of Meredith, Ibsen, and Shaw. Just as the Hay hero can always be sure that the more deeply he suffers at one woman's hands, the more gently, bravely, and selflessly he will be consoled by those of another, so the heroine seems to accept, and expect, that her sufferings, the demands made on her courage, will be proportioned to the sufferings inflicted on the hero by the devil-woman. What she craves is not to be protected by male chivalry, but to vindicate female chivalry. Thus it is practically stated, in a long authorial digression which presumably reflects Heans's own notions (p.55), that good women like Matilda have been "evolved" specifically to be used, and misused, by man. But in any case his long (and almost unique) soliloquy shortly after his interview with Franklin, ending with the exclamation, "Heaven deal with me, if ever I trouble her!" (p.90), suggests that his compunction stays alive even if it sometimes appears to sleep.

There are, it must be allowed, a few other aspects of Heans's behaviour towards women that raise awkward questions, not least his readiness to sunder himself from Matilda forever for the sake of his "liberty", and his refusal to give up his own chance of escape when it is put to him that by doing so he would improve that of Madame Ruth. Part of the answer to these questions lies, I believe, in the particular romantic tradition, attaching a supreme value to liberty, within which Hay is working. Although his novels are full of warnings against "reform" and reformers—on the grounds that they don't take enough account of the necessity to keep curbs on the evil in human nature[5]—the unspoken but unquestioned assumption in all his convict novels that the need to be free, the instinct to escape imprisonment, will take precedence over every other desire is squarely in the French revolutionary tradition. It is thus axiomatic that a man of spirit will strive to resist lawful arrest (as, for example, Alfred Doubt does) and to escape from lawful detention (as Heans does). In nearly all the novels the law, indeed all constituted authority, is almost synonymous with the threat of more or less arbitrary imprisonment. And lawbreakers, such as the bushranger Martin Cash and the murderess Madame Ruth, appear to be allowed their right to freedom with the same romantic generosity as persecuted law-abiders.

Much of this, as I have suggested, can be ascribed simply to the influence of a radical tradition which goes back to the border ballads and is continued by Schiller (in *Die Räuber*), Godwin (in *Caleb Williams*), Hugo (especially in *Les Misérables*), and to some extent Byron, Dickens, and Marcus Clarke. But Heans's conviction that an "honoured life" is impossible to him as a prisoner, that it would be dishonourable not to do all he can to escape, is obviously genuine and meant to be taken seriously. Though there are moments when he half-senses that all life may be a prison and wonders, in particular, whether liberty without love is an illusion ("Liberty! What was liberty? It was life! What was life? A little while! Oh, fair young head! Oh, kind heart! Oh, lost affection!", p.89), the novel as a whole overwhelmingly affirms his vision of prison as a "lie", poisoning all true human feelings, a denial of life itself:

> "There's not a word of truth in it, or in any of us, or Life, sir—in man, woman, or child. It is a lie. You and I are a lie, sir; and that prison; and the confounded, jangling bell. And the hills in their shadow—what a pitiful lie! Everything—hurt or joy, or faithfulness like yours, or hope like mine ... all a damnable fancy! Why should I be brave enough to hope—or you mad enough to care!" (P.125.)

For the man who utters these words, the educative value of imprisonment surely cannot be as great as most critics have implied. And though, like the Prisoner of Chillon, he finally regains his freedom "with a sigh", and with a suspicion that, bereft of love, "the whole earth would henceforth be/ A wider prison unto me", it remains a matter of course that liberty must be pursued at whatever sacrifice except that of personal honour.

Apart from the moral to be inferred from Heans's humiliations and eventual release, the most problematical element in the novel is the motivation and moral significance of Daunt, his chief persecutor. In considering this, Hay's other novels are again helpful, but most of them in a less direct and obvious way; more help can be got, I believe, from a careful weighing of the multifarious "influences" that can be, and have been, detected in his work.[6] In particular I suggest that the influence of Stevenson has been underestimated.

The remarkable difference between Daunt and nearly all of

Hay's other persecutor-villains is that he is not simply and unmistakably evil, that he appears to have good impulses contending strongly with his evil ones. Hence Heans's baffled cry, in a parenthesis which in fact may even be an editorial-authorial aside, "Devil or philanthropist, which was Daunt?" (p.79). Generally in Hay evil is unalloyed, like that of Spafield, the secondary villain in *Sir William Heans*. It is, moreover, a phenomenon for which one doesn't expect rational explanations: it simply exists, presumably always has existed since the Fall. This is not to say that it is ever entirely unmotivated. Even the apparent "hate with no motive" of Spafield is found to be based on a special, and not unintelligible, "antipathy" towards the "gentlemanlike" (pp.243,244). But the scope and intensity of evil tend to seem out of all proportion to its motive. Its malice, like that of Melville's white whale, is a natural manifestation of a supernatural principle, and in its extremest form, as the narrator of *Strabane* observes, it almost ceases to appear human, almost becomes "animal" (p.55). Even in milder form, that of simple "nastiness" or "unkindness" (two of Hay's favourite terms of opprobrium), it is apt to appear quite gratuitous.[7]

Apart from *Sir William Heans*, the only important exception to this sharp polarization of good and evil occurs in *Captain Quadring*. In all the other novels the principal agent of persecution appears absolutely evil. In *Stifled Laughter* he is a hunchback who is paid by the authorities to spy on his fellow-convicts. He haunts the rocky cliffs above the house of the hero and heroine, secretly watching all their comings and goings like a perverted, malevolent Quasimodo. (His official function, like Quasimodo's, is that of bellringer, summoning the convict fishermen home at dusk by ringing a bell on the cliff-top.) When he thinks he has his prey trapped he becomes a "jester", like another of Hugo's hunchbacks, Triboulet.[8] The ostensible motive for his vendetta is sexual jealousy, but it is ingrained malice that really rules him. In *Herridge* also, sexual jealousy, wounded sexual vanity, is the pretext for the vicious persecution of the hero by the villainess. But what really feeds her hatred, and that of all his persecutors, male and female, is the quixotic goodness which had made him think he could save her from her own evil nature, and which later impels him, in spite of crushing disappointments, to go on trying to christianize the convicts in his care. At the climax her hatred becomes transcendental: "She was beaten; and in

229

her anger, she rose, for the moment, above herself—that careful and cunning self at prey upon the world. Her next action was perhaps the highest one of her life. For the moment, I fully believe, she put aside all *reason* for it. Hate—pure, unreasoning hate—flooded in and swamped her being." (P. 250.) Hate had been shown reaching a similar ecstatic orgasm in *Stifled Laughter*, at the instant when the convict Ben resolved to murder the hunchbacked villain (p.287). At such moments of concentration it becomes pure, subsumes all other emotions, including love; doubt and self-division vanish, and the character becomes his ideal self.

As we shall see, however, doubt returns in Hay's next two novels, *Captain Quadring* and *Sir William Heans*, dominating the central confrontation between good and evil to such an extent that the hero and villain, far from being defined by their enmity—and feeling able, at the climactic moment, to define themselves by it—display a measure of common identity, a tendency to exchange attributes and roles that muddles and perplexes their feeling towards each other. Subsequently, perhaps dismayed by the moral uncertainties he had exposed in these two novels, Hay reverted in *Strabane* to a pattern in which the gulf between sheep and goats is wide and unbridgeable. Of all his novels this is the one where his vision of life as a clear and ceaseless conflict between "kindness" and "unkindness", good and evil, is most insistent and explicit. Evil again becomes simply inexplicable and unredeemable, a "tragic mystery" like "the 'fault' in the geological strata of our lives" (pp.55—56). And the bald message that the good must never lower their guard against it, never even parley with it, smacks of self-admonishment on the part of the man who wrote *Sir William Heans*.

The idea of a partial identity and exchange of roles between hero and villain stands out more clearly in *Captain Quadring* than in *Sir William Heans*. Andrew and Henry Fairservice, the hero and "villain" of *Captain Quadring*, are brothers and show a strong family likeness. Being men of "ancient Cromwellian stock", both are hard and selfrighteous; hence their respective nicknames, "Iron" and "Steel". But whereas Andrew, the elder, is "drab and close", living soberly, industriously, and frugally, Henry has a "generous, dark, and fiery temperament" that leads him into loose and extravagant ways (pp.83ff.). Eventually, when the family estate is threatened by Henry's extravagance, Andrew proposes to restrict him to a fixed allowance. Stung in his pride, Henry retaliates by paying court to Andrew's fiancée and winning her affections. Upon learning that Henry cares not for her but only for his revenge against Andrew, she quickly dies and the hatred between the brothers now becomes implacable. Andrew allows Henry to be convicted and transported for stealing a sum of money from him. He also exiles himself, unable to continue living at home after the loss of his fiancée. They accidentally meet again in the convict colony and Andrew, in a fit of fury, shoots and apparently kills his brother. He now becomes the criminal, the moral outcast, changing places with Henry. At the same time Henry, who has not died but has "resurrected" (p.176) under the name of Captain Quadring, has become a martinet like his brother, controlling an establishment of rebellious convicts with savage severity, courage, and self-discipline. They are finally reconciled through the good offices of a young woman who is able to "soften" them both. Henry, however, dies straight after from wounds received in a battle with the convicts. For solace, Andrew is left with the woman.

I have given the story in some detail in the hope that, as well as its relevance to the story of Heans and Daunt, its close resemblance to one of the masterpieces of English romantic fiction will be noticed. Stevenson's *The Master of Ballantrae* also deals with two feuding brothers of high rank, who exhibit a similar contrast of temperaments to that between the Fairservice brothers, and who also quarrel over money but more crucially over a woman. The woman, again, is pledged (indeed married) to the stern sober brother but prefers the dashing romantic one. Like the Fairservice brothers they eventually fight, and the wastrel brother is apparently killed but later "resurrected". Thereafter the two stories diverge, but Hay's continues to follow Stevenson's in one highly important respect, the manner in which the behaviour of the sober brother becomes more and more assimilated to that of the wild one, until finally he is hardly less cunning, ruthless, and irresponsible than his brother.

Hay, as has often been noted, recorded his sense of affinity with the Scottish romantic tradition on a number of occasions. He was of Scottish parentage himself and was obviously brought up on the border ballads, Scott, and Stevenson. More than once he remarked that what most attracted him to Australian history as a subject for fiction was its "ballad-like" quality, the same quality that attracted

Scott and Stevenson to Scottish history. He found in Australian history those "narratives of the dramatic deeds of men of a passionate or tragic nature" which, like Scott, he believed were the fittest subjects for fiction.[9] In both *Herridge* and *Captain Quadring* there are discussions of the concept of "reality" which recall the terms of Stevenson's well known disagreement with Henry James about the novel of "adventure",[10] and which make it clear that Hay would side with Stevenson against James (see *Herridge*, part 2, chapter 5; *Quadring*, pp.140ff.). To Hay and his heroes the "real life" is not the familiar one of simpering sociability but that of high adventure, testing one's courage and physical endurance to the limit—the life that most readers can live only in their imagination. (By contrast, Hay's idea of James's reality is represented, presumably, in the brittle, nasty gossip and underlying violence of the "art circle" in *Strabane*, which he called his "Henry James novel".)[11]

The psychological dualism that finds expression in *The Master of Ballantrae*—with one brother in many respects absorbing the personality of the other—reflects a deep ambivalence running right through Stevenson's work, and Scott's also. Imaginatively, as has often been noted, both writers are drawn to what we may call the "Jacobite" figure—aristocratic, adventurous, stylish, but not altogether scrupulous. Morally, however, their allegiance is to the "Whig"—bourgeois, stolid, honest, but rather priggish. Being in reality a conflict between different aspects of the novelist himself, the conflict seldom resolves itself as smoothly as it appears to on the surface. Our sober realistic judgment must favour Sir William Ashton against the Master of Ravenswood, Evandale and Morton against the more rabid of the Cameronians, David Balfour against Alan Breck, Dr. Livesey against Long John Silver, James Durie against his brother the Master of Ballantrae, and most emphatically Dr. Jekyll against Mr. Hyde. But it is the outlaw or semi-outlaw, no matter how *passé* and morally tattered, with whom we side imaginatively. If it were possible we, and often the characters themselves, would like to be both Whig and Jacobite, to act both roles. But as Dr. Jekyll and James Durie discover, though we may perhaps replace one role by the other, we cannot for long play both.

At first glance the resemblance of the story of Heans and Daunt to those of the Fairservice and Durie brothers may not seem very close. Like the Fairservice brothers, however, Heans and Daunt in-itially are rivals for the same woman. Initially, too, they appear as contrasting personalities, the one (Heans) elegant, ingratiating, highborn, with a reputation as a ruthless womanizer, the other (Daunt) dutiful, efficient, hard working, perhaps rather puritanical. Their enmity, again like that of the Fairservice brothers, gradually leads to some curious interchanging of roles, so that the staunch up-holder of the law (Daunt) is driven by his hatred to lawless ex-pedients (the use of Spafield against Heans), and the supposed betrayer of women's honour emerges as their defender while the former defender traduces a woman's honour unforgivably. By the time of Daunt's death his upright character is ruined even more thoroughly than Andrew Fairservice's appears to be at the time when he "kills" his brother, and Heans has shown himself capable, as Henry Fairservice does, of all the virtues upon which his enemy had most prided himself. More important still, it is constantly sug-gested, from their very first meeting in the novel, that there exists between Heans and Daunt some intimate connexion which they can both sense but cannot understand. On Heans's side this expresses itself chiefly as a vague, immanent uneasiness reflecting his awareness of Daunt's irrational, intensely personal hostility and almost uncanny familiarity with his secret designs. Up to a point he, and the reader, can extrapolate plausible motives for this hostility— sexual jealousy and class-envy, for example—and can put it down glibly to repulsion of opposites, Daunt being a man of business, Heans a man of pleasure; Daunt a sober Victorian, Heans a Regency beau, a Skimpole, a Carlylean dandy; Daunt a self-righteous English Whig, Heans a merry Irish Jacobite. But no less striking than the general contrast between the two men are the likenesses. Both are middle-aged men, often (and I submit more typically than other characters to whom the epithets are applied) "pale", "grey", and "tragic". Both fall in love with the same young woman. Under stress, Heans, as I have noted, can become almost as grim and hec-toring a tyrant as Daunt, and Daunt, in sociable mood, can turn a phrase with quite as Meredithean a felicity as Heans. Above all, however, it is obvious that Daunt feels haunted and daunted by Heans, or what Heans in his eyes stands for, no less than Heans does by Daunt. The cumulative impression we obtain is that Daunt makes another man, Heans, the scapegoat for all that he most fears and distrusts in himself, all the cynical, irresponsible urges that he dares not acknowledge or give rein to: he makes Heans a projection of his own suppressed self.

Curiously, it is the ex-convict Oughtryn who comes closest to pinpointing this. As his daughter tells Heans, "Father says his [Daunt's] mind is on you too much—as if you were the place of a crime he had committed." (p.128) But every step Daunt takes against Heans confirms Oughtryn's insight: the harder he tries to catch Heans out, to uncover the evils in Heans's nature, the more he uncovers the same evils in his own. The most extreme example is the way in which, by gossiping about Matilda's part in Heans's first escape attempt, presumably with the object of showing how little care Heans had had for her honour, he grossly traduces her honour himself. But he also in effect becomes the moral outlaw he believes Heans to be when he resorts to violence by manhandling Heans in front of the naval officers and when he turns loose the criminal maniac Spafield against him. It can hardly be coincidence that when he dies his idea of Heans effectively dies with him, dies in the public mind and ceases to daunt Heans himself. The words which he had tried to utter to Heans on his deathbed—words which would have been to Heans's "advantage" though uttered with hatred—must surely have signified, directly or otherwise, that he, Daunt, had taken up the burden of Heans's sins and was about to relieve him of it finally.

That Hay did intend Heans and Daunt to be perceived as overlapping identities, each potentially or actually embodying aspects of the other, is borne out by the symbolism he employs to emphasize the duality of Daunt's nature and to relate it to the ambivalent moral vision of the novel as a whole. Unlike Hay's usual world, that of *Sir William Heans* is one in which the worst is nearly always glimpsed as a corruption of the best. In this world it seems appropriate that the "Christian" name of Oughtryn's spotless daughter should be a rough anagram of "Belial", the nickname he had borne as a lag (p.66), that the Shaxtons, whose country house is at Jerusalem, should finally unite with the Oughtryns of pagan Bagdad to help the fine but tarnished Heans, and that liberty for Heans should entail something close to loss of life. It is a world in which apparent contrarieties repeatedly dissolve. The images of Eden in the early part of the novel, associated mainly with Matilda's garden, all subsequently break down into contradictions, when golden-haired Matilda, whose "clever, invisible selflessness" had led Jarvis Carnt to call her "the carpet serpent" (p.5), lets other serpents into her garden by her "erring love" for Heans. Daunt denounces Heans as a "singed butterfly", telling him that he would "find a flower to trifle with in the Garden of Eden" (p.52), and the partial correctness of this forecast appears when "hollyhocks" like those which grow so "Englishly" in Matilda's garden (p.19) are almost lost sight of in the bush landscape—"Nature at her wildest"—over which Daunt's eye roves as he overhears Heans asking her to elope with him (p.99). (Later, we see hollyhocks growing at the Cascades prison where another carpet serpent, the red-haired Madame Ruth whose selfless sympathy inspires Carnt no less than Matilda's, languishes as a convicted murderer.) The duality of Daunt himself, who is so often seen as "hissing", as a "reptile" (p.144), as a "snake", albeit one whose "venom is for right" (p.100), is symbolically caught in the scene of showdown where we notice that one of his hands is "white as snow", the other "red as his jacket" (p.264). The white-red duality here·recalls that of the valerian: the white valerian that Matilda gathers in her garden to strew on the grave of a dead child, and the red valerian—"Bloody Warrior as it is playfully called"—which colours the grass of Abelia's garden with "an old stain of blood" (p.307). This garden, presided over by the carved figure of the soldier with a "look of terror" in his face (p.148)—in contrast to Maltilda's "star-like face like the head of some angelic soldier" (p.19)—is as far from, yet as near to, Matilda's pristine garden as is Bagdad from Jerusalem, Spafield from the "brave fellows" who sail the *Erebus* and the *Terror*, and the Daunt who descends to "satanic tyranny" (p.130) from the Daunt who would live by devotion to order and duty and by "belief in women" (p.135).

The "mystery" of Daunt, then, is in essence the mystery of Dr. Jekyll and Mr. Hyde; and the "escape" of Sir William Heans is the exorcizing of the Daunt that has invaded his own nature. In confronting each other the two men confront their own self-doubts; and if one of them is saved in the process and the other destroyed, the nightmarish vision that the novel as a whole gives of the ambiguity of man's moral nature remains firmly fixed in the reader's mind.

13

Australia of the Spirit:
Some Aspects of the Work of
Vance and Nettie Palmer
1938–48

VIVIAN SMITH

On 8 February 1938 Vance Palmer started a book called *Pioneers*, to consist of chapters of three thousand words each on the explorer, the orator, the politician, and other representative figures in Australian history. Nettie Palmer states (Journal, 1938) that Vance was quickened to writing the work partly by an article "What Our Students Know" by Professor Allan Fisher "in a Sydney Quarterly" which commented on the limited knowledge of Australian history of first year university students. Palmer's book, which began modestly enough, was intended to fill a gap.

Out of this preliminary work grew *National Portraits* (1940), one of Palmer's most immediately successful and reprinted books, and one of his most rewarding. It sprang out of his abiding concern with the figures who had shown a deep sense of responsibility to their country, "who had [originated] ideas and [tapped] springs that were later to enrich the national life".[1]

In *Fourteen Years* Nettie Palmer wrote (13 November 1937), on returning from the poorly attended unveiling of a statue to Higinbotham:

> The whole affair makes me wonder if there isn't some essential lack in us, something missing that keeps our life from having meaning and depth—interest in our past, reverence for those who have shown out-

standing qualities of mind or spirit. When we look back it is on great empty spaces; the significant dead have no memorials; the few statues in our parks are mainly of forgotten grandees and kings. It must be because we have no sense of ourselves as a people, with a yesterday and a to-morrow. I can't help remembering that little fishing-village in Britanny where we lived when we were first married; on some rock rising from a wheatfield a bronze plaque, in memory of a local poet or hero. How these simple memorials added another dimension to the day-to-day life of the village!

The Palmers had become increasingly concerned at what seemed to them not only a lack of proper respect for but a positive indifference to the achievements of the past, and *National Portraits* is a living memorial to significant figures in Australian history. Palmer concentrated on men "with some creative impulse", who worked, some of them unobtrusively, to reveal the character of the country they lived in. The guiding theme of *National Portraits* is its celebration of men of vision and energy who fought against the intellectual timidity that went with "Colonialism" in all its forms. This theme is particularly asserted in the striking portraits of John Dunmore Lang, George Higinbotham, and Alfred Deakin. Most of all it is the integrity of his subjects that Palmer admires; and his admiration, not uncritical, makes it possible for him to respond to the very different, even opposed, characters and personalities of figures like John Macarthur and Charles Sturt, J.F. Archibald and Cardinal Moran, Sir Charles Kingsford Smith and Ferdinand von Muller, who helped to create some of the values they transmitted or imposed. The unobtrusive chronological arrangement of the portraits subtly presents a sketch of the country's history; they move from the period of the first settlement through colonial times to federation and specific modern developments. But the book is also a study in the kinds and possibilities of imaginative enterprise that have been available in Australia and it is significant that its portraits are listed as a series of types, again arranged historically—the landtaker (John Macarthur), the currency lad (John Batman), the explorer (Charles Sturt), the painter (Louis Buvelot), the pastoralist (Robert Christison), the unionist (W.G. Spence), the writer (Henry Lawson), the industrialist (H.V. McKay), and so on. It is a highly personal choice, restricted to those who worked "within their own borders". But in this way, too, it manages to suggest and present an outline of Australian achievement.

VIVIAN SMITH

Given its partly pedagogic origin one might be tempted to read *National Portraits* as a moral text on the virtues of self-dependence and the well-directed will. But the essential spirit of the whole can best be gauged from the chapter on Louis Buvelot:

> It is natural to a human being to love the scenes among which he was bred, the hills and valleys on which his eyes first opened, yet this feeling may weaken or vanish, unless it find a sanction in art: particularly if the general influences of life are against it. In Australia, the hostility of the earlier settlers to their surroundings was partly bequeathed to their children, who read English books, pored over English pictures, and almost felt they were aliens in a harsh and remote world that had no beauty or significance. Only the work of artists, looking around with fresh eyes, could lift this imaginary burden. To the artist, in so far as he has an original gift, beauty and significance are not a matter of sentimental associations; they are something to be discovered and revealed. And it was the painters who first saw the Australian landscape as it really was.[3]

It is Palmer's happiest formulation of the deeply personal theme he had first tried to express in 1905 and which was to preoccupy him throughout much of his critical writing—the need for Australia to become a home to the imagination. It is the achievement of *National Portraits* as a whole that it shows the variety of ways in which it has become so.

By 1940 Vance Palmer was coming to be considered the leading figure in Australian letters and more and more the official tasks of warden of Australian culture fell to him. It was almost inevitable then that it should be he who was asked to assemble a commemorative volume in honor of A.G. Stephens. Like Stephens, Palmer had always maintained that the development of a vigorous Australian culture could not be achieved without a consistent critical attitude and that what Australia most needed was an impersonal critical atmosphere in which to develop its own dependent and assured values. Palmer felt enough sense of affinity with Stephens to be able to write of him with sympathy, and even a degree of identification, and enough detachment to be critically just in his appraisal. Palmer's interest in Stephens was threefold: personal, critical, and literary. They were fellow Queenslanders; Stephens in his *Bulletin* heyday impressed Palmer deeply as a critic, setting something of a standard for the young aspiring author ("his policy on the Red Page was to stimulate Australian writing, to assess its

238

value, and to connect it with the main stream of European culture")[4], and the frequent references to the *Bookfellow* in the Palmer diaries show with what attention Vance and Nettie continued to follow Stephens's work: they missed none of his fugitive publications.

There were other, perhaps even closer, causes of identification. Stephens had initiated the publication of *Such is Life* and Palmer had continued the work of finding an outlet for and of creating a fuller critical response to this remarkable national book. Palmer and Stephens had the capacity for responding to Australian books while knowing that "Australian criticism and creative writing could only reach maturity by keeping in touch with the larger world";[5] and both realized that only the development of flexible inner standards could save Australian literary culture from the twin evils of colonial defeatism and provincial or nationalistic self-assertion.

The Palmers were now convinced that critics and writers should be fruitfully engaged in a patient attentiveness to the past, in looking at what had been achieved, rather than restlessly clamouring for the great Australian novel or assertively dismissing what had been done. New movements were trying to develop, new magazines beginning; Nettie and Vance were critical of their rootlessness, of the way everything in Australia had to start from the beginning all over again. They saw that what the Australian writer needed was a sense of continuity with his own "useable past", and that the constant process of having to start all over again from the beginning would, if prolonged, hold back the development of Australian writing indefinitely. A series of local literary movements ending in frustration and defeat like the Pioneer Players or the Jindyworobak Movement, without the support of substantial individual literary achievement, was now unlikely to provide the sense of continuity needed. While responding to what was worthwhile in the Jindyworobak Movement, for instance, Nettie Palmer nevertheless condemned its cultural naivete, its uneducated brashness, its unawareness. She noted laconically in her diary (24 February 1939) "letter from R. Ingamells ... using all Vance's old slogans but exaggerated", and to C.B. Christesen in the early stages of *Meanjin*'s development she complains of "rootless reviews", absurd enthusiasms, and over-praise for minor writers, as well as failures of style, tone, and art, in letters that balance warmth of response and encouragement with critical astringency and detachment.

The Palmers now constantly stressed in letters, lectures and broadcasts that there could be no secure future development of an Australian literary culture without a mature understanding of the problems, limitations, and achievements of the past. *A.G. Stephens: His Life and Work* was an example of what they had in mind. It is both a tribute and a reconstruction. It gathers together a selection of Stephens's best criticism and in its unhurried, challenging foreword gives a clear outline of Stephens's career, his features as a commentator and a man.

The selection is largely taken from Stephens's earliest work, mainly because it was the least known, and diary entries reveal how much time the Palmers spent at "the pub"—their way of referring to a hard day's research in the Public Library—collecting the material and carefully transcribing it by hand. Palmer thought Stephens was outstanding in his judgment of black and white art, but found it hard either to suggest fully or to represent this side of his work (Diary, 15 May 1940, held in the Palmer Papers, National Library, Canberra). He seems to have shared the general view that Stephens's break with *The Bulletin* resulted in some impairment of his personal and critical capacities and that he was never again to be a mainstream critic.

Palmer's selection concentrates exclusively on Stephens's writing on Australian books and authors, and while he made no definitive claims for his study (he insisted "the way to a fuller collection of his essays is still open") it is arguable that he did less than full justice to Stephens's scope. There is no record of Stephens's interest in American writers, for instance, of the way he was reprinting Conrad Aiken, Vachel Lindsay, and Wallace Stevens in *The Bookfellow* in the early twenties. Palmer now saw it as his imperative duty to concentrate on Australia and things Australian, and his space was limited.

It is only necessary to add here that *A.G. Stephens: His Life and Work* sprang out of the convictions and conditions that first made Palmer undertake the writing of *National Portraits* and, indeed, if this memorial selection had not already been planned as early as May 1937,[6] Stephens would certainly have been included in the volume of pioneers as the critic.

It was to continue to be for the Palmers a time of memorials, tributes, sketches, and experiments, rather than of deeply sustained creative work. The death of Frank Wilmot ("Furnley Maurice") in

1942 had robbed Palmer of a close friend and the Frank Wilmot Memorial Committee asked him to prepare a commemorative brochure. Palmer's work on the portrait form had helped him develop his skill in presenting a composite image of a person, a period and a place and his monograph *Frank Wilmot* (1942) succeeds admirable in its limited task. It is an engaging sketch of an interesting minor poet, more valuable as a human document than as a critical assessment. Palmer greatly valued the contribution Wilmot had made to the development of a national Australian culture, a contribution made as much through his attitude as through his work:

> The truth was that he had little regard for his own reputation. You could imagine him writing anonymously at the end of his life as he did at the beginning. He saw his work as a contribution poured into the common pool—the end being the erection of a culture that would water the dry soil of this country and give it a richer life. This was a task in which personalities didn't count.[7]

Again one sees how Palmer looks for and emphasizes what he took to be the Australian artist's supreme task—the transformation of the environment. It was his one obsessive theme, and one of the motivating forces behind the writing of *Hail Tomorrow*.

Although not published until 1947, the play *Hail Tomorrow* was written between May and September 1943 and then revised and enlarged in June 1945. William Lane had been a figure in Palmer's mind for years, but he found it hard to find the adequate form in which to express his reflections about him. Palmer was unable to fit him into the world of *National Portraits* because he was fundamentally unsure about Lane's idealistic conception of an Australia that could be started afresh in the wilderness of Paraguay. There was enough in Palmer to respond to Lane's contempt for the spiritual emptiness of a society given to "Friday night booze, Saturday races, the pious torpor of Sunday", and the challenge Lane seemed to offer to his deepest imaginative convictions could not be sidestepped. Where and what is Australia? Is it a place and a people in a known and named place, or is it an idea, a concept that can be expressed anywhere—"written on the Andes"? Is there an Australia of the spirit, and if so, what does this, what could this, mean?

The four acts of *Hail Tomorrow* constitute four tableaux. The first begins at the time of the shearers' strikes in the nineties. The second is set partly in the great shearers' camp at Barcaldine, partly in

VIVIAN SMITH

the head-quarters of the Pastoralists' Association in Brisbane; the third in the Rockhampton office of the Shearers' Union, and the fourth in a large living room in Balmain where Lane's followers are preparing to leave for Paraguay. The whole action takes place over two years during which Glover, the leader of the shearers' strike (a fictitious creation), is imprisoned for his work for labour against capital and Lane determines to go to South America to found the real democratic Australia in which he believes. Glover, for all his defeats and disappointments, is determined to remain loyal to the here and now of Australia; there is never any question that he will join Lane. At the beginning, commenting to Ann Somers, Lane's assistant, on Lane's idealism, Glover insists "You belong to this country ... You've grown up with it and become part of its bone. Lane hasn't; the whole earth's one to him. Lately I've been afraid ... The last time I saw him he had some notion of trying to organise the new world in the Argentine. Or was it Brazil?''. He adds later: "If we begin dreaming of far-off Utopias, we're done before daybreak." Glover will not give up his country; for him that is running away. He is aware that the forces and the injustices of organized capital are working to drive men like Lane out of the country, but his fundamental convictions are merely strengthened by his term in prison. It is no surprise then that he refuses to join Lane. "My mind has no wings" he says to Lane. "It's rooted in what I know—in the blue-grass plains below Clermont and the billabongs of the Maranoa where I used to camp as a youngster".[8] Glover's loyalty is to the fellows he grew up with,

> men who didn't care a damn for money or power, but would give their lives or their last bean for a mate. They were the men who filled the camps two years ago, and they'll still be fighting for unionism and all it means back there among the billabongs. Those are my people, Will, and I believe they've got the spirit that will take hold of this country in the end and make it over.[9]

The last scene has been frequently praised, and it finely balances the opposed views of Lane and Glover:

> GLOVER: I understand, Will. The first night I met you—you talked like that then. It gave me a jolt—the first real jolt I'd had—made me realize there was more in the fight than a watertight union and a few more bob a hundred.
> LANE: But that's all it amounts to, Alec, if you won't look at humanity as a whole.

GLOVER: Sorry, Will, but I can't think or feel that way. You and me—we're different. Humanity—to me it's the fellows I know— some old whaler humping his drum, a couple of chaps yarning around a fire, Rennich and McCristal fighting to get a fair go for everyone.

LANE: For everyone? For everyone I know, that comes to mean in the end, for my particular crowd ... When I look ahead, Alec, I see the fire I tried to kindle on the plains of the west guttering out in ashes. Men thinking of nothing but a little extra comfort—longer smoke-ohs, better-built huts, a few more pounds for gambling. I see unionism grown corrupt and spiritless; the whole movement become a racket for officials, for politicians and bush-lawyers. There's hope for a people who've never been awakened; there's no hope for one that's heard the call and turned over to sleep again.

GLOVER: Maybe.

LANE: You feel that too, Alec?

GLOVER: Maybe I'm fooling myself when I say we can take hold of this country and make it over—make it a beacon for free men everywhere like the old Cross above it. Maybe, Will, the whole of life's a mirage, codding us to keep going by the promise of good water over the skyline—fine grassy country and flowing rivers ... Mirage? ... Yes, perhaps ... but I prefer to live as if it isn't.

LANE: It really is a parting of the ways, then, Alec?

GLOVER: I'm afraid so, Will.[10]

In spite of this effective directness, *Hail Tomorrow* is an unsuccessful drama as a whole. There is no real dialectical tension in the questions it asks (one senses that Palmer had resolved the issue to his own satisfaction before the play began) and it has insufficient dramatic life, except for the last scene, to succeed as a play of ideas. Palmer has no real liking for Lane—his own convictions are quite clearly Glover's—yet in addition he appears to be emotionally and imaginatively cramped by the necessity to convey a historically accurate image of Lane. Nevertheless, for all its limitations as theatre, *Hail Tomorrow* is an extraordinarily interesting document in the development of Palmer's thought at the time. In his work it belongs with *National Portraits* and *The Legend of the Nineties*, which it precedes, rather than with, say, *The Black Horse*. It shows that at this point Palmer's preoccupations with Australia's nature and her destiny through the theme of the imaginative possession of a country and the transformation of an environment (both in a sense pre- or post-literary questions) had grown beyond the resources of literature. It was proving intractable to the few literary forms at his disposal and he was unable to embody his ideas and feelings in works of creative art. The brief critical comment and the historical essay alone seemed adequate to his capacities and concerns.

A detailed chronological list of all the hard inconspicuous work the Palmers were engaged on in the early forties is hardly necessary. It had become a part of their lives to read the manuscripts submitted to them, to comment on the new works appearing, to act as judges to literary competitions and to take a friendly interest in various cultural activites. They continued to review; they regularly broadcasted and in fact the radio became their most important general outlet at this time. The A.B.C. Archives contain nearly four hundred book-review scripts and nearly one hundred other scripts written by the Palmers between 1941 and 1959, and while none of this seems to me to have quite the importance of their literary journalism of the twenties and thirties, all of it is marked by soundness of judgment, a sense of responsibility to literature as a whole, and a scrupulous fairness of response. They gave memorial broadcasts on the significance of the life and work of writers as different as A.B. Paterson, Louis Esson, Shaw Neilson, Randolph Bedford, and Furnley Maurice. They paid tribute to living writers such as Bernard O'Dowd, Katharine Susannah Prichard, Christina Stead, and others on the occasion of a birthday or an important new publication. As critics the Palmers retained the capacity for generously encouraging immature but promising work without compromising their standards, and the esteem in which they were held and the appreciation with which their help was received is fully attested by the various tributes offered to them throughout their careers. The extent of their backroom work is indicated in their diaries and in their correspondence, and it will probably only be the publication of their letters that will adequately suggest the range of intensity of their toil. It would be too space-consuming to list all the public lectures for the Commonwealth Literary Fund, University extension courses, and summer schools given by the Palmers in the last twenty-five years of their lives. Some of this material was used in broadcasts; Vance Palmer incorporated some of it in later publications like *The Legend of the Nineties*. Some of it is merely of a routine professional nature, some of it has a fugitive air. Like many professional writers the Palmers often found themselves obliged to use their material in multiple ways, so that in their literary journalism, lectures, and talks there is much overlapping, adaptation, and repetition. Most of this writing has gone uncollected. It is always hard to assess accurately the influence and impact of work of this kind, but not difficult to recognize its importance and value in the day-to-day life of letters and the way it contributes to the health of a national culture.

In November 1945 Vance Palmer was sent for review William Gaunt's *The Aesthetic Adventure*. He had already been contemplating for some time a study of the Australian 1890s, and Gaunt's book served both as a stimulus and a model.

Palmer always worked in thought on several books at once; and while he was planning his study of the 1890s his mind frequently turned to the Mt. Isa novel he had long planned. By the beginning of 1946 when *Louis Esson and the Australian Theatre* was complete— another tribute to a fine artist and a dead friend—a sudden concurrence of events further quickened and sharpened the Palmers' literary intentions and ambitions; on 21 March Henry Handel Richardson died, and on 11 July there appeared the first volume of Katharine Susannah Prichard's trilogy of the goldfields, *The Roaring Nineties*. For the rest of the year their plans were decided. Nettie Palmer would work at her long projected study of Henry Handel Richardson, Vance Palmer on *Golconda* and *The Legend of the Nineties*. On 2 August 1946 they left Melbourne for Queensland to spend the winter working there. In Brisbane Vance did research for the background of *Golconda*, reading files of the *North Queensland Register*, especially for 1924. Nettie helped transcribe reports of Trade Union Secretaries and general news of Mt. Isa (Diary, 22 August).

Vance Palmer worked steadily on *Golconda*, which was finished in draft by 29 May 1947, though revisions and additions and important changes were made throughout the year. Nettie Palmer was unable to work with full concentration at her literary concerns (her health had been failing for many years). But by August, her years of accumulated papers, notebooks, and diaries had been sorted. The idea of publishing extracts from her private journal now seemed to impose itself of its own accord. *Fourteen Years* was taking shape.

In assembling *Fourteen Years*, Nettie Palmer decided to begin at 1925 with the move to Caloundra—a very significant year in the Palmers' careers since it marked the beginning of their most mature literary work. But it was, too, an important date in the development of Australian literature between the wars; and for those involved at the time, 1929 in particular was to come to appear in retrospect a tiny *annus mirabilus*. It was the year of the publication of Henry Handel Richardson's *Ultima Thule*, a book which commanded attention throughout the English speaking world.

> Through this one novel, *Australia became a reality to overseas readers and, in consequence, to herself.* There was a change of climate. Improvement of communication and greater freedom of travel also had a quickening effect. Publication, both locally and in England, was easier to achieve than ever before. Suppressed talent was released by a change, partly economic and partly spiritual.[11]

Literary developments are always more organically complex than this, of course, and the importance of D.H. Lawrence's *Kangaroo* and Katharine Susannah Prichard's *Working Bullocks* which acted as catalysts on local writers needs to be taken into account. But it is interesting to read Palmer saying in an interview published in 1930

> I think the Australian novel is coming into its own at last. This is due to Henry Handel Richardson more than anyone else, for her amazing trilogy has carried us right into the broad stream of European literature. The influence of this book will do us no end of good, though, perhaps, its full effect won't be seen for another generation. It'll mature us, help us to grow up. Even the people who think Australian writing should be something like an immigration pamphlet with coloured illustrations have been forced to read it because of its notoriety abroad, and their minds won't remain as raw as before.
>
> But apart from Henry Handel Richardson there's been a lot of good writing in the last three or four years. Look at Katharine Prichard's "Working Bullocks" and "Coonardoo". What vitality and poetry on nearly every page! Out of slang, colloquial phrases, the common names of things, she has created a style that's all her own, and that corresponds with the rhythm of our life in some queer way. I suppose only literary people understand what she's done yet; to some extent, she's a writers' writer. Then there's Chester Francis Cobb, another experimentalist. If there's any virtue in being modern, his work is as modern as anything being done abroad, and the way the life of Sydney flows through his characters' minds is vivid and exciting. M. Barnard Eldershaw's "A House is Built" is a particularly good attempt to build up an historical background for us, and there's not a single cheap motive or false sentiment in the whole book: it's solid as stone. "The Montforts" does for Melbourne what Miss Eldershaw's book does for Sydney, though it's a more lightweight affair—rather a chronicle of families than a unified work of art.[12]

It now seems to me very likely that the writers of the Palmers' generation—which includes Katharine Susannah Prichard, Frank Dalby Davison, Barnard Eldershaw, Leonard Mann—will come to be looked on as a group, whatever individual distinctions and discriminations have to be observed. After Lawson and Furphy, whose talents coincided with the values and style of a society their work reflects, their generation belongs to a more genteel, lettered but still "colonial" tradition. Their problems were accentuated by the exceptional difficulties of the society and culture in which they found themselves. All were excessively self-conscious, even anxious, about being Australian writers—and more than merely Australian writers—and about adequately reflecting and interpreting their environment in ways acceptable to overseas readers. What one appreciates in their work is a general situation rather than a cogent or incisive point of view. The tones and modes—if not the fundamental convictions and attitudes—of Lawson and Furphy were not available to them except as weak imitation or pastiche. They had inherited no secure values or style; and they were not able to use the advanced experimental techniques and innovations of Europe to any sustained end. (It is worth noting that the rare "experimental" novelists of the period, Chester Cobb, Leslie Meller, and, on another level again, Robert Tate and Ernest Wells wrote only one or two novels each and were unable to sustain a body of work.) All were serious writers, each anxious to impose his own particular vision and world, but none was strong enough or talented enough to be able to reject the pressures of literary commercialism or the taints of amateurism which at one point or another vitiate their writing. And for all their interest in overseas writing, all remain "colonial-provincial", that is dependent authors, trying to interpret Australian reality through the English, American, and European authors of their time. Katharine Susannah Prichard's lyricism owes much to her way of assimilating D.H. Lawrence and some of the Scandinavian writers like Knut Hamsun, D.E. Rolvang, Martin Anderson Nexo, as well as the Polish writer Wladislaw Reymont whose epic novels of Polish rural life were widely translated in the twenties after he won the Nobel Prize in 1924. In all these cases Prichard has been influenced by writers whose visions of their own "pioneering", epic communities could help her to interpret her own. Eleanor Dark and Barnard Eldershaw are influenced by later writers like Aldous Huxley and Thornton Wilder and a somewhat diluted notion of the thirties novel of ideas. Galsworthy, among English novelists, was a pervasive influence especially on the Barnard Eldershaw of *A House is Built* and Palmer's *The Swayne Family* as well as on Henry Handel Richardson, while Frank Dalby Davison's studies of animal life with their images of a "frontier" life belong to an old literary tradition that had been recently revived in the work of writers like Jack London and Henry Williamson. It is now known that Mazo de la Roche's novels, the Whiteoaks series, which chronicle the life of a Canadian family from pioneering days to the present time, inspired Miles Franklin after a long break in her writing life to undertake her chronicles of Australian pioneering life, and one can see in writers like Velia Ercole and Godfrey Blunden the combined influences of writers as different as D.H. Lawrence and the Sinclair Lewis of *Main Street*. There are distinctions to observe here; but I think one can say that these writers were all intent on interpreting Australia and Australian experience in the light of overseas writers, whereas Lawson and Furphy—whatever influences they assimilated—remain landmarks of a national literature because they combine the two characteristics which T.S. Eliot maintained all such landmarks should possess: "The strong local flavour combined with unconscious universality".[13]

Fourteen Years in its unassuming way throws an exceptionally clear light on this generation in Australian writing, but by virtue of its style and its sense of personality, it completely transcends any ascription as an historical document. It is unique in Australian letters as a record of reminiscence and impressions and in its sense of intimacy with times and places that no later reconstructions can replace; it is unique too in its point of view. Nettie Palmer was fully aware of the problems which faced the writers of her time, but she was free of the peculiar tensions of the creative writer committed to pioneer a difficult field and running all the risks of artistic failure. She could sympathize and observe. This gives her work a particular purity and it frees her critical comments and asides from any invidious comparisons with her own creative output. One does not usually adduce a critic's creative work in this way, but with the Australian writers of this generation one always feels that their understanding and experience of their situation and their problems exceeded their creative potential for coping with them. They are

248

sometimes more interesting to read about than to read.

Fourteen Years is a remarkably flexible and wide ranging account of literary and personal encounters in Australia and Europe. Its portraits of, for instance, figures like Havlock Ellis, F.R. Leavis, Andre Gide, Christina Stead, H.B. Higgins, and Randolph Bedford, are impressive for their sympathetic detachment, their assured objectivity of response, their concreteness and immediacy. Of Havlock Ellis she writes:

> His profile was fine and balanced, with his white mane, his white beard not hiding the firm lips, large, clear-blue eyes almost untroubled-looking, almost childish, with a slight unstrained cast seeming to give a personal quality to them, as in Louis Esson's eyes. He was dressed as if he had ordered his suit perhaps forty years ago, and—his figure and habits not altering—had had it copied in some very uncrushable tweed, soft and silky-surfaced. Like a grand Whistler portrait he sat there, but not silhouetted against the wall; more fluid and ample, with the October light coming through remote bay windows behind him.[14]

Of A.G. Stephens:

> A downright, hearty man, not stout, but rather like that mature sea-captain of Conrad's who seemed "extremely full of healthy organs." A man who hadn't time to be anything but healthy. One noted that he was bald, his short, neat beard white. But these were not limitations—impossible to imagine him otherwise. The silver beard belonged to his remarkably fresh colouring; his baldness made a dome for his fine, candid eyes—childlike eyes, someone has said, but belonging to a child whose eagerness never let up. No one could believe, looking at his face, that he was pursued by petty financial worries.[15]

And there is this glimpse of a conversation with Masefield, not without its ironies for the present day reader:

> Strolling outside to a camp-fire supper I asked about these modernists:
> "Ah, yes, that interview," he said, "it was a very leading question." He thought these poets unorthodox and political; they certainly had their various talents, but he couldn't see that as poets they had much to say. Spender, perhaps? But Auden—well, Auden, he heard, had been a very good teacher before he was a poet: "and I don't think he'll write much more." Day Lewis too. His poetic gift was rather different, though he had been a teacher. "I don't think much more poetry is to be expected from him, either". He paused, sadly-gladly, then went on with more warmth:

"There's one still younger poet, though, Charles Madge, very promising indeed. He wrote poems already at Winchester and invented a new stanza for himself. Very fertile and original, and he has no politics. He's more likely to bring the general reader towards poetry again as the Georgian poets did, and as I think poets should."

But they were singing Waltzing Matilda under the trees in the light of the flames as the billy came to the boil.[16]

It is almost futile to try to cull appropriate extracts from *Fourteen Years*: each entry has its own value and charm. What cannot be conveyed is the ease with which it moves between Australia and Europe, following events and happenings in both; the way it registers life, at, say, Green Island or in Barcelona. It is not all a record of literary meetings. There is the lively account of being caught over-riding in a Spanish train, and the encounter with the hat-maker who paid her fare; descriptions of coral, stones, and birds. What most strikes one in this book is Nettie Palmer's sure grasp of the concrete, her clear perceptions of personalities, places, and things. She hardly ever generalizes, consequently encounters and incidents with people or books are allowed to speak simply for themselves. Nettie Palmer writes with the sureness and poise of what one can only call an inherited style. One can point to the beautiful arrangement of balanced sentences with a pungent incisiveness of comment, and the almost colloquial lilt—a combination that seems to guarantee its survival. *Fourteen Years* received no wider circulation than that of an edition limited to five hundred copies. It was published in 1948 and has never been reprinted, but it is likely to prove Nettie Palmer's most important contribution to Australian literature, a classic of its kind.

14

Norman Lindsay as Novelist

Novel writing was for Norman Lindsay a peripheral activity, and yet one that had great importance for him. From the outset his artwork was accompanied by attempts at imaginative writing, just as the inspiration for much of his art was drawn from literature. At Creswick Grammar School (says a contemporary F.G. Brinsden) he was "the prime mover in our publication, *The Boomerang*, being editor, illustrator, printer, and chief contributor of literary gems". His published works include twelve novels and the anomalous *Madam Life's Lovers* written in dialogue form, as well as two children's books, *Creative Effort*, a collection of essays, *The Scribblings of an Idle Mind* (1966), and two books of reminiscences, *Bohemians of the Bulletin* (1965) and *My Mask* (1970).

But he wrote much more than that. There were many short stories, of which I put a few into *Vision*; and many *contes drolatiques*, to which belongs *Hyperborea*, printed in *Vision* and done by me as a small separate book in London in 1929. My mother had two handwritten booklets of verse, which he had bound up in the early days of their relationship, one of them a poem of some length in *Omar Khayyam* quatrains. And he wrote poems now and then later, though he was shy about them. He introduced some of them into the first text of *Madam Life's Lovers*, but cut them out after a tactless comment of mine: that they weren't bad, but on the same level in poetry as drawings of mine would be in art. My mother told me that he did much writing in the first years when they were together. Illustrations, which have survived, show that about 1900 he wrote a Roman comedy, "The Pink Butterfly", based on his readings of Plautus in the Bohn translation, and a fantasy tale, *The Boy, the Girl and the Garden God*, about 1905. At the end of the 1890s, he, Lionel, and Ray Parkinson (my mother's brother) collaborated in writing a novel about pirates. Ray was to do the narrative proper, Norman to add humourous passages, and Lionel to add description and details about ships. (Not long after, in Sydney, Norman himself became an expert on sailing ships.) Around 1918—19 I had the manuscript of Ray's story, which I recall as a good workmanlike adventure narrative, not very original, indeed strongly influenced by R.L. Stevenson. (I left it behind in Brisbane and have no idea if it still exists. As every second page was blank, I am ashamed to say that I used them for writing poems in.) Hetherington tells us that about 1905—6 Norman attempted a fantasy novel, "The Thieves of Gaiety" which was too ambitious for his powers at that time and which he never finished. During the period when I was a visitor at Springwood, 1919—26, he always had manuscripts to produce, novels or stories, and he was continually revising works already written.

Because of his way of holding on to a novel for many years, during which he read out passages to friends in the evening—an activity which he much enjoyed—the publication dates of his works often give little idea of the dates of composition, especially of the date of the first version. *The Cautious Amorist* was written by the early 1920s, when he read it to me, but it did not get into print till 1934. Certainly much of *Rooms and Houses*, printed only in 1968, was also written by the early twenties; for I heard several sections of it read out with his infectiously chuckling gusto and occasional shouts of laughter, and with hand-claps on leg. I have forgotten what its name then was, but it was not *Rooms and Houses*. Either he had not then written the passages bearing directly on my mother, or he did not like to read them to me; my impression is that he had not made the work so strongly autobiographical in its first version and that it went through several rewritings.

I may add that while he clearly amused himself a great deal by writing during his lonely evenings and feeling the big watercolour studios filled with the rowdy life he conjured up, he found his work come truly alive when he read it aloud and gave it something of an objective existence. He liked the responses that he was sure to get from his friends; but he never let himself be quite carried away. The sense of an audience helped him to get the work in a new focus, which later led to reconsiderations and revisions. One odd way he had of getting a sense of the pattern of a novel was to lay the chapters out in a system known only to himself on the studio floor. Somehow, through the thicknesses of the chapters and the positions of those dealing with related themes, he got an idea of how things were shaping.

The only novelists that he ever talked about to me were Scott, Dickens, Balzac, Conrad. (Earlier he must have read many of Balzac's novels, but in later years Balzac meant for him the author of the *Contes Drolatiques*.) Lionel had made him read many French authors of the nineteenth century in translation, but the only one that left a strong impact on him was Gautier's *Mademoiselle de Maupin*. After throwing off Lionel's influence he rejected Flaubert, but I think that *Madame Bovary* had more effect on him than he knew. Rabelais, Petronius, and Cervantes were favourite authors from early years. Of Australian work he talked only of Louis Stone's *Jonah*, though he knew the work of Lawson, Ambrose Dyson and others quite well. I know from my mother's books that he had read Gissing and Meredith, though he never mentioned them to me. I feel sure that it was from Meredith he picked up an odd use of abstract nouns, to which he gave his own peculiar twist. For example:

> She had been observing these histrionics of renunciation from the courtyard door with annoyance, the annoyance of a mature concept of life which sees its purely rational phenomena made a mess by two infant adults ...
> All that afternoon Wally had so analysed the father as destructive inertia on the freed action of the son that Jerry's moral debility found itself served with a cocktail when he wished to order a small beer, as the meekest excuse for toping with a father. (*Miracles by Arrangement*, 1932)

I introduced him to Norman Douglas and Huxley; and of Douglas in particular he had a high opinion.

JACK LINDSAY

Clearly there is, apart from a few works which I shall discuss later, a big gap between his writings and his artwork. A large part of his fiction, certainly the best and liveliest part, is based on Creswick memories of boyhood and adolescence, whereas the drawings or paintings range through history for material and backgrounds, and often attempt imaginative judgments or definitions of life on a grand scale. I should say that one main function of the fiction was to bridge the gap between his artwork and the everyday life from which, after the return from his first visit to England, he had in effect retired. After the early years of journalistic activities, Norman lived much of his life alone; and he needed his fiction as well as his art-images to people the solitude that he preferred. In him a very amiable and gregarious element, after the years of youth, went on battling with a rejection of all forms of social life as pointless and illusory. He liked intermittent contacts with individuals whom he felt to have something of a kindred viewpoint on life; but he quickly tired even of that, and wanted to get back to his solitude.

In a letter of July 1958 he stated:

> I have never acquired the habit of thinking of myself as a writer in the professional sense. For me, it has been a release from the tension of thinking, for thinking can become damned oppressive for one who lives so much alone as I have done over many years. If I had been in frequent communication with the few intimate friends of my time, I daresay much that I have written would have evaporated in talk.

But he was not in frequent communication with friends because he chose to live that way; there was nothing to prevent him from living differently except his predilection for solitude. He preferred to fill the evenings with the characters from his fiction. Further, as he says, the work of writing was an escape from the problems of thought. His novels are not projections that involve the complex world of his thinking; they belong to quite another sphere, that of direct living, from which all the problems of thought are excluded as fully as is possible. The tales and novels summon up the daily or nightly scene as a protection; they fill the questioning silences of the mountain lair, the heavy emptiness of the studio after a day's work at drawing-board or easel. The last thing that the writer wants is to unite the difficult thoughts and the bustling picture. There is thus a magical element in what appears an objective picture of things going on in the world, and this element in turn is liable to transform the social scene into a phantasmagoria rather than to evolve any rational scheme.

The split of life and thought shows up most clearly in many of the fundamental ideas and characters of the novels, and in the comments usually made by someone in the story who is used as the author's mouthpiece, but also occasionally by the author in his own person. There is no justification or explanation of anything that occurs in social life, we are told, except as a mere explosion of unrelated personal energy.

> He put the designs away and began sorting his papers and tidying up his table. That brought him another spasm of revolt, which visualised in a flash the fatuous activities of earth forever imposing an exercise of order on a process incessantly falling into decay. Anarchy is the only retort on a system designed to go wrong. "You cannot alter, you can only smash ..."
>
> Repeating formulas on paper allowed him to dispense with thought on their account, and free speculation on the absurd spectacle of humanity, which was a harliquinade [*sic*] clearly designed for a wise man's entertainment. (*Miracles by Arrangement*)

Such attitudes are dominant throughout the novels and show the angle from which the writer is viewing his material, people in general. Yet art he looked on as an integrative process that created its own organic order and found in the harlequinade the revelation of the life-process and its abundant self-organizing energy. We see that the split between thought and fictional activity points to a deep split somewhere in the writer (and so also in the artist). In this essay I want to follow out further the consequences of the attitudes that Norman admitted, to find how those attitudes expressed themselves in his writings, and what they tell us in turn about his art.

First let us glance at each of the novels. *A Curate in Bohemia*, dated by Hetherington 1904—5 in his biography, was published in 1913. Here is a light-hearted account of art-student days in Melbourne in the later 1890s with Norman as Partridge and Max Meldrum as MacQuibble. Norman was still close to the events and there is nothing of the sceptical self-conscious philosophizing such as we see in the above quotations from *Miracles by Arrangement*. Round the same time he began writing stories about his boyhood in Creswick, the first of which appeared in *The Lone Hand* on 1 July 1908. Since these stories began in the years when we, his three sons, were still very young, one might suggest that his thoughts had been turned back to his own early years by the fact of his watching us at play. I cannot however find the least thing in the stories that relates to us; Norman was never at ease with children, but in his efforts to evade us his memories of Creswick must have been willynilly stimulated. Clearly what attracted him to small boys (at least in his mind) was the belief that they lived a quite amoral life without anything of the "tension of thinking" from which he wanted in his activity as a novelist to escape. The small boy thus became the perfect symbol of the state of mind of the novelist creating him, and it was no accident that Norman discovered his method as a novelist by turning to the feckless art-student life in Melbourne (where none of the normal responsibilities of life appear even in the ghostliest of forms), and then by going further back to his boyhood days when the individual is seen as existing, not only without any responsibilities, but in a permanent state of rejection of the adult world and its values. Within this field, which in fact reflects one aspect of early youth, but by no means all the aspects, he had much success, because of the completeness with which he could identify himself with the small boy.

Next, after his return from London, with his long illness and convalescence (during which he read many minor novels), he wrote *The Cautious Amorist*. A friend, Ralph Stock, had been wrecked with his sister and a friend on a reef off Norfolk Island; and the episode started Norman thinking of the possibilities in a story about a trio of males and one female on a desert island. He himself told me that the main stimulus came from De Vere Stackpool's *Blue Lagoon*, one of the novels given to him as he lay abed. He was so annoyed at the romantic treatment of the theme—though in its time *The Blue Lagoon* was thought daring—that he decided to write a satirically realistic account of the same sort of situation. For some reason the curate had become to him an emblem of all that was must futile and feeble, as we see from both *A Curate in Bohemia* and *Cousin from Fiji*; at the same time it gave him a convenient basis for lampooning the religion that he detested, without bringing him into a head-on collision with conventional views.

I should add that in the first decade of the century he did a vast number of joke-drawings for the *Bulletin*—as well as similar drawings for postcards, advertisements, and so on—in which he developed his sense of the comic character. He used much genuine

observation in depicting humorous types, and there was more sympathetic fellow-feeling here than is to be found often in his later
literary exercises in the comic. He told me that he did hundreds more
drawings than were ever printed, as a fire at the *Bulletin* office
destroyed a large number.

During the twenties, as I have said, he did much writing of
stories, novels, and droll stories (with Boccacio, Rabelais, and
Balzac as his models). But he did not publish any works of fiction
apart from *Madam Life's Lovers* (written around 1923—24), which
he gave to me when I set off on the Fanfrolico adventure, plus an
etching to be used as frontispiece. Then in 1930 came *Redheap*.
Brian Penton brought the manuscript over when he came in 1929. I
was then running the Fanfrolico Press and took Penton on as
business manager when P.R. Stephensen went off. He was vigorously trying to find a publisher for a novel of his own, which never got
into print, and among the firms he contacted were Faber and Faber.
We decided that it would be worth trying *Redheap* on them, and
when they accepted it he carried through the arrangements for its
publishing.

What made Norman decide at this point to try his fortunes as a
novelist? My brother Philip had also turned up in London as a
novelist seeking a publisher; and there had been much talk about
novels and the problems of print between Norman and the two
young aspirants. In 1950 Norman tells how Penton had read the
manuscript and proposed to take it with him to London. "I was
reluctant to let it go. I did not want to confuse the action of my work
as an artist by also figuring as a novelist. I knew damned well that I
ought not to write novels." Here, as so often, I think Norman is un-
intentionally getting his memories out of focus. He was certainly
delighted when we wrote and told him that Faber wanted the book,
and he promptly went on to publish more novels in England. One
must recall the impasse to which he had come around 1929. He
found himself deflated of all impulse, thrown back on himself in a
dead and frightening sort of way. In such a state he may well have
turned his thoughts once again to his origins, to the years when he
had been free from the "tension of thinking" that was now threatening to paralyze him. *Redheap*, written during the moral and
emotional crisis induced by the world war in 1918, was one of the
novels that he had read to me in the early twenties, and at all stages
it meant a great deal to him.

The original version, by the way, had the character Bandparts, based on a drunken schoolmaster of Creswick, who was something of a mathematician; but he did not talk in the Einsteinian idiom put to his mouth in the printed book. Norman had known nothing of Einstein—or of Freud—when we met again in 1919—20; but he was very excited at the imperfect account I gave him of the theory of relativity, especially the idea that an object moving at the speed of light would assume the mass of the universe. He at once decided that the art-image with its concentrated force (the image seen as a substance apart from the artwork in which, so to speak, its imprint was left) was such an object, moving into a new dimension beyond the earth. He could not resist making Bandparts something of an Einsteinian, regardless of the anachronism which mars the book. Similarly in *Pan in the Parlour*, where the setting is again essentially that of his early Creswick, he makes the feeble writer Treadwater an exponent of the modernism that he despised:

> You see, I'm trying the method of defining certain mental states by a series of images which recall an association of ideas. Each mental state has its special series of images, which represent the plastic speed of thought. To get that effect I've used a disarticulated prose—forms, colours, sensations, objects of contact, all of which are the emotional content of the mental states ...

The first version of *Redheap* had been written in an effort to escape the "tension of thinking" induced by the impact of the war of 1914—18. I have dealt elsewhere with the shattering effect that the war had upon him, tearing up the roots of his philosophy of earth-glorification (based on Rubens, Rabelais, Nietzsche) and making him reformulate his position in terms of a home-made variety of Neo-Platonism: a universe of hierarchical levels with the artist as a sort of saviour descending to the limits of contracting Matter. A crucial event in bringing about his changed outlook had been the death of his younger brother Reggie in action and the belief that a telepathic contact had been established with his mother at the moment of dying. Norman's thoughts returned to the township where he had grown up, unimplicated in the values of the adult world that had ended in the cataclysm of the war. Now in 1929, as his creative life seemed stricken with impotence, his thoughts must again have gone that way, giving him a renewed interest in the manuscript of *Redheap*. I may mention that his memory for the details of the early years was not so good as might be thought. He went to Creswick to refresh his recollections, and he sounded Lionel and Mary his sister a great deal. Lionel told me that he agreed to compile lists of juvenile jargon for him and that he lent him his Creswick diary. He was infuriated at the extensive use that Norman made of the latter. Take the humour gained, for example, by contrasting the factual account of Robert's hopeless fumbling in his attempt to seduce Millie with the high-faluting version in a letter to a friend, which ends "I'm glad I spared her". The letter-version was more or less a transcript from the diary. Norman through much of childhood had been kept at home on account of illness, and had grown accustomed to looking out at life through a window. Lionel had then been the admired leader, and Norman turned now to him for information about what had really happened. I make this point because it brings out that his fascination with the early years was based, not so much on vivid memories of schooldays, as on the meaning which they had now acquired for him.

The success of *Redheap*, which included its ridiculous banning in Australia, must have made him decide to take himself more seriously as a novelist. In 1933 Faber published his *Miracles by Arrangement*. This novel he certainly hadn't written in the 1920s; internally it bears all the marks of his efforts to settle down to middle-age after the years 1929—30. Also the concluding scene when the son leaves for England is clearly derived in part from Philip's departure to join me in 1929. Norman has used his relations to Philip and myself throughout the book, though in no way does he draw directly on them. The book, though from one angle an attempt to write a novel with a contemporary setting, keeps on returning to the Creswick focus, so strong is the pull of the early years (for example, the whole account of Jerry). Norman seems to feel himself simultaneously the bewildered adolescent and the lost middle-aged husband. But though the novel is insecurely based on the early 1930s, it represents the only effort that Norman made to deal directly with the world of his adult life, except for *Dust or Polish?*

Next came the collection of smallboy stories, *Saturdee*, in 1933, which I would define as Norman's central work. The same year came *Pan in the Parlour*. Here, though much less than in *Miracles*, there is some attempt to take a contemporary setting (indicated in a halfhearted way by a few motorcars and pianolas), but in fact the world depicted is an odd fusion of Creswick and Springwood. The predicaments of Gilbert with his difficult wife Irene are closely based on Norman's own troubles at the time (for which one may consult Jane Lindsay's *Living with Pa*); but he so strongly feels the need to put any significant relationship into the world of his childhood that Springwood fades out into Creswick. Laurence the intruder who upsets things is made epicene because for Norman the prime upsetter was the woman. In other respects he is based, I feel, on a conflation of Philip (an unpredictable descender on Springwood in the years before he left for England) and a friend of mine whom I had taken to Springwood. As the latter is still alive, I will not give his name. He was a fellow of much charm, but at root unscrupulous and mischievously pleased at embroiling people. Norman uses Laurence as an emblem of what he considered the malice of chance, a projection of the buried discontent felt by people at their safe and conventional lives.

    The Cautious Amorist (1932), was brought out from some drawer of discarded manuscripts; and in 1938 came *Age of Consent*. The latter work, dealing with the attempt of an artist to find material for work and escape from the city, down on the south coast of New South Wales, was indeed not Creswick-sited; and its emotional stimulus came from Norman's attempt to find some renewal of his life, away from Springwood, in the later 1930s. But it cannot be called contemporary in any serious sense. Its heroine and its general feeling look back to early years. In a letter to Mary, Norman mentions that the artist was based on a Creswick character. "His whole appearance and personality was so stamped on my mental retina that I used him as the central figure in a little novel called Age of Consent." We see again how Norman, even when trying to write a work originating from his own predicaments in the immediate present, could not help sliding back to a Creswick basis.

    The Cousin from Fiji (1954) returns unashamedly to the years of adolescence, though Ballarat and not Creswick is the setting. (Norman's mother had come from Fiji.) *Halfway to Anywhere* carried on the characters of *Saturdee* to the years of adolescence. In 1950 came the one effort to write something like an ordinary contemporary novel, *Dust or Polish?*, with its account of a shop-hand who becomes a secondhand furniture dealer in Sydney. Though competent enough, it is the least characteristic or lively of Norman's novels. After that there was only *Rooms and Houses* in 1968, forty-five or more years after its first version. Here there is a return to the world of *A Curate in Bohemia*, though in fact the work is a farrago of memories and fantasies, reaching several years forward into the Sydney years when he met Rose Soady. For some odd reason he builds his picture of my mother's family on that of Christopher Brennan (whom he knew only through the stories of Lionel, plus what I told him of Anna Brennan). I have dealt elsewhere with what I can only describe as a number of falsifications introduced in order to justify himself in his own eyes for his treatment of my mother. (Strictly one cannot speak of an author falsifying facts when he is giving a fictional account, but at so many points this novel deals with Norman's own life that it can only be regarded as a fictionalized autobiography.)

We see then to what a remarkable degree Norman's novels looked back to his early years, particularly to boyhood and youth at Creswick, and then to his art-student days before he was entangled in adult responsibilities. When, as in *Miracles*, questions of responsibility do come up, they are shrugged aside as unreal and irrelevant. We have an astonishing proof of the way in which his emotional life was tethered to his early years and above all to the family house at Creswick. The method of presentation has an effect of objectivity because of the busy series of characters who parade, gesticulate, babble, or bluster their way through the stories; but the essential focus is that of the boy or lad, puzzled and rebellious, whose perspective is limited to the family circle and to various plans for escape and self-assertion. Among the other boys he has to keep his end up; and as he grows aware of girls, he is obsessed by the problem of proving himself a licentious lover in his own eyes and in those of his companions. A give-away aside by the author occurs in *Mircales*. "Peter was a big fellow, short nosed and pugnacious, but his brown eyes adored Jerry. Jerry adored Peter. Friendship for them was in the only stage that friendship can exist, still on the borderland of adolescence, before the terrors of a defeated ego get to work on it." That declaration helps to explain why Norman felt driven back to these early years when he attempted a representation of people that involved a social background. Only in boyhood and adolescence, he felt, could friendship—any form of emotional union other than the sexual—exist and flourish. When an individual was driven by age and circumstances further out into the world, to stand on his own feet, his "defeated ego" cut him off from such unions in a series of disillusionments and frustrations. Experience thus revealed itself as nothing but an increasing self-isolation, in which the strong man affirmed himself over against the world of otherness, while the weak man succumbed and in varying degrees was obliterated. That is why love is shown in the novels as something to be afraid of; for to love is to deliver oneself up naked to the power of another, and that other, in his or her defeated ego, will take advantage of the surrender. To love is to lay oneself open to suffering. The wise course is to close oneself up in one's ego, as little defeated as possible, abandoning the unions of boyhood and youth, which now, if made the basis of one's living, only betray one to misery and exploitation.

Hence the contradictory qualities of these books. On the one side there is a vast gusto, as if of a careless abandonment of self to the joys and turmoils of living; on the other hand there is the defeated retreat into the self, a protective set of evasions based in fear, an acceptance of the alienation of oneself from one's fellows— and so ultimately from one's own deepest self. The second aspect, that of the retreat, is masked or obscured to the extent that the material treated is that of boyhood and youth, when, in Norman's phrase "friendship can exist". But because the desire and the experience of union reside only in the early layers and cannot be effectively carried forward into adult life when "the terrors of a defeated ego get to work" on them, the social element cannot be realized outside the bonds of play, mischief, display, girl-chasing and the like that unite the youngsters. The rest of the world, especially the other members of the family, are strange nuisances, obsessed and defeated characters carrying on with aims and motivations that seem insensate and absurd to the youthful eye. Only to the extent to which play, mischief, display, and girl-chasing survive and are perpetuated in the adult world is that world recognized as human, happy, and worthwhile. Against these elements which, because of their basis in childhood, are felt to have validly uniting force, there is set the phantasmagoria of the men and women who are controlled by their defeated egos. Here we meet Norman's humorous powers at full stretch, drawing to a considerable extent on Dickens for their method, but also derived in part from popular tradition. (Norman loved "Pitcher", Arthur Binstead, and he had illustrated works like those of Steele Rudd.) On this basis he developed his own systems of comic fantasy and created his crowded gallery of monsters, scoundrels, loons, monomaniacs, in whom we see personality reduced to a single dominant characteristic or a mad automatism, as with Annie Tregaskis in *Halfway* or Miss Biddlecombe in *Cousin from Fiji*. The comic impulse is a highly varied matter, but at one level it can reveal much cruelty or can spring from fear. When the feared object is made ridiculous, the fear lessens or fades out. Again, the comic approach can offer formulas for dealing with areas of humanity in which one does not feel at home; Dickens is not free from this aspect in the way he tends to keep the comic focus for dealing with the lower classes. Certainly these less estimable aspects of comic invention are present in Norman, mingled with something of his original feeling that all vigorous manifestations of life deserved to be acclaimed. His humorous figures thus belong to some extent to the smallboy level of spontaneous energy, into which the problems of the ego (in Norman's terms, the mature individual confronted with the demands of the external world, with money-making and marriage) do not intrude; but they also belong to the spheres that threaten the smallboy level, representing obsessed forms of activity that do not make any sense to the smallboy with his particular set of satisfactions. In the latter sense they become threatening manifestations of the alien enemy, for the most part bombinating in their own peculiar vacuum, but dangerous in the event of a collision.

The basic ingredients of this fictional world are then the small boys or adolescents and the phantasmagoria; but to complete the picture there has to be added a sprinkling of grown men with deflated egos, who often are the protagonists of the story and who in various ways reflect some of Norman's own inner conflicts, and the women who stand outside both the phantasmagoria and the sphere of deflated egos. Indeed it is they who above all do the deflating. "No man ever made a love affair or broke a love affair yet. It's entirely woman's work." I noted this passage down from one of the novels, but now can't trace it. The idea, however, can be seen set out in the action of any of the novels, for instance *Pan in the Parlour* where Irene, with her "ruthless femininity" is the *dea ex machina*, as it is Madame Life that arranges all the relationships in *Madame Life's Lovers*. I may add that this sort of attitude underlay Norman's talk about life. He sums up his position in *Pan*. "Man's business to be disturbed and woman's job to disturb him. I know all about it; the frictional contact of energy. Marriage as a dynamic for work—". In the activity of life (as distinct from work) woman is seen as the dominating factor. Women are rarely approached from the inside in the same way as the men. They are the objects of desire and the upsetters of the male's futile search for order, silly or lovely, shrewish or mysterious, but gifted with intelligence only in their sexual relations. The most fully drawn are Cecilia and her daughter in *Cousin from Fiji*, who exist only as sexual beings, full of animal magnetism. In the sense that they threaten the would-be rational world of the males, they belong to the phantasmagoria, but in a subtle and complex way which makes them desirable as well as frightening.

So far we have been considering works which supplement, but do not directly relate to, Norman's art, except for the link of the joke-drawings with the phantasmagoria. The many droll stories, unpublished, however have their close affinities with the lighter and more fantastic side of his art; and there is one book in which we find the tension of his thinking brought right into a work of fiction, *Madam Life's Lovers*. Here that tension pervades everything and determines the whole nature of the work. The assumption that there is nothing to be taken seriously in life outside the smallboy schemata is thrown overboard, and Norman is throughout concerned with the question of success or failure in self-fulfilment. But we are as far as ever from the social world proper. For Norman held, like the early Sartre, that everyone was the sole creator of himself. This severely existentialist position, held intuitively at first and then rationalized in the system of thought expounded in *Creative Effort*, is set out in *Madam Life's Lovers* in terms of the artist's struggle to maintain his creative purpose and individuality. In Norman's Neo-Platonist universe that struggle on earth is at every point linked with the struggle to maintain order and renew the sources of energy at higher levels. So the creative individual on earth is seen as entwined with spirit-forces in other dimensions. Norman certainly believed in the actual existence of those forces, but one could take the spirit-forms as symbols or embodiments of various aspects of the creative struggle on earth. The individual is defined as alone with his destiny, which ceaselessly oscillates between self-fulfilment and self-destruction, though on it ultimately depends the fate of earth and indeed the whole universe. I do not need here to analyze in detail this scheme of things; its importance for us is the way in which it reveals how Norman consciously excluded from his fiction proper the whole struggle of values, the complex patterns of development, which he recognized with another part of his mind. By making this division he cut his art away from life at the very point where he most wanted to make the connection; and his fiction played for him an important role in helping him to maintain this division.

The effects on his art were highly complicated and I am not here attempting to sort them out. My aim is rather to bring out certain deep conflicts and contradictions which need to be thoroughly understood before any such sorting-out can be made. But I would like to point out one more consequence of the division I have analyzed. Apart from the smallboy and adolescent level, the social essence of characters tended to be isolated and shut up in the phantasmagoric image. As questions of development had been limited to the artist, poet, musician, the ordinary individual was seen as a sort of explosive or fettered force enclosed in a solipsistic system. By itself such a force could at worst do only a limited amount of damage; but if by some chance or malevolent design the idiot forces came together and merged, the possibilities were horrific. Then one got what Norman called the Mob. Hence his panicked opposition to any forms of association, above all in the political field. In *Halfway* he describes the social patterns (class-patterns) of Redheap and how certain changes had come about through economic and other pressures: "But its codes and prejudices remained, and still remain; and a good thing, too, for any system that separates one class of mankind from another is better than a blind regimentation of all classes into one mob." For him any movement into fellowship (above the smallboy level) can only be blind regimentation. Thus we see how social prejudices were powerfully supported by his whole artistic position (which included his concept of the Novel) and his artistic position in turn was welded with his social prejudices.

15

Influence and Individuality: the Indebtedness of Patrick White's *The Ham Funeral* and *The Season at Sarsaparilla* to Strindberg and the German Expressionist Movement

DENNIS DOUGLAS

The first performance of *The Ham Funeral* took place in an atmosphere of lively controversy. The script had been offered, according to Geoffrey Dutton, to the Elizabethan Theatre Trust, who turned it down.[1] It then went, in Max Harris's version of the story (which eventually reached the columns of the *New Statesman*), to the Board of Governors of the Adelaide Festival, who rejected it, against the advice of their Drama Advisory Committee. A rescue operation was mounted by the Adelaide University Theatre Guild, apparently on the initiative of Dr. Harry Medlin, and a production placed in the hands of Colin Ballantyne. Max Harris, who later described himself as "the Billy Graham of the 'Ham Funeral' campaign", provided a good deal of publicity.[2] The season was a remarkable success, attracting favourable reviews from Geoffrey Dutton, in the *Bulletin* (25 November 1961, p.31), Brek, in *Nation*, who pointed out that something similar had happened to *The One Day of the Year* (2 December 1961, pp. 17—18), and Roger Covell, in the *Sydney Morning Herald* (18 November 1961, p.11). These notices paved the way for the presentation of *The Season at Sarsaparilla*, the following year, when Melbourne University's Union Theatre followed the Adelaide University Theatre Guild's production with one of their own, and Geoffrey Hutton of the Melbourne

Age added his voice to the chorus of approval (13 and 16 October, 1962). Neither play entirely escaped unfavourable comment, and *The Season at Sarsaparilla*, in particular, provoked a saturnine aside from David Martin,[3] but their reception was in the main sympathetic.

This turn of events is all the more surprising when one recalls that *The Summer of the Seventeenth Doll*, *The One Day of the Year*, and *The Shifting Heart* were representative examples of the "new" Australian drama of the fifties (White managed to ensure that his plays would be contrasted rather than compared with them by assiduously informing people that their naturalism of approach did not interest him), and that *Our Town* and *Under Milkwood* were offered as examples of the "lyrical" drama towards which he seemed to be moving.[4] There was little general awareness in Australia at the time of the symbolist-expressionist mode in which his plays were couched.[5] The possibility of estimating his aims more clearly today is directly related to the movement of drama syllabuses,[6] and of theatre practice in the experimental theatre groups, in directions which have awakened an awareness of Brecht's links with the expressionist school, and of Strindberg's anticipation, both of the expressionists and of the dramatic avante-garde of the last decade.

The characteristics that distinguish *The Ham Funeral* and *The Season at Sarsaparilla* from plays like *The Summer of the Seventeenth Doll* and *The Shifting Heart* might, at this distance in time, be worth stressing, for they relate to ever-present tendencies in drama which White's plays resist—the tendency to conform with, to express, and to appeal to, socialized habits of mind, and a leaning towards concreteness of action and reference. It would be a pity to let a sense of White's links, as a dramatist, with a thriving dramatic movement of the twenties and thirties obscure our feeling of his artistic individuality.

The Summer of the Seventeenth Doll and *The Shifting Heart* take received social sanctions as the basis of their moral position, embody their central conflicts in familiar objects which function in an emblematical way (like the seventeenth doll itself, or the stinking fish which flies over the fence into the backyard of the Italian immigrant family at the opening of *The Shifting Heart*), and employ for their action a plausible "slice of life", the kind of happening audiences can be led to regard as part of the recognizable material of common experience. White's plays take issue with socialized attitudes, *The Ham Funeral* in its bleak view of human interaction, and *The Season at Sarsaparilla* in its critical approach to accepted Australian ways of thought. One might expect them to have puzzled and irritated theatre-goers, though the tendencies in them which alienated, for example, the Board of Governors of the Adelaide Festival, involve White's inheritance of a nineteenth-century dramatic dilemma. As literature, and intellectual life generally, became, in the post-Romantic period, more and more aligned to a prevailing movement towards attitudes of moral and intellectual discrimination,[7] the writer's acceptance of a critical role in relation to society made involvement with the stage increasingly hazardous. The notable exceptions to the normal nineteenty-century pattern of a non-intellectual, if not anti-intellectual, bias within the theatre, Ibsen and Chekhov, found it no simple matter to reconcile their critical obligations as nineteenth-century intellectuals with the very different obligations of the working dramatist. In the light of this kind of perspective, an author as critical of mankind as White is in *The Ham Funeral*, and of Australian habits of mind as he is in *The Season at Sarsaparilla*, might well find his rigorous conception of the author's intellectual vocation incompatible with the suaver offices of theatrical craftsmanship.

The inward focus of White's dramatic characterization is most evident in his stress on emotional mechanisms of an obscure kind, like the psychic storm that sweeps Stella to her death in *Night on Bald Mountain*, or the impulse, to which I wish to return later, that sends Nola Boyle to bed with Rowley Masson in *The Season at Sarsaparilla*. Equally significant, and perhaps more alarming to theatre audiences, is his evocation of states of heightened consciousness. "One morning, you wake up," says Julia Sheen, "Dogs are barking. The sky is ablaze. People are asleep in other rooms. The furniture is so ... wooden ... It is suddenly TERRIFYING!"[8] "What is a man to do," asks Ern Boyle, "when his guts are twisted by his thoughts? And all the flickering pictures that he sees at the back of his eyes?" "Yes. Yes," answers his wife, "The dreadful things. The mad things. The long, velvety moments. You wonder afterwards if any of it happened" (p. 98).

Most distinctively of all, White often presents his characters as striving to come to terms with spiritual intimations of which the commonest objects are instruments. "There are the voices, too. Not only the voices of the walls. There are the voices of the gas-fires full of advice that we haven't the courage to take. And the mirrors in the deal dressing-tables" (p. 16). The universe of White's novels abounds in such mystic and unworldly apprehensions. They represent less of an anomaly there than in the plays, drama being, as I have tried to suggest, a public and inherently positivistic literary form, wedded, for better or for worse, to the finite, and to awareness at the level of basic common-sense.

The elevation of representation above all other artistic aims in the nineteenth century found its theatrical expression in the tight plotting and sober characterization of what is often, very properly, termed "bourgeois comedy", a theatrical form which can be shown to have derived its conventions from the habits of mind of the newly-culturally-dominant (and pardonably exultant) bourgeoisie. Not only did the kind of dramatic mode that resulted aim for confinement of scope, economy of action, and singleness of purpose. Its plotting took money seriously, not to mention business and political scandal. Erotic situations occur in such plays in the context of the threat they pose to respectable reputations.[9] The approach to drama involved was the circumscribed, inwardly harmonious reflection of an orderly and logical worldview. Its imaginative limitations and its essential secularity were of a piece with its basic premises.

The Ham Funeral lies at the opposite extreme of the dramatic spectrum. Much of its action involves the acting-out of fantasy material. Even apparently naturalistic scenes take on the shifting contours of the central character's dream world, divided as it is between lofty visions and surrealist nightmares.

The Season at Sarsaparilla appears to make larger concessions to naturalism; but there, too, White's aim is to penetrate the surface of character and event, to isolate mysteries of personality and behaviour, to make the mundane stream of incident and recollection deliver up its secret essence. The choric passages of stylized housewifely dialogue are intended to create a composite impression of the gap between inner being and outer life. Roy Child's elliptical shafts and metaphoric insights are literally lost in the razzle-dazzle. The function of the surface of events in *The Season at Sarsaparilla* is to operate in some ways as a blind. The "reality" of the play lies not in the action itself, but in a reconciliation of the action with a partly-critical, partly-transcendental level of perception reaching beneath and beyond it. The norms of Sarsaparilla are not self-justifying.

The distinctive characteristics of these two plays, their critical stance, and their inward focus, exemplify White's affinities with the alternative stream of theatrical evolution to "nineteenth-century realism", the symbolist impulse stemming from the plays of the second phase of Strindberg's career, which germinated in the line of development pursued in the next generation by the German expressionists.

It is tempting to treat Strindbergian-symbolist and expressionist elements in White's plays as one and the same, adopting John Gassner's view that Strindberg should be thought of as the first expressionist dramatist.[10] It seems a pity, however, to lose sight of the differences between the two movements, if only because of the radical contrast between the atmosphere of the nineties, in which Strindberg's later dramatic mode took shape—hence his use of images like Bocklin's "Isle of the Dead" for dramatic effect[11]—and the atmosphere of the period during and after the 1914—18 war, in which the expressionist dramatists pursued their careers.

Australian critics have been happier to acknowledge a symbolist intent in White's plays than an expressionist one, often without specifying very precisely what kind of symbolism they had in mind. The presence in them of expressionist devices has nevertheless been a matter of comment from shortly after their first performance. Roger Covell noted it in 1964, and wondered if the intermediaries between the German expressionists and White might not have been Auden and Isherwood, since their plays, popular in the late thirties, took over expressionist techniques from Brecht. He made much, in this connection, of the stylized crosstalk of the dead landlord's four relatives in *The Ham Funeral*, and also remarked on White's use of his experience writing revue sketches in the thirties in constructing the scene with the two "professional ladies" (*Quadrant*, no. 29, 1964, pp. 7—12). R. F. Brissenden then claimed Covell's warrant to make a slightly different point about expressionist techniques in *A Cheery Soul* (*Meanjin*, vol. 23, 1964, pp. 243—56). Three years afterwards, Barry Argyle asserted (in *Patrick White*, London, 1967, pp. 91—92) that the closest play in spirit to *The Ham Funeral* on the European stage was Borchert's neo-expressionist *Draussen vor der Tur*, which was first presented in 1947, the year White began *The Ham Funeral*—a connection to which I shall return.

It has so far been overlooked that in 1935, the year of White's graduation from Cambridge, where he had studied French and German, Toller, the best known of the expressionist playwrights outside Germany, was in England. The expressionists were regarded with extreme disfavour by the Nazis, and Toller was one of the fortunate few who escaped the gruesome penalty of his cultural misdemeanours. He directed *Draw the Fires* for Manchester Repertory Theatre, with Dominic Roche assisting, in February of 1935, and staged a single performance of it at the Cambridge Theatre, London, in May.

It is also noteworthy that the Gate Theatre, for which Brissenden, in the reference listed above, claimed White wrote during his pre-war years in London, had staged a succession of Toller's plays between 1924, the year of the premieres of *Masse-Mensch* in London and New York (and Sydney, where questions were asked in Parliament, and the actors provided with police protection), and 1936. *Masse-Mensch* was revived there in March 1926, under the title *Masses and the Man*; *Hinkemann* was presented in May and June of the same year; *Hoppla, Such is Life!* in February and March 1929; *Miracle in America* in October 1934; and *No More Peace* in June 1936.[12]

The references to the Spanish Civil War in *The Living and the Dead* suggest that White might have been more receptive in the thirties to the ideals Toller represented than one might expect from a reading of the works written later than the crisis of reassessment of 1942, described in "The Prodigal Son".[13]

It must be acknowledged, of course, that such an argument amounts to no more than a circumstantial extrapolation, and that the debt to Strindberg is much more evident at first glance than the links with the expressionists.

White's use of stage settings to embody dramatically functional concepts, such as the divisions between the houses in *The Season at Sarsaparilla*, and the divisions between the floors in *The Ham Funeral*, for example, is Strindbergian rather than expressionist, in the sense that symbolist dramatists used symbolic details of decor to mirror thematic material. At the end of *A Dream Play*, for example, the castle at the back of the stage bursts into flames, the chrysanthemum above bursts into flower, and the backdrop becomes a wall of anguished human faces.[14] The use White makes of his sets involves something closer to a schematization than a reflection of his themes. The set of *The Ham Funeral* offers a cross-section of the Young Man's personality just as that of *The Season at Sarsaparilla* parcels out Australian society into its strata of gentility. The decor embodies the vision of the personality that is acted out in the former play, and of social interaction in the latter. The three stage levels on the one hand, and the three backyards on the other, add up to a totality as large as life itself. The house in *The Ham Funeral*, like the one in *The Ghost Sonata*, is a symbolic House of Life, or Death, as well as a metaphor of a human soul.

The Young Man's fastidious distaste for existence, which he regards in the light of a "conflict of eels", in which one is condemned to take part, but which one must at the same time survive, has undertones of good humour; but the questions raised by the scenes with the four relatives and the two aged prostitutes are in no way resolved when he goes out to face the night. They recall the crimes and their consequences that bring the inhabitants of the house together in *The Ghost Sonata*, and the Daughter of Indra's discovery, in *A Dream Play*, that human happiness is only possible at the expense of the infliction of pain and sorrow on others.

By contrast with the "universal" symbolic meaning the house in *The Ham Funeral* can be interpreted as possessing, in the light of Strindberg's use of symbolic settings to embody aspects of the human condition, there is also a more confined and doctrinaire symbolic framework operative in the play, which accords to basement, hall, and upper landing in the house a specific correspondence with the three levels of the personality in Freudian psycho-analysis or Jungian analytic psychology: the id, the level of naked instinctual craving; the ego, the level of social interaction and self-concept; and the super-ego, the level of value-formation and moral awareness.

In communing with the beautiful girl whom he can never meet, since she is all spirit, the Young Man acts out a quest for integration as Jung conceived it, discovering the wisdom of the soul, always embodied in analytical psychology by the symbol of the anima, a pure and beautiful young woman.

Freud's conception of the processes of value-formation was rather different, and there is a sense in which what goes on in the basement in *The Ham Funeral* competes for attention with what goes on in the upper rooms, as though a doctrinaire Freudian sub-plot were coming into conflict with a doctrinaire Jungian main action.

In regarding these scenes as incorporating a doctrinaire Freudianism I have in mind their recapitulation of Freud's theory of the importance in the development of the male personality of incestuous attractions towards a mother-figure, consequent murderous hostility towards a father-figure, fear of punishment in the form of castration for these forbidden impulses, and the necessity of resolving these anxieties in such a way that no residual distress remains to disturb the adult mind.

The modifications of this pattern in White's play all serve to allay the anxiety attendant on these experiences. The Landlord and the Landlady are only quasi-parental, the Landlord dies of natural causes at the beginning of the play, the Landlady makes the sexual advance, and the Young Man escapes with his chastity and his self-respect intact. The threat of castration is part of the texture of the relationship between Landlord and Landlady, made much of in the First Relative's tale of how Alma Lusty robbed her husband of his strength and goodness. The metaphor of stabbing is employed when the four Relatives re-create the Landlady's fantasies of killing her husband, and the Young Man's rejection of the Landlady takes on the metaphoric function of a symbolic revenge-murder, being accompanied by physical violence.

In effect, the play substitutes a more ego-gratifying set of anxieties for those incurred in the acting-out of the Oedipus complex, by centring, as far as the Young Man is concerned, on the fear, not of incest and castration, but of domination and explicitly in this play, sexual exploitation by an older woman. A psycho-analyst would argue that this fear is the product of a reassuring subconscious subterfuge, by means of which disturbing emotions, such as sexual longing, with its attendant guilt, are disowned and transferred to the other person. So far as the play centres on the Young Man, it represents, from a Freudian point of view, a safely discreet, perhaps even self-indulgent, treatment of adolescent stresses. It lays its main emphasis on the threat implied in surrender to sexual desire. White may have had in mind a low-life parody of myths like that of Samson and Delilah, or Venus and Adonis, in which masculine energy is imprisoned or reduced to subservience by a female will, in his account of the Landlord's life.

273

Inside this very considerate play, however, there is a sadder and more honest one struggling to get out. Critics from the first have commented on the forcefulness of the Landlady's part. As the action of the play proceeds on the stage, it centres more and more on her agony, anticipated in the scene with the prostitutes, and in her baiting by the mourners, crystallized in the Young Man's brutal rejection of her, and driven home by her rueful oscillation at the end between uncomprehending remorse and uncomprehending self-acceptance. Her attempt to seduce the Young Man, and his escape, form the central crisis and turning-point of the play, and her suffering the play's emotional kernel.

The doctrinaire Freudianism of *The Ham Funeral* recalls the enacting of rituals of self-liberation in two early German expressionist plays, Walter Hasenclever's *Der Sohn* (Munich, 1917), in which a young man frees himself from his father's brutal domestic tyranny, and instigates a crusade against paternal domination, and Paul Kornfeld's *Die Verehrung* (Berlin, 1916), in which an apparent psychopath rather implausibly wins the favour of almost everybody he meets in the course of acting out his sexual and homicidal impulses. To German intellectuals of the expressionist generation, Freud's writings endorsed their own revolt against the repressions of the "Prussiert" German Empire, with its stifling authoritarianism, and its reduction of authorised intellectual pursuits to those that served the needs of dominant cultural institutions. Freud's recognition of the mechanism of repression implied the possibility of a psychic revolt against the deforming influences of their culture. A social revolution demanded a revolution within the human personality. The period was one of intense activity in psycho-analytical circles. Among expressionist texts which went further in the more positive directions suggested by a deeper knowledge of psycho-analytical theory, Sokel's *The Writer in Extremis* lays stress on Leonhard Frank's *Die Ursache*, Werfel's *Barbara*, and *Die Schwarze Messe*, and Toller's *Die Wandlung*.[15]

Turning from *The Ham Funeral* to *The Season at Sarsaparilla*, we find less contriving of events to suit preconceived notions of the personality. The most fully realized figure in the play, however, is Nola Boyle, whose adultery with Rowley Masson is as central to *The Season at Sarsaparilla* as the Landlady's attempted seduction of the Young Man is to *The Ham Funeral*.

The differences all lie in the direction of tough-mindedness. Nola's insistence on "acting a bit honest in dishonesty" (p. 147) takes the theme of sexual temptation onto a new plane altogether. The Landlady's "You know, I quite like you, yer little bugger" (p. 73), just before the Young Man leaves, is a gesture of exoneration. Nola's "Choke yourself, Rowley. Ern's here" (p. 148), belongs to a bleaker world. The development of the sexual triangle in the play has overtones of Strindberg's (or Pirandello's) insight into the obscurer hostilities of heterosexual relationships. To the betrayal of Ern with Rowley is added her covert betrayal of the two men in coming between them, an achievement denied Pearl in *The Summer of the Seventeenth Doll*. The working-out of the relationship between Nola and Ern touches on subtler temptations than are contemplated in *The Ham Funeral*. The quarrel scene following Ern's return home constitutes a ritual self-abasement on Nola's part, a display of remorse acted out as a form of courtship. To the paradox of desire and disgust explored, gingerly enough, in *The Ham Funeral*, is added the paradox of the desire to be loved and at the same time despised.

It will be evident that on this reading of the play the reconciliation between Nola and Ern must be regarded as no happy ending, but as qualified by Pippy's inexorable "But it's gunna begin again" (p. 175), and Roy Child's "The sanitary man's wife is sad. She's between her times. Something has ended and nothing has begun" (p. 174). To regard her, on the other hand, as the stock suburban swinger of current television serials would be a gross misreading. There is about her determination to face her sexual nature honestly something of the coarse demotic stoicism of Miss Quodling, in digger hat and gum boots, defying the "something that knows more ... something that gets us all in the end" to destroy the silence that "will breed again ... in peace" (pp. 355—56).

Along with the tedious vulgarities of Pippy and Deedree, Nola's craving for self-abasement focusses in terms of character an aspect of *The Season at Sarsaparilla* that literally refuses to be ignored, the theme of the relation of socially derived values to self-images in a coarsely self-hating society, a society that bolsters its collective self-esteem by nurturing snobbery and shame, to put White's case in the strong terms it seems to demand. The image of the bitch on heat pursued by the local mongrel pack embodies an indictment, in that it reflects the crudity of Australian prudishness. White's overstatement of the point, by having the barking of the dogs as a continual accompaniment to the action, is central to the truculent strategy of the play. By conferring on Nola the status of a nightcart driver's wife, White is confronting his audience with an aggressive attack on conventional attitudes in the society to which he, she, and they belong.

The aggressive criticisms of their society made by the German expressionists are preserved for us in the harsh visual outlines of Erich Heckel and Emil Nolde and in Trakl's violent imagery; but there is a significant difference between White's stance and theirs. There is no doubt that his writings contain an astringent critique of ruling Australian mores. Nor need one hesitate to ascribe regenerative aspirations to them. His vision of a need for personal re-integration based on a necessary purification of insight and motive, however, expressed, for example, in the characterization of Himmelfarb in *Riders in the Chariot*, and the bleak sense of a peculiarly Australian variety of spiritual decay conveyed in Himmelfarb's terrible journey back to Sarsaparilla after his Passover visit to the Rosetrees (*The Season at Sarsaparilla* and *Riders in the Chariot* have the same geographical location),[16] are very unlike expressionist dreams of the collapse of a social order based on ruthless industrial exploitation, on militarism, and on the dehumanization of the individual. The expressionist vision of a New Mankind was a secularized one. White's regenerative ideals are conceived, like Strindberg's, in terms of an eclectical mysticism.

There is a significant difference, too, in White's use of stylization and caricature in characterization. The unnamed characters in *The Ham Funeral* are not intended to embody universal responsibilities and destinies, like the unnamed characters in expressionist plays, but given exaggerations and distortions required to fit them into a hallucinatory scheme of things. The "professional ladies" and the Relatives are clear caricatures. The central figures, too, are incomplete. The Young Girl must be all spirit, the Landlady all earth, the Young Man, though hungry for self-realization, essentially passive. There is a parodic feeling, a feeling of the revue sketch, about the entire piece.

The more "realistic" atmosphere of *The Season at Sarsaparilla* is continually being subverted by a like nightmarish undertone of grotesquerie, most disconcertingly in the sub-plot concerning the love affair between Julia Sheen, the model, and Mr. Erbage, the public servant who hopes to become a councillor, which culminates in her pregnancy and suicide. Mr. Erbage is permitted no more substance than a businessman in a Grosz lithograph.[17] His lines are as wooden as his personality is two-dimensional, and dramatically functional by virtue of their woodenness, as when he announces Julie's death to Roy Child, "Your friend, Miss Julia Sheen, has taken her father's car, and driven it against a wall" (p. 169). White's attitude to Julia seems to have been ambiguous. He appears to have wanted her to leave an impression only of synthetic glamour and a shapely pair of legs (pp. 90—91), but he also shows her receiving sympathetic respect from Roy, and from Judy Pogson, and he gives her a forceful revelation scene.

One might be tempted to localize another central difference from the German expressionists in White's use of comic and ironic devices. The expressionist dramatists were on the whole rather serious in their social criticism; White employs a savage wit in his. Two things need to be borne in mind, however. One is that though there are only traces of sardonic humour in expressionist drama (one notable exception, perhaps comparable with *The Ham Funeral*, being Kaiser's *Die Judische Witwe*, which takes for its plot the legend of Judith and Holofernes), a mordant wit is strongly evident in expressionist paintings, such as Ernst Ludwig Kirchner's "Five Women in the Street", and Max Beckmann's "The Night". William Dobell's "The Dead Landlord", the painting that is said to have inspired *The Ham Funeral*, lies in a similar line of artistic development. The other is that Borchert's neo-expressionist play of 1947, *Draussen vor der Tur* (to which, as I pointed out earlier, Barry Argyle first drew attention), though not a comedy, is full of a wry, gruesome sense of humour. Faithfully mirroring the state of demoralization in which Borchert was himself to die shortly before its first performance, it brings to the plight of Beckmann, the central character, a courageous spirit of self-mockery, to balance the self-pity that is also present in it.

Apart from the parallels suggested by Argyle between Will Lusty and Borchert's God, "in whom no one believes any more"[18] there are echoes of Borchert's dialogue in two scenes of *The Ham Funeral*. As White's Young Man announces that he could have been born in "in Birmingham ... or Brooklyn ... or Murwillumbah" (p.

15),[19] Beckmann sees himself as the universal man who stands "outside the door ... By the Elbe, by the Seine, by the Volga, by the Mississippi" (p.113). As White's Girl reminds the Young Man of childhood experiences when she first appears (pp.31—32), Beckmann's alter ego, The Other, introduces himself by recalling Beckmann's childhood, and some of his frontline memories as well (pp. 83—84). In the light of such coincidences, it does not seem unlikely that a copy of *Draussen vor der Tur* was in White's hands at some time during his post-war sojourn in Erbury St., London. It had caused a considerable stir in Germany at the time, still has a respectable following among German drama critics, and was included in an anthology of Borchert's prose in English translation issued in 1952, with an introduction by Stephen Spender. The great distinction between the two plays is that whereas *The Ham Funeral* is a farce with tragic undertones, *Draussen vor der Tur* is a tragedy with undertones of farce.

In White's plays the desire to turn a sardonic sense of humour to good account betrays him into a simple-minded *épatisme*. Almost every commentator has remarked that Nola Boyle did not have to be a nightcart driver's wife. Nor did Pippy Pogson have to learn so much from watching the frolicsome dogs of the neighbourhood.

No doubt the coarseness and brutality of Australian attitudes demanded , as I suggested earlier, sardonic treatment; but there is a world of difference between Patrick White's revolt, as a stifled intellectual, against the regimented mediocrity of a mass society, which covertly worships, with awe rather than comprehension, its stifled intellectuals, and the revolt of the expressionist generation against the constraints of a brutally authoritarian cultural system.

One is continually aware, in *The Ham Funeral* and *The Season at Sarsaparilla*, of intellectual role-playing. The irreducible distinction between White and the German expressionists lies in this direction. It is almost impossible to compare the Young Man's fastidious probing of the tedium and squalor that surround him, in *The Ham Funeral*, and, to take one example, the painful involvement of the central characters in Toller's *Masse-Mensch* in the debate over the morality of revolution that provides the basis of the dramatic action. The moral regeneration of the other prisoners' lives affected by the Woman's sacrifice of her own life, rather than commit a murder in escaping from prison, may be as insubstantial, in the light of rigorous critical scrutiny, as the Young Man's sense of liberation, in *The Ham Funeral*, when he goes bounding up the stairs for the last time, but it seems to betoken a less narcissistic range of basic concerns.

The moral or spiritual insufficiency of White's intellectual commentators emerges even more strongly in Roy Child's bland epitome of culturally privileged detachment, "Of course, We-Who-Know-All-This hate it, and promise ourselves to escape to something better. But wonder if that exists ... and depend on those twin dazzlers, time and motion, to help us believe we are doing and being" (p. 99). The uncertainty of such convictions is reflected in the relation of the intellectual commentators to the central action of the two plays. It falls to the lot of others to act and suffer, to break, to confess and survive their confession. Roy Child and the Young Man are there to observe, and to escape.

White's general influence, as a leading defender of intellectual standards in the Australian community, has been wholly salutary, but in these two plays he seems as awkward and embarrassed with regard to the place of cultural interests in common life as any suburbanite. The Young Man in *The Ham Funeral* does not know whether he is a poet or not, but the role of the poet places him above the characters drawn from his surroundings, and he can only communicate on equal terms with the symbol of his soul's wisdom, who descends into the next room to speak to him through the dividing wall. Ron Suddards's references to music are introduced into *The Season at Sarsaparilla* (pp. 89, 165) as unconvincingly as Pippy Pogson's encounter with the depravities of empresses in Gibbon's *Decline and Fall* (pp. 136, 155). The awkwardness and embarrassment cannot be entirely salvaged by the suggestion, in the plotting of *The Season at Sarsaparilla*, that cultural pretensions represent a delusion from which Judy Pogson, for one, is awakened when she falls out of love with Roy Child (pp. 103, 136). The question seems to have been a focus of conflict for White, to which he was not able to give satisfactory artistic embodiment in the plays, though it is treated effectively in the novels.

For these reasons I am inclined to concede to White's critics of ten years ago,[20] though with some reluctance, the presence of a certain priggishness, akin to a vitiating class-consciousness, in the position that the author confers on the intellectual as a culturally

DENNIS DOUGLAS

privileged figure in these two plays, and to allow that, while *The Ham Funeral* may be an avowedly adolescent play, *The Season at Sarsaparilla* can scarcely be held up as a model of artistic maturity.

Despite that reservation, these two plays remain a significant contribution to Australian theatre history, for reasons which bear an analogy, again and for the last time, with the plays of the German expressionists. Their plays, though often awkward in production, foreshadow later work of a more enduring kind, and provide a valuable reflection of a general movement in European intellectual life. In the same way, these two plays of White's, in themselves works of no mean achievement, must be regarded as finding their full artistic fruition in qualities that his work on them imparted to his fiction, and in their anticipation of later developments in Australian drama, which within a decade was to move away from the kind of play our writers were turning out in the fifties, and the kind of patronage on which they were then dependent.

16

The Rhetoric of
Patrick White's
"Down at the Dump"

R. B. J. WILSON

This typical and very effective example of White's prose is a reminder of how fully he has exploited the resources of language to create his literature and how well he has assimilated some of those more successful technical experiments that have given to the prose of Joyce and of Faulkner such extreme flexibility and intensity, and how White has in fact produced a mode of discourse that generates a distinctly new rhetoric. The elements comprising it have undergone further sophistication; the new mix is full of surprises, sudden switches of kind and of key and of pace. Interestingly, the prevailing tone produced by all this variety and flux most often resembles low-keyed, casual chat. Next to it, the remarkable closing paragraphs of "The Dead" and the equally remarkable eloquence of "Barn Burning" seem to have achieved their effects by means much more familiar and obvious. All three writers are concerned with moments of self-awareness: Gabriel Conroy and Sarty Snopes and the two youngsters Lum and Meg have their confrontation with selfhood; and there is in White's rendering of this experience a protean quality that derives from stylistic subtleties representing an important advance in the art of fiction.

White tells of the funeral of Daise Morrow, a woman of abundant compassion for those who have been rejected by the Philistine middle-class suburban society of the small Australian town. While Daise's relatives make their hypocritical self-centred visit to the graveside, the town rubbish-dump next door to it is visited by the Whalleys, a rough and earthy family whose directness and humanity White obviously prefers. He presents the story in nineteen sections, marshalled to throw into significant relationship the various human values involved—especially the relationship of all these people to the dead woman. He alternates our attention between on the one hand such figures as Daise's limited, mean-minded, and mercenary sister Myrtle, whose boorish husband Les, a corrupt town-councillor,* was only sensually aware of Daise, and on the other hand figures such as the dead-beat Ossie and Daise's niece Meg, who have recognized and been fortified by Daise's great capacity for loving-kindness. White juxtaposes a section on Meg's sadly superficial parents, Myrtle and Les Hogben, with one on the vitally alive Whalleys, the neighbours who so shock their pretensions and pretences. He follows a section on citizens such as the Hogbens and the like-minded Lasts, imprisoned in loveless marriages, with one on Meg and young Lum Whalley drawn to each other as they explore their private adolescent fantasies. The method affords mobility and speed. Implicit ironies and poignancies are made swiftly and variously clear, and eventually White is ready to resurrect Daise in a section to which I now devote closer attention.

It embodies in microcosm a dynamic and fluid illustration of the idea developed in the story as a whole. White darts from description to comment, from one character to another, from irony to admiration, from one kind of narrative voice or tone to another—whether satiric, compassionate, or philosophical—working always in sentences free in syntax and often fragmentary in form. He begins the scene by the graveside thus: "Even if their rage, grief, contempt, boredom, apathy, and sense of injustice had not occupied the mourners, it is doubtful whether they would have realized the dead woman was standing amongst them."[1] The sentence is part of the frankly omniscient manner that allows him from time to time to distance his people: even Daise is for him at this point so treated; she is "the dead woman". He then touches briefly, sceptically, on the religious notion of resurrection which he soon uses figuratively. "The risen dead—that was something which happened, or didn't happen, in the Bible". And this is immediately followed by the ironic: "Fanfares of light did not blare for a loose woman in floral cotton."—with its quick synaesthetic linking of the sublime and the mundane. From these concrete images, he moves to speculation: "Those who had known her remembered her by now only fitfully in some of the wooden attitudes of life. How could they have heard, let alone believed in, her affirmation?" So to the directness of the dramatic mode: he gives voice to her spirit. "Yet Daise Morrow continued to proclaim".

The affirmative proclamation that follows, revealing her insights and her understanding and her urgent gesture of salvation, moves us away from White's authorial conducting of the story and gives us Daise's own racy idiom.

> Listen, all of you, I'm not leaving, except those who want to be left, and even those aren't so sure—they might be parting with a bit of themselves. Listen to me, all you successful no-hopers, all of you who wake in the night, jittery because something may be escaping you, or terrified to think there may never have been anything to find. Come to me, you sour women, public servants, anxious children, and old scabby, desperate men ...

It is daring of White to have risked such an explicit statement of his theme, and he makes provisions for guarding this higher-pitched rhetoric from too naked a didacticism: one is the context provided by the preceding narrative with its sharp realism and astringent ironies; another is the way this hypothetical statement—the words she might have used if she could have spoken—are characterized by Daise's own attractive humanity; a further precaution is the tempering of this passionate altruistic plea by having it include also her candid impatience; and finally White, who has had to use words to evoke his idea of a someone whose medium was not words, resumes thus: "Physically small, words had seemed too big for her. She would push back her hair in exasperation. And take refuge in acts." We are reminded of his feeling for Miss Hare and Mrs. Godbold when he continues: "Because her feet had been planted in the earth, she would have been the last to resent its pressure now, while her always rather hoarse voice continued to exhort in borrowed syllables of dust." And an old idiomatic dead-metaphor gains from this phrasing and this context a new force.

The exhortation switches us back to the immediacy of her own voice:

> Truly, we needn't experience tortures, unless we build chambers in our minds to house instruments of hatred in. Don't you know, my darling creatures, that death isn't death, unless it's the death of love? Love should be the greatest explosion it is reasonable to expect. Which sends us whirling, spinning, creating millions of other worlds. Never destroying.

In sustaining the figurative language just noted in White's own preceding intrusion, this passage raises the pitch of her peroration one step even higher, and, as is usual at such points in his prose, the ensuing language becomes commensurately complex: able to bear the emotional intensities he seeks with it, and also able to express with clarity and force the metaphysical notion of an all-embracing, all-redeeming love, so central to this story and indeed so fundamental in most of White. "From the fresh mound which they had formed unimaginatively in the shape of her earthly body, she persisted in appealing to them." Immediately after this he gives us on a separate line three sentences printed in the italics that have hitherto been reserved for the utterances of the clergyman as he reads the burial service. "*I will comfort you. If you will let me. Do you understand?*" The formal religious idea of divine succour and compassion is thus translated into the human love and understanding that the voice of the dead woman is offering to those about her.

For obvious reasons of emphasis, the fragmentary nature of the prose is continued by three similarly isolated lines. The first, in roman typeface again, gives White's rejoinder: "But nobody did, being only human." The rancorous satire of his earlier comments on most of the spectators of Daise's life and burial is thus replaced by a new acceptance and forgiveness. He instantly underlines this by reverting to italics for another line from her in the liturgical mode: "*For ever and ever. And ever.*" And the next, the last, of these carefully isolated elements of prose that are introduced at this climatic stage in the narrative, shows us White rendering the story in a manner even more indirect; by taking the storytelling away from even the vocal spirit of the dead woman and by inserting a single line of scenic description that expresses the woman's benedictory words in symbolic terms which, in the immediate context, are unmistakeably clear, and in the general context of the whole antecedent narrative, intensely potent: "Leaves quivered lifted in the first suggestion of a breeze." The grammar and the lack of commas make the word "lifted" ambiguous, but both of the allowable functions of the word reinforce the same meaning: the leaves did lift and the leaves were lifted, and each interpretation continues the idea of a living, quivering energy returning to all things.

These crucial isolated lines work like verse, and White is here using the poet's device at the novelist's leisure. Or, again, they have the impact of lines delivered in a well-acted drama where the protagonist and chorus time their pauses and then break the stillness and quietness with words that reverberate portentously. They shift the discourse from the naturalistic and humorous one with its photographic snapshots of the human scene, to one concerned with abstractions, with ideas and spiritual qualities. The movement is from spectatorship to contemplation and it is achieved by means just as subtle and fluent as the move back to a note of wry affectionate irony which now follows: "So the aspirations of Daise Morrow were laid alongside her small-boned wrists, smooth thighs and pretty ankles. She surrendered at last to the formal crumbling which, it was hoped, would make an honest woman of her." To be followed by the single quiet: "But had not altogether died."

With which White turns from Daise to young Meg who, in her fresh faith and sensibility, has always felt awe for this woman's command of life. "Meg Hogben had never exactly succeeded in interpreting her aunt's messages, nor could she have witnessed the last moments of the burial, because the sun was dazzling her." It is her next sentence, the final one in this whole section, which rewards the closest attention. "She did experience, however, along with a shiver of recollected joy, the down laid against her cheek, the little breeze trickling through the moist roots of her hair, as she got inside the car, and waited for whatever next." Its principal clause, linking her with the breeze that "lifted" and "quivered" the leaves, links her too with the redeeming and energizing spirit of which White has made it symbolic; and its final clause insists on the forward-looking, hope-sustaining nature of this force by which Meg will be equipped to face with good faith her future. It is a sentence that balances finely between what is felt and thought and what is seen and heard; it shows the outward while still keeping central to our attention the inward. It demonstrates in particular terms what Daise's hypothetical exhortation can mean. The whole story, with its diversity of human types and reactions and its general ramifications is resolved into a meaningful unity by the girl's dim, excited but certain apprehending or "interpreting" of "her aunt's message".

285

The interesting *difference* of this rhetoric is quickly seen when comparison is made with sentences from peaks of significance in the "The Dead" and "Barn Burning". Here are the famous concluding words in Joyce's account of Gabriel Conroy's epiphany: "His soul swooned slowly as he heard the snow falling faintly through the universe and faintly falling, like the descent of their last end, upon all the living and the dead."[2] And here is the Faulkner sentence in which Sarty Snopes first glimpses the southern mansion that his vicious father may threaten, a sentence that moves from the boy's own words ("Hit's big as a courthouse") to hypothetical language attributed to him and then returns to the familiar Faulknerian manner:

> *People whose lives are part of this peace and dignity are beyond his touch, he no more to them than a buzzing wasp: capable of stinging for a little moment but that's all; the spell of this peace and dignity rendering even the barns and stables and cribs which belong to it impervious to the puny flames he might contrive* ... this, the peace and joy, ebbing for an instant as he looked again at the stiff black back, the stiff and implacable limp of the figure which was not dwarfed by the house, for the reason that it had never looked big anywhere and which now, against the serene columned back-drop, had more than ever that impervious quality of something cut ruthlessly from tin, depthless, as though, sideways to the sun, it would cast no shadow.[3]

As might be expected in declamatory prose, the vocabulary and diction in these passages are abstract. We find in key positions in the Joyce, "soul", "descent", "end", the "living" and the "dead", and in the given context, even the material fact of the "universe" loses most of its concreteness. Similarly, in the Faulkner, except for the strong particularity of the "wasp" and the "flames", the really operative positions are occupied by "peace" and "dignity"—both of them repeated—and by "spell". All the other nouns itemized are robbed of a considerable degree of their concreteness by being cast in the plural and by the emphasis thus being placed on their representative qualities: "barns", "cribs", "people", "lives". Both these writers derive a considerable rhetorical force from the connotative values of words generally renowned for being highly charged with emotional overtones. White, on the other hand, seems concerned with casual conversation even with the mundane, and he appears to take pains to qualify each of the essential abstract quantities by a phrasing that emphasizes a very concrete and physical manifestation. So: the "recollected joy" is experienced by Meg with a "shiver"; this "joy" she felt with Lum is embodied in "the down" of the adolescent's incipient beard that he laid against her cheek; "the little breeze" that, in the context of the prose, connotes the spirit of loving-kindness central to Daise's gospel, is described as "trickling through the moist roots of her hair" and is thus made part of her physical response to the boy's expression of his feelings. The rendering of this crucial incident appears almost off-hand; the more familiar agencies of rhetoric have been eschewed. The fervour is there but it is all the girl's, and it is generated without the use of the more standard devices of persuasion.

The same is true of the use of rhythm. The Joyce sentence makes immense music with its alliterative, almost fugal, account of the snowfall and moves to its conclusions with majestic solemnity. The Faulkner one is frankly hortatory, calculated to make a direct appeal to the ear; it is high in pitch and elaborate in cadence, almost frenetic in its mass appeal. The White one is by comparison designed for familiar discourse; even for subdued yarning. The seven distinct parts into which it falls have been selected by him to meet the needs of analysis and arranged for the achievement of clarity, and as each comma checks our progress through it, we ponder the various ideas it contains and those relationships among them that White offers for appreciation. These are: the whole tender question of young Meg's experience; the impact upon her of her first encounter with physical love; her dim but very relevant awareness of what her aunt's life and death may mean; her obedience to her present immediate circumstances in which parents bid her to enter a car and be driven home; and her frankly eager anticipation of her future, for which her experiences with the aunt and the boy have now prepared her. This is the rhythm not of the onward rush but of deliberation, and the impact of the whole sentence is derived not from elements in it that are intrinsic to conventional rhetoric but from the context provided by the antecedent narrative, to which it deftly makes indirect allusion and reference. The ramifications of the girl's excited awareness are all the more penetrating for having been signalled by such quiet means.

As a piece of shorter fiction, ever grateful for prose of great economy, "Down at the Dump" demonstrates the superb adroitness with which White can modulate his discourse among many functions—satiric, compassionate, speculative—and give it a dimension that is metaphysical, even religious, in its range. Only the later E.M. Forster has achieved such breadth of reference with so little overt apparatus and with such throwaway eloquence. White's dramatic modes prove his ear for the mimetic to be fully as faithful, for idioms and tones, as is Joyce's, and his technical adventurousness is every bit as bold as Faulkner's. His important difference lies in his undercutting of the strident to a point where passages that are in fact declamatory in function come through as almost laconic. His is indeed chameleon prose; or, to change the figure, experimenters in fiction during the earlier years of this century have provided him with a loom on which he now weaves a fabric of lustrous texture which is not necessarily "better" but is certainly important in its kind, for it suggests one more way in which even art that has the most manifold effects can conceal its means; and one more way in which an arresting treatment of particulars in time and place can be released from the particularity of that time and of that place.

17

Quest or Question?
Perilous Journey to the Chapel

REBA GOSTAND

Dorothy Hewett's *The Chapel Perilous (or The Perilous Adventures of Sally Banner)*[1] is a contemporary morality play imaging the "confused and confusing experience" of a "demanding, gifted woman" in the twentieth century (preface, p.4); it recreates Sally Banner's passionate struggle with both self and society with an intensity of feeling and a structural complexity that are as yet rare in Australian drama.

In her preface to the play Sylvia Lawson points briefly to the underlying allegory that relates the solitude of the pilgrim to the solitude of the artist, and she notes links with Malory, Spenser, Sir Gawayne, medieval French lore and legend, and also with pre-Christian myths of quest going back to the *Odyssey*. Aarne Neeme in the introduction develops this:

> beyond the surface reality of the characters ... lies an area of symbolic and ritual significance ... The Authority Figures represent the three types of leader in our society, who manipulate and dictate our ethical and moral standards ... In direct contrast ... is Michael, the archetypal nature figure, brandishing those weapons of passion, irrationality and disorder that are a constant danger to the veneer of civilisation ... [Sally] is the artist, flaunting her individuality but in constant search for someone or something worthy of her commitment ... Only when she has overthrown Michael, discovered the emptiness

behind the Authority Figures, reconciled herself to the derision of the crowd and to her own life and purpose, can she come before the Chapel Perilous ...

The Chapel Perilous treads a perilous line between an intensely personal, even at times sentimental, involvement and an objective, critical, cynical disengagement ... The constant tension between Sally's self-assertion and the Chorus's response:

"Poor Sally, she never made it,
No matter how hard she tried ... "

reflects a basic human problem: endeavour versus self-doubt.

But the play makes no such clear-cut distinction as, for instance, a conflict between "endeavour versus self-doubt", nor is the underlying allegorical pattern as clearly defined as Lawson and Neeme seem to suggest. Ambiguities of theme and characterization combine with the ironic and paradoxical complexities of structure and dramatic treatment to create a much richer—and at the same time much more "confused and confusing experience"—for leading character and playgoer alike. And there is "constant tension" not only "between Sally's self-assertion and the Chorus's response" but also—and often most disconcertingly—between the realistic elements of characterization and action and the "allegory", at least as Sylvia Lawson and Aarne Neeme have interpreted it. Quest and question are both opposed and fused until, in the words of Sally's poem: "*Such contradictions mock mortality.*" (P.69.)

Through the leading character the play images the self-absorption of the creative artist, and this self-absorption is judged and condemned by all the other characters—in their turn also judged and condemned. If Sally's rebellious self-absorption is intended to reflect the "necessary arrogance for a person to act" against the "approval-disapproval pressures of our society" (introduction, p.7), it is difficult to accept her final achievement of her goal simply as either an act of affirmation or as an indication of virtue rewarded, because Sally's rebellion has been repeatedly shown by the action to reveal her weakness, not her strength. The satire in the play is aimed equally at Sally and at the society that is frightened by so much individuality (p.20). Both the emotional tone and the dramatic action place Sally on trial, at the same time as they relentlessly reveal the hypocrisy, the materialism, the moral turpitude of our society. The emotional texture of the play involves even more than merely tension between an "intensely personal ... involvement and an objective, critical, cynical disengagement"—shifts of tone and of point-of-view constantly require the playgoer or reader to reassess his judgments.

Consider the tone at the beginning of the prologue. In spite of the fact that Sally claims "courage and great heart", the Chorus tells her that she is "neither pure in heart nor humble", and warns her: "Your worldly renown can avail thee nothing in matter of the spirit. Repent yet for ye do not belong to the blessed, and we fortell your death." (P.13.) This sombre, admonitory tone, the allusion to medieval legend, hints of ritual, religious sanctions, judgment, all give a serious significance to the words of the Chorus here, a significance that is ironically undercut throughout the remainder of the play by the way the Chorus is used. But the emotional tone of the prologue may *not* be intended to reflect—as the audience might initially suppose—human endeavour struggling towards a spiritual goal, erring Everyman on the final journey, Sir Gawayne on his heroic quest; instead the tone may be ironically parodying the smug judgment of the society (the Chorus) that rejects the aspiring soul, the artist; condemning to social and hence (in their view) spiritual death one who dares to be different because she does not belong to the "blessed", that is, those who conform and are accepted. Or perhaps the Chorus is predicting the eventual death of Sally's "flaunted individuality", the time ahead when "the heyday in the blood is tame" and she finally joins the conformists, the "humble":

> JUDITH: Sally Banner, what is your opinion of full frontal nudity?
> SALLY: None of my friends ever looked very good naked. *
> CANON: Sally Banner, what do you really think about Australia?
> SALLY: It's better to be a big frog in a small puddle. (P.88.)

Consider the ambivalent portrayal of Sally. "Know thyself" was the rule of the ancients, one of the principal philosophical tenets inherited by the Renaissance, and a favourite theme for allegorical treatment in all ages. On the level of realistic character-portrayal as well as on the level of allegory Sally undoubtedly does *not* know herself. She rebels passionately against authority, against the Establishment and its attitudes and values, but she falls in love with, and offers herself to, a succession of Authority Figures (who, significantly, all bear Biblical names). Sally, the "arch-rebel", is constantly shown by the action to be incapable of functioning

---

* Compare with Judith's own use of these words on p.85. This passage is of course full of echoes from earlier scenes.

without the support of a relationship with authority in some form. She has a love-hate relationship with authority—the men (and the one woman Judith) she loves are all variations on Authority Figures. Sally rejects religious faith and ceremony ("SHE WOULD NOT BOW", p.16) with its ritual of observance, only to embrace instead the faith of the blood with its ritual of promiscuity, then political faith with its ritual of dogma. Both the latter eventually reject *her*—indeed, far from overthrowing Michael (Neeme, introduction, p.6), Sally finds that he wants neither her body nor her love poems: "I've got ... conservative tastes. I'm a plain, uncomplicated man and I like my women virtuous. It's as simple as that." (P.75.) Saul, too, casts her out: "But of course you have no discretion: politically unreliable, your career in the Party finished. I'm almost sorry for you, Sally." (P.71.) And at the end "As it was in the beginning" (p.89) the authority of religion apparently re-asserts its claim and Sally bows to the altar. She then climbs her tower (ironically the scene of her first suicide threat), achieving the symbolic goal of her "questing", her pilgrimage through life. But she reaches it only after she has acknowledged that "I wasted my substance." (P.85.) Indeed her whole life, she realizes "has been a struggle to be identified with someone, something, anything that gave me even a brief sense of my own immortality" (p.85.)—a confession that is hardly in keeping with the image of the self-absorption of the artist. It suggests rather the desperate search for a mother- or father-image by an emotionally immature adolescent:

> PSYCHOLOGIST: (*to parents*) All adolescents go through a period of role-taking. The only cure is time. (P.34.)

Sally is in many ways the perpetual adolescent, and she certainly rushes headlong from one role to another, recklessly over-acting most of her self-chosen parts. She "always goes for broke" as Michael says; to which she agrees "I don't play for halves. I take it all the way" (p.52). And although she seems to see this as the symbol of her independence, she contradicts this "independence" in every relationship. The men make the rules, call the tunes to which she dances:

> SALLY: Somebody walked over my grave. Promise you won't leave me?
> MICHAEL: (*stopping her*) We're alive now. You're in my arms. That's enough. Nobody can promise past that.

SALLY: No ... nobody can promise more than that.
MICHAEL: So. Shut your mouth and take off your clothes.
  (P.27.)

and

DAVID: ... The game's over, Sally.
SALLY: You made the rules.
DAVID: I didn't want to be like all the others. I wanted you to
think of me differently. (P.39.)

and

SALLY: It is worth it. It's got to be.
THOMAS: No, quite worthless Sally. The things that matter
aren't our own little egos, our happiness, our satisfactions. The
things that matter are building a new shining life for everyone ...
  (P.57.)

and

SAUL: ... If there's to be anything at all, it's got to be on my
terms. And when I say finish, it's finished. (P.65.)

Far from being independent, in her "questing sexuality" or in
anything else, Sally is quite pitifully dependent upon others. As each
of her lovers rejects her she begs him (her) not to leave her (compare
with Everyman asking each in turn to accompany him to his death?).
She begs the men for marriage, security, reassurance—the ritual of
the Establishment. Thus the repetitions in the structural pattern of
the play reinforce this ambivalent picture of Sally. Her first thought
on being rejected by Thomas is "Who'll look after me?" (P.71.)
When almost at the end of her road, she goes back to her mother in
the hope of being looked after (p.87), but her mother has gone
beyond her reach, into the protective sanctuary of senility, so Sally
turns again to her first love Judith. Judith too has gone beyond her
reach, into the protective sanctuary of religion (p.87).

Is it this dependence upon others that makes Sally a "minor
poet"—she is *not* ruthlessly self-sufficient as the true artist must be?
When she tests Michael (pp.28—29) and he fails her—but wasn't
that failure a mutual one, disappointing and disillusioning them
both?—Sally says that she wanted a "kind of unique communion",
and the essence of her "rebellion" does seem indeed to be a constant
search for someone or something with which she can identify. Later
in the play she explains to Michael the reason for her promiscuity;

after he left, she gave herself to anyone: "I wanted to destroy myself, because I didn't exist any more. Not as a whole, loving, complete human being." (P.53.) But it is difficult to avoid passing a judgment on this at the realistic level—Sally was already after men before she met Michael in the first place:

> lst GIRL: Sister, Sally Banner's got another one. (p.26)

After David (the intellect?) rejects her, Sally feels again that she does not exist, that she has no identity, she is NOBODY (p.41), and she tries to turn this state into a reality by swallowing lysol. Is it relevant to the interpretation of the allegory that her most serious attempt at suicide comes after she is rejected by the one intellectual in her life? She always denies the intellect: "I believe strongly in the blood, the flesh, as being wiser than the intellect." (P.34.) But has she the same love-hate relationship with the intellect as she has with authority?

Sally makes a number of attempts at self-destruction, threatening to jump from the tower, taking the lysol, having the abortion (suicide by proxy?). After the abortion she apologizes to her husband Thomas for the death of the child (Michael's), giving as the excuse for her affair with Michael that she wanted "some kind of immortality" (p.57)—mightn't the child have given her this? And when Thomas offers her political immortality, she eventually rejects this too just as she rejects the second child (Thomas's). Is Sally's belief in the blood and the flesh as being wiser than the intellect actually a contradiction of the artist's role, instead of a symbol of it? No matter how much Sally tries to answer with the blood direct, she finds with every experience that the blood does *not* answer, does *not* satisfy her. She always wants something the other characters can't or won't offer her. She does not give them what they want from her. Is this symbolic of the confusion, the emotional uncertainty, in her personal rebellion, her challenge to life? Or is it a comment on the essential ambiguity of the artist's role?

Although Sally talks of wanting to be an actress, or a poet, and fancies herself also as a singer and artist (p.24), not one of these is what, in the course of the action, she *gets on with being*. Even her poetry is related to her changing enthusiasms for people or ideologies, and—at least as reflected in the action of the play—seems to be almost an accidental by-product of them. She uses most of her energy not for writing but for sex—is this what she means when she admits at the final trial that she has wasted her substance?

Any attempt to confine the total play within a neatly explicated allegorical pattern must stumble over the changing roles of Michael. Does Michael symbolize the Green Knight, the Keeper of the Chapel Perilous in *Sir Gawayne and the Green Knight*? The Green Knight and Sir Gawayne do ritual battle, and Sir Gawayne fails the test because he kept the gift that could save his life. The essence of Gawayne's story is "not the proof of herohood or of chastity, but of a failure, even in the best of knights, to keep a perfect integrity ... 'A little you failed and loyalty you lacked ... you loved your life.'"[2] or, as Sally Banner confesses in the prologue to the play: "I have seen such things that are beyond the power of the tongue to describe or the heart to recall, and had I not sinned I would have seen much more." (p.13) and the relationship between Michael and Sally throughout the play frequently takes on the implication of a ritual battle with no quarter given on either side.

Neeme, however, calls Michael "the archetypal nature figure" (introduction, p.6). If Michael is a nature figure, why is he so shocked, so much the frightened, angry, cornered male, when he learns that Sally is carrying his child? What could be more "natural" than a baby? Michael leaves the decision about bearing the child to Sally (that is, in terms of allegory she must stand on her own feet, make her own decisions), but why does he sound so completely "Establishment" as he tells her that she "can't break the rules" (p.55)? Is even nature bound by rules?

There is a further confusing reversal when Michael becomes one of the workers, and finally rejects Sally completely. Does nature-Michael reject Sally because the vehemence of her attack on life is "unnatural": she is too sexually demanding, a sexual cannibal?

MICHAEL: You want to use me up ... Eat me alive. (P.75.)

How can this be explained if Sally's "sexual questing" is to be accepted as a *positive* image, a reflection of the artist's struggle? When Sally, as usual when rejected, begs him for assurance, for marriage, for security, Michael tells her bluntly: "Marry you, an amateur moll like you? Marry a crow who deserted her husband and kid!" (P.76.) But why then does Michael cry? Is it at the waste of potential in the life Sally has chosen? Nature abhors waste? And when Michael is burning Sally's poems, calling them lies, how does this fit into the allegory? Is art all lies? Or is this Michael's way of saying what the song of the schoolgirls says: "*She was a minor poet*". Does this recurring phrase image *not* Sally's self-doubt (introduction, p.7) but the *real truth* about her ability? In the face of this possibility, the next question clearly is: If, like Everyman on the road to death, Sally is to be rejected by each companion in turn, who—or what—is her "Good Deeds?" One might have assumed that her poetry would fulfil this role—how then to fit Michael's burning of the poems into such an allegorical pattern? If Michael is a symbolic figure, then realistic characterization and allegory are decidedly at war.

With Saul, once again realistic and allegorical patterns appear to be in conflict. However hard Sally tries to reject the illusions of the Establishment, she needs illusions to sustain herself, she needs a hero-figure to worship, perhaps to substitute for the worship she refuses to give as a schoolgirl at the altar. She tries to cast Saul in this role (p.65). But in embracing communism it is obvious that Sally is merely substituting another form of authority, of regimentation, a new faith, for those she has already tried and found wanting. In this part of her experience is she expressing the social commitment that one might relate to the responsibility of the artist,* or is she mindlessly repeating the clichés of the political enthusiast? While politically active Sally is "dumb" poetically—can one only serve one god?

> SALLY: In the public square I forgot ... the private virtues.
> JUDITH: Creativity, love, warmth, freedom. YOU forgot those?
> (P.84.)

Saul seems to manage to serve two gods—sex and politics—why one law for him, another for Sally? And why does Saul say that Sally will be finished politically if she leaves him for Michael? Is this normal sex jealousy or is the contrast between the two men (politics are "unnatural"?) to be fitted into the allegory? And if so, what are we to do with the fact that Michael becomes a "worker"? Realistic objections insinuate themselves whenever the male characters take on a form that promises "meaning" —or are all the males in the play

---

* Of course, the autobiographical strands within the play need to be taken into account too—the author's own experience is intricately and inextricably woven into the pattern. I have made no attempt to deal with this side of the play here.

mirror-images of that supreme Authority Figure, the Male Chauvinist Pig? If so, Sally finds them all—Saul, Thomas, but chiefly Michael—irresistible:

> *I see myself in you, yourself in me,*
> *We love and hate ourselves most tenderly;*
> *Lover to lover lost in fierce caress,*
> *Such contradictions mock mortality.* (P. 69.)

When Saul rejects her, however, Sally counter-attacks by accusing him of suffering from the cowardice common to all Authority Figures. Diagnosing their trouble as fear of life, she attempts to "define" life itself—characteristically enough by a set of emotionally-charged negatives topped off by a passionate generalization: "Life's not an abstraction. It's not a set of rules or a great sacrifice of the self. It's all we've got, and I'm going to live it to the fullest stretch of my imagination ... " (p.71) but does she really use her *imagination* on life at all—or does she only use her body?

> 1st BOY: I gave her a bunch of dandelions yesterday. She took them and smiled. She's a goddess.
> 2nd BOY: She's the University bike.
> 1st BOY: She wears her hair like a coat of armour.
> 2nd GIRL: She doesn't wear any pants. (P.38.)

Can one divorce imagination completely from the mind or intellect?

> SALLY: The intellect is only a bit and bridle. What do I care about knowledge? All I want is to answer to my blood direct without fribbling intervention of mind or moral or what not. (P.43.)

Undoubtedly great works of art are created out of passionate feeling, but wouldn't feeling by itself create something inchoate, unless there were some (however slight) shaping process of thought? How significant is it that the "creations" of her blood and flesh—her children—both die?

Obsessed by her twin needs to reject the world around her and yet to find someone or something external to herself worthy of her total commitment, how can Sally chart a coherent emotional course? In spite of her glib political slogans—"It's a question for the whole human race ... I sign with the millions: thou shalt not kill ... " (p.74)—she not only survives with apparent minimal scarring the deaths of two children, but at times the action shows Sally refusing to see what is *really* happening in the world: "I don't want to listen ...

It's nothing to do with me ... I'm a pacifist ... " (p.23) and she seems ultimately more concerned with her own personal fear of annihilation than she does with the fate of mankind:

> SALLY: It was annihilation. I could never accept annihilation. The shadow of it lay over everything I did ... I've always known, even when I struggled hardest, that annihilation was the end of it. Even when—no, especially when—I was wild with joy because I thought I'd found, even for a moment that immortal otherness at last. (P.84.)

Does Sally fail as artist, as saviour of a corrupt world, as a human being in her relationships with other human beings, precisely because the essential self-absorption of the artist is in her case not directed with utter concentration upon creative work but upon herself as a sentient being?

> SALLY: ... I want to feel everything. To tell everything, to walk naked. That's my protection. (P.18.)

But it offers her no protection at all. She is utterly vulnerable:

> MICHAEL: Choose, Sally, choose.
> SALLY: All I know is I'm happy when I'm with him and miserable when we're apart.
> THOMAS: Happiness, what's happiness? Why is happiness so important?
> SALLY: What else is there? (P.70.)

In spite of her rebellion, in spite of her "sincere ... dishonesty" (p.84), her belief in freedom (p.83), Sally always struggles "to be identified with someone, something" (p.84); she is looking for *herself in relation to a mutually demanding and yet satisfying relationship with others*, a "kind of ... unique communion" (p.29), never understanding that she must look within herself, that she must draw her strength from *within herself alone*:

> SALLY: Jude, stay with me.
> JUDITH: No, I'm going too. You don't need me Sally. You don't really need anyone ... only you don't know it yet. (P.30.)

She tries to defend herself in the final trial scene by pleading that she destroyed her children "For a great love":

> JUDITH: What was that great love?
> SALLY: Love of myself. You said it. I wanted to live so completely a dozen lives; to suffer everything. (P.85)

A capacity to suffer and ample opportunity for suffering (even if it is sometimes self-inflicted suffering?) have marked the lives of the greatest artists and the greatest saviours. But surely some admixture of *selfless* compassion is also needed: except during her political phase (when her responses to the world around her are clearly mechanical—conditioned reflexes to slogans and catch-cries), Sally's compassion is lavished chiefly on herself.

Is the point of the artist's struggle that he *should express himself*, however misguided the means may seem to society at large or to some representatives of it? Is Sally Banner trying to say, through her way of living, that "Those who live also create"? These are the words of the Girl, the anima figure in Patrick White's *The Ham Funeral*, a play with which *The Chapel Perilous* has much thematically in common. Sally reaches her tower after her confession in the final trial scene, and one is reminded of the Young Man's closing speech in *The Ham Funeral*: "How warm her face was ... and touching ... lovely in its way ... the way of those who've lived, and confessed, and survived their own confessions."[3] And like the Young Man, Sally does mature, does progress beyond the search for a fetish-figure—or does she perhaps merely substitute herself as Heroine? She comes to realize in the end that one is forced to accept onself, "to be finally and irrevocably responsible for oneself" (p.88) and immediately after this she achieves the fame she had always been hungering for, *bows to the altar at last*, and climbs her tower. Does this suggest that the strictures of society expressed through the other characters and especially the Chorus figures are to be taken as a judgment Sally ultimately accepts and bows to, in spite of the satire directed against them in earlier scenes? Or can Sally join Authority in an "elevated position" now that she at last understands, knows, herself? How can one explain in terms of allegory the fact that the stained glass window has been endowed by Sally herself?

> CANON: (*Coming from behind mast*) Parents, teachers, young ladies, dear brethren, children of Christ: on this speech day, we pause to honour Sally Banner, born Widgiemooltha, 1923. As canon of this college of young and foolish virgins I bear a great responsibility, and I rejoice today that we are gathered together here to offer up our humble thanks to Miss Banner, who has so liberally endowed our little chapel with a stained glass window in her image and likeness ... (Pp.14—15.)

On the level of satire this is a condemnation of society: once Sally is successful she is acceptable, and society accedes to the value Sally places upon herself. But on the level of allegory is Sally in the end so far responsible for herself that she alone can honour herself? If she ascended the tower *without bowing* the latter would seem a valid interpretation, but the apparent acknowledgment of the values and rituals she had previously rejected so strenuously is hard to reconcile with either realistic characterization or a consistent allegorical pattern. Is this one last attempt to turn her back on what she has so painfully learned, a final effort to identify herself with all she has fought against—or is it simply wishful thinking in defeat?

In spite of the temptation to do so—a temptation to which I have clearly succumbed—it is no use looking for naturalistic motivation in this play, except possibly in the character of Sally herself, and even here as I have indicated I have reservations. The play is an emotional montage, an expressionistic dream or phantasmagoria in which one episode shades off into another and characters merge with endless mirrored versions of themselves. Past and present coalesce in Sally's mind when she is in hospital recovering from her suicide attempt, and again in the trial (self-trial?) scenes. Characters constantly recall past events, past phrases, and these gather momentum and rise to a nightmare crescendo of accusations in the final trial scene. And once again there are suggestions of *The Ham Funeral*. The surrealistic trial scene recalls the "conscience" scenes between the Relatives and Mrs. Lusty, and also the interrogation scenes in Pinter's *The Birthday Party*, and awakens echoes of Brecht and Beckett.

The circular structure of the play, the successive rejection scenes, image the Wheel of Fortune, the repetitive pattern of all experience, the eternal recurrence of life. In the end, faced with Judith her first love, Sally finds that love has assumed the robes of one of the Authority Figures and is still demanding that Sally bow. Sally has taken "a ride on a roundabout. Close the circle and I end where I began." (p.87), an allusion to Donne's 'A Valediction: forbidding mourning'. Although it is possible to interpret this as suggesting that Judith is the other "soule" of Donne's image, it seems far more likely that it is the altar, or the sanctuary of religion, that is the "fixt foot" of the compass figure; and no matter how far Sally might "rome" or "obliquely runne", the firmness of this "fixt foot" draws her "home" at last. But home to honour or defeat? Sanctuary for the struggling, comfortless soul who at last sees upon a slope "a glimpse of light" (p.13), or a complete recantation of everything she has ever believed in and striven for?

Throughout the play there is a constant juxtaposition of parallel characters (the masks reinforcing the parallels and emphasizing relationships between their attitudes, beliefs, illusions, or hypocrisies), parallel situations, ideas, motives, interpretations, "received opinion", or clichés. Reality and illusion are played off relentlessly through these parallels; for instance, act I ends with the march of the Chorus to the words of the workers' song (the ideal), act 2 opens with politics imaged as a side-show (the reality). The reality and the illusion of physical satisfaction are ironically explored in the action: Sally finds no permanent satisfaction with anyone—indeed her sexual aggressiveness helps to destroy most of her relationships with others—and she comes to realize that this kind of love does not last: "Every time the surf falls on the beach I think this is forever, and every time the tide sucks it back again I know we're lost, we've got no future and never can have." (Pp.53—54.) The reality and the illusion of social rituals, moral and religious attitudes, the slogans of war and peace, are also explored. Characters give contradictory pictures of themselves and of Sally; contradictory versions of incidents are given in different parts of the play, for instance, the parting of Sally and Michael, and of Sally and David. Nothing is ever as it seems ...

Irony and paradox are Dorothy Hewett's favourite weapons: the Authority Figures join in lewd song and dance routines (sex and politics, with religion to justify it all?). The amplifier-voice is used to give the real thoughts that underlie a character's spoken words (an updated form of the old dramatic convention of the aside), allowing Dorothy Hewett to expose the many levels of hypocrisy that go to make up not only those caricatures the Authority Figures, but Sally herself.

Certain phrases echo and re-echo through the play: Sally's desire to answer to her blood direct; walk naked through the world; big frog in a small puddle ... There is something dream-like (or is it more truly nightmare?) in the way that a remark by one character is repeated by another character, sometimes in almost identical words, sometimes in a slightly altered form—for instance, the phrase used

301

by the psychologist, "The only cure is time" (p.34). Apart from her poem a few seconds later, Sally's final speech in the play, when she returns to Australia as a celebrity and is being interviewed, is "I was a rebel in word and deed. The latter usually tones with time." (P.88.) And the repetition of the words "time ... time ... time" repeats the bell-like tolling ("Ring out wild bells"?) * that closes the prologue with identical words.

The richness and variety of form and tone in the language might be compared with that in the plays of Patrick White: it ranges from the passionate prose-poetry of the declaration of love for Judith, through poems of intense feeling, passages of realistic, idiomatic dialogue, to nursery-rhyme jingles and to the obscene and derisive songs of the Chorus. Miss Hewett shares an interest in word-play with Hibberd, Williamson, Buzo, and Blair—not to mention Shakespeare—and her jokes and puns range from comic irony to the macabre and the salacious. There is a good deal of slapstick verbal humour in the play, and jargon and cliché are mercilessly parodied. Allusions from many sources (but especially from religious ceremonial, the Bible, and literature) are woven into the dialogue, particularly in the trial scenes where, in addition to enriching the emotional tone or extending the satire, they reflect the movement of Sally's mind as it travels back over the "oblique" road she has "runne".

The trial scenes combine theatrical excitement with cynical observation of character, and reach their climax with the final trial that joins the farce of Gilbert and Sullivan and the fantasy-satire of the trial in *Alice's Adventures in Wonderland* to the menace of Pinter. The comic, the absurd, the surreal fuse together as the tension mounts steadily to nightmare. The accused is proclaimed guilty even before the judge calls the first witness (pp.79—81). The judge and witnesses all accuse Sally of things they do or think themselves, exposing their own "hangups", obsessions, complexes, (examples are the mother and father, and the Canon, on sex; the Sister and Mistress on freedom of thought and smearing of reputation; the mother on lies, etc.)—it is an *Alice Through the Looking Glass* reversal (suggested by: FATHER: "Come through the glass, Sally,", poem, p.81), an ironic mass self-indictment by society, all of which was adumbrated in the prologue.

---

* The Canon uses this phrase from Tennyson's "In Memoriam A.H.H." when the schoolgirl Sally climbs on to the parapet of the Chapel tower (p.22).

The final trial develops at one stage into a "classical" communist witch-hunt and the farcical variety of charges pressed against Sally many of them obviously based on gossip and scandal-mongering, symbolizes the unreliability of evidence, the uncertainty of justice:

> SALLY: There is no justice.
> SISTER: This is not a court of justice.
> MISTRESS: This is a court of law. (P.80.)

Sally makes her plea that she believes "in the brotherhood of man" (p.82), yet has the play provided us with convincing evidence of the truth of this? She is charged with "betraying the system" and pleads guilty to this charge, but when the whole court takes up the cry:

> MISTRESS: Sally Banner, for all our sakes, it is necessary that you be guilty.
> ALL: GUILTY ... GUILTY ... GUILTY ... (P.83.)

Sally (according to the stage directions) "steps down, moves centre, still very much mistress of the situation. She faces the audience, with her back to AUTHORITY FIGURES":

> SALLY: *It matters not how strait the gate,*
> *How charged with punishment the scroll,*
> *I am the master of my fate,*
> *I am the captain of my soul.* (P.83.)

This too is unproven, and Judith and Michael (the two she loved best) step forward to shatter her composure by accusing her of self-love. This is the most telling charge of all; and she defends herself in vain:

> SALLY: (*proudly*) I heard a voice from Heaven say unto me ... "WRITE".
> JUDITH: And what did you do?
> SALLY: (*defeated*) I wasted my substance. (P.85.)

and a little later:

> SALLY: Jude, I wanted to find in this dirty, scheming, contemptible world something, some kind of miraculous insight ... (*To audience*) I had a tremendous world in my head and more than three-quarters of it will be buried with me. (P.88.)

Surely the saddest moment in all the complex and confusing emotional patterning of this demanding play?

Triumph or defeat? Does this play image a spiritual quest—or an ambivalent question? It seems to me that the very uncertainties and ambiguities of the action and the characterization create a *positive* image. The play is indeed an allegory in the sense that it is composed of several levels of meaning, some of which are not necessarily consistent with others, though they are never mutually exclusive. *The Chapel Perilous* recreates not only Sally Banner's struggle with self and society; it also presents the whole ambivalent question of what *is* self, what *is* society other than self-in-action-and-interaction-with-other-selves. The characters form a circular chain of mirror-images that represent not only the Authority Figures against whom Sally rebels, but also aspects of Sally's own soul:

We love and hate ourselves most tenderly;
Lover to lover lost in fierce caress,
Such contradictions mock mortality. (P.69.)

The action forms a circular chain that represents the "roundabout" of human experience, human aspirations, physical and spiritual striving, trial and self-trial, and when the "circle is closed" the questing, questioning soul ends

back at that lonely place
where I began.

Anything's possible
now that I am alone,
anything at all,
now Heaven is impossible
and all's well.

CANON: As it was in the beginning, is now and ever shall be.
ALL: World without end, Amen. (P.89.)

and the lone schoolgirl's voice closes the play with the siren-song of temptation and paradox ...

In whatever way the reader or playgoer tries to grapple with the ambiguities or attempts to interpret the details of the "allegory" the emotional impact and the dramatic impetus of the total play are undeniable. The intensity of feeling and language, the evocative richness of the imagery with which Dorothy Hewett expresses the dilemma of her protagonist-self, the theatrical panache of the many-faceted form she has chosen, have few counterparts in our drama. This is an exiting and disturbing play.

18

Jack Hibberd and the
New Wave Drama

ALRENE SYKES

In any account of the "new wave" Australian drama, the name that is likely to recur most frequently is that of Jack Hibberd.[1] Hibberd holds the improbable record of having on the one hand written *A Stretch of the Imagination*,[2] the Australian play most likely to appeal to academics, for its complexity and verbal subtlety; and on the other hand, the play that must hold the Australian record as a money-spinner in theatre restaurants all round the country, "Dimboola"—a sketch, variously fleshed out by different companies, which takes the audience as guests to a country wedding, with bad food, excruciating vocal renditions, lewd telegrams, and a bridal party which manages to get inebriated in record time.

Jack Hibberd was of course one of the founding fathers of what is sometimes called Australia's latest drama renaissance. 1967 was the year when Betty Burstall, returning to Melbourne fired by the inspiration of New York's Off Off-Broadway theatres, rented a small disused shirt-factory in Carlton and turned it into an experimental theatre (called, after its American inspiration, the "La Mama") for frustrated actors, playwrights, and directors. It was also the year when Hibberd's first substantial and full-length play, *White With Wire Wheels*,[3] was performed at the University of Melbourne. Hibberd was from the beginning associated with La Mama; in fact, one

305

of his short plays, "Three Old Friends", was the first drama performed in the little theatre. Graeme Blundell, describing the early
days of La Mama, says:

> In the beginning it was used mainly for poetry readings and folk-song
> afternoons. But after the performance of some of Jack Hibberd's
> "micro-plays", a variety of *ad hoc* ensembles began producing plays
> there by local writers ... The foundations of the La Mama company
> were laid in mid 1968 when a few of us who had worked together on a
> season of Jack Hibberd's *Brainrot*, at the Architecture Theatre,
> Melbourne University, started an actor's workshop at La Mama.[4]

From the La Mama Company, the Australian Performing Group
evolved, and in 1970 moved into their own premises, close to La
Mama: the Pram Factory. It is now history that the A.P.G. has
become highly respected, fashionable, and the recipient of substantial grants, while it struggles to maintain its independence and anti-
establishment vehemence. The group's policy has modified sufficiently for non-Australian dramas to be included among the
productions. Some of the early stalwarts, including Graeme Blundell
and David Williamson, have moved outside the group, but not so
Jack Hibberd; in 1974 he is still very much part of the A.P.G. and,
with John Romeril, its most prolific writer.

Anyone who considers the work of A.P.G. playwrights such as
Jack Hibberd ignores at his or her peril the influence of the group as
a whole. To take just one example: in 1974 one of the group's major
preoccupations was women's liberation; women in the A.P.G.
have argued consistently for plays showing the woman's point
of view, plays with better parts for women; an early objection to
the first draft of David Williamson's *Don's Party* was that the
female roles were sketchy and stereotyped. The A.P.G. women in
1972 together evolved "Betty Can Jump", one of the surprisingly
few women's liberation theatre pieces. Even in *White With Wire
Wheels*, performed in 1967, Hibberd showed an unusually sympathetic understanding of the woman's point of view, as the play
spelled out its message that the average Australian male is more interested in beer, cars, and his mates, than in women, who in fact ter-
rify him; but in later plays he has intensified this sympathy to a more
specifically women's lib point of view, particularly in his latest (at
time of writing) play, "Peggy Sue". *White With Wire Wheels*
tempered the satire undercutting the males with some sympathy and

understanding; in "Peggy Sue", man is purely villain and victimizer. *White With Wire Wheels* has seven characters, three men and four women; all four female roles are played by the same actress, helping to make the point that to the three men, all women are alike. The doubling makes its point very effectively, and provides a splendid opportunity for one actress, but is rather limiting for a group which has a number of good actresses. In "Peggy Sue", the position is reversed. All the varied male roles are played by the same actor (suggesting that all men are alike in exploiting women?) but each of the three women is played by a different actress; admittedly there is some doubling in the women's roles also.

The implication is not, of course, that the A.P.G. playwrights simply soak up and reproduce the interests of the group: clearly they must themselves exert considerable influence. It seems, however, inevitable that writers, actors, and everyone else, must—working so closely—tend to reinforce each other in their shared beliefs and commitments; and further, that the group's style of acting, and particularly their interest in street theatre, influences the writing styles of the playwrights, including Hibberd, though he has not in fact written much specifically for street theatre. Graeme Blundell describes Romeril's street theatre in terms which could, in part at least, apply equally to Hibberd: "His street plays were 'rough theatre' pieces: cartoon-like, sloganeering, blending stock caricature figures, comic exaggeration, pantomine, narration, audience participation: the whole bundle of tricks from the anti-illusionist theatre."[5]

Given that Jack Hibberd is so breathtakingly prolific a writer, it is not surprising that his plays are uneven in quality and variable in style, ranging from the brief, delicate precision of *Just Before the Honeymoon*[6] to the massive, first-draft turgidity of plays like "Klag" and "Aorta". Nevertheless, despite the variety, one soon begins to recognize certain Hibberd characteristics that are almost as much a trade mark as Harold Pinter's pauses. If I could use only one adjective to describe Hibberd's plays, I think that adjective would have to be "vigorous"; good and bad, the plays are exuberantly lively, essentially physical, and very often aggressive. Almost every play explodes into physical violence, quite a number of characters are killed, a good punch up is the normal outlet for male frustrations, and on the rare occasions when a play contains no physical violence, verbal conflict takes its place. (It seems of a piece that Hibberd obviously admires the legendary Australian middleweight boxer, Les Darcy; there are references to him in several plays, and he has a play of his own in the recent "The Les Darcy Show".) Violence is not of course characteristic of Hibberd alone; it is equally present in most of the new wave drama, and indeed in Australian drama of any period. People are knocked down in both *Summer of the Seventeenth Doll* and *The One Day of the Year*, the classics of the fifties; Douglas Stewart's plays are concerned with violence, though it is not so much on-stage violence as talk about violence; in Patrick White's plays, characters do not bloody their fists, but the passion of their repressed violence is more disturbing than all the rest. On the whole, it is more difficult to think of Australian plays in which people do not get knocked down than to think of plays in which they do.

The new wave Australian drama has been consistently critical of Australian manners and mores, to the point where one begins to expect each new play to be a savage indictment of "the Australian way of life". Again, a critical attitude is not new in Australian drama, it can be traced through Esson, Lawler and Seymour; but the drama of the late sixties and early seventies is more openly moralistic, didactic, and savage than ever before, and seems for the most part to be interested in society rather than the individual. (The conspicuous exception to this rule is David Williamson, who seems to be still concerned with the reasons why certain individuals do certain things, and whose plays are almost amoral, at least in the sense that they record, rather than apportion praise or blame.) Margaret Williams has suggested that "the greatest single factor in setting Australian playwrights free to explore the dramatic possibilities of their own society has been the decline of naturalism, particularly of the well-made naturalistic plays".[7] She says that the new drama has evolved its own style. "In spite of their veneer of devastatingly accurate sociological observation, few if any are naturalistic works; the device they exploit is the *stereotype*, in a formalized verbal and structural patterning that makes the apparent naturalism a brittle veneer as far removed from mere reportage as are the polished surfaces of a Noel Coward play."[8] This comment is eminently true of the plays of Hibberd, and nowhere better illustrated than in one of his earliest and best plays, *White With Wire Wheels*. The three young men in the play, at first sight almost interchangeable, are stereotypes of distinct classes of the Australian male, defined largely by their choice of a car: Mal, an average up-and-coming young executive, is obsessed with his new white (with wire wheels) Valiant; Simon, who goes in for pseudo-culture, dreams of a '62 Rover; Rod, who is even more insecure and aggressive than his friends, is determined one day to own a Mustang. All three break off with their girl friends, played, as mentioned earlier, by the same actress; each of the men makes a date with the new girl in the flats where they live, Helen (still the same actress), and is systematically humiliated by her. The play is funny, lively, and perceptive; and the only scene which falters dangerously is scene eight, where the author attempts to turn inwards, and suggest the other side of the male insensitivity and aggression: his fear. The scene is dream-like, symbolic; each of the men brings to Helen a car part, each one expresses to her his fear:

> I don't know what I'm doing,
> My dreams are thick with fear,
> I'm frightened,
> And unenlightened,
> I think there's something brewing.

Perhaps what the scene says is too obvious to need saying; perhaps the switch from savage satire to pathos is too abrupt; whatever the reason, scene eight does not quite integrate with the rest of the play, and it is a relief when we are returned to comedy-satire and the external lives of the characters. Society is where Hibberd seems to feel at home, and with later plays, to date, he has stayed with it, in dramas that cover a wide range of controversial topics, including, for instance, "Proud Flesh", a bawdy commentary on censorship and those who censor, and "Captain Midnight V.C.", in which Aborigines who have been persecuted by whites hit back with "bedroom guerillas" and take over Tasmania—which, when the play was produced in Brisbane, became Queensland.[9] Hibberd's most frequently recurring theme is conformity, the soul-destroying conformity of thinking and living which society seeks to impose on the individual. It is the informing theme of the epic plays, "The Last Days of Epic J. Remorse", "Klag", and "Aorta", but one is aware of it, obliquely, in almost every play.

The stereotype technique has obvious pitfalls, and they were pointed out by A.A. Phillips in a review of recent published

Australian drama. "The adoption of stereotyping imposes special demands. It usually shuts a dramatist off from the greatest achievement of naturalism, its power to probe deeply and accurately within the character, thereby bringing the audience to an awareness of the more significant movements of human impulse ... Symbolic methods frankly assert that the ultimate significance of the play lies in the ideas about living which the dramatist is presenting ... It follows that if a dramatist abandons truth of characterization, he must compensate by achieving depth of symbolized idea."[10] In plays like *A Stretch of the Imagination* and *White With Wire Wheels*, Hibberd does provide such compensation; but not in all his plays. Sometimes, urged perhaps by enthusiastic involvement in a cause he is supporting, Hibberd will reproduce, uncritically, an idea or symbol that is tired cliché or even inaccurate. "Captain Midnight V.C." is a lively play which should be savagely disturbing; its impact is lessened by the easy falsity of one of the central ideas of the play: the white fantasies about the limitless sexual prowess of the black man. Hibberd uses it, deliberately, as a cliché; but it is a cliché of how white Americans are supposed to feel about black Americans, and has never, I think, been part of the Australian myth or attitude towards Australian Aborigines. Sexual abuse by white men of Aboriginal women, certainly; but not the sexual supremacy of the Aboriginal man. It is therefore very amusing when Captain Midnight with a little help from his friends succeeds in filling white Australian suburbs with half-caste babies; but it does not exacerbate any exposed national nerve. Similarly, "Peggy Sue" has to battle against the old-fashioned triteness of its central situation, three women, betrayed and victimized by men, being forced into prostitution to support themselves and their children.

Jack Hibberd is a writer of contrasts. Having said that his plays are essentially physical, and often aggressively so, one must go on and add that the second Hibberd trade-mark is a thoroughly Pinter-like appreciation of words. Hibberd has a wide-ranging and subtle vocabulary and, like Pinter, he not only uses words but savours them. Like Pinter, he uses place names very frequently, investing the banality of the places themselves with an air of mystery: Ultima, Echuca, Sunraysia, Bundaberg, Leongatha. His characters, like Pinter's, sometimes use words as weapons, as do the man Conch and the woman Coco, in *Just Before the Honeymoon*, discussing the young couple upstairs.

310

CONCH: Never seen a happier couple. So young too.
COCO: Too young too.
CONCH: Too young to what?
COCO: What?
CONCH: To be married?
COCO: No.
CONCH: To be happy?
COCO: No.
CONCH: Well, what?
COCO: Just too young.
CONCH: Two young what?
COCO: Nothing.
CONCH: Two young nothings.
COCO: (*emphatically*) Too young, nothing.
CONCH: You're wrong.
COCO: I am not.
CONCH: Should be plural, nothings.
COCO: How can you have a plural of nothing? Nothing is nothing, nothing plus nothing makes nothing, nothing multiplied by thirty-five comes to nothing, n-o-t-h-i-n-g, nought, zero.
CONCH: I'll have to think about that one. Sure there's an escape clause somewhere. (*Pause*) I know, how about nothing's doing?
COCO: Nothing *is* doing. It's not plural. That was a pretty stupid clause, you know.
               Pause.
CONCH: Anything doing?
COCO: Nothing.
CONCH: And yesterday?
COCO: Nothing.
CONCH: And the day before that?
COCO: Nothing.
CONCH: A series of—(*he pauses*)
COCO: (*smiling*) Nothing.
CONCH: Pretty bloody smart, aren't you? An expert on nothing.
COCO: Well, it's something.
CONCH: No. It's nothing.
COCO: Touché.[11]

A good deal of the humour in Hibberd is verbal; he is even fond of puns: "What? No blood? A sanguine turn of events",[12] and "Conjunctivitis. As they say at funerals."[13] He uses medical terms and the names of medical products as Pinter uses the names of tools and machinery, for their innate absurdity; "Proud Flesh", for instance, opens with two suburban housewives discussing the physical effect of various types of contraceptive; their dialogue is casually clinical, dead-pan serious, and funny. *White With Wire Wheels* is another play with a verbally arresting opening; this time the startling effect is due to a combination of crudity and alliteration.

> ROD (*gloating*): ... The man who loses his load but once a decade. Too much. It was only a couple of weeks ago that you detonated over the dashboard of Don's new ...
> MAL: I know, I know. Don's new Daimler.
> ROD: He's still scraping it off the walnut woodwork.[14]

Not all Hibberd's humour is verbal, of course. There is a good deal of physical, knockabout farce in the new wave drama, fostered doubtless by the interest of groups like the A.P.G. in street theatre; and Hibberd's plays have their fair share of this physical farce. The kind of humour that interests me particularly in Hibberd is the humour that is at the same time funny—and horribly painful. One is reminded of Pinter's description of tragedy: "The point about tragedy is that it is *no longer funny*. It is funny, and then becomes no longer funny."[15] Hibberd's "Captain Midnight V.C." is built on this tension between what is funny, and what is no longer funny; ideally, the audience should laugh, and then with horrified realization understand what they are laughing at. One of the most daring combinations of shock and comedy in the play is probably the scene where the old one-legged Aboriginal woman, Ruby, is shot. Though the play is fiercely pro-Aborigine, Ruby is hardly an admirable figure. She is eager to sell her daughters for food, she is ingratiating to anyone whose colour happens to be white; and the play makes it clear that she has had to be like this to survive. In a good production she can retain something of the dignity of Brecht's Mother Courage. At one point in the play, one of the white characters kicks away her crutch so that the old woman falls to the floor, and moments later, the same character, shrieking with laughter, shoots her in the foot. (Ruby later dies of the wound.) The moment is horrifying: and at the same time, an audience is impelled towards laughter, not only for release of nervous tension, our long-standing excuse for such laughter, but because it *looks funny*. In the end, the indrawn breath of horror normally predominates. There is the same kind of tension, in a less extreme form, in Monk O'Neill running round the table, and at the second lap, grinding to a sudden astonished halt. "Jesus. They've locked. The compo's set. (*He tries in vain to walk*.) They've solidified. (*Pause*.) Doomed never to pad the earth's crust again. A fixture. I'll rot and weather just like this. A victim of the elements. A premature case of rigor mortis."[16] A human being suffering the onslaughts of arthritis is not really funny; but unless the audience laughs, the actor has failed. Audiences at Hibberd's plays become accustomed to being assaulted, undermined, and sometimes insulted; in "The Last Days of Epic J. Remorse", the characters hurl insults and obscenities at the audience, tell them to go home; and the character Magdalen says, "Some of them don't think we're serious."[17]

Despite the liveliness and vivacity of plays like *White With Wire Wheels*, "The Les Darcy Show", "Captain Midnight V.C.", "One of Nature's Gentlemen", and the rest, Hibberd's claim to be considered a substantial playwright rests at the moment solidly on one play, *A Stretch of the Imagination*. This is a fascinating and complex drama, with only one character, Monk O'Neill, a very old man who lives alone in a dilapidated corrugated iron hut on One Tree Hill. (In early productions of the play in Melbourne and Sydney, the role was played by Peter Cummins.) Though only Monk is physically present, the stage is soon crowded with a host of characters, men and women from Monk's past, summoned up through his long monologue, and visible to the audience in much the same way that the characters in a good radio play are always visible. This perhaps is one implication of the title of the play: it stretches the minds and the imaginations of the audience.

Monk spends the entire course of the play talking about himself. At last, one might think, the opportunity for the traditional "character analysis" approach. But Hibberd has not in fact changed his spots. He is no more concerned with in-depth character study in *A Stretch of the Imagination* than he is in his overtly sociological dramas. It soon becomes clear that only the very rash would put their trust in anything Monk tells us about himself; the only thing one could feel confident of saying about him would be that he has a splendid, subtle vocabulary, and a gift for the thought-provoking phrase. *A Stretch of the Imagination* is yet another play about collective man, and not for one moment is the audience eavesdropping while a lonely old man spills out his being. Instead, we watch while someone, who does appear to be a lonely old man, puts on a stage performance, essentially for an audience—the audience may be us, the ants, the unknown, himself, it hardly matters; the essential thing is that what we are watching is not involuntary self-revelation, but a performance. Monk presents us with a whole series of little sketches, often almost vaudeville routines, acting out a series of adventures in which he is the hero. Some of these anecdotes may be events truly remembered; but some at least are more likely to be fantasies. (This is perhaps a second implication of the title; not only the audience, but Monk also, is stretching his imagination.) It matters little whether the anecdotes are memory or fantasy; what does matter is that Monk through them paints a dramatic frieze of actions which he regards as acceptable, even heroic; and by implication, his values are also the values of our society. Monk's fantasy-memories cover a whole range of Australian myths. As Margaret Williams suggests in her preface to the play, "he is a distillation of the Australian legend of pioneer, old fossicker, footie hero, womaniser, and of solitary man pitted against the land."[18] I would add two more roles: Monk also sees himself as a man about town, and something of a scholar— "A classical education is a fine thing. I'm a great reader."[19]

Hibberd's attitude to these myths is sceptical; he undercuts them, makes comedy of them, shows up Monk's pretensions, but affectionately rather than cruelly. The scene in the restaurant where Monk dines on hot Shlong Arabesque à la Creme, set off by a Bordeaux, and instructs the waiter on the correct degree of stiffness for a table napkin[20] suggests irresistibly that Monk got his knowledge of high-class restaurants from romantic novels. He quotes impressively from the Carmina of Horace, "Nil desperandum Teucro duce et auspice Teucro",[21] solemnly tells us it is by Homer, and we wonder if he is making an (esoteric?) joke, or if in fact he got the line from a quiz show or a calendar. Monk is factually suspect more often than not, even in his little anecdote about Les Darcy[22] and his surmise whether it was Garibaldi or Peter Lalor who brought the Italian population out to Shepparton.[23] But what of his personal anecdotes, which we cannot, of course, check? Memory or fantasy, Monks presents them as the adventures of a tough, aggressive hero, ruthless with man, woman, and animal, taking what he wants from life, occasionally himself ill-used. What comes through to the audience, however, is that if these anecdotes are true, Monk has been a distinctly unlovable character in his time, and that his life has been destructive, wasteful, bordering on the tragic. Though he is now scrupulously careful in his relationship with the ants, his only living companions, Monk's relationships in the past with men, women, and animals have clearly been disastrous. He has made love to women and then abandoned them or been abandoned by them; his men friends he has normally either betrayed sexually or left to die alone (as he left both Mort and his brother Luke). His most successful human relationship seems to have been with Les Darcy, who merely knocked Monk unconscious. Monk killed his dog, and was in effect responsible for the death of his horse; he shows some grief for each of them, in fact almost weeps over the dog, but it is grief tempered by thoughts of self. He cut down the one tree on One Tree Hill; this is the only act in the play for which he expresses both responsibility and regret, and he is nurturing the sapling which replaced it with his "own nitrogenous waste".[24] After such a life, one might well opt out of society to die alone. Monk is comic, we laugh at his adventures, and at the tough ruthlessness with which he recounts them; at the same time, he is, as an old man dying alone, pathetic; and in fact his adventures are not really funny, they are often obviously painful and sometimes reprehensible. It is the familiar, violent Hibberd mixture: the mingling of what is funny and what is horrifying in the same breath. Moreover, above and beyond this, most people would feel for Monk considerable respect, for what seems genuine stoicism, and ability to endure without self-pity. He says early in the play, "A man should hurdle and pole-vault to his coffin",[25] and his last so-called classical quotation is "Nil desperandum". The myths, the place names, the values, make this play Australian to its bones—a production outside Australia might well prove incomprehensible—but at the same time Monk is a modern Everyman, facing death alone after a long journey, without his medieval predecessor's consolation of religion. Monk seems to express his creed when he says "I am blessed with some employment of limb. I contrive to walk. I breathe. I cerebrate. I have no soul. What more could a man desire?"[26] The cynical question suggests that indeed Monk desires a good deal more; but what he desires, the play does not say.

A Stretch of the Imagination has no formal division of act or scene; the only natural break occurs about two-thirds of the way through the play, when Monk falls asleep, and morning changes to afternoon.[27] In fact, *A Stretch of the Imagination* is as usual with Hibberd a series of little scenes, normally marked by Monk going in and out of his hut, acting out various encounters, performing various

ALRENE SYKES

tasks. The play as a whole has no point of climax, but instead, a series of minor climaxes in individual scenes—for instance, in the scene of his brother Luke's death, the climax comes as Monk shoots at the religious statue ("I always leave the serpent intact") and drives the nuns out of the room, before, in his turn, leaving his brother to die. "I left him to die alone. The only way."²⁸ Like most of Hibberd's plays, *A Stretch of the Imagination* works by repetition and cumulation. Monk's encounters with the men and women (and animals) in his past are varied; but they all come to surprisingly similar conclusions. Repetition is also a very important element in the present. Like the old style Englishman who changed for dinner in the middle of the jungle, Monk seems to be held together, kept alive, by his strict adherence to ritual. During the course of the play and the day, he changes his costume in some way, even if it is only a change of glasses, nineteen times; he eats four meals; he fusses obsessively with his clock, which stops, no doubt symbolically, dead on noon; he shaves; he sweeps; he digs the garden; goes through a bag containing the relics of his last wife; brings a pumpkin out of the hut and takes it inside again; alters his will, leaving his lands and property, goods and chattels, to the Aboriginal peoples of Australia, and in the event of their extinction before his own decease, to the populous Oriental nations of the north; he attempts to urinate on stage six times—only twice successfully. The point Hibberd is making may not be simply that Monk is kept alive by his rituals; he may also be suggesting that man becomes so imbued with the rituals of society that he constructs rituals even when he is no longer part of that society. Whatever the comment, Monk in his isolation is as frantically active as any nine to five suburban commuter.

Like many other writers, Jack Hibberd seems to dislike comparisons between his plays and those of other writers. In the introduction to *A Stretch of the Imagination* he says: " ... it is imperative to excorcise from thought and sensibility the feral figure of Samuel Beckett. Indeed, *A Stretch of the Imagination* can plausibly be viewed as an indirect riposte to that increasingly taciturn and impacted gent. For Monk O'Neill, though a self-willed exile and part-time misanthrope wrestling obsessively with his own imminent death, is ultimately on the side of growth and human perpetuity."²⁹ Nevertheless, some of the techniques if not in the end the spirit of Beckett are unmistakable in *A Stretch of the Imagination*, and to

316

say this is not to accuse Hibberd of plagiarism. Indeed, his most seemingly derivative work, the brilliant group of short plays collectively titled "Brainrot", relate not to Beckett but to Pinter—and were in fact written before Hibberd became acquainted with Pinter's plays. Harold Pinter seems to haunt Hibberd's plays, particularly, as suggested earlier, in their enjoyment of words, their unexpected use of words. Monk's invitation to Mort in *A Stretch of the Imagination*, "Would you fancy a bite to eat, a beaker of something cool, a hot poultice, a kick in the crotch?"[30] would not be out of place in, say, Pinter's *A Slight Ache*; the formal language used to express fairly outrageous sentiments in "Proud Flesh" has on occasion the ring of *The Homecoming*. But the resemblances are not only verbal. In "Three Old Friends" three men discuss the past, or, as they say, they are "reliving old times".[31] Their memories of the past differ wildly, and the play ends with the death of one of them, casually strangled by the other two, who then go on talking of days gone by. (Pinter's *Old Times* was first produced in 1971, "Three Old Friends" in 1968.) *Who?*,[32] one of the best of the "Brainrot" plays, is almost pure Pinter, with three men struggling for a room and a bed, one of them in the end displaced (*The Caretaker*); menace; guilt; a silent entrance, unobserved by the characters on stage (*The Caretaker*); Alex reading aloud from a newspaper to the incredulous Paddy (*The Dumb Waiter*); Alex and Dinga standing on either side of Paddy and menacing him in a well orchestrated duet of threats (*The Birthday Party*). *Who?* has in fact been performed by the A.P.G. in a double bill with Pinter's *The Dumb Waiter*—or rather, according to a review in *The National Times*, on the same evening as *The Dumb Waiter*, Pinter's agent objecting on principle to the double billing of Pinter's plays with those of other writers.[33] In the end, in spite of irresistible similarities, Hibberd's plays do not in essence resemble Pinter's. Harold Pinter's plays are pervaded by a sense of the inexplicable, even the supernatural; Hibberd's are firmly anchored in reality. Even *Who?*, although the action is puzzling, is in fact Pinter without the impenetrable mystery.

Beckett's pessimism is open to debate; but essentially Hibberd is even further removed from "that increasingly taciturn and impacted gent" than from Pinter, if only in that his characters are not passive, as Beckett's so often seem to be; whatever their circumstances, Hibberd's characters mostly try to fight back, savagely, and if they are inescapably victims, they are palpably victims of other people, not of a metaphysical human condition. However, *A Stretch of the Imagination* resounds with echoes of Beckett: a solitary old man reminiscing, intermittently dashing off stage (*Krapp's Last Tape*); the waiting; the way of filling the stage with action even though very little is actually happening; the suggestions of violence off-stage; even the *Godot*-like tree and urination. Beckett's *Happy Days*, like *A Stretch of the Imagination*, opens under a blazing sun, with Winnie immobilized in her mound of earth more completely than Monk is by his arthritis; a bell rings piercingly, for ten seconds, Winnie wakes and says "Another heavenly day",[34] while in *A Stretch of the Imagination*, an alarm clock rings, Monk wakes, stops the noise, says "Thank Christ for that ... Dawn ... The inauguration of another beautiful day."[35] Both Monk and Winnie are oppressed by the heat; Monk has a black umbrella which he opens at the beginning of the play and closes at the end, Winnie has a parasol which half way through bursts into flame;[36] they are both concerned with their appearance, and each has a bag to rummage in. Winnie shares Monk's fondness for the odd learned word and literary reference, though as she says, "One loses one's classics."[37] Winnie sings one song,[38] Monk sings several,[39] and of course whistles,[40] plays the mouth organ,[41] and an old Kriesler record.[42] Monk talks constantly to the ants; Winnie watches fascinated the progress of an emmet.[43] Winnie is not alone; but the almost silent, almost motionless Willie is barely more visible to the imagination than Monk's unseen companions. I find these resemblances fascinating, pace Dr. Hibberd, not because they suggest that one writer has borrowed from another, but because two writers, making images of the human condition in fundamentally quite dissimilar plays, have drawn on such closely related observations of it.

Plays by Jack Hibberd

"Three Old Friends". July 1967, La Mama, Melbourne.
White With Wire Wheels. 28 September 1967, University of Melbourne.
"Brainrot". 17 April 1968, University of Melbourne. (The plays comprising "Brainrot" were: *Who?*, *Just Before the Honeymoon*, "O", "One of Nature's Gentlemen", "This Great Gap

of Time", "No Time Like the Present", and a musical drama, "Jack Juan", libretto by Hibberd and music by Stuart Challender.

"Commitment". August 1968, Saturday Morning Club, Melbourne Theatre Company.

"The Last Days of Epic J. Remorse". Written 1969.

Dimboola. July 1969, La Mama, Melbourne.

"Customs and Excise" (later "Proud Flesh"). May 1970, La Mama, Melbourne.

"Klag". Written 1970.

"Marvellous Melbourne" (with John Romeril). Two versions: 11 December 1970; and 3 March 1971, at the opening of the Pram Factory, Melbourne.

"Aorta". Written 1971.

A Stretch of the Imagination. 8 March 1972, Pram Factory, Melbourne.

"Women!" An Adaptation with James McCaughey of Aristophanes' *Ecclesiazusai*. 14 June 1972, Union Theatre, Melbourne.

"Captain Midnight V. C.". 20 December 1972, Melbourne University Theatre.

"See You Tomorrow at Maxims", a sketch in John Romeril's "Earth, Air, Fire and Water". 26 October 1973, Pram Factory, Melbourne.

"The Architect and the Emperor of Assyria", translated from the French of Arrabal. February 1974, Pram Factory, Melbourne.

"The Les Darcy Show". 14 March 1974, Flinders University, Adelaide.

"Peggy Sue". 6 June 1974, Pram Factory, Melbourne.

"An Easter Groom" (previously "Love at First Sight"). A television play, at the time of writing produced but not broadcast.

"Goodbye Ted" (with John Timlin). 9 April 1975, Chevron Hotel, Melbourne.

"A Toast to Melba". 6 March 1976, Theatre 62, Adelaide (Adelaide Festival of the Arts).

19

Aust. Lit. &c.—A Chaplet of Wattle Blossom?

BRIAN ELLIOTT

I often wonder, said Omar, what the vintners buy, one half so precious as the goods they sell.

If literature is the merchandise, what proportion should be kept between the imported and the exportable article? Is the case for Protection good? Does the tag, Made in Australia, enhance or diminish the goods?

Or is this a wrong way of thinking altogether?

The proliferation of new academies has sent up the price of Australiana. That would have happened in any case, as a scarcity item. A question does arise, though. Do we *read* Australian books, regarding them as literature, or merely *collect* them?

Centres of Australian activity seem to be springing up everywhere. Some have a longish history already, and valuable collections, others have just come up lately. Is it a vogue or a permanency? To name a few: Philadelphia; Austin, Texas; Aarhus in Denmark; Venice at the Ca' d'Oro; Montpelier in France; Leeds, Exeter, Hull, and elsewhere in England; various places in Canada. Sometimes it happens as an independent activity, more often as part of a package-deal called Commonwealth Literature (or some such). What does it all really amount to?

I am not absolutely sceptical about it but I find some difficulty in sorting out my ideas. If I attempt to read West African books I find one here and there which is spellbinding. But I cannot really find my way in that field; the whole tenor of my assumptions is different. I can hardly offer to assess that literature, because I have no basis from which to begin. I could collect examples and make a survey of them. Would that lead me to criticism? Yes, no doubt; provided there were "critical" rewards, which there no doubt would be. But still where do I stand? What is "literature"?

The assessment of an unfamiliar tradition is a very vexed question and one which, as soon as I raise it, I can only drop. I can't solve it, neither can I forget it.

The one thing which will not do, is to take a merely theoretical attitude. Problems *must* surround any new literature as they surround the rest of the local culture. At present we are concerned to be practical. That is why it does really seem relevant to ask, how fond are the vintners of the vintage they sell? Is the wine noble, passable, or barely of commercial quality? And what quantity of it shall we put down in the cellar?

There is some uneasiness in the thought that academics who profess "Australian Literature" may actually be doing so less for their devotion to the subject, than because it affords them a cosy corner with room to expand. The pride of the nation automatically justifies it and the press nods approval. Inside the universities there is not exactly a wild enthusiasm but there is toleration. And for the present, at any rate, there is still a comfortable scope for Ph.D's. One can get on. I personally do not much like the thought that it is the job, and not the subject of it, that holds the attraction. But one can't blame the postgraduates. They all need a job as well as an interest in life.

These thoughts are preliminary to the question of approach, which is really what I want to look at. Implicit in what I have said so far is the idea of an academic study called "Australian Literature". It is not my notion of a good thing. But I will speak with enthusiasm of the same material approached in a different way. I would distinguish between them by calling the second subject "Australian Literary Studies".

It seems trivial to make a fuss about a phrase. I hope to make clear why I think it isn't. First, however, to clear up a little of the confusion which hovers over the interest and importance, relatively regarded, of English and Australian literary materials. Given time and experience most people can sort this debate out for themselves but the beginner can be tangled and uncomfortable and it may be convenient to have an argument ready to offer him.

It is fair enough to suggest that in schools and universities the subject called *English* could do with a bit of an overhaul. It has over the years developed into an institution and its emphases have become somewhat out of date. I do not aim here to correct them; I merely point to the clear fact that young people have become critical and discontented. When there is so much else available that lies nearer to their modern interests, university students especially tend to shy off formal English if they can. Not all of them; for many English is still the most rewarding experience of their undergraduate years. But many do rebel, and there could be various explanations. The chief, if I am any judge, is this: that there is a discrepancy between the natural interests (I do not mean whims) of genuine students and the formulas which they are asked to apply. Modern youngsters are not categorically fools and incompetents; by and large they are much more able in various ways than I believe I was at their age—much more alert and perceptive, perhaps I should say sophisticated or urbane. In some, certainly, complex modern pressures have produced disturbing confusions; but these are not the generality. The old approaches to literature have become discredited, mostly because they are out of touch with common experience. So, at any rate, younger students see them. Especially the guts (excuse vulgarism) seem to have gone out of the aesthetic and moral programme: both moral pragmatism and free aestheticism, viewed as a rule of life, worry them. I would think it reasonable to suggest that students come up to university classes expecting literature to illuminate and open up the whole of life to their growing experience of it: and they do not like what seems so partial. It will not satisfy them at all to be told, "This is beautiful, this is harmonious, admire this work of art!"—they may have some crude and elementary ideas about the total reality, but it is nevertheless life, and for the most part not just art, that they are hungry for. When English—or worse, Australian—literature is offered to them as an augmentation merely of their more tender sensibilities, they are inclined to reject it. It is difficult to blame them. In their young way they are on firm ground and they know not merely what they want, but what they need.

Education is not only for the young. But in schools and universities it is mostly the young who get it. There are few pleasures available to an older person equal to seeing younger ones avidly following an aroused interest.

The place of English literature in the curriculum, then, is not one hundred per cent plain. I wish it were. Again I have no suggestions. I am only saying there is a sadness in the thought that this good discipline seems to have become compromised. That remark stands as preliminary to another, which is that we need to remember that England has a mature tradition, Australian only a nascent one. The approach to English literature can properly be made from within the scope of the literature itself; whereas Australian literature requires an approach made very largely from outside it—I mean, from *within* the culture, but often *outside* the particular piece of writing.

The nascent literature needs to gain by being set against a proper study of the mature one. I don't think logic absolutely requires that the comparison must be with English—if there is another literature that the student knows better, that will equally make sense—but for practical purposes in Australia, let us suggest that a study of the main English stream is indispensable for a proper awareness of what literature itself is and does, and even though some proportion of the older heritage may not be assimilable in its every last detail (Wordsworth's Cumberland? Hopkins's world of wildness and wet?), it is nevertheless from this experience of an established literature understood *per se* that he will set up many important primary criteria in his mind. These, and then others formed by analogy, he will apply to the Australian comparison. They should not so much freeze his judgment as give him independence and supply him with perspectives.

On the other hand, I believe the student who argues that other literatures are irrelevant if they are likely to prejudice or distort his opinions, has a point of view. I would hope to persuade him to be more liberal but I would listen to him.

If one has a clear understanding of the difference between a formed and a forming literary tradition, some cluttering notions can be got rid of. One doesn't have to claim reciprocal equality with English literature in order to dismiss the sneer of inferiority. As an academic subject, Australian literature is by no means a second rate study suitable only for second rate and colonial minds. There may be some who are mean-spirited enough to think so but we can afford to ignore them. And by the same token it is not necessary for postgraduate students of the literature to apologize for carrying their interest through to a higher degree, once they have become engrossed in it.

But here I return to the distinction I wish to draw between the two phrases. It seems to me that as designations of courses of university enterprise, "Australian Literature" and "Australian Literary Studies" are two quite clearly different plates of witchetty grubs. "Literature" implies a continuing tradition, and so far so good; we expect the tradition to continue. But continuity, if urged alone, will take us too far back in time and too far away from common experience; it will impose models and precedents which we cannot genially accept, or which, if we do accept them, may a little bend and pervert our judgment of the actual. And even though it *were* but that little, any little is too much, is disproportionate. We are trying to go forward by looking back; our heads are screwed on the wrong way, we are critical anthropophagi. On the other hand, "Literary Studies" can carry us forward without impeding our capacity to look both around and back at need—or beyond, if it comes to that: to America and elsewhere.

Let me state again, then, and perhaps overstate, this distinction. The concept "literature" is hermetic; it implies a community for which it speaks. That community is the reality. Socially, culturally, and to a degree physically, the word takes for granted certain limits, a certain homogeneity. Also an integrity, a concentrated heart of substance, appropriate to the facts. Analysis and classification lie naturally within it—embracing historical and all other sorts of mental, moral, and spiritual differentia—and so on. The position is complex because as we must remember there is one large and most important element that we share: the English language (which we also share with Americans and others). But it is merely a banally obvious argument that this common element binds all the English-speaking tribes together. It is no less obvious to those who make a study of language itself, that in subtle ways it also marks us off and separates us. Some attention should be given within the discipline of "Australian Literary Studies" to the Australian uses of English; it is a legitimate and necessary part of the scope. But in the main it can be set aside from present reasoning. Attention needs more urgently to be directed to the effective equation between the general culture and the general literary repertoire. Where a nation is still growing, the formula "Literature expresses the community", rough as it is, is a reliable one to operate on. I suppose I am saying, in other words, that what we are concerned with is still, what some years ago we called "the search for identity". I detest that way of talking because it sounds so parochial. But some more sophisticated perception of such issues does still underlie our natural interest, and until we have finally struggled through it, will continue to do so. It is more or less an accident of the times. The phrase "literary studies" embraces a good deal more than this old obsession which "identity" implies.

"Australian Literary Studies", then, covers the scope of the Australian literary experience as a whole. It aims to encompass not merely the books, but the circumstances which prompted the books. It aims to explore the people, their way of life, their kind of world, their spiritual resources; their ways of thinking and feeling. At the summit of all this, literature provides the expression which gives outlet to all these intimacies. If our subject is "literature" in general, for its own sake, and the supply of it in a major tradition is plentiful and stimulating, well and good: we can ask questions like, "How good is this book and how does it compare with that other book?" But it depends upon the supply of such books being not merely abundant, but virtually inexhaustible. If our subject is "literary studies", then we are not quite so hard-pushed. We must and may still ask those questions, but others will also arise that will sometimes seem even more urgent: "What is the place of this book in its environment?" Then we will examine it, perhaps, not merely as a success, but possibly even as an interesting failure. Failure itself in certain circumstances *can* be interesting. What was the book trying to do, and how did it fall short? What were the criteria?

The student who asks such questions must understand not only the high qualities and colours of the literature regarded critically; he must pay heed to its mere function and purpose, its natural teleology. He must be able to view the work not as art—as achievement—*only*; but with particularity and penetration, as *process*. Only when he does understand that, can he—more especially in the case of a younger literature—judge the matter coherently.

Objectivity is essential. Only by working objectively can we hope to keep any kind of proportion. There will be problems, especially, in striking a balance between some old but short-sighted Australian enthusiasms. The *Bulletin* in its palmy days preached "Australia for the Australians": jingoistic, xenophobic. Are we to swallow that doctrine or repudiate it? Must we be gulls about it, or else prigs, or trimmers? Shall we worship at the parish pump? Or look rather to draw water from deeper artesian wells?

It is only at the end of a longish academic career devoted very largely to Australian criticism that I come so positively to insist on these points. Partly it is because experience teaches; partly, too, I suppose, because times change *et nos matamur cum illis*. Be that as it may, I am more convinced of the expedience of looking at the academic picture from the point of view of young learners than once I was, and this geriatric sympathy prompts a little what I now want to say about tactics.

The problem is to arrive, if possible, at a critical end-result, a trained judgment and the augmentation of natural sensibilities, by means not themselves invariably or exclusively bookish. The way to do it, I suggest, is to proceed by step and step from accessible experience—not to attempt right at the beginning the literary tightrope. We deceive ourselves if we think that all our students, including some who are naturally very able, must needs love literary sophistication at first sight—on the contrary, literature like all the other arts is vulnerable to hysterical and hypocritical misinterpretation, or say, vogues and pressures; and practical-minded students are never slow to challenge insincerity. Nor are they always able to tell what is insincere; much of what is merely beyond their inexperienced grasp seems humbug. Agreed, such students may not have been well trained, but these days their backgrounds can be very miscellaneous and we must resign ourselves with sympathy and patience. Again and again one has had the happiness of finding initial sceptics who, once invited to proceed from the known to the unknown (which is more easily done in "Australian Literary Studies" than in some subjects), have become vitalized and ended up as enthusiasts. (That is not to say first-class scholars, which must depend on other factors also; but it is a beginning.) I believe it may be one of the special rewards of the Australian Studies plan that it happens often. It can happen anywhere but the advantage with "A.L.S." is that the already known details are likely to be *well* known, and the sense of progression seems therefore to come home more vividly. Certainly students who are brought along in this way seem to get better value from their courses than those for whom the horizon is formal literature alone. If you ask most students nowadays to write essays on "Character and Destiny in *Richard Mahony*" or "Classical Allusion in A.D. Hope" (not absolutely unhopeful topics in themselves), they will play along and produce a result, but you will get no glow in their prose. Give them a "Go-and-find-out" type of task, however, and they—beginners especially—will become natural gatherers and come together eagerly to compare results. Chaotic results, perhaps often; but the business will be to arrive at an abundance first and put order into it later. In the end literary order becomes not only necessary but inevitable—because (as they discover) it is the *only* practical and satisfactory way of putting down what is pressing to be said. For reasons much like these it would seem better not to ask undergraduates to concentrate on aesthetic and technical comparisons when actual experience can have so much more satisfying a meaning for them. Therefore one will not expect them to compare Rolf Boldrewood with Scott or Dickens or Fenimore Cooper as a novelist, but will rather ask, "What were the facts about bushranging and how true is the picture given in *Robbery Under Arms*? Does the story relate in any way to Ned Kelly? Is colonial Australia a man's or a woman's world? How far, either in fiction or life, did colonial life depend on the use of horses? Can you pick out the various threads of fact and fiction in the book and see how the writer has managed to combine them?" And so on. Certainly there will be few students capable of exhausting every such suggestion that can be made, nor will there be time for that. The tutor must guide. He too must be open-minded. The bower-birds among his students may bring many discoveries to him that he has not made for himself. Abundance first, order afterwards—but order will, and does come, and is alive and healthy.

Looking beyond the undergraduate interest, it is possible to point to one gratifying result of this approach. Students no longer come to me and say, "Now I am a B.A. (hons), I can attempt an Australian Literary M.A. or Ph.D. What should I write it on?"—the student of "A.L.S." does not ask such questions. He has developed his interest long since and already formed an idea of its scope and viability. He *knows* what he wants to write his dissertation about.

Appendix

Cecil Huddlestone Hadgraft: The Man and His Work

LEON CANTRELL AND SPENCER ROUTH

Cecil Huddlestone Hadgraft was born in Melbourne in 1904 and raised in the port of Rockhampton, central Queensland, where his father worked for the Harbour Board. As a student at Rockhampton Grammar his headmaster was the distinguished H.A. Kellow, whose later *Queensland Poets* (1930) remains a definitive book. Coming up to the University of Queensland as a science student in 1922, Cecil Hadgraft became involved in student literary activities, being editor or sub-editor of *Galmahra* in each of his three undergraduate years. Jack Lindsay, a previous editor, had graduated before Cec arrived but Lord Roberthall and P.R. Stephensen were among his contemporaries.

In 1925 he returned to Rockhampton Grammar as science master and began an external degree in Arts, staying in Brisbane in 1931 for his English honours year. By this time Professor F.W. Robinson had begun the university collection now known as the Fryer Memorial Library of Australian Literature, with which, in more recent years, Cec Hadgraft has been closely associated.

For ten years after graduation he taught in schools in New South Wales and Queensland and in 1942 joined the Education Division of the R.A.A.F. where, as Flight Lieutenant Hadgraft, he was stationed in Kingaroy, Melbourne, and Darwin. After the war, and

postgraduate work at the University of Manchester, he was appointed to the staff of Queensland University as lecturer in English
in the Department of External Studies and then to the main English
department in 1954. By his retirement he had been promoted to the
position of Reader.

Cecil Hadgraft's interest in Australian literature has earned
him a distinguished reputation. His Commonwealth Literary Fund
lectures in 1951 (which included the first major critical accounts of
Christina Stead and Patrick White) were followed by a number of
monographs and editions which remain standard works. After introducing into the University of Queensland the first ever academic
course in Australian literature he was appointed a John Hay
Whitney Fellow in 1956 and served as Visiting Professor at the
University of Omaha and the Loiusiana State University. His
Queensland and its Writers (1959) was a notable successor to Kellow's book and his *Australian Literature: A Critical Survey to 1955*
(1960) the first book of its kind in thirty years. His editions of the
first Australian novel, *Quintus Servinton*, and of the first major
piece of Australian literary criticism, Sinnett's *Fiction Fields of
Australia*, indicate his special interest in nineteenth-century writing,
which this book records.

To his colleagues and students, Cec Hadgraft's retirement in
1974 marked the end of an era at Queensland University. Val Vallis
pays tribute to the learning, warmth, and integrity we all know:

Cec and I both joined External Studies in January 1950, Cec in
English and I in Philosophy. Even then when I was writing my
poetry I soon discovered that what was "good enough" for me—in
other words, vague poetic expression—was certainly not good
enough for him; and what are generally considered to this day to be
my most spontaneous lyrics were the result of long critical sessions
with Cec.

In 1965 I joined the English Department and ever since have
shared lecturing in Australian literature and literary theory with
Cec. And shared does not simply mean a division of duties. I believe
Cec has sat in and actively participated in every lecture I have given
in these fields over the last nine years, the lectures imperceptibly taking on a "Gallagher and Sheehan" flavour; my excessive
enthusiasms for the expressive image, Cec's love for and belief in the
ultimate authority of the language itself. No vagueness or shod-

diness of expression passed without his comment or censure. And this (to use an image totally wrong in every other respect) is but the tip of the iceberg. Beneath it lies the vast dimension of his learning and that rare accumulation of information that so often gives rise to the remark: "Don't bother going to the library, ask Cec!"

A Select Bibliography by the Fryer Memorial Library

Books

Exercises in Subjunior English. Brisbane: William Brooks, 1941.

An Approach to English Literature. Brisbane: William Brooks [1945].

Senior English: Notes and Exercises. Brisbane, Sydney: William Brooks, 1947. [2nd ed., 1948].

Essays and Adventures: English and Australian Prose Selections. [Edited by] A.K. Thomson and C.H. Hadgraft. Brisbane: Jacaranda Press, 1955.

English Prose Styles: Passages Illustrating the Development of English Prose. Edited with notes by A.K. Thomson and C.H. Hadgraft. Brisbane: Jacaranda Press, 1956.

Queensland and Its Writers. Brisbane: University of Queensland Press, 1959.

Australian Literature: A Critical Account to 1955. London, Melbourne, Toronto: Heinemann, 1960. [Corrected reprint, 1962].

Coast to Coast: Australian Stories, 1959—1960. Selected by Cecil Hadgraft. Sydney: Angus and Robertson, 1961.

Henry Savery. *Quintus Servinton: A Tale Founded upon Incidents of Real Occurrence.* Edited with a biographical introduction by Cecil H. Hadgraft. Brisbane, Melbourne: Jacaranda Press, 1962.

A Century of Australian Short Stories. Edited by Cecil Hadgraft and Richard Wilson. Melbourne, Sydney, London: Heinemann, 1963.

Henry Savery. *The Hermit in Van Diemen's Land.* Edited with a biographical introduction by Cecil Hadgraft and notes on the persons by Margriet Roe. St. Lucia: University of Queensland Press, 1964.

Frederick Sinnett. *The Fiction Fields of Australia*. Edited with a
  biographical introduction and notes by Cecil Hadgraft. St.
  Lucia: University of Queensland Press, 1966.
James Brunton Stephens. St. Lucia: University of Queensland Press,
  1969.
"Tasma". *Uncle Piper of Piper's Hill*. Edited by Cecil Hadgraft and
  Ray Beilby. Melbourne: Thomas Nelson (Australia), 1969.

Periodical Articles and Other Publications

Sub-editor of *Galmahra*, 1922—23, Editor 1924. Cecil Hadgraft's
  own essays in *Galmahra* were signed "Q.E.D."
"Murdoch's Mask". *Southerly* 8 (1947): 20—25.
"The Novels of Henry Handel Richardson". *Southerly* 9 (1948): 2—
  17.
"Australian Fiction". *Southerly* 9 (1948): 116—18. [Review of C.
  Roderick, *Twenty Australian Novelists*.]
"The Fiction of Vance Palmer". *Southerly* 10 (1949): 28—37.
"Australian Literary Scene". *South-West Pacific* (Canberra) n.s.
  no. 24 (1950): 47—49.
Commonwealth Literary Fund Lectures, 1951. Lectures on
  Christina Stead, Joseph Furphy, Australian literary criticism,
  Patrick White, Christopher Brennan. (Fryer Memorial
  Library.)
"Four Ages: Youth and Norman Lindsay". *Southerly* 12 (1951):
  62—68.
"Diagnosis of Mahony". *Australian Quarterly* 27, no. 2 (1955): 87—
  95.
"Innocent Abroad". *News Bulletin of the Institute of International
  Education* 32 (February, 1957): 9—12.
"No Power, No Glory". *Nation*, 6 December 1958, p. 25. [Review
  of F. Hardy, *The Four-Legged Lottery*.]
"Writers of Queensland". *Bulletin*, 26 August 1959, pp. 2, 61, 66.
Review of T. Astley, *A Descant for Gossips*. *Makar*, no. 3 (1960):
  28—29.
"Green's *History of Australian Literature*". *Meanjin Quarterly* 20
  (1961): 441—44. [Review of H.M. Green, *A History of
  Australian Literature*, vol. 1]
"A Green Imprimatur". *Bulletin*, 10 February 1962, p. 47. [Review
  of H.M. Green, *A History of Australian Literature*.]

Review of H.M. Green, *A History of Australian Literature*, vol. 1. *Books Abroad* 36 (1962): 427—28.

"Charles Harpur". *Nation*. 17 November 1962, pp. 23—24. [Review of J. Normington-Rawling, *Charles Harpur*.]

"In Quest of a Quaker: A Note on Henry Savery's *Nom de Plume*". *Australian Literary Studies* 1 (1963): 57—58.

"Literature," in *The Pattern of Australian Culture*, edited by A.L. McLeod (Melbourne: Oxford University Press; Ithaca, N.Y.: Cornell University Press, 1963), 42—101.

"Histories of Australian Literature". *Literary Criterion* (Mysore) 6, no. 3 (1964): 102—6. [This journal issue was reprinted as *An Introduction to Australian Literature*, edited by C.D. Narasimhaiah. Brisbane: Jacaranda Press, 1965.]

"A Tribute to James Devaney". *Meanjin Quarterly* 24 (1965): 215—21.

"Memorial to Dame Mary Gilmore". *Meanjin Quarterly* 24 (1965): 535—37. [Review of Dymphna Cusack and others, *Mary Gilmore: A Tribute*.]

"Charles Rowcroft, for Example". *Australian Literary Studies* 2 (1966): 171—78.

"Undeserving Laureate". *Bulletin*, 29 October 1966, p. 39. [Review of C. Roderick, *Henry Lawson: Poet and Short Story Writer*, and *Henry Lawson's Best Stories*, chosen by Cecil Mann.]

Articles on Henry Savery, and, with J.C. Horner, Charles Rowcroft. *Australian Dictionary of Biography. Vol.2: 1788—1850, I—Z*. Carlton: Melbourne University Press; London, New York: Cambridge University Press, 1967.

"More Substance to Fisher's Ghost?" [By Cecil Hadgraft and Elizabeth Webby.] *Australian Literary Studies* 3 (1968): 190—200.

"Frederick T. Macartney's Autobiography". *Meanjin Quarterly* 28 (1969): 552—57.

Article on Barcroft Henry Thomas Boake. *Australian Dictionary of Biography. Vol.3: 1851—1890, A—C*. Carlton: Melbourne University Press; London, New York: Cambridge University Press, 1969.

"It's Not on the Tip of My Tongue". *Southerly* 20 (1970): 65—68. [On R.H. Croll's quatrain, "Whalers, damper, swag and nose-bag", etc.]

"The Last Word on Vance Palmer?" *Makar* 6, no. 4 (1970): 46—48. [Review of H. Heseltine, *Vance Palmer.*]

"Henrietta Huxley". *Southerly* 32 (1972): 227—32.

"Stroking, Not Scratching". *Meanjin Quarterly* 31 (1972): 233—34. [Review of C.B. Christesen, *The Hand of Memory.*]

Articles on Mary Hannay Foott and William Anderson Forbes. *Australian Dictionary of Biography. Vol.4: 1851—1890, D— J.* Carlton: Melbourne University Press, 1972.

"Paul Grano. Witness". *Meanjin Quarterly* 32 (1973): 459—65.

Review of J. Hetherington, *Norman Lindsay: The Embattled Olympian. Australian Literary Studies* 6 (1974): 328—32.

Article on Philip Durham Lorimer. *Australian Dictionary of Biography. Vol.5: 1851—1890, K—Q.* Carlton: Melbourne University Press, 1974.

Review of R.G. Geering, *Recent fiction*; H. Heseltine, *Xavier Herbert*; M. Lord, *Hal Porter*; B. Niall, *Martin Boyd. Australian Literary Studies* 6 (1974): 437—42.

Review of Clement Semmler, *Douglas Stewart*, and Vivian Smith, *Vance and Nettie Palmer. Australian Literary Studies* 7 (1975): 217—21.

Notes to Text

1. Literature, History, and Literary History: Perspectives on the Nineteenth Century in Australia

1. George Nadel, *Australia's Colonial Culture* (Melbourne: Cheshire, 1957), p. 69.
2. Desmond Byrne, *Australian Writers* (London: Bentley, 1896), p. 5.
3. Arthur W. Jose, *History of Australasia* (Sydney: Angus and Robertson, 1909), p. 253.
4. H.M. Green, *An Outline of Australian Literature* (Sydney: Whitcombe and Tombs, 1930), pp. 14—15.
5. W.K. Hancock, *Australia* (London: Benn, 1930), p. 58.
6. Hancock, *Australia*, pp. 297—98.
7. H.M. Green, *A History of Australian Literature* (Sydney: Angus and Robertson, 1961), Vol. I, p. xi.
8. Green, *History*, Vol. I, pp. 8—9.
9. Ibid., p. 348.
10. Cecil Hadgraft, *Australian Literature: A Critical Account to 1955* (London: Heinemann, 1960), p. 53.
11. Hadgraft, *Australian Literature*, p. 169.
12. G.A. Wilkes, "The Eighteen Nineties", *Arts* I (1958): 17.

2. "Parents rather than Critics": Some Early Reviews of Australian Literature

1. Woolls was identified as the author of this review in his obituary notice in the *Sydney Mail*, 18 March 1893.
2. In his *People's Advocate* for 17 February 1849, E.J. Hawksley attributed the *Gazette* review to its then editor, Patrick Grant, and the *Examiner* notice to the poet E.K. Silvester.
3. See S.J. Routh, "The Australian Career of John Lang, Novelist", *Australian Literary Studies* I (1964): 206.

3. Towards Seeing Minor Poets Steadily and Whole

1. Harpur MSS, Mitchell Library, Sydney.
2. Brian Elliott, *The Landscape of Australian Poetry*, (Melbourne: 1972) p. 72.
3. James McAuley, *The Personal Element in Australian Poetry*, (Sydney: 1970) p. 7.
4. Judith Wright, *Preoccupations in Australian Poetry*, (Melbourne: 1965) p. 18.
5. For example, J. Mornington-Rawling, *Charles Harpur, An Australian*, (Sydney: 1962); Michael Roe, *Quest for Authority in Eastern Australia 1835—1851*, (Melbourne: 1965); G.H. Nadel, *Australia's Colonial Culture*, (Melbourne: 1957); Manning Clark, "The Beginning of an Australian Intelligentsia", *Southerly*, No. 3, 1973.
6. Alec King, "Australian Poet and Settler—Tough or Sentimental", *Westerly* (November 1962): 93—96.
7. A.C. Mitchell, "The Radiant Dream: notes on Henry Kendall", *Australian Literary Studies*, vol. 4, 1969.
   D.P. Peterson, "Henry Kendall: The Quest for Eden", unpublished thesis, James Cook University, Townsville.
8. Marcus Clarke, preface to Gordon's *Poems*, (Melbourne: 1897), p. viii.
9. H.M. Green, *A History of Australian Literature*, Vol. 1, p. 157.
10. H.G. Turner, and A. Sutherland, *The Development of Australian Literature*, (Melbourne: 1898), p. 170
11. E. Humphries and D. Sladen, *Adam Lindsay Gordon and his Friends in England and Australia*, (London: 1912), p. 65.
12. Ibid., p. 67.
13. Clarke, preface to Gordon's *Poems*, p. x.
14. Elliott, *The Landscape of Australian Poetry*, p. 84.
15. Alec King, review of five poets in *Australian Poets* series, *Australian Literary Studies* I (December 1964): 280.

4. English Publication of Australian Novels in the Nineteenth Century: The Case of *His Natural Life*

1. Frederick Sinnett, *The Fiction Fields of Australia*, ed. Cecil Hadgraft (Brisbane: University of Queensland Press, 1966), p. 31; first published in the *Journal of Australia* 1 (June-December 1866).
2. No doubt essays on this subject in nineteenth century newspapers and journals await collection. The published works I have found useful are: Simon Nowell-Smith, *International Copyright Law and the Publisher in the Reign of Queen Victoria* (London: Oxford University Press, 1968); John Holroyd, *George Robertson of Melbourne 1825—1898* (Melbourne: Robertson and Mullens, 1968); Wallace Kirsop, *The Australian Book Trade, Prospects for a History* (Sydney: Wentworth Books, 1969).
3. Melbourne *Herald*, 2 March 1909.
4. Ronald G. Campbell, *The First Ninety Years, The Printing House of Massina, Melbourne 1859—1949* (Melbourne: Massina, 1949[?]), pp. 83—85.
5. Quoted by Brian Elliott, *Marcus Clarke* (Oxford: Clarendon Press, 1958), p. 151. Subsequent quotations from Massina's interview are from the same source.
6. Massina had published Clarke's first novel, *Long Odds*, in 1869.
7. Elliott, *Marcus Clarke*, p. 151.
8. Elliott, p. 156.
9. Campbell, *First Ninety Years*, p. 82.
10. Elliott, p. 164.
11. Elliott, pp. 164—65.
12. Elliott, p. 165.
13. (London and Los Angeles, 1951), vol I, pp. 88—89.
14. Kirsop, p. 15; see also p. 29, fn 70. The Melbourne Baillière was probably a friend of Clarke who had given him an inscribed copy of *Old Tales of a Young Country*

and who spoke French fluently. Clarke owed Baillière—and others—money at the time (Elliott, p. 176) and was later to have some works published by him.

15. For example, Barry Argyle speaks of Dawes and Sylvia "responding not as Christians leaping 'into the arms of God', but as a lady and gentleman who are found in each others'" (*An Introduction to the Australian Novel 1830—1930*, Oxford: Clarendon Press, 1972, p. 147). Compare fn 19 which shows Clarke intended to show that transportation could be "a fate worse than death".

16. The first English review appeared in the *Athenaeum*, 2 October 1875.

17. Royal A. Gettmann, *A Victorian Publisher: A study of the Bentley Papers* (Cambridge: Cambridge University Press, 1960), p. 205.

18. For example, the revisions Geraldine Jewsbury (Bentley's reader) suggested for *East Lynne* were not made (Gettmann, pp. 204—5).

19. Elliott, p. 165. Miss Joan E. Poole questions whether these changes were "minor" though a thorough collation has yet to be made. Miss Poole has drawn my attention to some changes: a quotation (appearing on the verso of the 1874 title page) from the 1837-38 Transportation Report (the "Molesworth" Report) to the effect that transportation may be made "one of the most horrible punishments that the human mind ever depicted [sic]", that it "may be made a fate worse than death", was omitted; the 1874 Letter of Dedication is shortened by the omission of the statement that "a portion of the story has appeared as an Australian serial" and of the reference to "the publication of the book in its present form" being due to Duffy's advice and encouragement, another reason for the dedication—in other words, all references to prior Australian publication are omitted. Minor alternations include the considerable addition of commas throughout the novel and some word changes presumably in the interests of "elegance". Miss Poole raises the interesting question of whether the 1874 edition was ever reprinted, the first English edition apparently serving as the source for all later ones (except serial reprintings), and the dedication being eventually cut down to an "Introduction".

20. Mrs. Hoey was a novelist, journalist, translator, publisher's reader, and the first to send a "Lady's letter" from England to an Australian newspaper, a fortnightly contribution she continued for more than twenty years. Her husband, John Cashel Hoey, was a well known Dublin journalist associated with Duffy both in this work and in the Young Ireland Movement. In 1861 he was called to the Bar of the Middle Temple and was Secretary to the London agent-general of Victoria (1872—73), possibly appointed by Duffy, as Victorian Premier, and 1879—92) and of New Zealand (1874—79). (Information from *Dictionary of National Biography*, second supplement, vol. 2, London, 1912.)

21. Elliott, p. 165. Clarke thanked Gavan Duffy and Mrs. Hoey (presumably for their help in the English publication of the novel) in a letter of 30 November 1875, quoted in Charles Gavan Duffy, *My Life in two Hemispheres* (London: T. Fisher Unwin, 1898), II, 367.

22. Nowell-Smith, *International Copyright Law*, p. 93. London publishers had no full-scale Australian branch until 1884.

23. Nowell-Smith, pp. 13—14. Part of this author's thesis is "the perplexity of the poor publisher".

24. "Recent British novels might appear as local newspaper serials, with or without authority " (Nowell-Smith, p. 94).

25. On 13 September 1875, quoted Holroyd, p. 53. A.G. Stephens is quoted by Holroyd as writing: "Back in the nineteenth century, when Melbourne led Australian letters, the old bookselling firm of George Robertson tried its publishing hand at cheap books, but never reached large editions" (p. 56). Holroyd adds: "Local production costs were high and few printers or binders could turn out a pleasing volume. Moreover, although George Robertson loved his adopted land, he never acquired an Australian outlook" (p. 56).

26. Duffy had been a member of the House of Commons, and "had always thought of himself as a 'poet-statesman', above all enjoying talking about ideas and literature. The Carlyles were his lifelong friends and through them he met many English men of letters"—as well as being acquainted with leading politicians (see

entry by Joy E. Parnaby, *Australian Dictionary of Biography*, General Editor Douglas Pike, Vol. 4, Melbourne University Press,1972, pp. 109—13).

27. For alterations made to the dedication in the 1875 edition see fn 19 above. Duffy's suggestions about the revisions to the serial version for the 1874 edition—suggestions Clarke followed to a large extent—are outlined in *My Life*, pp. 312—14.

28. See for instance figures quoted by Gettmann, *A Victorian Publisher*, p. 85.

29. Gettmann, p. 87.

30. Gettmann, p. 116.

31. The Bentley Papers are divided between the British Museum and the library of the University of Illinois. The only Clarke letter in the latter refers to his unfinished novel "Felix and Felicitas" (see Elliott, p. 235). I wish to thank my friend and a former colleague, Mr. E. Stokes of the English Department, University of Tasmania, for searching out and transcribing some of the Clarke correspondence at the British Museum. See note 40 for later letters about sales.

32. The title was of course *His Natural Life*.

33. A reference to *The Marcus Clarke Memorial Volume Containing Selections from the Writings of Marcus Clarke ... And a Biography of the Deceased*, compiled and edited by Hamilton Mackinnon (Melbourne: Cameron Laing and Co., 1884).

34. Clarke wrote modestly, but with implicit pride, that it had "been fairly reviewed in the [English] Press" (quoted in the MS "Bibliographical Notice of the Life and Work of Marcus Clarke" by Cyril Hopkins, ch. 27, p. 8, Mitchell Library, Sydney). In another letter Clarke had noted with disappointment that the first Australian edition had not been reviewed in London (Hopkins, ch. 27, p. 3). See also L.T. Hergenhan, "The Contemporary Reception of *His Natural Life*", *Southerly* 21 (1971): 50—63.

35. *Athenaeum* (London), 20 November 1869, quoted by Nowell-Smith, p. 87, with the note that the first of the paragraphs was adopted almost verbatim in *Copinger on Copyright, 1870*, and later editions.

36. Quoted by Nowell-Smith, p. 85.

37. The Bentley letter of 1881 wrongly attributes the longer title to this edition as does Sadleir. The latter also states that this edition was part of "Bentley's Favourite Novels" series, a fact recorded in no other bibliography, library catalogue (including that of the British Museum), nor anywhere else to my knowledge. One may wonder, then, whether Sadleir was relying on Bentley's "Private Catalogue" (A *List of the Principal Publications Issued from New Burlington Street During the Last Three Months of the Year 1829—part of the year 1898, etc*, London: Richard Bentley and Son, 1893—1923, privately printed in an edition of 50 copies according to the British Museum *Catalogue*). Sadleir does show that this source is erroneous in stating that "the original Melbourne edition which they [the compilers] ascribe to the wrong publisher was 'very different' from the Bentley three-decker". Sadleir adds: "Clearly they never saw a copy of the Australian edition, guessed at the publisher and took the above two letters [from Clarke in 1874 and 1875, discussing an ending specially written for the English edition but not used, as we have seen] at face value."

38. Bentley published "Australian editions", without mention of Robertson, but with the same claim to proprietorship on the verso of the title page as with the 1885 and 1888 editions, in 1890 and 1897; and one in 1892 that was not an Australian edition and had no verso comment.

39. There were editions in Macmillan's Colonial Library series in 1904 and 1907 (the latter has been examined for copyright information and states on the title page "all rights reserved"), and the same publisher subsequently issued a number of cheap editions, as did Ward Lock and Co.

40. I have traced in the Bentley Papers the following five letters, all concerned with the sales of *His Natural Life*, to Mackinnon in Melbourne. That of 24 June 1884 shows Bentley not in favour of a cheaper edition at 2/6 as there was "still a satisfactory sale of the more expensive forms" (presumably the 1875 edition and the 1878 6/-) which were more remunerative for author and publisher. Bentley

wrote again on 13 February 1885 to the same effect, adding in answer to Mackinnon's "information of copies from America" that these were "illegal, and all such copies might be confiscated and the seller proceeded against". The next letter of 30 October 1885 expresses a hope that the Australian public will be pleased with the new (1884—1885) cheap edition at 2/6, and adds that Bentley would be happy to be associated with publication of other works of Clarke if as well produced (presumably in Australia), and depending on terms. Bentley wrote on 24 November 1890, however, suggesting that *Chidiock Tichbourne* would be best issued in Australia where Clarke was "so well known", and expressing a hope that the next account of profit (probably from the 1890 edition of *For the Term*) would be better, as "the initiatory accounts of each edition are always severely handicapped by construction expenses—paper, print, etc.". The same letter spells out year by year, 1880—1890, the amounts spent on advertising the novel (a "good deal" of which "in late years has been diverted to the Australian press"), a total of £130, and adds that Bentley is steadily extending its agencies throughout the Australian colonies. On 18 April 1893, the year of the next colonial edition, Bentley was "glad to find that the demand for it is steadily maintained ... [and] except the times of 1885—86, when there was a special run on the first starting of the Colonial issue, the amounts earned have been much the same". In answer to obvious concern on the part of Mackinnon and Mrs. Clarke about profits, Bentley went on to point out that although amounts remitted to the latter had been smaller they had been sent at shorter intervals; that there was always fluctuation in profit over a period of years, depending on expenses; and that "a cheaper issue in this country would not produce, we feel, the effect you desire" (i.e. increased profit). It would appear, then, from these letters as a whole that profits over the years were mainly from Australian sales of colonial editions, and that these profits, though reasonable in Bentley's experience, were of little solace to the impecunious Mrs. Clarke.

41. Elliott, p. 165.
42. The unfinished "Felix and Felicitas". A copy of the first four chapters in print (presumably to interest publishers) is in the Mitchell Library.
43. Nowell-Smith, p. 94.
44. Nowell-Smith, p. 85.
45. Excerpt from a letter to the *Australasian*, 6 April 1872, p. 434. Apparently no study has been made of "intercolonial" copyright, and performing rights sometimes differ from copyright of books. It may be relevant that when Clarke's *Sensational Tales* appeared posthumously in 1886 it was "published" separately in five Australian states: Melbourne (M'Carron , Bird & Co.); Adelaide (E.S. Wigg); Sydney (E.R. Cole); Hobart (publisher unknown to me); Brisbane (Watson and Ferguson and Co.).

5. The Short Stories of Marcus Clarke

Abbreviations used in the notes:

Mackinnon. Hamilton Mackinnon, ed., *The Austral Edition of the Selected Works of Marcus Clarke* (Melbourne: Fergusson & Mitchell, 1890). Part II of this *Austral Edition*—"Australian Tales and Sketches"—together with Mackinnon's introductory "Biography" were reissued as *Australian Tales* (Melbourne: A. & W. Bruce, 1896) and as *Australian Tales of the Bush* (Melbourne: George Robertson, 1897), so the Mackinnon reference applies to these also; however, though the setting is the same as the *Austral Edition*, the pagination is different.
Hergenhan. L.T. Hergenhan ed., *A Colonial City: High and Low Life—Selected Journalism of Marcus Clarke* (St. Lucia: University of Queensland Press, 1972).
Wannan. Bill Wannan, ed., *A Marcus Clarke Reader* (Melbourne: Lansdowne Press, 1963).

1. C. Hartley Grattan, *Australian Literature* (Seattle: University of Washington Bookstore, 1929), p. 8.
2. *The Australasian*, 5 September 1868. Partially reprinted in *The Peripatetic Philosopher* by "Q", i.e. Marcus Clarke (Melbourne: George Robertson, 1869), pp. 42—43. Reprinted Hergenhan, pp. 32—33.
3. *The Australasian*, 26 February 1870. Reprinted *Holiday Peak and Other Tales* (Melbourne: George Robertson, 1873), pp. 79—84; Hergenhan, pp. 67—72; and Mackinnon, pp. 324—28.
4. *Holiday Peak*, p. 79.
5. *Holiday Peak*, p. 81.
6. *Holiday Peak*, p. 84.
7. Mackinnon, p. iv.
8. *Holiday Peak*, p. 18.
9. *Holiday Peak*, p. 19.
10. *Holiday Peak*, p. 32.
11. *Holiday Peak*, p. 33.
12. *All the Year Round*, 22 February 1873, pp. 352—57.
13. "The Curse of the Country", *Humbug*, 15 September 1869; reprinted Hergenhan, pp. 195—98.
14. *The Future Australian Race* (Melbourne: A.H. Massina, 1877), p. 21. Partially reprinted Mackinnon, pp. 329—40; Wannan, p. 29.
15. *Holiday Peak*, p. 67.
16. *Holiday Peak*, p. 65.
17. H.G. Turner, "Marcus Clarke", *The Melbourne Review* no. 25, January 1882, p. 7.
18. A copy of this letter in Hugh McCrae's hand is held in Fisher Library, University of Sydney, bound into a copy of *Holiday Peak* (RB1165.29) inscribed to George Gordon McCrae in Clarke's hand.
19. *The Australian Journal*, March 1871, p. 389; reprinted Hergenhan, p. 236.
20. *Australian Journal*, March 1871, p. 389; Hergenhan, p. 237.
21. *Holiday Peak*, p. 78.
22. Henry G. Turner, "Marcus Clarke, Australian Author and Journalist" (No. 11 in "Gallery of Eminent Australians"), *Once A Month*, 15 October 1885, p. 242.
23. Arthur Patchett Martin, "An Australian Novelist", *Temple Bar* 71 (May 1884): 99.
24. "Pretty Dick" by the author of "Long Odds", *The Colonial Monthly* 20 (April 1869): 128—41.
25. *Holiday Peak*, p. 53—54.
26. *Holiday Peak*, p. 56.
27. *The Argus*, 18 July 1870; reprinted Hergenhan, p. 232.
28. Cited Mackinnon, p. xii.
29. H.G. Turner, "Marcus Clarke", *The Melbourne Review*, No. 25, January 1882, p. 5.
30. Ibid., p. 7.
31. Arthur Patchett Martin, "An Australian Novelist", *Temple Bar* 71 (May 1884): 100—101.
32. Francis W.L. Adams, "The Prose Work of Marcus Clarke", *The Sydney Quarterly Magazine* 4 (June 1887): 126.
33. Ibid., pp. 126,127.
34. Francis Adams, *The Australians* (London: Unwin, 1893), p. 110.
35. A.G. Stephens, "Marcus Clarke's Minor Writings", *The Bulletin*, 29 April 1899, red page. Partially reprinted in Vance Palmer, ed., *A.G. Stephens: His Life and Work* (Sydney: Angus & Robertson, 1941), pp. 38—41. Reworked as "Australian Writers II. Marcus Clarke", *The Bookfellow*, 15 January 1920, pp. 41—43.
36. H.M. Green, *An Outline of Australian Literature* (Sydney: Whitcombe and Tombs, 1930), p. 49.
37. Vance Palmer, "Marcus Clarke and His Critics", *Meanjin Papers* 5 (Autumn 1946): 9.; reprinted Clement Semmler, ed., *Twentieth Century Australian Literary Criticism* (Melbourne: Oxford University Press, 1967).

38. *Holiday Peak*, p. 55
39. "Cannabis Indica", *Colonial Monthly*, February 1868. Reprinted in Hamilton Mackinnon's *Marcus Clarke Memorial Volume* (Melbourne: Cameron, Laing, 1884) and *Austral Edition*, and in *Thorunka*, November 1970, pp. 16—19. On his opium smoking, see Charles Bright, "Marcus Clarke", *Cosmos Magazine*, 30 April 1895, p. 418.
40. H.G. Turner on Clarke in H.G. Turner and Alexander Sutherland, *The Development of Australian Literature* (London: Longmans, 1898), p. 303. Turner's chapter on Clarke draws on his two earlier essays in *The Melbourne Review* and *Once a Month* and adds some new commentary.
41. *Holiday Peak*, p. 34.
42. *Holiday Peak*, pp. 1—2.
43. Brian Elliott, *The Landscape of Australian Poetry* (Melbourne: Cheshire, 1967).
44. Elliott, *Australian Poetry*, p. 96.
45. Leslie Fiedler, *The Return of the Vanishing American* (first published 1968; Paladin edition, London, 1972) p. 41.
46. *Holiday Peak*, p. 9; Mackinnon changed Chapman and Hall to Bentley for the *Austral* edition (p. 309).
47. *Holiday Peak*, pp. 9—10.
48. *Holiday Peak*, p. 8.
49. *Holiday Peak*, p. 8.
50. On Clarke and Hopkins see Brian Elliott, "Gerard Hopkins and Marcus Clarke", *Southerly*, 8 (1947): 218—27.
51. See Brian Elliott, *Marcus Clarke* (Oxford: Clarendon Press, 1958).
52. Turner, p. v, n. 17.
53. *Holiday Peak*, p. 9.
54. *Four Stories High* (Melbourne: A.H. Massina, 1877), p. 27.
55. "Balzac and Modern French Literature", *The Australasian*, 3 August 1867; reprinted Mackinnon, pp. 481—88; Wannan, pp. 37—45. Clarke also discusses Balzac in "Of French Novels" in "The Buncle Correspondence", *Argus*, 2 February 1872; reprinted Hergenhan, pp. 286—93; and makes him the Rev. North's reading in *His Natural Life* (Book IV, chapter 3).
56. *Four Stories High*, p. 8.
57. *Four Stories High*, p. 9.
58. "The Romance of Lively Creek", 23 August 1873; "La Béguine", 8 February 1873; "The Poor Artist", 13 July 1872; "King Billy's Breeches", 12 August 1871; "The Acclimatised Sparrow", 29 January 1870—all in *The Australasian*.
59. *The Mystery of Major Molineux and Human Repetends* (Melbourne: Cameron, Laing, 1881), p. 83.
60. *Major Molineux*, p. 82.
61. *Major Molineux*, p. 83.
62. Plato and Pythagoras—v. "Distinguished Authors" by V.J.D [aley]. *The Bulletin*, 24 October 1903, red page.
    Cleopatra—"As to Marcus Clarke's Fads" by "Old Penjostler" *The Bulletin*, 9 November 1903, red page.
63. L.H. Allen, introduction to *For The Term of His Natural Life* (London: World's Classics, Oxford University Press, 1952), pp. ix—x.
64. Marcus Clarke, *Sensational Tales* (Melbourne: M'Carron, Bird; Adelaide: E.S. Wigg; Sydney: E.R. Cole; Brisbane: Watson & Ferguson; Hobart; 1886).
65. Francis W.L. Adams, "The Prose Work of Marcus Clarke", *Sydney Quarterly Magazine* 4 (June 1887): 125.
66. Francis Adams, *The Australians* (London: Unwin, 1893), p. 105.
67. *The Colonial Monthly*, July 1866.
68. *Melbourne Herald*, 24 December 1874.
69. *Sensational Tales*, pp.7—8.
70. *The Australasian*, 27 September, 18 October, 1 November, 1873.

6. A.G. Stephens, *The Bulletin*, and the 1890s

1. "The Eighteen Nineties", in Grahame Johnston, ed., *Australian Literary Criticism*, (Melbourne: Oxford University Press, 1962).
2. *Bulletin*, 21 January 1899, Red Page.
3. *Bookfellow* 2 (February 1899), 22.
4. A.B. Paterson, *The Man From Snowy River* (Sydney: Angus and Robertson, 1895), p. 9.
5. Bernard O'Dowd, *Poems* (Melbourne: Lothian, 1941), p. 35.
6. *Such is Life* (Sydney: *Bulletin* Newspaper Company, 1903), p. 65.
7. *In the Days when the World was Wide*, (Sydney: Angus and Robertson, 1896), p. 36.
8. Henry Lawson, *Short Stories and Sketches 1888—1922*, ed. Colin Roderick (Sydney: Angus and Robertson, 1972), pp. 83—84.
9. *The Australian Legend* (Melbourne: Oxford University Press, 1958).
10. *Bulletin*, 18 May 1901, p. 6.
11. *The Lone Hand* I (August 1907): 432.
12. *The Times*, 31 August 1903. Quoted in C.M.H. Clark, *Select Documents in Australian History*, II (Sydney: Angus and Robertson, 1955), p. 807.
13. *Bulletin*, 12 March 1892, p. 16.
14. Quoted by Bernard Bergonzi in his introduction to Gissing's *New Grub Street* (Harmondsworth: Penguin, 1968), p. 24.
15. *Bulletin*, 10 October 1896, Red Page.
16. S.E. Lee, "*The Bulletin*—J.F. Archibald and A.G. Stephens", in Geoffrey Dutton, ed., *The Literature of Australia* (Ringwood: Penguin, 1964), p. 282.
17. John Barnes, ed. *The Writer in Australia: A Collection of Literary Documents 1856—1964* (Melbourne: Oxford University Press, 1969), p. 65.
18. *Bulletin*, 13 February 1897, Red Page.
19. *Bulletin*, 23 February 1897, Red Page.
20. *Bulletin*, 23 May 1896, Red Page.
21. *The Receding Wave: Henry Lawson's Prose* (Melbourne: Melbourne University Press, 1972).
22. *Bulletin*, 15 February 1896, Red Page.
23. *Bookfellow*, 2 (February 1899): 22.
24. Brian Kiernan, *Criticism*, (Melbourne: Oxford University Press, 1974), p. 18.
25. "Narcissus and some Tadpoles", *Bookfellow* 4 (April 1899): 14.

7. The Structure of Brennan's *The Wanderer*

1. "Symbolism in Nineteenth Century Literature", Six Lectures, June-July 1904, *The Prose of Christopher Brennan*, eds. A.R. Chisholm and J.J. Quinn (Sydney: Angus and Robertson, 1962), p.76. In all subsequent references to this book, the designation *Prose* is used.
2. The only article devoted wholly to *The Wanderer* is G.A. Wilkes's "Brennan's *The Wanderer*: A Progressive Romanticism?", *Southerly* 4 (1970).
3. The eight poems were nos. 1,2,3, and 6 from the first movement of the final version, and nos. 8,9,13, and 14 from the second movement. (The text of *Poems* (1913) used in this article is the facsimile edition, ed. G.A. Wilkes, Sydney University Press, 1972. In the text itself the poems are not numbered. For purposes of reference, I have used the notation 1—14.)
4. Quoted by G.A. Wilkes, *New Perspectives on Brennan's Poetry* (Sydney, 1953), p.22. The letter is dated 28 September 1906.
5. Annette Stewart, "Christopher Brennan: The Disunity of *Poems* (1913)" *Meanjin* (September 1970): 301.
6. See, for example, A.L. French's "The Verse of C.J. Brennan", *Southerly* 1 (1964): 10: "The verse of *The Wanderer* ... looks at first glance more 'natural', easier in manner, than that of the first two sections. But the self-pity and self-

dramatisation (the Wanderer is exiled but unbowed) show still more clearly when deprived of perplexing syntax and grandiose gestures: the trouble with the Wanderer is not that he is pretentious but that he is sentimental. Even so, what looks like greater freedom in the verse turns out, on closer examination, to be invertebracy."

7. *Prose*, p.42.
8. Annette Stewart singles out Brennan's "falsely prophetic language" as evidence of *The Wanderer*'s "obvious limitations as poetry": "too much of 'ye' and 'thou' to cover an ultimate indecisiveness". ("Christopher Brennan: The Disunity of *Poems* (1913)", p.290). In fact the archaism "thou" never occurs in *The Wanderer*, and its *omission* provides a significant tonal difference from the poetry of earlier phases of *Poems* (1913), where it occurs quite commonly. And "ye" is used significantly in only *two* of *The Wanderer*'s fourteen poems (nos.9 and 10), where it occurs repeatedly (fifteen times in all) along with other rhetorical devices, in order to establish an oracular tone. In other words, these two poems deliberately assert their special character as passionate oracular utterance, and they do so not by their similarity to other poems in the sequence, but by their *difference* from them.
9. Reprinted in *Prose*, pp.254—56.

8. "Cyrus Brown of Sydney Town": Christopher Brennan and Dowell O'Reilly

1. Printed in G.A. Wilkes, "The Uncollected Verse of C.J. Brennan", *Southerly* 23 (1963): 188. The date of the letter is supplied in Harry F. Chaplin, *A Brennan Collection: An Annotated Catalogue* (Sydney: Wentworth Press, 1966), p.34.
2. T.L. Sturm, "The Social Context of Brennan's Thought", *Southerly* 28 (1968): 270.
3. A.R. Chisholm and J.J. Quinn, eds., *The Verse of Christopher John Brennan* (Sydney: Angus & Robertson, 1960), p.23.
4. Chaplin, *Catalogue* pp.34—35. A copy of the letter is also held at MSS. 344/9, Mitchell Library, Sydney.
5. The Papers of Dowell O'Reilly, MSS. 231/7, Mitchell Library, Sydney. A pencilled date at the beginning of the letter ascribes it to 1908. References within the letter itself indicate that it must come from 1900.
6. The Papers of J. Le Gay Brereton, Jnr., Uncat. MSS. 281/5, Mitchell Library, Sydney.
7. Dowell O'Reilly, *A Pedlar's Pack* (Sydney: W.M. Maclardy, 1888), pp.68—70.
8. Brereton Papers, Uncat. MSS. 281/5. "Cities" appears in *Poems 1913* as "The yellow gas is fired from street to street" (no.10), and "Imogen" as "And shall the living waters heed" (no.18).
9. Brereton Papers, Uncat. MSS. 281/5. The lines are here titled "Thank-Gift".
10. Brereton Papers, Uncat. MSS. 281/1.
11. Wilkes, "Uncollected Verse", p.379; the lines are reprinted in Chisholm and Quinn, *Verse*, p.219.
12. Wilkes, "Uncollected Verse", p.178.
13. Brereton Papers, Uncat. MSS. 281/1.
14. Chisholm and Quinn, *Verse*, p.212.
15. Sturm, "The Social Context of Brennan's Thought", p.267.
16. Wilkes, "Uncollected Verse", p.185. The final stanza of "Simple Addition" is printed on p.187.
17. Chisholm and Quinn, *Verse*, p.231.
18. Brereton Papers, Uncat. MSS. 281/5.
19. Brereton Papers, Uncat. MSS. 281/1.
20. Brereton Papers, Uncat. MSS. 281/5.
21. Note to poem 23, Wilkes, "Uncollected Verse", p.200.
22. Brereton Papers, Uncat. MSS. 281/5.
23. Brereton Papers, Uncat. MSS. 281/5.

24. Wilkes, "Uncollected Verse", p.182.
25. *Hermes* 7 (2 November 1901): 17.
26. Brereton Papers, Uncat. MSS. 281/5.
27. O'Reilly Papers, MSS. 231/7.
28. O'Reilly Papers, MSS. 231/7. The anthology O'Reilly refers to in Bertram Stevens's *An Anthology of Australian Verse* (Sydney: Angus & Robertson, 1906).
29. O'Reilly Papers, MSS. 231/7.
.30. See Bertram Stevens's letter to O'Reilly dated 16 May 1907 in the O'Reilly Papers, MSS. 231/9.
31. O'Reilly Papers, MSS. 231/7.
32. O'Reilly Papers, MSS. 231/7.
33. O'Reilly Papers, MSS. 231/7.
34. Brereton Papers, Uncat. MSS. 281/1.
35. Brereton Papers, Uncat. MSS. 281/5. Since 1910 O'Reilly had held a post in the Federal Land Tax Office.
36. Chaplin, *Catalogue*, p.32.
37. See Brennan's letter to O'Reilly of 11 August 1920 in the Brereton Papers, Uncat. MSS. 281/5. The earlier letter of condolence is at Uncat. MSS. 289/1.
38. O'Reilly Papers, MSS. 231/11.

9. *Such is Life* and the Observant Reader

1. Barry Argyle, *An Introduction to the English Novel 1830—1930* (Oxford: Clarendon Press, 1972), p.182.
2. Brian Kiernan, Review of Argyle's *Introduction to the English Novel* in *Australian Literary Studies* 6 (October 1973): 211.
3. Frank Dalby Davison, "Tom Collins and his books", *Bulletin* 9 June 1937, Red Page.
4. *The Buln-buln and the Brolga and Other Stories* (Adelaide: Rigby, 1971), includes portion of the original chapter 2 of *Such is Life*, together with a valuable introduction by Kevin Gilding.
5. Recent research by Judith Rodriguez has established the identity of Johanna Jorgenson whom Furphy indicates was the model for Nosey Alf. (Letter to Cathels, n.d., Mitchell Library, Sydney.) See Judith Rodriguez, "The Original Nosey Alf", *Australian Literary Studies*, vol. 7, no. 2 (1975).
6. Judith Rodriguez has established that De Lacy Evans was an actual woman who lived disguised as a man. Collins's remark is ironical, not literal.
7. Brian Kiernan, *Images of Society and Nature* (Melbourne: Oxford University Press, 1971), p.11.

10. Henry Lawson's Fictional World

1. Chris Wallace-Crabbe, in his introduction to *While the Billy Boils* (Sydney: Arkon Paperbacks, Angus and Robertson, 1973), concludes: "It is not a provincial assessment to dub the work a classic." All references to *While the Billy Boils* in this essay are based on that edition.
2. David G. Ferguson, "Mr. Lawson's New Book", August, 1896, in *Henry Lawson Criticism 1894—1971*, ed. Colin Roderick (Sydney: Angus and Robertson, 1972), p.48.
3. Anon, "A Voice From The Bush", August 1896, *Henry Lawson Criticism*, p.55.
4. *Henry Lawson Criticism*, p.48.
5. Ibid., p.51.
6. Wallace-Crabbe, introduction to *While the Billy Boils*.
7. "PM", "Henry Lawson's Prose", September 1896, *Henry Lawson Criticism*, pp.58—59.
8. *Henry Lawson Letters 1890—1922* ed. Colin Roderick (Sydney: Angus and Robertson, 1970), p.63.

9. Ibid., p.93.
10. Ibid., p.63.
11. Ibid., p.66.
12. Stephens notes the same characteristics in his "Lawson and Literature", February 1899, *Henry Lawson Criticism*, p.79.
13. *Henry Lawson Letters*, p.92.
14. Stephen Murray-Smith, *Henry Lawson*, Australian Writers and Their Work Series (Melbourne: Oxford University Press, 1963), p.40.
15. Wallace-Crabbe, introduction to *While the Billy Boils*.
16. I am applying to Lawson's work, with various modifications and adaptations, the idea of "three worlds" as it has emerged in the debate about William Faulkner's fictional world. I am grateful to Mick Gidley, my colleague at Exeter University, for suggesting this tactic to me and recommending some relevant reading. Probably the central reference, in this connection, is Arnold Goldman, "Faulkner and the Revision of Yoknapatawpha History", *The American Novel and The Nineteen Twenties*, Stratford-Upon-Avon Studies, 13 (London: Arnold, 1971), pp.165—95. But also very relevant are: Malcolm Cowley, "Introduction to *The Portable Faulkner*", in *Faulkner*, Twentieth Century Views Series (Englewood Cliffs, N.J.: Prentice-Hall, 1968); and "Interview with Jean Stein Vanden Heuvel", in, among other places, *Lion in The Garden*, ed. J.B. Meriwether and M. Mellgate (New York: Random House, 1968), pp.237—56.
17. *Henry Lawson Criticism*, pp.48—49.
18. Ibid., p.52.
19. Ibid., p.48.
20. Wallace-Crabbe, introduction to *While the Billy Boils*.
21. Murray-Smith, p.40.
22. *Henry Lawson Letters*, p.99.
23. A.A. Phillips, "The Craftsmanship of Lawson", *Henry Lawson Criticism*, p.281.
24. Ibid.; on this point Phillips remarks on "the imperceptiveness of his academic critics. They hopelessly underestimated the conscientiousness and skill of his craftsmanship, either patronising what they took for an inspired naivete or nagging him to adopt more conventional methods". p.285.
25. Cf. Cecil Mann, *The Stories of Henry Lawson*, First Series (Sydney: Angus & Robertson, 1964), p.171, where he speaks of "... the various Mitchells, Steelmans, Stiffners, etc., such name repeats for entirely different people ... being almost a Lawson trade mark."
26. *Henry Lawson Letters*, p.63.

12. The Daunting Doubts of William Hay

1. Quoted in F. Earle Hooper's "A Memoir" (of Hay), *Southerly* 7 (1946): 128—41, on p.136. In later notes this article is referred to as "Memoir".
2. This line of argument, with variations, is adopted by R.G. Howarth, "*The Escape of Sir William Heans*; the Technique", *Southerly* 7 (1946): 156—58; by Thelma Herring, "*The Escape of Sir William Heans*; Hay's Debt to Hawthorne and Meredith", *Southerly* 26 (1966): 75—92; and by Fayette Gosse, *William Gosse Hay* (Melbourne: Lansdowne Press, 1965). A dissenting view, with which my own has some points of agreement, is put by L.T. Hergenhan, "The Strange World of Sir William Heans (and the Mystery of William Hay)", *Southerly* 27 (1967): 118—37.
3. The saintly James Herridge shows noticeably less pride of rank than the other heroes. He resembles Rufus Dawes (as the others do not) in that his sufferings are to a considerable extent voluntary, and also in that they become too acute and continuous for mere wounded pride to figure prominently among them. In the early stages, however, he is hardly less sensitive to snubs than Heans.
4. The bare facts of Cash's life are compatible with Hay's interpretation of his character; but Hay relied mainly on Cash's own sentimentalized version of his

career in his "reflections and recollections" as edited by Joseph Lester Burke, *Martin Cash, the Bushranger of Van Diemen's Land* (1870). That Hay knew this book is recorded in I.D. Muecke's "William Hay and History; a Comment on Aims, Sources and Method", *Australian Literary Studies* 2 (1965): 125.

5. See *Strabane*, pp. 103—4, 258—59, and 412—13 ("The danger of liberty is that you may find yourself dying for a fresh tyranny — some rubbish in vogue — some reform too difficult for life.").

6. I have not space for the "careful weighing" in this paper. Briefly, however, I submit that the influence of Hawthorne and Meredith has been exaggerated, that of Dickens underrated, and that of Hugo's *Les Misérables* practically overlooked. Notwithstanding the very obvious (and acknowledged) imitation of Hawthorne in book 1, chapter 15, Hay's essentially secular moral vision, as well as his romantic atmospherics, to me recall Dickens (and perhaps, through him, the Gothic novel) much more strongly than Hawthorne. Stylistically, as I suggest in this paper, the influence of Meredith is sometimes noticeable, but in the main I accept the view, propounded by L.T. Hergenhan, that Heans's ordeal includes too pronounced an element of physical and external (or at least externalized) danger to be comparable with the Meredithean "ordeal". The relationship between the convict Valjean and the policeman Javert in *Les Misérables* looks an obvious model for that between Heans and Daunt, though without the same psychological intensity and intricacy and with a simpler, more tendentious message. *For the Term of His Natural Life*, I feel, is a pervasive, but never more than a superficial influence. For discussions of influences, see especially the articles by Howarth, Herring, and Hergenhan listed in note 2 above.

7. At the end of his article L.T. Hergenhan quotes a number of passages from Hay's notebooks which suggest that, like most of his heroes, he suffered in real life from a persecution complex. Like them, he also found that a woman (his wife) was the sole buffer between himself and the hostile world all round him.

8. In the play *Le roi s'amuse*, upon which Verdi based *Rigoletto*.

9. See "Memoir", p.134. Thelma Herring has noted the frequent references to Scott in the novel, along with Hay's comment, in a letter, that his "art ... approaches rather in the direction of Stevenson than of Scott" because of his more finical methods. Scottish comparisons are suggested also by the Scottish novels on Heans's shelves (*Lochandu* and *The Wolf of Badenoch*), by Abelia's playing of "Robin Adair" at a crucial moment (it is broken in upon by the "Indian or Native ditty" which Spafield chants), and by the performance of scenes from Talfourd's *The Massacre of Glencoe* by the Hobarton ladies and gentlemen while, outside, Heans is fighting for his life against Spafield. Heans is loosely associated with beleaguered Highland chivalry, just as he is with the figures and situations he reads about in Langhorne's *Plutarch*.

10. See Janet Adam Smith, ed., *Henry James and Robert Louis Stevenson* (London: Hart-Davis, 1948), pp.77—81, 93—95; James's later essay on Stevenson, published in *Partial Portraits* (1888), shows a juster appreciation of his art (see especially pp.151—52 of Janet Adam Smith's compilation). In Hay's essay "Novels as a Guide to the More Worldly Life", included in his *An Australian Rip Van Winkle and Other Pieces* (1921), he speaks of Stevenson with strong affection but admits that, except for *The Master of Ballantrae* and "perhaps" *The Ebb Tide*, his novels "hardly help youth much in his struggle with the world" (p.170) — a view that James, by the way, would certainly not have endorsed. Hay's own novels, it may be supposed, *are* meant to help youth in this struggle, and it is worth noting that the narrator of *Strabane* has "young readers" particularly in mind (p.104) and that Heans himself writes to the narrator of his story: "The tragic distresses of portions of our lives make at worst a pleasant interest for the young of future ages." (p.134.) This remark is exactly in the spirit of Stevenson.

11. In a letter, quoted by Thelma Herring on p.88 of her *Southerly* article. Miss Herring rightly suggests that Hay's remark needs "explication". If my interpretation of it is correct, it would be the over-sophisticated artiness — and artfulness — of some of James's characters that Hay tried to catch in *Strabane*: he might, for example, have had a novel like *The Awkward Age* particularly in mind.

13. Australia of the Spirit: Some Aspects of the Work of Vance and Nettie Palmer 1938—48

1. Vance Palmer, *National Portraits*, third, enlarged edition (Melbourne: Melbourne University Press, 1954), p.v.
2. Nettie Palmer, *Fourteen Years: Extracts from a Private Journal 1925—1939* (Melbourne: Meanjin Press, 1948).
3. Palmer, *National Portraits*, p.76.
4. Vance Palmer, ed., *A.G. Stephens: His Life and Work* (Melbourne: Robertson & Mullens, 1941), p.16.
5. Palmer, *A.G. Stephens*, p.17.
6. See *All About Books*, vol.9, no.5, 12 May 1937.
7. Vance Palmer, *Frank Wilmot* (Melbourne: Frank Wilmot Memorial Committee, 1942), p.35.
8. Vance Palmer, *Hail Tomorrow: A Play in Four Acts* (Sydney: Angus & Robertson, 1947), p.68.
9. Palmer, *Hail Tomorrow*, p.69.
10. Palmer, *Hail Tomorrow*, p.71.
11. Marjorie Barnard, in *Books Abroad* 29 (1955): 280—84.
12. *All About Books*, 19 April 1930, p.87.
13. T.S. Eliot, *To Criticise the Critic* (London: Faber & Faber, 1965), p.54.
14. Palmer, *Fourteen Years*, p.183.
15. Ibid., p.115.
16. Ibid., p.139.

14. Norman Lindsay as Novelist

The references to analyses by myself elsewhere are to my book *The Roaring Twenties* (London, 1960) and to an essay in *Meanjin Quarterly*, 29 (1970): 39—48. See also my review of John Hetherington's *Norman Lindsay: The Embattled Olympian* (Melbourne, 1973) in *Meanjin Quarterly*, 33 (1974): 27—41.

For Brinsden, see J.A. Graham, *The Creswick Grammar School History* (1940), and Harry Chaplin, *Norman Lindsay* (Sydney, 1969), pp.1—2; also for a piece in *Boomerang* on Mark Twain. For the Creswick basis of *Age of Consent*, Chaplin p.45; of *Cousin*, p.49. The characters in *Rooms and Houses*, Chaplin, p.66. *The Flyaway Highway* was derived from *Thieves of Gaiety*; letter of Norman Lindsay in Chaplin, p.44. Penton and *Redheap*, Chaplin, p.30. For letter on "tension of thinking" see Hetherington, *Norman Lindsay* (Melbourne, 1969), p.42.

For the stories, I printed "Black Bill's Friendship" in *The London Aphrodite*; see manuscripts in Chaplin's collection, pp.71—77; the droll stories of Micomicon are in Jane Lindsay's possession and will doubtless be printed. I may add that the Preface to *Poetry in Australia*, though written by myself, was signed by Norman; we felt that it would give me undue importance in the book to introduce it.

15. Influence and Individuality: the Indebtedness of Patrick White's *The Ham Funeral* and *The Season at Sarsaparilla* to Strindberg and the German Expressionist Movement

1. *Bulletin*, 25 November 1961, p.31. No other account of the misfortunes of the play mentions a rejection by the Trust, though Max Harris makes much of the hostility to it of the Trust's director, Mr. Neil Hutchison. Notices of the first production both of *The Ham Funeral* and of *The Season at Sarsaparilla* were found for me by Miss Mimi Colligan, of the English Department, Monash University. Since I am many thousands of miles from a comprehensive collection of Australian research material, these pages could not have been written without her ready and efficient assistance, for which I should like to record my gratitude.

2. *New Statesman*, 24 November 1961, p.806; *Nation*, 2 December 1961, pp.19—20.

3. "On a fine day, from the Trades Hall roof,/ The class struggle can still be clearly seen/ Beyond the university where, lately,/ The dogs of Patrick White made love off stage." "Letter to a Friend in Israel", *The Gift: Poems 1959—1965* (Brisbane: Jacaranda, 1966), pp.11—12.

4. Geoffrey Hutton's notice of the Melbourne production of *The Season at Sarsaparilla* made this suggestion, which I do not wish to reject out of hand. *Our Town* also came into Brek's notice of the Adelaide production, *Nation*, 22 September 1962, pp.15—17.

5. Brek's notice of *The Ham Funeral* described it as "using no techniques more novel or forbidding than those pioneered by Strindberg half a century ago". The comparison does not seem to have occurred to any one else at that time.

6. See for example the treatment of Strindberg and the German expressionists in Raymond Williams, *Drama from Ibsen to Brecht*, second revised edition (London, 1968), pp.297—98, which is a reference work widely consulted by students of modern drama.

7. Arnold's insistence that such was the predominant impulse of the best minds of his century, which he contrived to place, for example, on the very first page of the first edition of the first series of *Essays in Criticism*, (London, 1865) was no doubt influenced by his solid grounding in biblical and historical criticism; but it was also a widely-stressed principle for continental thinkers that any serious exercise of the mind was by its nature critical. See, for example, George Eliot's translation of Feuerbach's *The Essence of Christianity* (London, 1854), p.96.

8. Patrick White, *Four Plays* (London, 1965), p.143. All references are to this text.

9. One finds these conventions everywhere in Victorian and Edwardian, and in nineteenth-century European, drama, from Hugo's *Ruy Blas*, which purports to be a historical tragedy, to their inversion by Wilde and Ibsen. The examples usually given are Scribe's comedies of ambition.

10. Gassner put together a collection of Strindberg's later plays under the title *Eight Expressionist Plays* (New York, 1965). A similar emphasis is present in Dahlstrom's *Strindberg's Dramatic Expressionism* (Ann Arbor, 1930). The suggestion that two different kinds of issue were involved was made to me by Mr. Iain Topliss, of Pembroke College, Cambridge, when he saw an early draft of this paper. I am very grateful for this and other comments of his, as for the advice of Mr. Michael Meehan, also of Pembroke, who looked over the same draft.

11. See the stage directions for the final curtain of *The Ghost Sonata*.

12. The information in the last two paragraphs is available in John M. Spalek, *Ernst Toller and his Critics: a Bibliography* (Charlottesville, 1968), pp.718—63, especially pp.725—28, 742, and 750, 874, 877, 879, 885—87, 889.

13. *Australian Letters* I (1958): 38.

14. The cost of staging such effects has deterred most companies from attempting the play, and actual performances have been few. I had the good fortune to see the Traverse Theatre, Edinburgh's presentation of it in May 1974, but that was in Ingmar Bergman's adapted version, which presents fewer problems.

15. Stanford, 1959, pp.169—70, 185—89.

16. Links between *The Ham Funeral* and *Riders in the Chariot* were pointed out by J.J. Bray, *"The Ham Funeral"*, *Meanjin* 21 (1962): 34, and Elizabeth Loder, "*The Ham Funeral*: its Place in the Development of Patrick White", *Southerly* 23 (1963): 78—91.

17. James Murphy's notice of the Melbourne production in the *Bulletin*, 27 October 1962, linked Mr. Eubage, as he was then called, with the stock caricature of the "important man" in *Smith's Weekly*, a now extinct publication, which ran the work of many Australian cartoonists, some of them satirical.

18. *The Man Outside*, tr. David Porter (London, 1952), p. 77. All references are to this text.

19. Early scripts apparently gave "Moose Jaw" and "Brooklyn". See Brek's notice, listed above.

20. See, for example, the doctrinaire stand adopted by the editorial board of the *Realist Writer*, no. 12 (1963): pp. 3—4.

16. The Rhetoric of Patrick White's "Down at the Dump"

1. All references are to the first book publication of this story in Patrick White, *The Burnt Ones* (London: Eyre & Spottiswoode, 1964), pp. 283—314. Section occupies pp. 309—10.
2. James Joyce, *Dubliners*, (London: Jonathan Cape, 1956), p. 256.
3. *The Collected Stories of William Faulkner*, vol. 3 (London: Chatto & Windus, 1958), p. 16.

17. Quest or Question? Perilous Journey to the Chapel

1. Currency Playtext Series 1, no. 4 (Sydney: Currency Press, 1972). All page references are to this edition.
2. Quoted from the foreword by Laura Hibberd Loomis to "Sir Gawain and the Green Knight", *Medieval Romances*, ed. R.S. and L.H. Loomis (New York: Modern Library, 1957), p. 327.
3. Patrick White, *Four Plays* (Melbourne: Sun Books, 1967), p.73.

18. Jack Hibberd and the New Wave Drama

1. A list of Hibberd's plays will be found at the end of this essay.
2. *A Stretch of the Imagination* (Sydney: The Currency Press, 1973).
3. Buzo, Hibberd, Romeril, *Plays* (Ringwood: Penguin, 1970).
4. Introduction to John Romeril, *I Don't Know Who to Feel Sorry For* (Sydney: Currency Methuen, 1973), p.7.
5. Ibid., p.8.
6. *Komos* 2 (May 1969): 16—22.
7. "Mask and Cage: Stereotype in Recent Drama", *Meanjin Quarterly* 31 (September 1972): 308.
8. Ibid., p.309.
9. Brisbane Repertory Theatre (La Boite), 17 April 1974.
10. "Assaying the New Drama", *Meanjin Quarterly* 32 (June 1973): 192—93.
11. *Komos* 2 (May 1969): 19—20.
12. *A Stretch of the Imagination*, p.13.
13. Ibid., p.20.
14. Buzo, Hibberd, Romeril, *Plays*, p.154.
15. Quoted in Martin Esslin, *The Theatre of the Absurd* (London: Eyre and Spottiswoode, 1962), p.212.
16. *A Stretch of the Imagination*, p.6.
17. Typescript held in Fryer Library, University of Queensland, p.74.
18. *A Stretch of the Imagination*, p.iii.
19. Ibid., p.42.
20. Ibid., p.18.
21. Ibid., p.47.
22. Ibid., pp.36—37.
23. Ibid., p.4.
24. Ibid., p.44.
25. Ibid., p.6.
26. Ibid., p.41.
27. Ibid., pp.30—31.
28. Ibid., p.28.
29. Ibid., p.v.
30. Ibid., p.8.
31. Typescript held in Fryer Library, University of Queensland, p.4.
32. Buzo, Hibberd, Romeril, *Plays* (Ringwood: Penguin, 1970).
33. "Pinter outplays Hibberd in a one-act contest", *The National Times*, 17—22 September 1973, p.22.

34. *Happy Days* (London: Faber and Faber, 1966), p.9.
35. *A Stretch of the Imagination*, p.3.
36. *Happy Days*, p.28.
37. Ibid., p.43.
38. Ibid., p.47.
39. *A Stretch of the Imagination*, pp.12, 14, 24, 26, 30, 33—34, 48.
40. Ibid., pp.8, 23, 24, 38.
41. Ibid., pp.20, 38.
42. Ibid., p.30.
43. *Happy Days*, p.23.

Leon Cantrell is a graduate of the University of Sydney and now lectures at the University of Queensland. He has edited several little magazines and published widely on Australian and English Literature. His edition of the work of influential Australian critic A. G. Stephens will soon be published.